Time Gone

Time Gone

The Story of a 20th-Century Family

Elizabeth Edwards-Stuart

The Pentland Press
Edinburgh – Cambridge – Durham – USA

First published in 2000 by
The Pentland Press Ltd
1 Hutton Close
South Church
Bishop Auckland
Durham

ISBN 1-85821-743-1

Typeset by Carnegie Publishing, Carnegie House, Chatsworth Road, Lancaster
Printed and bound by Bookcraft (Bath) Ltd

For my grandchildren –
Luke, Anna, Thomas and Rachel

When as a child I laughed and wept, time crept,
When as a youth I dreamed and talked, time walked.
When I became a full grown man, time ran,
And later as I older grew, time flew.
Soon I shall find while travelling on, time gone.
Will Christ have saved my soul by then? Amen.

attributed to Henry Twells.
Copyright © E. Edwards-Stuart.

Contents

Introduction

THIS STORY IS TOLD FOR MY FAMILY and their descendants. It starts by describing the lifestyle of their Victorian forebears and goes on to chronicle their progress through five reigns.

The story is told largely through their letters from Australia, Canada and Hongkong in the 19th Century, and from the trenches of the First World War through the inter-war years and on to World War Two.

The first volume ends in 1947 and volume II will bring the story up to the present day.

The Victorian letters of William LeMesurier have been well summarised in Appendix 1, for which I am indebted to Eric Lummis.

Acknowledgements

Firstly to my husband, whose gift of a personal computer saddled him with a constantly distracted wife. This wonder machine I call 'the sorcerer'. It enabled me to write and re-write the story which follows.

Secondly to my friend Elise Rhodes (née Dunn), who returned to me in 1984 letters I had written her in 1945 and onwards. And, of course, to my dear Mother who kept all the other letters.

Thirdly, to all those kind relatives and friends who have read various chapters and given me so much encouragement to carry on with the book.

Fourthly to Bob Brown of S.E.S. Ltd, Weymouth, whose unfailing help and patience has helped me to disentangle from the sorcerer when I became hopelessly enmeshed in its mysteries. Also to Martin Howe for photocopying all the maps.

Lastly again to my long-suffering husband who read and corrected the worst of the mistakes.

Part One

Grandparents and Parents 1725–1920

Chapter One

My Parents' Childhood and Adolescence

AN ATTRACTIVE AND LIVELY YOUNG WOMAN, her beautiful hair hidden beneath her topi, was driving along the dusty track across the African plain returning home to the 'Boma' in her pony trap. She had only recently given up riding as she was expecting the birth of her first child at any time. A rustle in the grass and a quick movement frightened the pony. It shied and the woman was thrown from the trap. All this took place in British East Africa, now Kenya, at the end of March, 1918 and the young woman was my mother. Luckily she was not far from the house and the natives soon alerted someone to the accident. The doctor and the monthly European nurse, booked at the start of the pregnancy, were hastily summoned from Nairobi, 15 miles away.

My mother was born Nancy Aileen LeMesurier Croll in 1891. On her mother's side she came of an interesting Channel Island family, the LeMesuriers (See Appendix 2), three generations of which had served in the Commissariat.

Lucie, my grandmother, married a brewer, David Hay Croll, who later failed in his business. By 1895 the family had moved to Watford, where the boys went to Berkhamstead School and Nancy eventually to the Girls' School. But money was running out and something had to be done to keep the roof over their heads and the family clothed and fed. Lucie was clever at design as well as with her needle, so she set to and devised and developed the 'Dolls' Cut-Out Clothes Company'. In 1896 it was under way and as it was run as a mail-order business, Nancy soon learned how to wrap and pack the orders. In a couple of years Lucie had a flourishing little workshop employing her husband, David, as well as a couple of girls. Later she developed the business further and ventured, likewise successfully, into 'Adults' Cut-Out Clothing'. Eventually she sold the business to Selfridges and moved to a smaller house in the Fulham Road. The two of her children still living with her, Cedric and Nancy, supported and protected her in every way, and especially when David, her husband, became difficult.

In 1910, when she was 19, Nancy was invited to be bridesmaid to her cousin Effie Saul at her wedding in Bournemouth. The best man was Samuel Frederick Deck. Nancy could not take her eyes off this very handsome man and when his blue eyes met hers, it was love at first sight.

Sam, known to all his friends as 'Skipper', came of good old Suffolk yeoman stock. His family traced its roots back to Clement Deck of Vezelay, goldsmith at the Court of King René of Anjou, who granted him armorial bearings in 1496. Sam was the fourth of five children and his grandfather and father both farmed in Suffolk, where he grew up amidst many cousins, all countrymen to the core, well versed in the ways of the countryside and the life of the fields and woods by which they were surrounded.

Sam was educated at Faulkenberg School in Beccles, where he gained a scholarship to Felstead School in Essex. From there a further scholarship enabled him to go up to Caius College, Cambridge. He was a History Scholar and a prizeman, gaining a BA 2nd Class Honours in History in 1905. He was in the College cricket and football teams. After gaining his degree he went to the University of Poitiers from 1905–6, and was awarded the Diploma for French. Then followed a year teaching French at Tyttenhanger Lodge School, St. Albans, under Mr Harvey Trollope. In 1907 he entered the Colonial Civil Service as Assistant District Commissioner.

In the same year Sam set sail for the British East African Protectorate. The Nairobi that he first saw had had a very short history. It had been established as the railhead camp in 1899, only a few years before he arrived. The name comes from the Masai for 'place of cold water' and it was on swampy ground in the vast Athi plain. It became a quagmire in the rains and a dustbowl in dry weather. The plain teemed with wildlife: herds of hartebeest and many varieties of buck and gazelle, giraffe, ostriches, zebra, buffalo, rhino, lion and many small unseen creatures. It was a constantly moving mass. Lions prowled round the new camp and wrought havoc amongst the people there.

This was the 'Dark Continent', the land of mystery and hostile terrain and climate; of dread diseases, malaria, dysentery, blackwater fever, smallpox, cholera and plague; of man-eating ants called siafu, ferocious lions, poisonous snakes and jiggers that ate into one's toes. It was peopled by enigmatic natives whose habitations were sparse and widely scattered.

Nairobi became the headquarters of the railway construction at the turn of the century and consisted mainly of shacks and the Indian bazaar. Gradually officials and merchants built their houses and trees were planted. The European community divided itself into 'officials' and 'settlers' and Sam found that the administration both of the native tribes and of the settlers was still very much in its infancy. To a young man starting out on his career, here were challenges aplenty. Sam set about learning the languages of the country and achieved proficiency in three of them: Swahili, Masai and Arabic. I still have his New Testament translation into Masai. President Theodore Roosevelt was in British East Africa in 1909 and Sam may well have heard the speech in which he said: 'You young people are doing great work. You have brought freedom where there was slavery. You are bringing health where there was disease. You are bringing food where there was famine. You are bringing peace where there is continual war. Be proud of yourselves and the world will be proud of you.'

Sadly, however, fifty years later, the world was not proud of them. What perversity held my son's and grandchildren's generations in ignorance of the historic feats and achievements of their forebears?

In 1910 Sam was on his first home leave when George Crisford, a fellow officer, asked him to be best man at his wedding to Effie Saul. Sam was spending his leave in Suffolk, but before the wedding reception was over he had Nancy's address and within the next week he had penned the following two letters to her:-

----

Halesworth,
Suffolk
Oct. 2nd, 1910

Dear Miss Croll,

Lots of things I want to know. 1. Name and address of the photographer who took the wedding group. 2. Name of Bournemouth paper with an account of the wedding. 3. What was the matter with me on Saturday as I left my boots and keys behind in one place and my overcoat in another! 4. Whether you are going to turn up on Saturday – 'sure'.

Ever yours sincerely,
S.F. Deck

Halesworth
Suffolk
7.X.10

Dear Miss Croll,

Very many thanks for your letter. It's very good of you to send the paper. I feel very insulted because they did not mention my wedding present.

I wish you could fix up Saturday afternoon somehow. I'll call at No.9 anyway at 12.30 and we'll have lunch together. Do try and manage the afternoon, 'chap' or no 'chap'. Get some dear lady who doesn't mind being left alone in the National Gallery or some such edifying place, for three or four hours, while you are lost in London. But don't worry about it if it's a nuisance. We'll put our heads together at lunch and work out some little scheme. A taxi driver might take quite a long time to find his way to Fulham Road if he goes the right way to work.
Very sorry I couldn't answer your letter yesterday. I was away the whole day. Till 12.30 tomorrow.

Ever yours sincerely,
S.F. Deck

A postcard indicates that he sailed, with George Crisford, back to British East Africa at the end of 1910. It bore the sad little message: 'Marseilles, 10.45 Monday. Found George at Paris. He went by 9 from Charing Cross. This is our boat. Goodbye. S.D.'

It was addressed to Miss Nancy Croll, 477 Fulham Palace Road, London S.W.

Chapter Two

My Parents' Engagement and Marriage and World War I. 1911–1920

I DARE SAY NANCY AND SAM'S FAREWELLS at the station were less sombre than the postcard suggests. Sam sent a picture postcard of Mombasa when he arrived back in B.E.A. in January, 1911, as well as three more from Nairobi. However, though communication was kept open, it was not easy, especially when Sam was sent back to the Northern Frontier District. This was a wild, troubled and troublesome area. It consisted of vast tracts of uninteresting country which was grazed sparsely by the cattle, camels and goats of the various nomadic tribes. Tsetse Fly was a menace to livestock and the areas of its prevalence had to be avoided by the nomads grazing their herds. Somalis of various tribes inhabited much of the district and were squeezing out the traditional native tribes. In one particular raid a tribe called the Ogaden raided villages occupied by another, the Sakuye, 26 people being killed, 25 women and children carried off, and 5000 goats and camels seized. Subsequently Sam visited the District and succeeded in recovering the captives and part of the stock. To control the situation, a temporary boma was made at Waghalla in the Wajir District and eventually Sam was given permanent charge of the District. On 4th February, 1911 he wrote to Nancy:

K.A.R,. Wajir
N.F.D.
4th February, 1911

Dearest Nancy,

Excuse this filthy sheet of note paper, it belongs to the 'Lieut'. I have just received a long letter from you posted on Nov 5th, which amused and delighted me till I reached the postscript, which reduced me to a state of mental depression the like of which I've never known since I first came out to Africa. It's no good because it has led me to offend you. Well you said a lot of hard words about myself, and it's no good going on piling on the agony because after all you may only think I'm a hypocrite. However, there is one thing about it all, I'm pretty certain I'm not incorrigible, in spite of the fact that I honestly believe all that I've said about myself. Most men degenerate if they stay long away from civilization. There is such a thing as too free a life. I hoped to be able to keep up appearances till I saw you again. But it is not to be so and now I hardly dare hope you'll continue to write to me. So now, Nancy, the only thing I want to know is if I may come and see you next October. If you refuse me this, I certainly shan't come home then. From your letter which I have now I know you've partly forgiven me or you wouldn't have posted it. But I'm thinking of all the letters I've written since. I shall go on writing to you. The letters will be very dull and dismal I'm afraid. I've a period of penance ahead. You know it has an answer. I'm hoping that rather than stop writing altogether, you'll write just one more letter if only to tell me that I'm hopeless. I won't go on any longer, as even if the best has happened and you've forgiven me it can only make very dismal reading.

Just the same old love from

Your miserable Sammy.

By now policy for the North West Frontier District was developing from one of observation only to one of taxation of the boundary tribes and the necessity to protect those natives who were contributing to the revenue. This was another reason for the need to occupy Wajir.

Communications, as described in the report submitted by Sam Deck, were as follows:

Mails to the Northern Frontier District were brought from Meru (200 miles north of Thika railhead) twice weekly, the mail from Nairobi on Saturday reaching Archer's Post (50 miles north of Meru on the Uaso Nyiro River) on Sunday night 8 days later. Mails for Marsabit (100 miles north of Archer's Post), Moyale (100 miles north of Marsabit on the Abyssinian border) leave Archer's Post on the 1st and 15th of each month, being carried by donkeys to Merille, where they are met by donkeys from Marsabit. They reach Marsabit about the 7th and 21st of the month and are taken on to Moyale on camels, reaching there about the 15th and 29th of the month. The down mail from Moyale leaves for Marsabit on the 6th and 22nd of each month and connects with the donkeys going down from there to fetch the up mail. They reach Archer's Post about the 23rd and 8th of each month. Thus for a letter posted at Archer's Post on the 1st of the month, a reply can be received from Moyale on the 8th of the month following. Mails for Addis Ababa were formerly sent off from Moyale monthly by runners. This was found to be most unsatisfactory and a new system has been started by which the arrangements are made by Addis Ababa. Mails for Wajir (approximately 200 miles NE of Archer's Post) leave Archer's Post by donkeys on the 1st of each month to Arrodima, where they are met by a camel from Wajir with the down mail. They arrive in Wajir about the 16th of the month and a reply can reach Archer's Post about the 20th of the month following. There is no regular service between Wajir and Moyale.

The wonder must remain that Nancy ever got a letter from Sam under these circumstances.

Such was the place and the work required of Sam until his next home leave fell due, early in 1913, and he went on his way to Nairobi, first to Thika railhead by camel, donkey or on foot, thence by train to Mombasa and home by sea.

Shortly after Sam arrived back in England, he was quickly in touch with Nancy at No.9 Kensington High Street and their engagement was announced shortly afterwards. Happy snapshots survive to illustrate what must have been an idyllic summer. Sam rented a house for Lucie in Southwold and she and Nancy, sometimes joined by Nancy's brothers, Cedric and Graham, spent happy days on the beach and visiting Sam's relations and their farms. He bought a motorbike and sidecar, so he was able to drive Nancy around his beloved Suffolk. It was arranged that they would be married on his next home leave. Sam knew he would be returning to Northern Frontier District. He had, of course, described to Nancy the life he led. In the days before wireless and aeroplanes it was hard, lonely and isolated. He would have explained to her that as well as being administrator and judge, he was doctor and protector too. A wounded man whose arm he had had to amputate recovered, and returned north of the border. Many months later he was back to show himself and present Sam with a native Coptic Cross in gratitude. Sam must have left it in Nancy's safe keeping, as I still have it and sometimes wear it. Nancy will by now have had a better understanding of the means of communication from these outlandish places, where Sam moved around from well to well and from tribe to tribe.

Sam had actually been coping with serious episodes of tribal unrest and raiding and had put forward a number of proposals for the transfer of tribes to different areas of the region so as to separate the warring factions from one another and achieve a fairer distribution of the land and grazing grounds available. His suggestions were approved, but were not implemented because of the outbreak of the First World War.

Meanwhile Nancy waited impatiently for news of Sam and prayed that the camels and donkeys carrying his letters did not fail. She was rewarded at Christmas time with a home-made Christmas card on a sheet of old cardboard, which remains in her collection of photos of the Northern Frontier which accompanied Sam's letters home.

This then was the scene in Africa at the time when Nancy, in England, was packing up her bottom drawer. She would have described to Sam their lives in wartime London and the devastating news of her brother Graham's death 'going over the top' in the trench warfare in Flanders in May 1915. The news came to Lucie from Graham's friend serving with him in the 1st London Regiment. Nancy had been in constant touch with her cousin, Effie Crisford, who had found herself stranded in England. Her husband too had been on the Northern Frontier, but was transferred to Mombasa too late for Effie to join him before the War broke out. Nancy and Effie decided that they would sail together, Effie acting as chaperone to Nancy, the one to join her husband and the other to marry Sam when he came down from the N.F.D. in 1916. They sailed on RMS *Balmoral Castle* early in 1916, being chased by a German submarine across the Atlantic almost to the South American coast, before rounding the Cape of Good Hope and calling at Durban.

On arriving at Mombasa, Nancy stayed with Effie and George Crisford awaiting news of Sam. She remained in Mombasa for some weeks, but communication with Sam proved very slow and uncertain. She therefore decided to accept an invitation from the Rigbys in Nairobi, where at least she would be at the centre of news and information and in the hub of wartime activity. She would have taken a full part in the social and sporting activities of Nairobi, which included hunting, polo, tennis, cricket, squash and dinners galore. Nevertheless she was impatient to be re-united with Sam, so she used to go unchaperoned by train to the Blue Post at Thika so as to watch for him coming from Wajir. One evening a cloud of dust could be seen as she perched on her favourite rock beside the trail. Sure enough it was Sam's party at last. However, the joy of their reunion was somewhat marred by his shock at seeing her there. He was apprehensive for her safety and, since she was unchaperoned, for her reputation! Nancy failed to see that it mattered much in the wilds of war-time Kenya.

Back in Nairobi they were married on 16th May, 1916, her wedding ring fashioned from a gold sovereign. An announcement in *The Tatler* of June 1916 shows a photograph of Nancy with the caption, 'Mrs S.F. Deck' and reports her marriage in Nairobi. Coincidentally, the same issue carried the announcement, with photograph, of a further forthcoming marriage in the family, that of Miss Hilda (Tat) Phillips to Lieutenant Irvine LeMesurier Croll, Royal West Kent Regiment, Nancy's eldest brother.

My father's new posting was to Kisumu, which was in the grip of bubonic plague. A wire was sent off from the Secretariat in Nairobi, 'Is Kisumu safe for D.C.'s wife?' It elicited the reply, 'Yes, if the A.D.C.s are on safari'. So to Kisumu they went, after a brief honeymoon in Mombasa, and set up their first home in the D.C.'s house. Their first task was to try to elmininate the rats which infested the place. With the fighting now away in the south, it was possible to lighten the rigours of life by boat trips across Lake Victoria Nyanza. In 1917 Sam was moved to the Masai Reserve as D.C. Ngong, and they moved into the old D.C.'s house, then nearer to the M'bagathi River than the new Boma.

After their move he penned this little ditty to his bride:

Nancy Aileen LeMesurier Croll
Was a dainty attractive and charming young soul.
Her figure was trim and her ankles were neat,
The soldiers and sailors all fell at her feet.
But in spite of their ardours she gave them the sack,
And married old District Commissioner Deck.
She gave up her flirting and gave up her dancing
And vowed she found Africa cool and entrancing!
Now she lives at Ngong amidst naked niggers
With her house full of fleas and her feet full of jiggers.
But for all these small worries she don't give a damn
For the sake of old District Commissioner Sam.

The fall from the pony trap with which this story opens caused much consternation at the Boma. The doctor and the European monthly nurse had been hastily summoned. I had wrapped my arm around my head, so it was a difficult birth, of which she was to be reminded, since I bore a streak of white hair behind my left ear all my life. My mother's first pregnancy had ended in the miscarriage of a baby boy, so to the anxieties and agonies of my birth was added the disappointment that I was a girl. Nevertheless many joyful letters, accompanied by snapshots, were arriving at regular intervals, month by month, at Lucie's home in England. I was her first grandchild.

In 1919 with the War over, Skipper, my father, took some well-earned leave and they sailed for England via Durban. His service on the Northern Frontier had earned him the Africa General Service medal with the Bar 'East Africa 1915'. This Bar was awarded for an expedition under Lieutenant-Colonel W.F.S. Edwards, D.S.O., against the Turkhanas between 4th February and 28th March 1915.

Skipper's leave was spent mainly in Suffolk in a rented house in Southwold, where Lucie and Cedric joined them again. Lucie was able to enjoy her first grandchild in its infancy. Skipper too was in the midst of his family. His mother, after whom I was called, lived in Westleton, and they were frequent visitors to Skipper's sister Amy at St.Helena.

Chapter Three

My Childhood – Kenya 1920–1930

BACK IN BRITISH EAST AFRICA at the end of 1919 – its status now to be changed to a Crown Colony, Kenya Colony, my father was sent to Nyeri in the foothills of Mount Kenya in the Kikuyu country. There my brother Arthur Graham, known as Tom, was born on 14th September 1920. Shortly afterwards they were moved back to Nairobi. My father was now official interpreter and examiner in three of the native languages in Kenya, and he served as member and Chairman of the Kenya Colony Languages Board.

In Nairobi I attended the Montesori School. My parents enjoyed to the full the social life at the Muthaiga and the Nairobi Clubs. The Nairobi Club had many sporting facilities, especially tennis and cricket. My mother was a keen tennis player and my father played in the cricket XI. Tom and I enjoyed the occasions when the band played and we could dance round. It was a great meeting place for the officials and the settlers from up country, who would come to Nairobi for the shows and the race meetings.

From Nairobi my father was moved again and the family went to Dagoretti, back in Kikuyu country. There my sister Rosemary was born on 4th October 1922. And it was there that I became very seriously ill with dysentery at the age of four.

1923 saw the whole family back in England on leave again. This time they rented a cottage in Thorpeness called 'Montenot'. Skipper's and Nancy's families were reunited. Lucie joined them, as did Cedric and his wife Elise. Skipper's brother Jim, his wife Violet and their five children were also home on leave from the Argentine and had rented a house in Suffolk.

Skipper and Nancy and their brothers, cousins and assorted nieces and nephews joined in picnics and family cricket matches on the commons at Southwold and Dunwich. Bathing parties and golf in Thorpeness, tennis parties at Field End, Leiston, home of the Cooper cousins, as well as the tennis tournament in Aldeburgh, occupied their time. Tom and I were introduced to boating on the magical fairytale Thorpeness Mere.

My father had been warned by the Kenya authorities that his next tour of duty would be peripatetic, mainly on the burgeoning railway network. Because he and Nancy would be constantly on the move living under canvas or in bandas, Nancy decided that she should leave her children in England, but at the last moment she could not face total separation and took my three year-old brother Tom back with her. Rosemary and I were settled with my grandmother Lucie and my father's sister Amy. She was now a widow with her youngest son Robert, a youth of 14, at Merchant Taylor's School. A house was rented, 'Amwell' in Romford, a most appropriate name as we could not have had kinder or more loving guardians. My gentle grandmother and my scholarly aunt were ideal companions and a very happy household settled down for a two-year stay. My parents sailed away with Tom on S.S. *Llanstephen Castle* in October 1923.

My mother had heard of a plot of woodland for sale on the Karen estates between Nairobi and Ngong. Friends of my parents, Dr and Mrs Hemsted, had already built themselves a house on another plot. Nancy decided to buy it and build a house to her own design while Skipper was away on his travels. The land was in the woodland near the spot we later knew as 'Hassan's Duka', a little Indian emporium selling everything needed by surrounding natives and Europeans alike. Also nearby were the McQueens, one of the earliest settler families, a blacksmith and his large wife who had trekked from the coast inland as far as Uganda and finally settled by the M'bagathi River and built their house on land they claimed beside the river, where the rhino came down to drink. McQueen had fashioned his own building materials including all nails and door hinges. His wife saw no need to employ domestic servants except for a toto to fetch and carry. Here they raised a large family. At the farthest end of the wood lived Baroness Blixen, who became a great friend of my mother's. Nancy was also near her friends the Sprotts, who kept and bred Great Danes.

Nancy's first task was to build herself a shelter. So some bandas were put together, grass huts with thatched roofs, to house herself and Tom, and others for the servants and the native workforce. She also had two stables built for the horses on which she depended for transport and for haulage. Next she had to clear enough of the woodland for space for the house and garden. The wood was useful for fuel, but she had far more than she needed and she started a charcoal burning operation, got a contract with the Norfolk Hotel in Nairobi to supply their needs, and bought a second-hand lorry in which to deliver it. She was to be seen delivering her goods to the Norfolk Hotel and then calling on her friends in Nairobi, especially the Spencers, in her ramshackle truck. Having cleared enough space for the house, she hired an Indian stonemason and supervised the whole of the building operation herself.

The centre of the house was to be the large living room with a big open fireplace, for evenings there were quite cold. This room faced the forest edge and the view she had cleared of the Ngong Hills across the plain and the M'bagathi River. The front door opened into a small hall which led directly to the living room. On either side of the living room she built two wings, one for bedrooms and bathrooms, and the other leading out of the living room to the dining room and kitchen area and the back door.

Many were the alarms and excitements in her woodland adventure. Probably the most alarming was the night that a lion jumped over the stable door and killed one of the horses and dragged most of it away. Walking to visit her neighbours, the Hemsted family or Karen Blixen, black mambas were likely to drop from where they lay along the branches of trees on to passers-by beneath. Once one narrowly missed a friend's baby in a pram. This episode led to a hunt for the snake, which had missed its prey and taken refuge in the thatch of a nearby banda. Bare-footed natives, nothing daunted, climbed on to the thatch to prod the snake out into the path of my mother's shotgun.

Natives on the prowl at night would put their hands through the window spaces protected only by sacking, and lift anything within reach. Once she lost her sewing machine this way. My mother slept with her shotgun beside her, and the servants nearby for protection. Apart from the petty thieving, I never heard that she had fear of molestation.

Meanwhile back in Romford my recollections of those days are dim, but they are happy ones. I remember the little dame school I attended in Gidea Park. It was in a rambling old mansion which fascinated me. I remember dancing lessons in a beautiful room, probably a ballroom once. I loved dancing and I imagined myself waltzing through mirrored halls as a ballerina. I also loved exploring the old house and have had a love of old mansions ever since, with their closed-off rooms and their secret gardens. Next door to Amwell lived a little boy of my age, Charles, and we became great friends and playmates.

It was not long before my parents were back again on leave. My mother had completed her house and sold it to the Principal Medical Officer, Dr Patterson, who was my sister's godfather. The family was once again reunited. Rosemary had no recollection of her parents, having been left at the age of one year, but we were both young enough to take these things in our stride and I do not think it had any adverse effect upon us.

After my father's leave, he was again on secondment in 1926 and he rented Diphouse on the Karen estates. It was so-called because it was near to the cattle and sheep dip and was surrounded by the coffee plantations. It was approached by a track along a ridge which turned off the Nairobi-Ngong road. The track was lined with tall palm trees, high straight trunks with palm fronds at the very top. My mother was again near to all her friends, including Mu and Henry Hemsted and their three children, Rupert, Pen and Toby, as well as the Sprotts and Karen Blixen. I remember her as an aloof and dignified woman of whom I stood in great awe. One of the rare occasions when I behaved myself was in her presence. She had a lovely house with a huge sitting room and a big log fire which used to burn in the grate on cold evenings. She told wonderful tales and was very kind to me.

Before leaving England my mother had engaged a governess who travelled with us to Kenya. Our school room was adjacent to the house in a large wooden shed and under Doris Slight's quiet direction we lived an idyllic life. She allowed us a lot of freedom, and in the school room her magical way with children held our attention. Every day she would have new ideas to interest us, and it was she who started me learning and from whom I learnt most. My little sister could read fluently before she was four by simply listening and watching as Miss Slight tried to drag my reluctant brother into the world of literacy. Away from the school room, she allowed our imaginations free rein and we devised splendid games at the bottom of the garden.

My mother would not allow us to mix with the natives. She had an instinctive distrust of them, born no doubt of a lack of understanding of their primitive culture. Africa was a rather frightening place in those days. To the East African the wheel and the coin were unknown until the Europeans introduced them in the late 19th century. They had never used oxen as working animals, as they were cherished as their main source of wealth. This cultural gap was breached more readily by the settlers' wives, who had to deal with the farm workforce as well as train domestic servants.

The settlers made provision for their labourers to live on the farm and to bring their families. They granted them strips of land for their own use, and they were known as squatters. It fell to the wives of the settlers to look after the health and wellbeing of their squatters, and they became, ipso facto, doctor, health visitor and midwife rolled into one.

While the settlers' wives were helping to tame their own local workforce, the officials' wives had little part in the work of their husbands, although many of them ran charitable enterprises. Their husband's task was to look after the tribes in the district to which he was assigned and to endeavour to improve their lot. His was the task of providing roads, hospitals, and schools for all the local inhabitants, as well as to keep the peace and mete out justice.

It was, therefore, an added excitement for us when the coffee picking season arrived and all around us were the boys and bibis from Karen Blixen's squatters with their babies slung on their backs chattering and chanting as they picked. Disobeying our mother's instructions, we would hide in the coffee and join in with the pickers until a grown-up missed us and we were called back to the garden.

The women, the bibis, always fascinated me. Whenever we drove out in the car, we would see them trundling along in single file on the winding footpaths. They were bent double with loads of firewood tied with throngs and held by a leather strap across their foreheads, often a baby on top as well. Their arms covered with coils of copper wire from wrist to elbow and their earlobes dragged down by heavy ornaments or simply large pieces of wood, their only clothing a piece of leather tied round their waists back and front. They were the beasts of burden, the toilers and the child-bearers – their gait so different from the Somali women, who carried everything on their heads and their babies on their hips or slung on their backs.

We grew up with animals around us, a Sealyham called Punch and one or two cats, and the occasional mongoose. But by far the most fun were the chameleons we found on the bushes, and the little duikers which natives would bring in from the wild, usually a young one taken from its mother which they would try to sell us. However, although we always took them in to rear them on a bottle until they were strong enough to go back to the wild, we never paid for them so as not to encourage what my mother considered to be an undesirable practice.

One of the disagreeable aspects of our lives were jiggers. These tiny insects lived in the dust and would burrow under our toenails and lay their sack of eggs. If they were not removed immediately, the eggs hatched and the toe became infected and eventually eaten away. My mother became very skilled at their removal. Once we were asleep and were unlikely to move, she would roll back the bed clothes and work away with a sharp needle to remove jigger and sack. She knew whether or not we had picked one up as they caused intense irritation.

Because I was so fond of dancing, my mother took me to dancing lessons in Nairobi and I took part in several shows put on by the dancing school.

Another joy for us was old Mr Gorringe, an elderly bachelor, tall and willowy with bushy eyebrows and a moustache. He had been in the Boer War and had come north to Kenya to settle, and he had the farm adjacent to us. He was always on horseback with a hound or two at his heel, for he ran a pack of fox terriers crossed with blue bedlingtons, which he claimed were more suitable for hunting locally than English foxhounds. He hunted steinbuck and jackal and he fell in love with our governess. We thought him very old, but he could only have been about 50. He used the sheep dip near our house and our governess always took us to watch the farm animals being pushed through it and hauled out by the natives the other side. He taught me to ride on a very ancient mare called Kisuwani. Her ears were in a straight line with her tail and I perched on the top, feet not reaching below the saddle flap. She lolloped along in a rocking horse canter and I loved her dearly. I was even allowed to follow Mr Gorringe's hounds and loved the days I spent on the plains below the Ngong Hills on Kisuwani's back. Sometimes she would put both forelegs into a pig hole and I would topple over her head. She waited patiently while I picked myself up and led her to the nearest tree stump or rock on to which I could clamber to enable me to get back into the saddle. I then fell behind the rest of the field, but someone always appeared, and I don't recall getting lost. Kisuwani would have known her way home anyway. Mr Gorringe always had a rifle to hand by his saddle in case hounds encountered a leopard, or a lion, or a python, as sometimes happened. This added greatly to the excitement of the occasion. After the day's hunt the path homeward usually led through 'Lady MacMillan's Wood'. Here there was always much shouting and whipping in of hounds, since if they strayed from the path, a wary leopard was ready to spring and devour them. It was not unusual to emerge from the wood with a couple of hounds missing – never to be seen again. Hunting stopped when the grass grew too high. Before the rains the natives would set it alight, and when the rain came, it sprang up young and green and after a bit we started hunting again.

After two years of this idyllic life, my father's next leave was due at the end of 1927. The excitement of the impending journey to England was somewhat subdued by our sadness at parting from our governess. It had been decided we would go to boarding school after my father's leave. So Doris Slight got another job in Kenya. Mr Gorringe gave up trying to persuade her to marry him and married a widow called Queenie. Doris finally disappeared from our lives when she left Kenya some years later to take up a post in Brazil.

Our journey began in Nairobi when we boarded the train for Mombasa. This part of the journey was a particular treat as we had such a wonderful view of all the game – herds of buck and gazelle as well as the giraffe, zebra and ostriches – which would move away as the train chuffed past. We needed to have no fear that an unseen lioness would spring, as we always had when travelling by car, although the ill-tempered rhino had been known to charge the train in a fury. We stopped at stations down the line for our meals and for the engine to fill up with water and fuel. When we came to Tsavo, where man-eating lions had decimated the Indian workforce when the railway was being built only 30 years before, my father told us of the lone Indian clerk in the station office. A lion had been prowling around so he telegraphed for help to Nairobi for Askaris to come and shoot it. Two men were sent, but they also took fright and the desperate clerk telegraphed again: 'Askaris not so brave at time of roaring'.

As we approached Mombasa the country changed from the dried-up plains to the lush tropical growth of the coastal strip with its curious beobab trees. The humid heat bothered us and my father drove us round and round the place until it was time for us to embark. We boarded the ship with great glee, there was so much to explore. We loved the ports of call, particularly Port Sudan. There we would be frightened by the 'Fuzzie-Wuzzies', little dark men with huge mops of fuzzy black hair powdered by the coal dust as they moved chanting and shouting to and fro refuelling the ship. The greatest treat was to be taken in the glass-bottomed boats, from which we could gaze at the wonderland of the sea life below us. Myriads of highly coloured fish of all shapes and sizes flashing about and glittering in the clear water. Port Said was another joy, when the gully gully man came on board and entertained us with his conjuring tricks with little fluffy day-old chicks, as he had done for generations of children travelling to and from the East. Vendors in little bobbing boats below our high vantage point on deck offered all manner of wares, and much shouting and bargaining went on over the deck rail, until money and goods were exchanged by baskets hauled up from below. What interested us even more were the small boys of our own age diving for coins, which, when retrieved, they held in their mouths. These were wonderful exciting days for the three of us.

This time our leave was in winter and for part of it we shared a house with Cedric and Elise Croll, and Barbara and Graham her brother, in Wedderburn Road, Hampstead. My mother was reunited with her mother Lucie, now living with her sister Aunt Eva and Winnie Marshall in Acacia Cottage, Harrow. Our near neighbours were Gordon Cooper, Skipper's cousin and his wife Dorothy. They had no children but Gordon was devoted to all his young nephews and nieces and small cousins. He would arrange large parties of us and take us to the theatre, which was a tremendous treat. It was also a cold winter and we went tobogganing on Hampstead Heath, something we had never before experienced. We had never seen snow, we only knew of its existence because both Mount Kenya and Kilimanjaro were topped in white.

It was 1928 and my father was posted back to Ngong in the Masai Reserve and we moved into the new Boma at Ngong. The previous incumbent had supervised the building of this modern stone two-storey house perched on a knoll at the foot of the Ngong Hills. It was in a beautiful position with wide views of the plains and across the M'bagathi River towards Nairobi and the Ngong hills rose up behind it. The new Boma was a few miles further into the reserve than the old Boma, the house where I was born, had been.

The lives of the three of us children now changed, as we were to start at our new boarding schools. I was sent to the Hill School, Limuru, then quite newly established with only about 30 girls. It later grew into the well-known girls' school. Tom went to a prep. school, Kenton College, Kijabe, and Rosemary to the Loretto Convent, Nairobi the only school that catered for one so young. She was only 5 years old.

In August, after a long hot and dusty drive without her dark glasses, Nancy noticed a hair-line streak across her right eye. This slowly expanded until she had no sight in that eye at all. She consulted a specialist in Nairobi, who said there was nothing they could do for her in Nairobi and she should go to England immediately. Accordingly she sailed in the middle of the summer holidays, leaving Skipper to cope with the three of us. Kind friends offered hospitality to us and I went to stay in Nairobi with Alex and 'C' Spencer and their son Marlay, who was my age. I thoroughly enjoyed myself there as Alex was a very keen horsewoman and had some nice ponies, some of which she allowed me to ride. She was also a keen race-goer. It had been arranged that in my mother's absence Doris Slight would spend the Christmas holidays with us. We had a wonderful make-believe Christmas. A blue-clad Santa Claus presided over a sleighful of presents at the foot of the stairs, whilst his magnificent cut-out reindeer climbed up the stairway stuck to the bannisters. Santa Claus was clad in blue because we had been reading that enchanting story 'Santa Claus in Summer' by Compton Mackenzie. I remember leaping out of a papier maché Christmas pudding during an entertainment we put on to greet our mother's return from England. What a happy Christmas that was.

My grandmother's last letter arrived in December, 1928, and before it reached my mother, she had received the following cables from England only a few days after her joyous return to her family:

'Mother dangerously ill. Pneumonia. Cedric.'

'London 1st January 1929. Mother passed away peacefully last night. Irvine and I present. Funeral Watford Friday. Cedric.'

'Mother with us Christmas Day. Taken ill Eva's twenty-sixth. Removed Harrow hospital Thursday. Seemed much better Sunday. Monday morning crisis. Monday evening died nine p.m. Irvine and Cedric present from 7 p.m. Suffered no pain. Very peaceful. Cedric.'

My grandmother had just had her 71st birthday.

It was a sad start for the New Year for my poor mother. However, with us to pack off to school and Aunt Tat to entertain, and my father's joy at her return, she had much to take her mind from her grief.

We pursued our usual holiday activities, searched for our chameleons and cherished our duikers when they came our way. We had Punch to play with and a horse called Sofie to ride. We learnt to play tennis on the tennis court and golf on the golf course my father had laid out around the house. The first tee was a short step from where the driveway came round the hill up to the house. The first green was not visible from the tee as the ground fell away steeply and the ball was driven over the drop. A particularly long pole with its little flag marked the hole. Once, having driven off, we reached the brow of the hill and there on the green sat a lion with a very big mane. Golf hurriedly gave way to the hunt and we dashed back to the house for a rifle. The skin subsequently adorned the drawing room. The holidays came to an end and we went off to school again.

I wrote during that term from the Hill School Limuru on 15 April 1929: 'this is my last term, worse luck!' I was to move to join Rosemary at Loretto Convent.

The following holidays were filled with activity as we had Aunt Tat to entertain. We took her for picnics up into the Ngong Hills. On one of these picnics we reached the top and were able to look over the steep escarpment that dropped down to the plains towards Narok. It was always teeming with game. Giraffe, zebra, kongoni, ostriches, as well as Grants and Thomsons gazelles, duiker, rhino, elephant, buck of all sorts and lions. Vultures would wheel over carcasses, a lion's kill maybe or human remains, for natives were often victims of accident, attack or encounter with wild animals.

We often went in the box-body car to visit Narok or Kajiado. Sometimes my mother had to fetch my father if he had been away with his ADC. On one such journey my mother saw a lioness at the side of the road. Anticipating correctly that she had cubs, Nancy took a wide diversion off the road to avoid her, little knowing that the lioness had left her cubs on that side of the road. The lioness sprang, caught the spare wheel attached to the back of the box body, and the boy who always accompanied us on such trips threw himself on to the front seat. Mercifully all that was lost was the spare tyre. Families of baboons were another source of amusement as they gambolled alongside the car. They were great mimics and a nuisance too, as they tore down the telegraph wires to make bracelets, copying the bibis.

Sometimes during the holidays I would walk down to my father's office. It lay at the foot of the hill on which the house stood. There were always men waiting outside. The old men would be squatting in the shade of a tree, the young men, each one standing on one leg, the other tucked behind his knee and leaning on his spear. He would wear a blanket knotted over one shoulder and his hair well greased and plaited. Often at nights we heard the sound of their 'ngomas', the dances in celebration of season or anniversary. The throbbing of the drums carried up to the house and I always found the sound intimidating. I would snuggle down into the bed clothes. My mother taught us to shoot with a .22 rifle and she also taught us to drive the car as soon as our feet could reach the pedals. She felt we might need both skills if we were out in the bush and one or other of our parents were to be incapacitated. Ever a possibility in the wild and isolated places we visited in my father's province.

The first term at Loretto Convent was not particularly happy for me and I thought I was near enough home to run away, which I did with two friends. We followed the winding native footpaths which I thought led in the direction of Ngong. On 13th November 1929 my mother wrote to Aunt Eva:

> The children are all well, but Elizabeth does not seem to settle down at the Convent. Instead of it having a good, moral and holy effect on her, it seems to bring out all her worst points. I think I told you that she lost her temper with one of the Mothers and called her a 'fat fool'. The other day she and two other girls ran away for the day. I live in terror lest she should be expelled! As a matter of fact I really feel rather worried about her, as there is no other place to send her in the way of a school out here and if she can't settle down, it will mean sending her home before we come in 1931. I enclose her last letter. She is always imagining things. I don't for a moment think there is chicken pox at the school. The last time I went to see her, there was some other sickness she imagined some of the girls had, so altogether you can see she hates the school and is doing everything in her power to get me to take her away. On the other hand Rosemary is quite happy there and we think the school very good and the Mothers perfect dears.

The good news in this letter was that my father's promotion to Senior Commissioner (P.C.) had come through and meant an increase in income of £150. per year, as well as additional pension.

For some time I had been having to visit the dentist. My mother had large and protruding teeth which caused her much embarrassment. She was determined I should not be so handicapped and she insisted the dentist remove four of my new molars. This was an extremely painful business, reluctantly undertaken by the dentist, anaesthetics then being rather primitive. However, I have been grateful all my life and I am fortunate in my mid-seventies to have all my strong and healthy teeth. Just as well as our favorite food was 'mahindi', East African corn on the cob, the staple diet of the pastoral natives which they ate in the form of posho. The Masai, on the other hand, lived on milk mixed with fresh blood drawn from the jugular veins of their bullocks.

In the summer holiday of 1930 we stayed with the Hemsteds, who had moved from Ngong (Karen) to Naivasha and had a house with a garden running down to the lake. They were very keen on sailing and were, I think, founder members of the Sailing Club. Lake Naivasha had floating islands and a lot of hippo. These great lumbering beasts would lie mostly hidden below the surface and were a real threat to small boats, which they could easily capsize. Rupert, who was my age, was a very proficient sailor.

For the three of us our time in Kenya was now running out. My brother was down for Marlborough College and we were all destined for school in Europe.

We moved to Dr Patterson's house, which my mother had built in 1924–5. Dr Patterson, my sister's godfather, had bought the house from my mother when he returned to Kenya from leave with a young Swiss bride. He had continued to develop the garden which my mother had laid out, and house and garden were now a show place in what became known as 'Karen'.

Two particular occasions I remember from those few months. One was the night we were chased from room to room by invading siafu or safari ants, those dreaded flesh-eating ants which can kill a horse. They swarmed through the house undeterred by hot coals on the stone slabs in between the doorways, which my mother had incorporated for just such an occasion. They fell from the ceilings and were everywhere. We spent the night sleeping under the stars on the lawn. In the morning there was not a trace of them. They had moved forward on their relentless journey, devouring anything in their path.

The other episode was when my mother told me I would not be going to school in England, but in Germany. My protestations were loud, persistent and vehement. I spent a very unhappy few months contemplating my fate, for the idea appalled me. For some reason I was not sent back to school after Christmas 1930. I found a playmate in a girl of my own age who lived with the McQueens, possibly their granddaughter. The house fascinated me for it was very primitive, and so did Mrs McQueen, a very large and buxom woman who had no native servants, which seemed very strange to me. For no one of my acquaintance cleaned their own houses or did their own cooking. I used to walk down to the house alone through the wood to the edge of the river where they lived, keeping a sharp eye open for any puff adders on the path – horrid snakes the size of a man's arm and very poisonous. My mother had once shot one found in the house.

For the last time we anticipated the sea journey home but this time with some anxiety as to what lay ahead of us. Somehow my mother managed to arrange that we three children travelled second-class whilst my parents travelled first. This had the great advantage, from their point of view, that they could visit us in second-class, but we were debarred from visiting them! Tom and I immediately spotted an unfortunate boy, about my age and rather large, dressed in immaculate starched white drill bush shirt and shorts. We singled him out for persecution until his outraged parents complained bitterly to our parents, whom they had some difficulty in identifying. We pilfered the deck steward's locker for useful items like chalk and rope and generally caused consternation to passengers and crew alike. We had such fun, but we paid for it. My brother was whacked fairly regularly, but my parents disapproved of spanking girls, especially since Alex Spencer took it upon herself to beat me once, for which punishment I held a long resentment against her.

But Tom and I had another happy hunting ground ahead – the Hotel Centrale in the square at Alassio, where we had stayed on our previous leave. The church and the cafés in the square, with their tables and chairs outside, provided ample opportunity for mischief. Tom's favourite escapade was to run into the church and kick the metal spitoon, which would clatter and clank with resounding echo half the length of the aisle. Also in Alassio at the time was Winnie Marshall's brother Archie Marshall. He was a great delight to us and kept us out of mischief by arranging fancy dress parties and little pantomimes in which we and all the other English-speaking children took part. Days were spent walking up the steep salitas into the hills to join Aunt Eva at whatever spot she had decided to spend the day painting. My parents had a fair amount of difficulty controlling their wild offspring and I remember one walk we took along the coast road when Tom decided to walk on the parapet wall. There was a steep drop down on to the rocks and the boiling sea below. My parents were in a fearful quandary. Eventually Tom climbed down and was grabbed in an iron grip for the rest of the way. Punishment usually involved confinement to our rooms and this meant that my father had to sit in with one or other of us to ensure we did not wreck the hotel property.

The dreaded departure to Germany now came upon us, and we travelled through and under the Alps to Basel. Here we stayed another night in a very grand hotel whose bedrooms all had double doors leading on to the passage. As was customary on our travels, we three children shared one room and my parents another. The hotel porter cleaning the passage in the early morning was intrigued by strange thumps coming from behind one of the outer bedroom doors. He opened it and out tumbled two bloodstained struggling children – my brother and I engaged in one of our fights. He rushed screaming to my parents who eventually separated us. My brother and I, although a well-knit team when faced with outsiders, fought out a prolonged battle for supremacy. My case being that I was the eldest, his being that he was the boy! We were both very protective towards our little sister and excesses, real or imagined, perpetrated against her were often the cause of our violent disagreement.

My parents had received lists of schools from the agents in London, albeit finishing schools, there being no other boarding schools for girls and none, it seemed, for my age group. Several of these were in Freiburg in Breisgau in the Black Forest, and so this is where we went. We stayed in the Pension Schotzky. My mother fell in love with the place, and it was decided that here I would stay to learn German, providing of course someone could be prevailed upon to take me in. The visits began, hampered somewhat by Tom, who would get on to trams going in the wrong direction and then get lost. Finding him wasted quite a lot of time, but he always turned up in the end. We must have been a strange looking trio in our scanty tropical clothes and our sandalled feet, quite unsuited to the chill air of April with the snow-clad hills around. After visiting several schools who said firmly they took no one under 16, my mother came across one run by Frau Dr Scholtz, a gentle and worn-out looking woman and her partner Fraulein Wemans, a pear-shaped spinster of jovial demeanour and waddling gait. Frau Dr had a motherless niece aged 12 whom she had taken under her care. My mother insisted that I would be the ideal companion to Liselotte and so it was to be. It certainly took some time to persuade Frau Dr of this arrangement, not helped by the behaviour of Tom and me. We were left sitting on a narrow bench inside the front door with Rosemary. It was not long before we were pushing each other off, Rosemary was crying and Tom and I were locked in battle. That Frau Dr accepted this bundle of trouble says a lot for Frau Dr. The arrangement was that Frau Dr would coach me in German during the summer term, and get me into the Hohemädchenschule in the Holzmarktplatz in September. I have never understood why I was accepted there, but somehow Frau Dr managed it. As a last treat with my parents we were all taken up to the Schauinsland in the cable car – a great thrill – to see the snow. It was all very exciting. We got soaking wet and absolutely frozen and had to be thawed out in the cable car restaurant.

The next day my parents, brother and sister bade me farewell and set off for England.

Chapter Four

My Schooling – Germany and England

1931–1934

I WAS JUST 13 in the spring of 1931 when my parents left me with Frau Dr Scholtz and Fraulein Wemans in their Pensionnat Scholtz-Wemans in the Sternwaldstrasse in Freiburg im Breisgau. Frau Dr's niece Liselotte, Lilo for short, to whom I was to be companion, was my age and spoke no English. I spoke no German so we had little point of contact. Lilo was at school all day in the town, so I didn't see much of her that summer.

An English girl, Margaret McCurdy, aged about 18, took me under her wing, her eyebrows raised at such a strange apparition amongst the mostly 17 and 18 year-olds who were the girls in this finishing school. They were of various nationalities, mostly there to learn the language and absorb a bit of the local culture.

It was not long before Frau Mez, in a routine invitation to Frau Dr for any English girls in her establishment to come to tea, found me at her tea-table. Frau Mez was born Ethel Edwards and had married Herr Paul Mez, manufacturer of cottons and threads, who had met her on one of his visits to cotton mills in England shortly after the turn of the century. Their eldest son, Paul, was born in 1909, followed by Godfried (Dudu) in 1911 and Rudolf (Brutz or Bubi) in 1913. She had lived stoically through the First World War with her English relatives on one side and her German in-laws on the other. Communication was kept open through her Mez relations in Switzerland. In the terrible aftermath in 1919 she gave birth to their twin daughters, Anna and Maria. Now in 1931 the factory in the Karthauserstrasse was part of the Coates combine and still making threads with Herr Paul Mez as its Managing Director. A Scottish associate had been appointed from the parent company and when I was in Freiburg this was Mr Moncur, with his wife and teenage daughter. They lived in a flat just across the River Dreisam from the factory and the Mez family lived in a large house next door to it. Mrs Mez, who was to become a substitute mother to me, made it her business to offer hospitality to any English people who came to Freiburg. And so it was that I arrived one summer afternoon on her doorstep. I was somewhat overwhelmed to find myself in such a large house surrounded by a large family, for there were almost always friends or relations staying and the twins always had their friends in and out. Amongst the relations was an English cousin, Hugh Edwards, who was to become a staunch friend in later life. The whole family was bilingual and the twins were summoned to look after me. We gazed at each other in surprise across the end of the tea table in the large upstairs dining room. In spite of their mother's admonitions, they had no particular desire to befriend such a waif from 'das dumme England' as Maiu put it, or worse from the wilds of Africa. Maiu recalls 'a very small Elizabeth wearing an English school straw hat and a very short skirt and she looked like a mushroom. We nicknamed her 'Der Deckel (the lid)', a name she carries to this day'. The twins of course resolutely refused to speak English although to my relief they understood everything I said. Mrs Mez was most concerned about me and what she considered my orphan state. I was included in the family parties whenever Frau Dr would allow me out. So hesitatingly I became well used to being with the easy going Annu, with whom I shared a love of animals, particularly horses and dogs. We all played tennis on their tennis court and scrambled up their Rebberg, the vineyard which reached up the hillside immediately behind their house. We crossed the little brook, diverted from the Dreisam, which fed machinery in the factory, and mounted the steps to the terraces where the vines grew to the little Rebberghäusle half way up the hillside. It was fitted out as a cosy little 'Stüble' and there we picnicked and played with the dog, Arno, Annu's main delight. The dragging summer term was relieved by these interludes and at last it was time to travel to England to join my family. I travelled by train in the care of Margaret McCurdy, who had finished her time in Freiburg. My father met me at Victoria Station in London and we travelled together by train to Thorpeness, where we had rented a beachside cottage, 'Seacote', which was being shared as usual with the Cedric Crolls, who now numbered three in family, Barbara, Graham and Michelle. In those days the train still went to Thorpeness on a branch line which ran from Saxmundham to Aldeburgh.

It was a wonderful summer. My Argentine cousins were in England again, staying in a farmhouse near Southwold. I was about the same age as their youngest, Charles, and my sister Rosemary was a year older than Barbara, the eldest of the Crolls. So there was a wide age range. Nearby we also had the Grimsey and Cooper cousins, the girls now married and with their own children. Ruth Hancock's children were Jane (later Perrett) and William at the Red House, and Tilly Rope's were Richard and Golly (later Nottingham) at the Lower Abbey, Leiston. We always had friends staying, and we children all slept in a shed behind Seacote, which was full of a variety of camp-beds jammed in, leaving almost no floor space. All the seaside paraphernalia was draped around drying, sand was in everything, and we ran free through the village and along the shore. Kind uncles gave us money for an hour on the Mere, where we had the choice of rowing boats, canoes, punts and sailing dinghies, in which we explored the channels and islands in which the lake area abounded. The islands were furnished with little secret houses and dens all named after the characters in Peter Pan. Big family parties assembled on Westleton Heath to play cricket and picnic. Some days were spent sailing in family parties up the Alde. Otherwise it was tennis and golf and the statutory pre-luncheon bathing party on Thorpeness beach. It was a truly idyllic holiday and one of my happiest memories.

As a final treat at the end of this gorgeous holiday, my father's cousin Gordon Cooper took us all to London to see *The White Horse Inn*, then all the rage in London as well as in Germany. The music haunts me still and brings back the happy memories of those sunlit days, but also the frequent partings which have peppered my life.

September 1931 saw the family split up. We three children to different places and my parents back to Kenya. Tom went back to his hated prep. school in Deal, which was also attended by Marlay Spencer. Rosemary aged 9, no longer *en famille* with the Crisfords, went to a vicarage family in Bedfordshire and attended Bedford High School by the day with the vicarage children. Tom was to join her there for the school holidays and I was to join them in the long summer holidays.

Back in Freiburg I went off with Lilo and found myself amongst a crowd of girls scrambling for desks and hooks. I could understand very little as I had paid scant attention to my German lessons in the summer and had made little effort to talk the language and make myself understood. Much to my relief, I was in the same group as Annu and I clung to her for as long as possible. All the girls had come up from the Volkschule. Maiu had gone to the 'Gymnasium', equivalent to our grammar schools, and Annu to the Hohemädchenschule in the Holzmarktplatz, which is where I was too. It was a difficult term.

It was not long before the German Christmas celebrations engulfed and enchanted me. It began on Advent Sunday when the first of four candles on the 'Adventskranz' was lit before the evening meal. The Adventskranz was a garland of spruce and red ribbons suspended over the dining room table where it stayed until Christmas Eve, a candle being lit for every Sunday in Advent. How we looked forward to the days passing until Christmas time. We had 'Adventskalender', as every child nowadays knows, and opened a little door or window each day until Christmas Eve. On the feast of St. Nicholas, the 6th December, 'Sankt Nikolaus' called at each house where there were children, in his monk's habit and sack of goodies, and with a birch switch for the naughty children. Little rhymes were made up about each child and I remember Frau Dr's ditty about me began 'Kleine Topfe kochen schnell über', 'little pots boil over quickly'. She can't have been too unkind as I was only threatened with the birch, and got my apple and share of nuts from his sack. All around the Munsterplatz were the stalls of the 'Weihnachtsmesse'. They sold the lovely Black Forest carved angels and candleholders and the prettiest decorations of fir sprigs and red ribbons. I was quite enchanted by it all. Presents were exchanged on Christmas Eve in celebration of the birthday of the Christkind. I have always preferred the German celebrations to ours, to my mind so much more appropriate.

Christmas was over and the snow was accumulating on the hills above Freiburg. All my schoolfriends were going skiing. It must have been Mrs Mez, I think, who included me in one of their day trips. I had got a pair of skis and boots for Christmas and made do with my riding breeches and some stout stockings and joined the party. I can't remember having lessons; we just strapped things together and slid as best we could! There were no pistes in those days. We would take the early train crowded with young skiers from Wiehre station to Bärental and then on to the Feldberg, and spend the day sliding down the slopes, picking ourselves up, walking up the slopes again and skiing down again. After lunchtime refreshment at the local Gasthof, we would start the descent as far as the snow would take us, usually to Hinterzarten. It was not often there was enough snow to ski the whole way to Freiburg. In the Easter term of 1933 I would go with Annu and friends and we would stay over Saturday night in a friend's 'Hütte' – little Black Forest houses built of wood, cosy and warm.

The other excitement in the Easter term was 'Fastnacht'. Everyone at school dressed up and ran through the streets to school; it was a mad few days before the Lenten fast. By the end of the first term I was quite fluent in German and was fast forgetting the proper use of my mother tongue. Mrs Moncur was shocked and insisted I go to her every Sunday for tea and to speak English. This became a burden, but Frau Dr concurred and I had trouble getting out of this well-meaning engagement.

A new arrival at the pensionnat that year was a flamboyant American girl, Polly Peabody. She was only about 15 but mature and sophisticated beyond her years. She aspired to modelling or the stage and fitted in neither with the older girls nor with us. We called her Polleen. Some photographs show her sharing a sick room with me and another new arrival Anneliese Paulus who was the same age as Lilo and me. The picture shows me with my kaross on the bed, a rug of hyrax skins, so much in use in Kenya, which the old chiefs used to wear and the Europeans used as rugs. It was my dearest possession and went with me throughout my young days. I still have it, now wrapped up against moth. Anneliese was, like Lilo, left with only one parent. She was crazy about the boys and Frau Dr had a lot of trouble with her on that account. We were of course all palling up with the boys and one I remember in particular was Jochen a cousin of Annu's. He was always in our group. He was very sweet on Maiu, as were most of the boys, for she was very attractive and teased them unmercifully. After I had left Freiburg two of the University students had a duel over her and Papa Mez decided enough was enough and packed her off to an English boarding school for girls. Maiu describes this episode as 'being sent to England to be retarded.'

At weekends I was often invited to join the Mez twins and take my bike to the Wiehre station where we caught the early train again to Baerental and on to the Feldberg as in winter, only this time instead of skis we took our bikes and spent the day freewheeling downhill to Freiburg. We usually spent some of the morning either on the Feldberg or more likely at Titisee, where we would swim. We were always on our own in a group on these occasions without any adult supervision. Once, I remember, we decided to swim across the lake, a very risky undertaking. The water was very, very cold and the lake very, very deep. Mercifully there were a number of boats on it. We managed not to drown, but I remember it was very cold and very frightening and I never tried it again. The homeward bike ride to Freiburg was an exhilarating 20 miles of hairpin bends and steep hills down, down through the Hollental. Our back-pedalling breaks ran hot and we had to stop on some of the bends to let them cool off. We would sit on the parapet wall looking down into the valley, dark and mysterious, a long long way below us.

Other happy weekend trips were to the Kaiserstuhl in summer or autumn. In summer the roads, which were lined with cherry trees, provided plenty of free refreshment. Sometimes we would go as far as the Rhein at Breisach about 10 miles from Freiburg. There again we would swim, this time in the river, where I had another frightening experience. The river flowed very swiftly and although I was in reach of the bank, I was swept downstream by the current and had great difficulty getting a handhold to pull myself out. I didn't do that again either.

At the end of the summer term I was to travel to England to join Tom and Rosemary at the Vicarage at Sharnbrook in Bedfordshire. Mrs Mez arranged with Frau Dr that the twins and I would travel together on our own. Mrs Mez had great faith in me. 'You are in charge, Elizabeth,' she would say. The twins were to stay with Mrs Mez's sister, Miss Edwards, known as 'the little Aunt', in Edenbridge, and she would meet us at Dover, and I would stay with them for a few days before going on to the Vicarage. The twins were to visit their various English cousins.

The Vicar and his wife took in several children of Kenya families, so together with their four, Bob, Peter, Barbara and Robin and the three of us, we were a large crowd. Peter was my age and the younger two the same ages as Tom and Rosemary. The Vicar's wife was highly organized and managed this large household plus her parish duties with the help of all of us and one village girl to do the hard scrubbing. We youngsters had our allotted tasks in house and garden, and other than our duties, we made our own amusements. No entertainment was ever arranged for us. We all had bikes and would bike off to the river across the meadows and bathe. Part of those holidays were spent by the three of us with our Argentine cousins in their farmhouse accommodation outside Southwold. My cousins were also at school in England and Aunt Violet came over from Argentine for the summer holidays to look after them all. We arrived with the minimum of luggage and in our shirts and shorts and sandals. Aunt Violet was horrified and I remember being asked what I had to change into for dinner. The answer was nothing. She found an outgrown lacey garment of my namesake cousin Elizabeth (Lippy). I think I decided bed was the preferred option to facing a formal dinner in a dress to which I had taken an instant dislike. I don't think that this interlude was a great success. For one thing the age ranges were too great, only their youngest and I being of the same age, and Tom and I were constantly in trouble. Soon I was back in Edenbridge with Annu and Maiu, and this time delighted to be returning to my now beloved Freiburg.

We had a new form master that term, Herr Professor Goll, a fanatical National Socialist. This was something new on our horizons for we took no interest in politics, but the general excitement and the atmosphere of optimism and hope infected us all after the depressing years following the First World War. Jochen had joined the 'Hitlerjugend' and of course we took a great interest in his activities and put little swastika flags on our bikes. Herr Goll took a dislike to me because I was English and had come from the colonies, which he considered should by rights have been German. So I had a thin time from him but much sympathy from my school friends. The only consolation was that we were now, in our new form, considered to be mature enough to be addressed by the teaching staff in the formal manner of 'Sie' instead of 'Du', as we had been the year before. That tickled me as there was no such distinction in English. About this time, to my acute embarrassment, Fraulein Wemans, in her impish manner, announced to all assembled at the breakfast table, 'Der Deckel ist Dame geworden'. (Deckel has become a lady).

One of the delights of this autumn was to accompany Annu and Maiu to the Rebberg when the grapes were being harvested and later plunged into enormous tubs to be trodden. Herr Mez had a wonderful cellar with huge vats containing each year's vintage. He would instruct one of his sons to fetch wine when he wanted it and always specified precisely which year. He knew immediately if it had been drawn from the wrong vat. Annu remembers one dreadful occasion when the tap on his favourite vat was left on by a maid sent to get wine from it and the cellar was flooded.

Annu was a very keen and accomplished horsewoman and used to go regularly to a riding school outside Freiburg. To my great joy, Mrs Mez treated me to several rides with Annu. We would bike out to Herr Rosenstihl's stables and ride out in the countryside, or be schooled in the big indoor riding school.

In the Christmas term we joined a ball-room dancing class with the boys. I took part in a display and won a prize – a German beer mug – which I still have.

My time in Freiburg was coming to an end and I dreaded leaving to go to Bedford High School to take my School Certificate. My mother arrived from Kenya to collect me, and although I was pleased to see her and able to show her to my friends, I was devastated at the thought of leaving all my friends. My mother paid calls on all my kind hostesses, particularly Mrs Mez and Mrs Moncur, and found them somewhat critical of my unconventional education – unsurprisingly. Many were the farewells and the parting presents, some of which I still have. At last the dreaded day came and to my amazement most of my class and many of my friends were gathered on the platform to wave me good-bye. Jochen ran all along the platform as the train drew out. My mother was astonished. It was a ghastly wrench for me to be separated from so many friends at the age of just 15, with all of whom I had had so much fun. It was going to take me a long time to recover from it. Years later I heard that Jochen had joined the German Parachute Regiment and had been killed in the Battle of the River Gari in Italy in 1944.

Now began a forlorn decade in my young life. I found it very difficult to adjust to English life. It was good to be re-united with my mother and Tom and Rosemary, but I missed my friends dreadfully and spent my days writing letters back to Freiburg. I became hostile and anti-social.

My mother had rented a cottage in Sharnbrook and Rosemary joined us from the Vicarage and Tom from school. My parents' friends, the Spencers, had retired and were living in Westward Ho. We went there with Marlay their son, who was at school with Tom, for some of the Easter holidays. As was usual when in England, we stayed some time with the Cedric Crolls, then at Holmdale, Temple Sheen. Back in Sharnbrook my mother's interview with the Headmistress of Bedford High School was not a happy one. 'What have you done to this child's education?' she demanded to know. 'And how do you expect me to get her through her School Certificate?' My mother was not amused.

My mother had left my father in Eldoret, where he had been posted early in 1933 for his last tour in Kenya. It was one of the original resting places of the Boer trekkers after the Boer War. In 1908 they had chartered a ship to bring them, their houses, their horses, wagons, stock and families from South Africa to Mombasa. There they chartered trains to take them up country to Nakuru and then trekked on and staked out their land on the Uasin Gishu Plateau. On Farm 64 a town slowly grew. It happened by chance to be 64 miles from the railhead at Londiani. This was Eldoret and was known in its early days simply as '64'. Hard on the heels of the Boer settlers came the Indian merchants, and a large Goanese colony grew up there.

On the 26th May 1933 Skipper writes hoping to catch Nancy at a port of call on her journey back to Kenya.

Eldoret, P.O. 26 May 1933.

My own darlingest,

Your letter of the 16th received yesterday .... . I shall send my next letter to Aden by the ordinary mail which leaves June 3rd. I doubt whether it will catch you but it's worth trying. This week I started with a very good duck shoot with Hunter in the Nandi Swamp. We got thirty birds between us, duck, snipe and partridge. Unfortunately the right barrel of my gun wouldn't work; so I had only one barrel to shoot with. I got 12 birds to his 18. On Monday Donald Williams turned up and stayed the night. On Tuesday Judge Thomas arrived for the High Court. Wednesday was Empire Day and I turned out in full war paint and inspected the Kenya Defence Force, Boy Scouts and Girl Guides and what nots and then lectured them for about quarter of an hour in the School Hall on their duty to the Empire! In the afternoon there was a fete in aid of the Church which raised over £60. – and in the evening I went to the Shaws for dinner and bridge. Miss Mummick, the nurse, engaged to old Shaw's nephew, was there. She plays quite well. Last night I was sick! (This sounds like Tom!) Must have eaten something funny at the Shaws'. Was better to-day and took Bob Illingworth to the Mother Superior who was very anxious to hear all about you and the children. To-morrow, Friday, I am going with Donald Williams to Tambach, thence to Marakwet, then to Kapsabet and Kakamega, and back via Kitale on Monday. The 29th – the King's Birthday – is a tremendous affair; apparently about 150 people turn up: so I'm going to hold the 'levee' in the School Hall which is the only place big enough in Eldoret. That's on Saturday the 3rd June. I shall get Wilson to do the sandwiches and drinks – cup and sherry. I'm getting rather sick of these 'doings'. I don't mind making speeches but I hate putting on that beastly comic uniform with the hat stuffed with newspapers. At the Empire Day show there was a cinema man taking pictures of me as I walked round inspecting the guards!

I'll send the cash to Jonah at Mombasa to meet you, and I will be at Nairobi Station. Hurrah, I'm sick of being in cold storage! All my love darling,

Ever your S.

I joined Rosemary at the Vicarage when my mother had seen us all off to school and returned to Kenya. I started off badly at my new school. I disapproved of the straw hat and sought to improve it by severing brim from crown, cutting a piece off and sewing it together again. It lost its shape, of course, and I had to fit the school hatband on as well as keep it on my head by means of an elastic band under my chin. This brought me to the immediate attention of the Headmistress. I did not fit in with the girls either, as I was exempted from the German lessons, which did not please them, and then showed my dislike of team games. Cricket I found boring, and hockey painful, and to add insult to injury, I discovered that both Tom and Rosemary could beat me at tennis. In class, however, I held my own; English and History I loved, Geography was always a reality to me because of my travels, French had been very well taught in Germany and of course German was no problem. I attended only the last lesson of the term and digested the whole syllabus then. But arithmetic, algebra and geometry were a mystery to me and have so remained all my life. I had missed out on Latin sadly, and science was not then given the priority it enjoys to-day, and neither subject had ever been part of my curriculum.

At the Vicarage where we lived I did not take to the children of the house. Robert, the eldest, was pompous and condescending, Peter, my age, was a loner, Barbara was an unpleasant girl who bullied Rosemary, and Robin, Rosemary's age, was the best of the bunch. We all went to school daily on the bus and in the next village, Milton Ernest, three children from the Manor house joined us, John and Pauline Hedges and their younger brother. Pauline was my age and also disliked school and we became friends on that common sentiment. Many were the days I spent at their house. Her father collected butterflies and was a great lepidopterist. At the end of the year Pauline's mother died, and Pauline stepped into her shoes to look after the family and run the house. She grew very responsible and mature.

In the summer holidays we were joined by Tom and Evan and Daphne Williams, also from Kenya. I thought Evan was wonderful, and he used to take me on his motor bike riding pillion. We all had tasks in the Vicarage, and he and I were detailed to shut up the chickens each evening. We strolled through the summer fields and kissed and cuddled in the hay. We were the cause of much ribaldry when we got back to the 'schoolroom' where our lives in the Vicarage were centred.

The Vicar's wife made good use of every pair of hands, and we were all detailed to duties in house and grounds. We shut up and opened up the chickens and collected the eggs. Peter milked the cow and brought the milk into the dairy. There we girls were taught to skim the pans where the surplus milk lay and put the cream into the churn for buttermaking. Another of us fed the pig. We also helped the maid on laundry days – turning the handle of the large mangle which dealt with the sheets and heavy garments. Even waiting in the hall for meals or for interviews in the Vicar's study for some misdemeanour, we were not to be idle and a 'tisbut' lay on the hall table. This was a piece of knitting ('t'is but a moment' said the Vicar's wife) which we were to pick up and work on while waiting. She made all the boys' socks and jerseys and their shirts, and most of Barbara's clothes. Such domestic economy as I was ever taught I learnt at the Vicarage. The Vicar used to vanish for the day to his workshop, a hut in the grounds, or to do his bees, usually in the company of a jovial spinster lady from a nearby country house. We enjoyed the days she came to lunch as she lightened the usual tense atmosphere which prevailed at the meal table. The Vicar as I remember him was a strict disciplinarian and seldom known to smile. His workshop was, of course, strictly out of bounds.

So passed the summer holidays, and when term started we carried on our duties at week-ends and as long as daylight permitted into the winter term. Peter and I carried on a desultory teenage flirtation in the schoolroom after the younger ones had gone to bed. Robert had been promoted out of the schoolroom and was allowed to work downstairs.

Early in 1934 my father retired, and after the ceremonial farewells, and the presentation by the Goanese community of a little wooden casket duly inscribed, my parents embarked at Mombasa for the homeward journey. My father had arranged to leave the ship at Aden in order to go to Australia to visit his sister Mabel, and my mother travelled on to England, back to a rented cottage in Sharnbrook, where we spent some of the Easter holidays, visiting the Cedric Crolls at Holmdale, Temple Sheen and various of my mother's friends.

When my father returned in early summer, Rosemary and I went back to the Vicarage, and my parents went to Suffolk to look for a house. They rented Amor Hall, Washbrook from the Ipswich Co-op for £80. a year, and the Co-op continued their farming enterprise there so we shared a common access. At last after three and a half years we children had a home we could call our own.

At Whitsun the Vicar arranged for me to be confirmed into the Church of England along with some of the others, and we walked across the field full of summer flowers to the Parish Church as we did every Sunday. Later on I sat my School Certificate, after which our parents collected us for the summer holidays before the term ended, so the Headmistress refused to say good-bye to us!

Amor Hall was a lovely old Tudor farmhouse with Elizabethan chimneys, and indoors uneven floors, walk-in cupboards in the bedrooms, and was full of nooks and crannies. A wonderful house for our favourite game of 'sardines'. I had my own bedroom for the first time ever. It was painted yellow and Aunt Eva painted a still-life of marigolds for me to hang on the wall. I still treasure this picture. The drawing room was furnished with a baby grand piano, round which we gathered for sing-songs in the winter evenings, with me at the piano. The kitchen premises were extensive with a real Suffolk 'backhus'. There was electricity from our own generator, and water was pumped from a large pump outside one of the scullerys. The rule was 100 pumps if you wanted a bath! We children were not allowed in the kitchen in case we 'upset the servants'.

The garden was mature with lovely herbaceous borders round an hour-glass shaped lawn which led down to a wooded dell full of snowdrops in late winter, followed by all the spring flowers in succession. Across a field on top of a hill was a fenced-off tennis court which my father set about putting to rights. My mother was soon arranging tennis parties and she established a lively social round of tennis, golf and bridge parties. I was not a success on the tennis court and when my mother had tennis parties I would hide, usually up a tree. This infuriated her and a rift arose between us, the only result of which was a social inferiority complex I acquired and which lasted for a long time. My mother had invited Annu to stay with us when the twins were on their usual summer visit to English relations. Mrs Mez's married sister lived near Woodbridge and Annu combined her visit to us with a visit to her aunt. Annu's arrival eased the tension between my mother and me considerably.

The summer holidays drew to a close. Tom was to start at Marlborough College and Rosemary was sent to a convent in Verviers, Belgium. Her letters were miserable – 'I cry every day', she wrote. Eventually my father brought her back and she went to Ipswich High School until she could enter Felixstowe College in September 1935.

But what to do with Elizabeth? I had passed my School Certificate with exemption from Matriculation, so I was equipped for higher education and possibly Cambridge University, which was where I wanted to go. But with Tom's and Rosemary's school fees to meet, not to mention the cost of the social round, it was impressed upon me that I must earn my living. The quickest route to this was a secretarial training. As I was just 16, and it was considered I needed another language, I was given the option of going to France or Spain. I had not appreciated my father's connections in France and unwisely chose Spain. Whether or not my parents were aware of the social mores of Spain I do not know, but the arrangements made were extremely unconventional. Educational options for girls of my age in Spain were limited to convents. My sister's experience in Belgium was not a happy one and I decided that foreign convents were out. Eventually it was decided I would spend the time until New Year at home whilst arrangements were made for me to go to Spain.

This was a happy interlude and restored some of my lost confidence. It was the shooting season and I accompanied my father when he joined the shoots on the various farms owned by his relations. He had acquired a springer spaniel called Ross whom I loved dearly. I took it upon myself to help my father with Ross' training. I also followed the local beagles and as a special treat my father would hire me a mount to follow the Eastern Harriers.

January 1935 saw me despatched c/o the Vice-Consul, San Sebastian. I was 16, and I set off alone to this unknown destination. My mother kept my letters and they tell the story of that episode in my life.

Chapter Five

Travelling and Training –
Spain 1935 – London 1936

M Y FIRST IMPRESSION OF SAN SEBASTIAN was that it was a filthy place. Outside the station paper and muck was scattered about, but I have since then changed my mind. The streets are wide and spacious and clean, compared to what I had expected them to be.

———————

3.2.1935.

Darling Parents,

I hope you got my letter alright. I received yours yesterday. I've been waiting all this week for some money, but up to now none has arrived. After I had posted my letter to you on Wednesday, we went and interviewed Mme Duplan, my piano mistress. She is very young and very clever. She asked me to go with her to a concert that evening. She is actually French, but she has lived here all her life and speaks Spanish perfectly. I like her awfully. On Wednesday evening lots of friends of the Greens came before I went to the concert, and as usual all sat in the kitchen. I also had my first Spanish lesson with Mr Green, who, I've come to the conclusion, is not an intelligent man. Since I arrived he has had a cold and for four days has not been to the office. He's an awful old fusser about his health. I'm afraid he does not get much sympathy from me. I tell him he should go out into the fresh air and not take so much medicine. I think everyone now knows that I sleep with my window open and they can't get over my appetite. Mr Green is always boasting about how much they eat here. I tell him that it is greedy and very bad for his health. They are very slovenly people here and if you go to the market you find everyone slipper-slopping about in bedroom slippers. It was very cold here when I arrived and for 2 days it snowed a little. I didn't feel it very much, but the people here were moaning and groaning and I told them I didn't wonder if they walked about in slippers and thin clothes. However it is warmer now.

The Greens are most obliging to me and I have only to give the word and whatever I ask for is done. I had no difficulty about my bath and everything is most comfortable and the food very good. They drink red wine here like water and get quite surprised if I don't drink at least two glasses, but I keep it to a half. It's quite good and rather drier than port.

On Thursday I went to practise at Mme. Duplan's, as the man in the flat below is still very ill. When I got there, there were several people, so I joined in the conversation when possible. I discovered that a man, whom I took at first to be English, was German. So we spoke German. He complimented my German very highly and said I had a marvellous pronunciation, you might be glad to hear. He gave me his card and said if I took it to the German school here I could get some German books to read, which I shall do at the next possible opportunity. Of course I didn't do any practising.

That evening a friend of Mr G.'s came in. They began playing a silly card game, so when they had finished I said I'd teach them one. I taught them 'Beg-of-my-neighbour'. It took them about half an hour to understand it, but when they did, they played it with tremendous enthusiasm. I also managed to drum 'Old Maid' into their rather wooden heads. The friend was Spanish, hair as black as night, but quite amusing. The next evening he came with another man and some women. We played the card games of the night before, and then I told them that I knew some more, but that I thought they were too dense to understand them. I said it all in Spanish. After about an hour of sweat I had taught them rummy, which they seemed to enjoy.

Every morning after going to the market, the Senora and I and the child go for a walk. The boy is most intelligent and I have promised to teach him to ride the bike he has. San Sebastian is a most charming place. Unfortunately I have not yet seen it in the sun, that is a treat in store. The promenades are most beautifully built up. Apparently in February there are very high seas, which sweep right over the promenades.

Yesterday, Saturday, I went for my music lesson. I had to wait about 20 minutes for someone to finish, and then I began. She certainly is most efficient and I think I'll learn a good bit from her. She is giving a concert on February 19th. After the lesson had been going for about ten minutes, a friend of hers turned up in a car, so we all went for a drive. It was very nice, and they asked me to go to the cinema with them that evening. The friend is a singer, and when we got back she came in with us and sang to us most beautifully. It was so late that I had to come home and postponed the lesson until Monday. It's a most entertaining household and very musical. This morning I'm going for a stroll with Mme Duplan.

Tons of love to you both, and a nice long walk for Ross.

Your very loving, Elizabeth.

16.3.1935.

Queridos padres!

Muchas gracias para su carta que recibe el martes. En el ultima carta que escribe, yo dije que la proxima sea una en Español! (Roughly translated). I cannot express myself very well so far so I will not write much.

Quite a lot happened last week. On Tuesday I told the English girl Mignonne that I would meet her at twelve, thinking she would be at work. But after waiting for half an hour I came home. When she asked me where I had been I found out I had been waiting in the street next to the one where she had waited. Now she and I go for a walk together every day. It is more interesting than with Spaniards. The women here have voices like trumpets and they make so much noise I can't work in the evening in my room. On Wednesday we went to the theatre to see a 'zarzuela', *La del manojo de rosas*. It was lovely, but we did not get back until one o'clock in the morning, so I am very tired. Last night we went to see *Katuiska* again, and now I'm so tired I can't do anything. Mignonne knows some Germans here and tomorrow they are going on an excursion and she has promised to introduce me to them. The Senora is annoyed because I don't work here, but she doesn't understand that there is too much noise.

I've more or less given up going for walks alone, as you never quite know what you are going to meet round the next corner. I'm sorry Green finds me very reserved and bored. At table I'm the centre of conversation, but I am bored at times and I don't like the Spaniards much, but still I'm quite enjoying life. Now that I have made friends with Mignonne, she'll introduce me to some of her friends, who, by the way are all either German or something else, but not Spaniards. She too finds them difficult to get on with.

Tons of love and don't forget to write to me. Take great care of Ross, I love hearing about him in your letters. I wish I could see the garden, it must be glorious now. Send me some *Daily Mirrors* and also some of Tom's and Rosy's letters.

Liza.

30.3.1935.

Darling Parents.

On Monday Mignonne moved into new digs. She has left the family she was living with as they had no more room for her. I went with her to inspect the new room and it looked very nice and clean, but, what do you think? That night she found a bed bug. They are very frequent out here, and the people aren't a bit ashamed of them. As for fleas, well that is nothing, everyone has fleas. I have often found one in my bed, but they don't like me much as I have too many baths. No one here has had a bath since I've been here. The Senora keeps making hints to me, when she tells her husband that the water bill has never been so much before, and always in front of me. But I don't take hints. They don't light the fire any more and I have to heat my bath water on the gas-stove. Every time I ask to put on the water, she mutters something about the gas bill.

Twice this week Mignonne and I have had a game of chess. Now that Mignonne has her own digs, I always go to her in the evenings. Although we speak English, I think it doesn't make any difference whether I'm speaking English or thinking it, because if I'm not with her I'm alone. To-morrow I'm going for an 'Ausflug' with Mignonne, an Irish girl called May and three Germans.

The G's have been very annoying lately. The other day, just because I wasn't feeling hungry, he would keep asking: 'Are you ill, are you sad, are you frightened of growing fat?' I felt like throwing the food in his silly old face. I'm greatly relieved to be able to go to Mignonne's now, as it shortens those awfully long evenings when I used to sit and listen to the mother of Jose Luis and the Senora fighting over Jose Luis, who was being extremely naughty and annoying. Now I go at 4 p.m. and return about 8 p.m. just in time to do my homework, a little knitting and put my bath water on. Yesterday I went to the German school. I got four books and four magazines. Your idea that the Spaniards don't like the Germans is quite wrong. It is quite the contrary. During the war (WWI) most of the Spaniards were pro-German, and still are. They do not care particularly for the English.

No more news for you, so here is some Spanish to translate.

Tons and tons of love from your loving Eliza.

20.4.1935.

Darling parents, Tom and Rosemary.

Thank you very much for your various letters. I'm sorry Tom thought I made a fuss about nothing, I should like to see him in my place. I didn't think it could be so awful until I came here. Being all alone all the time, except when I'm with Mignonne, one is inclined to go a bit funny. Anyway these last few days have been quite fun, as Mignonne's dentist has gone away on a holiday for Easter, so she has been free.

On Thursday we went from San Sebastian over Monte Ulia to Pasajes, that is the next bay to San Sebastian. It was a very pleasant walk and took us about two hours. Yesterday we took the tram to Pasajes, and from here we crossed the bay in a motor-boat and landed in the little old town. It was most picturesque and very Spanish. Pasajes is a port where a few cargo boats call. If I had come by sea I would have arrived there. There were German and Swedish boats in. A narrow neck of sea leads to the harbour so it is excellently protected. From the old town we walked along a very narrow path which led to the sea. It ended abruptly and we climbed a few rocks and sat perched on the top of a precipice. I took a few photos. The scenery along this coast is absolutely magnificent, much more beautiful than along the Italian Riviera. The people here are all Basques and they are most insulted if you call them Spaniards.

Last Sunday was the feast of the Republic. In the evening there were fireworks, they were jolly good. The Boulevard, one of the places of fashion here, was all decorated with lights, it looked very pretty and there were four bands all playing different tunes at once and everyone was dancing. To-day we are going to Zarauz. It is a town about 25 kms along the coast.
Best of luck to Rosy and her scholarship. No more,

Tons and tons of love from your loving Liza.

———————

25.4.1935.

Darling Mummy and Daddy.

I expect you'll wonder at getting a letter at this time of the week. But since I've had so much time for thinking since I've been here, I've thought over a lot what I shall take up, and have decided my talents won't reach far in the dancing line, and that a career connected with languages is the best thing. It therefore strikes me as a pity that I should return home at the end of May, not knowing the language particularly well and not knowing any Spaniards. Mignonne suggested that I should go into one of the richer families who come up here in the summer as an English companion to a daughter and thus earn my board and lodging and pocket money. It is obviously no use staying any longer with the Greens as they can't introduce me to any decent class of people as they don't know them. As you very rightly said, 'They don't move in very high circles.'

It would mean staying out here until the end of September, when the summer season ends. As these families don't come up from Madrid until the end of June, it would mean staying with the Greens until then. It's also quite possible they would think me too young, but you could always add a year on to my age! One gets hold of these families through the Consulate. I should learn Spanish properly, and I would get to know decent people. My time would be fully occupied and I would probably get an entirely different outlook on the Spaniards.

If you agree with this, please write to old Green and say you can't afford to keep me here any longer at this rate, and that as you would like me to be in Spain a bit longer to learn the language better, ask him if it would be possible to find me a place in a family as an English companion for the summer. Put it tactfully as if the idea came from you, because if he gets wind that I wrote to you about it, he'll probably jump to the conclusion that Mignonne and I had been discussing the subject. As Mignonne's 'foster mother' out here is a certain Mrs Lagarde, who also works at the Consulate, he, being petty, as this sort of person is, will make things very unpleasant all round. It seems funny to have to warn you of such things but one must make allowances for these people. I've been most terribly sweet lately and have even given in to them about the baths.

Think this over, while I'm out here I might as well make the best of a bad job. When you write to Green, if you do, tell him that if he can't find me such a family I shall have to leave the country, so that he sees that he won't make anything out of it.

Enclosed two photos, I was awfully bucked as the German in the photo shop where I have my films done only discovered the other day that I am English. She thought I was German, and that's not bad after not having spoken the language since the summer when Annu was over! I do envy you all having such a glorious time. I'm so glad Tom has taken an interest in Ross, the darling (Ross).

Tons and tons of love, your loving, Ibbish.

5.5.1935.

Darling, darling Family,

Thank you very much for your letter. I'm glad you thought my plan a good one. I accept that it is mouldy having to stick in this place all the summer, still one can't have everything. I asked old G this morning if he'd had a letter from you this week, and he said he had. He said I could either go 'au pair' or go and exchange English for board and lodging. If I went 'au pair' it would mean having a Spaniard back to our place next year. I would prefer exchange as I would be more occupied. The only trouble is that those sort of people are harder to get hold of than the others.

I still spend every afternoon and evening with Mignonne. We've bought our own chess board and men, which cost us pts 2.95, 1.45 each. So we have tea in her room and then play or knit or go for a walk. If we're feeling particularly bored, we visit Willy Koch, a German who has been here for years and keeps a photo shop and studio.

May 1st was a great holiday here. It passed quite peacefully, though everything was well guarded by soldiers in all sorts of uniforms. They were in all the trams and buses. Mignonne and I took our lunch to Pasajes, crossed the harbour and climbed up the mountains for a little way. We daren't go too far as two Germans were held up the other day by bandits and had all their money pinched. However, they caught the culprits. We are having filthy weather just now. It rained all yesterday and again to-day. Mignonne is still killing bugs and she is probably going to move at the end of this month as they only get worse as the weather gets warmer.

Tomorrow being Jubilee Day, Mr Goodman, the Consul, has arranged a banquet at the Hotel Maria Christina, the posh one of San Sebastian, costing 30 pesetas each person. Everyone told him he was mad, still he would do it. I am not going, but as both the Greens are, they suggested Mignonne should come here to lunch with me, which was a bright suggestion on the part of old G.

My arm is aching so I'm going to stop. Tons and tons of love to you all, and don't stop writing and don't forget to send some papers.

Tons of love, your loving Ibbish.

12.5.1935.

Darling parents,

Thank you very much for your letters and the papers. The *Punch* was most amusing and thoroughly appreciated by Mignonne and other English people with whom we swop papers. Mignonne is English, or rather Scottish, her surname is Mackenzie. She has been out here since August 1934. At present she is giving English lessons here and supporting herself entirely. Anything else you want to know about her?

Yesterday I went to interview the wife of the Civil Governor out here, who said she knew of someone wanting somebody to look after their children during the summer months. I don't think it's much cop as I'm not going to be a bally nurse and I think the people are going to Valencia for their holidays. Green has heard of a family in Irun who might be wanting someone like me, either as exchange or as a companion to 2 girls, I think. He's not quite sure and is going to write to them. They sound quite satisfactory to me, and Irun is very close here, so I shouldn't mind that. The weather is foul, we haven't had a decent day this week.

Tons of love to everyone, your loving daughter Ibbish.

17.5.1935.

Darling parents,

I'm terribly thrilled because old G's found a family that is by way of taking me either from the beginning of June or the beginning of July. It's a doctor's family in Irun, who live in a villa and have a garden. They have twin daughters of 17. Yesterday afternoon I went to interview them at the Consulate. Their name is Galliano, or something like it. They seem very pleasant people and I ought to be ok there. If they go to Madrid next month, it will mean I can't go there until the beginning of July, but if not I'll go in June. They don't pay me, but I presume they pay all my expenses, but I don't know about that. I saw one of the girls yesterday, she looked very Spanish. I'm to speak English to the girls, but I can speak Spanish to the rest of the family. I hope they don't suddenly decide they don't want me, you never know with Spaniards. I suppose you wouldn't mind me staying at the Gs until July? I mind a lot but still —.

Mignonne has got hold of a woman who will board and lodge her for 6 pesetas a day. That's about 3/-, and it's a very respectable house with lift and everything.

I haven't had a letter from you yet this week so there's nothing to answer. I hope Ross is ok. I do so miss him. Tons and tons of love and write soon and send the money,

your very loving Ibbish.

———————

9.6.1935.

Darling, darling parents.

I'm awfully sorry to hear Tom has measles. He's a marvellous person at catching things. May, who teaches in one of the convents here, had an awful shock the other day. It turned out that two pupils in her class, who had been absent had developed smallpox. She was in an awful panic and rushed off to be vaccinated.

I discovered what had bitten G. It was because the money for June hadn't arrived. The silly ass never told me that the Irun people had told him that they were going to Madrid. Of course I couldn't tell you as I didn't know. He makes out it was all my fault for not writing and telling you that I should be here until July.

I thought you would want me to continue my Spanish lessons. It's probably just as well. I had a sudden brain wave, and asked G. to buy a Spanish history book. So now we study Spanish history in the lesson instead of ploughing through the stodgy grammar, which I now know off by heart.

I'm now out of debt. Mignonne very kindly helped me out with the hat. In return, as I had helped her out at the end of last month. I'm so glad you've got a wireless. I hope I shall be able to play you some marvellous Spanish dances when I come home, if I don't forget them in Irun.

My love and luck to Rosie in her exams, and with tons and tons of love to you all and Ross,

your very loving, Elizabeth.

10.6.1935.

Darling parents,

Just a scribble to tell you that this morning I asked G. what I was to do when Mrs G. went to Pau, and he said he would square up with me for half the month and I could find my own digs until July. Do you agree with this? I shan't be able to get a room with Mignonne, but I shall feed with her and look for a room somewhere else. I shall come everyday to G. for a lesson and go everyday to practise at Caroline's. I think that is quite satisfactory from 15th June. Send my letters still to the Consulate and he'll give them to me.

Tons of love to everyone, your loving daughter, Elizabeth.

16.6.1935.

Darlingest Parents,

Thank you for your letter and the blazer. PLEASE don't worry about me, it's most unnecessary. On Friday G. squared up with me and gave me 132pts. He charged me for the wireless which I knocked against and in which I broke two valves. It was an accident and I'm sorry about it. That is what brought the amount down.

G. was perfectly horrid to me. When he gave me the money he started by saying 'I consider it very rude of you to say it was cheek of me to charge you for the telephone calls to Irun.' I couldn't think what he meant or how he got to know that I thought it cheek and he told me that ever since I'd been here he'd been reading my diary. Just imagine, the little swine! He must have gone every day to my drawer and read it and also read your letters that I sometimes didn't tear up immediately. Luckily for me, Mignonne had told me about a fortnight ago that G. had been reading my diary, as apparently he has told everyone in San Sebastian what's in it. There's nothing much in it except my opinion of him, and I wrote how I hated him. So I hope he got a good shock! When he told me, I simply said that in England it was considered the height of dishonesty to read letters and diaries without the owner's consent. Don't you think he is a cad?

I've got very nice digs with Mignonne and you need have no fear that there's any disease or bugs. Fleas there are, but they are everywhere in Spain.

49

I have a room in the other flat on this floor. It's a nice little room and the furniture is entirely new. The flat is owned by a woman who is a cook in some hotel. There's no one in the house after 10 a.m. There's another inhabitant besides the cook, but I haven't seen him, or her, yet. I swamped my room in flea powder and slept like a log. I spend all day with Mignonne. I have breakfast with her, for which we are given tea, toast and butter. Then I go to the beach and to-morrow an English girl is coming with me who is staying with May until the 1st July and then going to a family like me. For lunch we have soup, eggs or fish or vegetable dish, meat and potatoes, fruit. For tea we just have tea, for supper a vegetable dish, meat or eggs and fruit. It all costs 8 pts a day – room, food and laundry. I paid the woman who feeds me and she's going to pay my room. The people are awfully nice, the milliner, who has a little shop in the Boulevard, and her husband and her sister who does the cooking. Mignonne is being very sweet to me and most comforting when I rushed in from the Greens. She says you may be reassured that I shall be ok here under her eagle eye.

I'm not continuing my lessons with G. The day I told him I didn't want to go to Pau and we fixed up that I should move, I said that, of course, I should be continuing my lessons till the end of the month. However, after he'd been so beastly and seemed to have taken it for granted that I wasn't having my lessons, I said no more about it. I hope this is not against your wishes, Papa. I promise I'll do an hour of Spanish history every day, and keep my brain from getting rusty. I'll be going every day to the Consulate to see if there are any letters for me, so continue to send them there. Next week sometime I'll go to Irun to see the people and fix up when I shall go to them. It would make a great difference if you would write to them. It will be nice to get there, and feel I've something definite in front of me.

I feel so much happier now I'm away from the Greens. It was so awful having that horrid woman always fussing about if I kept the light on for two minutes or if I wanted any water heated to wash in or anything, and all the shouting and the awful child and his awful mother. It will be nice in Irun too, to have company of my own age. Everyone I know here is so much older than I am, even Mignonne. I've heard from different quarters that the Galianas in Irun are highly esteemed people, so I'm sure I shall be ok there.

This morning we had a ripping bathe, the water was simply super! I've bought myself a very modest bathing costume as the other was a bit small. I've just been told that the people in Irun will probably want me to wear a bathing dress with a skirt down to my knees! You see lots of them on the beach, probably like the one Mummy wore in the 19th century! How glorious it will be to be home again. I haven't met an English or a German living here who likes the country. It's a different matter for tourists, of course.

Don't worry, I know it's very hard for you not to, but I can assure you

I'm just as well off here as with the Greens. You are very brave to let me do this, but the fortnight will soon be over and then I shall be well off. My best love to Uncle Jim and family and Uncle Bodkin. I hope they'll still be in England when I return. Tons and tons of love and take Ross for a long walk and see he is well brushed and not getting too fat.

Your loving daughter, Elizabeth.

Cheque £12.10.0 at 35 pesetas ptas 448.75
17 days at 12 ptas 204.00
Half a month Spanish lessons 37.50
Piano lessons 25.00
2 new valves to set 50.00 316.50
Balance given to Miss Deck Ptas. 132.25

24.6.35.

Darling parents,

Thank you so much for your letter which I got this afternoon. I'm surprised G. wrote and told you that I had refused to go to Pau and the boarding house that Mrs G. had found for me. It's the first I've heard of any boarding house. On the morning I was leaving she said to me that of course I was going of my own free will and that I could have had my food out with G. and slept where I was. I can assure you that the Gallanos (not Galiano) are very sound people. I've heard that they are very well-known and respected in Irun. Would you please send me another cheque. I hate asking again so soon for money, but as you say, I don't want to run short there. They are still in Madrid but they will be returning this week and then I'll ring them up. Send the money by cheque and to the Consulate so that it arrives before Monday 1st.

We had a marvellous time on the beach this morning. There were several Germans there. The town is simply swarming with English people. I'm having a lovely holiday, Peggy and I are usually together in the morning while Mignonne is working, but she too has a holiday for the next few days.

I'm sorry not to be at home with all the Argentine cousins and everything. I hope Ross doesn't love you too much or he'll forget all about me. Has he grown much? My heartiest congratulations to Rosy. I hope old Tom gets over his measles, he seems to have had a mouldy time. I like your description of Lippy! I don't think you'll find me with red lips. I've seen so many red lips and red nails and all those disgusting things, that I'd do anything to look as un-Spanish as possible! I'm assured by everyone that I look very English, so I feel ok.

My love to everyone and to Tom and Rosy when you see them,

Your loving daughter, Elizabeth.

Time Gone

c/o Dr Gallano, Mendivil, Irun.

2.7.1935.

Darling parents,

Thank you very much for the cheque, which arrived in the nick of time. Well here I am in Irun. I was sorry to leave San Sebastian and Mignonne, but I have soon got over that.

The Gallanos have a very nice villa here. The architecture is Basque, and looks just like a Swiss chalet. It is very comfortable inside and nicely furnished. You enter into a hall, which has a huge fireplace in one corner with copper urns hanging about. Half of it serves as sitting room and opens out on to a terrace overlooking the garden. A wide staircase leads up out of the hall to the next floor. The dining room is panelled and has heavy wooden furniture. I haven't explored the other wing, but I think it consists of his study and reception room. I have a very nice room upstairs next to the bathroom. It has two windows, one a French window opening on to the balcony. I also have a basin with H & C running water. The bathroom is huge and has a shower and all sorts of luxuries! And I can have a bath whenever I want one. The twins have a very nice room. All painted in an orangey shade with counterpanes of white material with huge blue and red spots, very Basque. Altogether it is very comfortable and it seems hard for me to realise that I'm still in Spain. The Basques are so very different from the Spaniards, I much prefer them. I haven't explored the garden yet.

The family consists of Ma and Pa, and son and the twins, whose names are Maria Dolores and Maria Angeles. There are some cousins of theirs staying in the house, a girl of about 14 and a boy the same age as their son. I haven't yet discovered which is the son and which is the nephew! One is called Ignacio and the other Jaime. Ignacio is an awful wet and talks continuously at the top of his voice. Jaime doesn't look so wet and yesterday had lost his voice, which is just as well. We only see them at meals. They have several animals. The chickens I have heard but not seen, two dogs, one a black Alsatian which is seldom at home, the other a terrier of the 57 varieties, who is rather inclined to snap, but hasn't snapped at me. There are two canaries which sing at the tops of their voices, one in the dining-room and the other outside my room upstairs, and there is a cat who sleeps all day except at meal times. There are two maids and a cook, and the food is very good. The manners are a bit peculiar, and various courses one has to eat off the same plate, but apart from that, it is well dished up and well served. Yesterday we had lunch in the garden under an awning. Breakfast is served for each person as they come down. Dinner (midday) at 1.30 p.m., tea at 6 (not high tea) and supper at 9.30 p.m., and bed anytime afterwards.

This last week-end has been the 'Fiesta of San Marcial' who is the Patron

Saint of Irun, and yesterday was the last day, so we went to the fair. I haven't seen much of Irun yet, but it's only a village, and it's lovely after San Sebastian. It's quite like living in the country.

To-day we are going to Hendaye in France! If I can change the cheque to-day, I shall send a wire as I expect you'll be worrying about me! The twins don't and won't understand English which is a bit trying! If I just persist in talking to them, I suppose they'll soon get the nack of it. They have a Standard 9, but I think they are getting another car.

I think I've told you everything of interest. PLEASE send my klepperles. They must be somewhere at home, as I certainly haven't them with me, and they would be so useful here. Don't forget to send me as many papers as possible as now I'm utterly and entirely without news from England. I must stop now as I still have my trunk to unpack.

Tons and tons of love to everyone, from your very loving daughter, Ibbish.

Sunday, 7th July 1935.

Darlingest parents,

I'm sorry I didn't sent the telegram as I said in my letter, but I didn't get the cheque changed until Thursday and my letter probably had arrived by then. I hope you weren't worrying. I'm thoroughly enjoying myself here. The people are really awfully nice. The only crab is that the twins seem entirely opposed to learning English. I read with them, or I should say to them as they refuse to, in the morning and for the rest of the day, everything I say to them I say in English and try to make them speak English to me. The son Ignacio is 17. I thought he was at least 20. The other boy Jaime is a cousin, also cousin to the other girl, Pili, who is here too. The other day a French boy arrived. Last year Ignacio went to France to his family, so this year the French boy has come here. He's a bit of a fool and never opens his mouth.

I have explored the house entirely now, it has two bathrooms. One frightfully posh, with shower complete, the other not quite so. I must stop now as they are laying the table, so goodbye, with tons and tons of love to everyone, your very loving daughter, Elizabeth.

Monday morning. P.S. Have just received your letter. Mrs Gallano is a nice motherly sort of person, and very kind. I'm glad Tom's got over his measles safely. My bathing dress reaches down to the knees and would have reached farther had I not cut some off!

Time Gone

Darling parents,

I'm still thoroughly enjoying myself, and actually beginning to appreciate the Spaniards. I still struggle trying to make the twins speak English. Maria Angeles is doing an English exam in the middle of September, so every day we do an hour's work at English grammar etc. Maria Dolores has private coaching at the Convent here in Chemistry and Physics as she has to take that part of the exam over again in September, as she failed in June. So I don't even get as far as reading with her. The weather here seems to divide itself into 2 days sunny and 4 days rain. At present we're experiencing the four days rain, and so for the last two or three days we've been indoors practically all the time. The last spell of sunny days we naturally spent on the beach. I'm actually getting quite brown, in spite of the Victorian bathing dress. But against the Spaniards I look as white as snow.

Last night there was an amateur variety show in aid of some charity at the local theatre got up by the 'Cultura Femenina'. The twins had a part in the last item, so we all went. It went off very well, and this morning we were all in bed until about half past eleven. To-day we're going to the flicks, also at the local theatre. Jaime, the cousin, left on Thursday, and Pili left to-day much to the sorrow of everyone. She was the life and soul of the party. Yesterday two girls came to tea and stayed on to see the play, and are still here. We played games last night and I taught them dumb charades.

Would you please send me my prayer-book. Also some more money. Journey expenses and the Victorian bathing dress made rather a hole in the last cheque. I also bought some wool for a cardigan for Mummy. I don't want to run short here, as it would be rather awkward.

Do you realise it's nearly a year now that we've been at Amor? How is Ross getting on? Is he still as obedient? Give my love to everyone, and tons of love,

from your loving daughter, Elizabeth.

———————

Monday 29th July 1935.

Darling parents,

I've still got no money, but as this letter won't go until I get it, that is unnecessary information. Yesterday was great. We all went to the 'Corrida de Toros'. At the present there is a Congress of Doctors on in San Sebastian. Doctors from practically all countries in Europe have come. Of course Dr Gallano plays an important part in it, and for the four days great festivities

54

have been arranged. The bull-fight was one, and the daughters of the doctors were the 'Senoritas de la Presidencia', who are the honoured guests at the bull fight. The twins were invited to take part, but as it involves wearing 'peineta y mantilla', it was decided that they were too young. We were all invited to lunch. The twins and I went to one house, and Dr and Mrs Gallano to the house of some doctor, where the other doctors were being entertained. Directly after lunch we joined them and saw all the Senoritas leave in a carriage entirely bedecked with flowers. It was most picturesque and colourful. We left the house after them in various cars and joined the procession of traffic that had, since half past two, been making its way to the bull-ring. When we arrived there was the most awful confusion parking the cars and a deafening noise of hooters and policemen shouting and losing their tempers. We got to our places at last, which were practically in the front row, very near and very frightening.

There were seven bulls. The first was a young one, and rather tamer than the rest, chosen especially so that they could do tricks with him. A table was put directly opposite the door where the bull entered, and as he charged it, the man standing on the table leapt over his back. It was very clever. Then with a long pole he pole-jumped it whilst it was charging. Then came the banderillas, which I explained in my last letter, only these ones had small birds inside them, and as they struck the bull the birds were released. There was also a picador mounted on a lovely horse which was free and not blindfolded like the other poor wretches. The bull didn't touch it. This was the only bull I've seen killed first go. The man did it very well, and in reward he was given the ear. The other six bulls were fought in the manner I described in one of my previous letters. One of the toreadors called Bienvenda fought very well, only killed very badly. The others weren't up to much. Nearly all the bulls were killed in front of us. Very obliging of the toreadors, but I don't think fully appreciated by the twins and myself. One of the bulls jumped over the barrier, behind which stand various members of the bull-fight, who at the moment weren't working. You should have seen them leap into the arena! One horse was killed, poor brute. It looked as though it had never had a square meal, literally a skeleton covered with skin.

After the bull-fight we went to a tea dansant at the Kursaal in San Sebastian. 'Miss Europe 1935' was also an honoured guest at the bull-fight, and as you can imagine, enthusiastically greeted by the crowd!

At the end of this week we are going up to Vera for the 'fiestas' for a few days. Mignonne leaves for England on August 1st, lucky blighter.

No more for now, tons of love, your loving daughter, Elizabeth.

4.8.1935.

Darling Family,

I'm now with the twins in Vera. We arrived here yesterday in the car. Yesterday afternoon the fiestas began, which consist of music in the village square and people dancing the jota and fireworks and a few side shows. It was quite fun and we danced until midnight. Vera is only a village of about 3000 inhabitants and very Basque as, being in the Pyrenees, they are more shut off from the rest of Spain. We are staying with the parents of Pili. She has three sisters all younger than herself. The house is pretty big, consisting of four storeys, the two top ones being let. We are staying until the end of the fiestas, which last four days. They have two most amusing dogs here, both puppies. One of six months old is a black terrier with pointed ears, a most comical creature. The other is a huge white dog with enormous paws, quite out of proportion to its body, and is about seven months old.

We're just going off again to dance in the village square. This morning we watched some Basque dances, and than a 'pelota' match. The local inhabitants played against some French Basques, the French won. Pelota is the national game and is very similar to fives.

Do you get my letters from Irun quicker now? The first ones I posted in the only pillarbox in the town, but apparently they only empty it about once a week, so now I post them at the station.

Tons of love to everyone, your loving daughter, Elizabeth.

11.8.1935.

Darling parents,

We have just arrived back from Vera. It was a great week and I thoroughly enjoyed it and also learnt a lot about the Basques. Most exciting was the final 'corre calles', when everyone dancing in the square ran down the hill through the main street. I was lucky not to have been knocked over, nor to have fallen down.

I wish you could have been there to enjoy the scenery. It's too glorious for words. Great mountains with fantastic peaks and rivers simply jumping with trout. We bathed twice in a lovely river which further down forms the boundary between Spain and France and flows into the sea at Fuenterabia. They wanted us to stay longer, but as Lolo (Maria Dolores) has lessons to do at school, we had to return.

One day we visited Pio Baroja, the famous Spanish novelist. I expect you've read some of his books, *Red Dawn* and *Caesar, or Nothing* and several others.

It's a fantastic house, very old and like a museum inside. His brother, who is an artist, showed us round, and he was the one, by the way, who was so thrilled by my dancing the 'jota'. He told me that while digging in the garden, they had dug up some skeletons of British soldiers who died fighting against Napoleon. Aunt Eva would have been thrilled. (N.B. I did not know, or had forgotten, that my great great grandfather Henry LeMesurier had lost his arm carrying the Regimental Colours at the Battle of Salamanca in the Peninsula War). We scooted about on bikes and took several photos. They have a very nice Chrysler here which we went about in a bit.

The last two days have been simply roasting and the family have flopped about in the hall, which was the only cool place. I've finished a lovely pair of socks for Daddy and am finishing Mummy's cardigan.

Tons and tons of love to you all, your loving daughter, Elizabeth.

————————

18.8.1935.

Darling parents,

I'm now halfway through my stay here, and rather wish I were more. One gets rather sick of the slap-dashness and slackness of the Spaniards. The last few days we've spent the morning at Fuenterabia bathing and the afternoon in San Sebastian or on excursions. Yesterday Pilar and Jose Marie (the niece and nephew of the Gallanos from Madrid who are staying here with their mother) and Pilar's fiancé and I went to San Marciel, which is a chapel situated on top of a fairly high hill near here. It commands the most marvellous view as far as San Sebastian on one side and Biarritz in France on the other. The twins had to stay at home as a punishment for all the arguing they did as regards where we should go! Mother was very firm, a quality I admire as it is so rare out here.

Last week was very low tide at Fuenterabia and every day we waded across the channel that divides France and Spain. It's such a funny feeling just walking from one country to another.

Every night after supper Ignacio tunes into London for the dance music from 10.30 to 12, here from 9.30 to 11, and he and the twins are by way of learning to dance. You never saw anything quite so hopeless, especially the waltz.

————————

2.9.1935.

Darlingest parents,

Only 25 more days. If I can I'm coming home on the 27th, leaving here on the 26th, so that I arrive in time for the weekend. I don't suppose these people mind what day I go. Everyone follows their secret heart in Spain.

Thank you for the letter and book of careers, which I studied very thoroughly. I'm terribly sorry to miss Uncle Bodkin. Will the Argentines have gone too when I return? When I next go to San Sebastian, I'll enquire at Cook's about the price of my journey home and then I'll let you know.

Maria Angeles is at last beginning to wake up to the fact that I'm here to converse with her in English! That is quite encouraging, Lolo hasn't even got that far. We've had quite fine weather for the last few days, and every day we go to the beach. Last week we went twice to Hendaye on various errands, and Maria Angeles and I walked over there this morning. On Wednesday the new car arrived. An Austin 9 and a natty little bus, and to celebrate the arrival, Dr Gallano took the twins and Pili and me for a picnic lunch near a village farther into the Pyrenees than Vera. We had lunch in a cool spot and then went up to the top of the mountain, half of which is Spanish and the other half French. But there is no sign of the boundary except a solitary stone. There were several men shooting pigeons which were flying over. It was lovely scenery. The other day we went to the theatre, it was not a bad show but I wasn't struck. We also went to the flicks and I saw a Spanish film for the second time since I've been out here.

Please send some *Daily Mirrors*, it's ages since I saw an English paper and the Spanish ones are so exaggerated. You must arrange a beagle meet at Amor for the next season, it would be ripping. I shall certainly be charming to Vera Churchill if there's any hope of getting a horse out of her!

Tons and tons of love to you all, from your very loving Ibbish.

P.S. I'm so thrilled about coming home.

————————————

9.9.1935.

Darlingst parents,

This week we've done practically nothing but go to Hendaye. I've never used my passport so much in all my life! This weekend Fuenterabia was plunged into 'fiestas'. In Fuenterabia, like in Irun, besides celebrating the day of their Patron Saint, they celebrate the anniversary of a battle which the 18th century inhabitants of that village won against the French. Hence it is a very special fiesta. Dr Gallano secured us a balcony in the house of one of his clients and from there we had a marvellous view of the 'march past' of various companies, all armed with shot-guns and dressed in a variety of peasant dress. Each Company halted in front of the Town Council, which was the building next door, and shot off blank cartridges. The idea was that they should all shoot together like one man, but very few succeeded. The other idea was to make as much noise as possible, in which they certainly did succeed. The church bells were ringing, each company had its own band, which played a different tune to the one preceding it and add to that the shoutings and shootings, and it was very noisy. Everything was crowded into the Calle Mayor about the only street in Fuenterabia and so narrow that I doubt whether two cars could pass each other. However it was all very picturesque, and I'm sure Aunt Eva and Aunt Winnie would have revelled in it.

Think of it – only 5 more days, isn't it glorious! This time next week I shall be at Amor. No more now as we're just off to bathe,

Tons and tons of love to you all from your loving daughter, Elizabeth.

Back from Spain in September 1935, I was granted another autumn at home at Amor. I was delighted to be reunited with Ross. Rosemary had left the convent in Seroule in Belgium and had spent the last term at Ipswich High School, whence she had been granted a scholarship to Felixstowe College, where she had now started in her first term. Once again I accompanied my father on his shooting expeditions looking after Ross the gun-dog, who was inclined to be rather wild.

At the Lower Abbey, living in one of the farm cottages, was a cousin of the Ropes, Vevita and her two little boys from Bogota, where war had broken out. Because she spoke little English, I was often sent to spend the day with her to help her with the boys and to ease her homesickness by speaking Spanish. Her cottage overlooked the marshes where my father used to go flighting with Geoff Rope, my cousin Tilly's husband. This was an early morning or late evening activity, and we would get home in the evenings absolutely famished, but instead of a welcoming high tea, we had to wait and change for dinner, by which time both of us were falling asleep. Happy days were also spent scrambling over the ploughed fields and meadows following the local beagles. My father also gave me another few days out following the Eastern Harriers on a hired mount.

Christmas 1935 was celebrated again with Aunt Eva and the Spencers coming to stay. I got very friendly with their son Marlay, whom I had known all my life and who was my age. My father's old Cambridge friend, Bodkin Wood, who was with the Colonial Agricultural Service in Trinidad, put up the money for my secretarial training, and in January 1936 I started at Kerr Saunders Secretarial Training College in Piccadilly, London W.1.

The College occupied the top floors of a show room in Piccadilly opposite

Green Park station. I lodged in the College hostel for the first few weeks, but soon joined forces with a girl from Kingsbridge called Bridget. We shared digs in St. John's Wood. I did not enjoy the training much and had few friends and no social life. I went home for week-ends when I could afford it, which wasn't often. London did not appeal to me and I longed for the countryside and the life I knew in Suffolk. During the summer months I became friendly with a red-headed girl called Sheila Marshall, who was also doing German on the course. She had spent some time in Munich, of which she was very fond. It was the year of the Olympic Games in Berlin and we decided we would spend our summer holidays in Germany. Sheila's widowed mother lived in Suffolk near Colchester, where her son was stationed with his Battery, and she had two younger daughters. Sheila had had a very select education at Westonbirt and she brought a touch of class to my sinking social life. I had lost touch with Pauline Hedges, who was still running her father's household and following the county social round in Bedfordshire. Sheila arranged with her brother David to let me ride one of his horses from the Colchester barracks. I push-biked from Amor Hall to Colchester one fine morning and found myself left to my own devices mounted on one of the battery chargers. I rode out along a track, but when my mount decided he had had enough of this inexperienced lightweight, he took the bit between the teeth and bolted back to his stable. Mercifully I managed to stay up and we clattered back to the stable yard to the entertainment of the gunners.

The Spanish Civil War had broken out and in July I got a most distressing letter from Maria Dolores Gallano.

Irun 7 – 1936.
¡Arriba Espana!

Dearest Elizabeth,

I cannot write you before because the communications are shut, but now they are open again.

All Irun was destroyed by the fire the reds set alight. I am 'fascist'. Every Sunday we parade and go to Mass with all the other people.

My Uncle Juan escaped from Bilbao in a ship with German people. When I have a snap of Irun burned I will sent it to you and also another in the fascist uniform.

My father has been at the front of Toledo and he was in the ruins of Alcazar.

Your affectionate friends,
Maria Dolores and M. Angeles.

Sheila and I set off on our jaunt to Germany. In my absence it was arranged that the Gallano twins would come to us at Amor for the rest of the summer holidays until they could enter a Weybridge convent for the September term.

Meanwhile Sheila and I were sight-seeing in Weimar and Dresden. One evening in Weimar we fell in with some young men in a Gasthaus and were plied with 'Viertel' – little jugs of wine – all evening, sitting and chatting round a table. When we got up to go I found to my horror my legs giving way. Somehow with super human effort and without disgracing ourselves, Sheila and I got back safely to our lodgings. The next day both of us felt very much the worse for wear and vowed to drink less next time. I had written to Annu to tell her I was in Germany again. She had tickets for the equestrian events at the Olympics, so we decided to join forces and meet in Berlin. Sheila was going to stay in Munich so we parted company. I joined Annu in Berlin and after the Games we returned to Freiburg. Mrs Mez lent a ready ear to my pleading for some opportunity or job to enable me to stay in Germany. Annu was starting at the Frauenschule Reifenstein. Maiu was at home awaiting her call-up for 'Arbeitsdienst' (work service) which she had to complete before being allowed to join the Dolmetscher-schule in Heidelberg. Mrs Mez sent us both off to Meersburg on the Lake of Constance for a week's recuperation. I was to look after Maiu! We spent our days swimming in the lake and sipping chocolate in the lakeside cafes. Maiu caught the eye of a not-so-young man in an open sports car, and before I could dissuade her, went off for a drive. I wondered how I was to break the news to Mrs Mez if she found out, or if anything untoward should befall Maiu. She returned safely, of course, and laughed at my concern. We spent our last day, which was very hot and sunny, on a raft with friends on the lake. I came back with a fearful sunburn, which gave me a blistered and painful back for my return by train on a wooden seat via Hook of Holland and Harwich. I could barely move my limbs for pain and my mother had to keep me back from College. This was just as well as the Gallano twins had arrived and Rosemary was getting a bit tired of acting as hostess.

At the end of the summer holidays the twins went to St. Maur's Convent in Weybridge and I returned to London. I found digs in Barkston Gardens and finally achieved my Leaving Certificate. However, I failed to get a permanent job and had to go on the College Temporary Secretary list, which at least meant I could start earning the minimum wage the College allowed us to accept, namely £2.10.0 per week. One incident from those days stands out in my memory. I had been confined to bed with a sore throat and fever. My mother asked my Aunt Elise Croll to visit me and check that I was all right. She turned up to find a Danish boy friend visiting me with a gift of a potted geranium, which for some reason caused her much amusement. I don't think she approved of the Dane!

In September I received another letter from Maria Dolores, which translated reads as follows:

Weybridge, St. Maur's Convent, Surrey.
10.9.1936.

Dear Friend,

I am writing to say that we cannot come on the 18th. My mother has written to ask if it would be possible for us to come on 1st October and stay with you for a few days before we return to Irun. At the moment we cannot return as everything is destroyed at the hands of the Communists before they left the town. But thanks be to God, our house is all right as Philomena and Isabel and Papa are there, but Mama and Ignacio and the grandparents are in Hendaye. Also with them is Concha Aleixandre with her five little children. But the most disgraceful and horrendous thing that they did was to murder Pepe, Concha's husband. He was shot on 1st September and they are absolutely ruined. They also ruined the family of Perez-Caballero, I wonder if you remember them, the parents of Casildita Taraquieta? What is happening is the most awful horror. The Paseo de Colon in Irun is completely destroyed.

Let me know if the arrangements suit you.

Good-bye and with greetings to your parents, M. Lolo.

Following this letter, I went home to be with the twins until they returned home to Irun. Sometime later there appeared in the newspapers an account of the arrest of a Mr Green, who had been caught smuggling items across the frontier at Irun in the British Diplomatic bag!

Christmas of 1936 followed the pattern of the previous years, with Aunt Eva and the Spencers staying as usual. My parents gave me a 'coming out dance'. It was a tremendous party, although most of the guests were better known to Tom and Rosemary, who had partied with them in the school holidays when I had been abroad. We went beagling, and we went beating for my Father's shoots and in the evenings we sang around the piano, played cards and charades.

1937 dawned for me still on the job hunting trail. Conscious of my inability to impress with my tomboyish looks, I dolled myself up with new make-up and a sophisticated outfit, or so I thought, and went along to see my Aunt Elise at East Sheen. 'What have you done to yourself?' she cried, 'you look awful!' Notwithstanding this rebuff, my confidence and self-respect were mercifully restored by a letter from Mrs Mez telling me that she could fix me up with an 'au pair' arrangement for the summer with an aristocratic family in the Uckermark, north of Berlin. The daughter of the house was at Reifenstein with Annu. My joy knew no bounds and my parents, somewhat exasperated, agreed to finance my trip.

The family living costs at Amor Hall were a constant worry to my father and he began to cast around for remunerative employment to supplement his pension. He had accepted a commission to go to the Gold Coast (Ghana) West Africa from my Uncle Cedric Croll who had interests in a timber concession there. He wanted my father to assess its viability. On 20th April 1937 my father wrote to my mother that he was enjoying the job in West Africa as it was just like being a District Commissioner again, roads, bridges, Government farms etc. He said he hoped to save quite a bit out of his £30 per month as he did not need to spend much out there. He said he was sorry she was having trouble letting the house, but not to bother over much about it, and that he should know more about the date of his return after a week or two.

After some introductory correspondence it was agreed that I should travel to Alexanderhof near Prenzlau to the von Heydens in May. There follow my letters home, which my mother kept.

Chapter Six

Travelling and Working –
Germany 1937 – London 1938

'Bei Frau von Heyden, Alexanderhof,
Prenzlau/Uckermark, Germany'
Saturday 22nd May 1937.

Darlingest Mummy,

I have just despatched a telegram to you with the intelligible message 'OK'. I had a very pleasant journey.

This is a colossal, self-contained farm. All the labourers live in cottages which line the upper end of the drive, which is two kms long. The house stands back from the cottages and the farm buildings. It looks very imposing from the front and the back. Downstairs it has some very large rooms. So far I've only discovered the hall, dining room, drawing room, with an ante-room leading off it and his study. Upstairs there is a very large landing, the stairs are at the extreme end of the house, with a long passage, off which lead all the rooms. There are multitudes of them and mine is at the extreme end of the passage furthest from the stairs. The bathroom I have not yet discovered. Its existence I doubt!

The family so far consists of father, mother, two daughters and a son. Father is very nice and quite English to look at, appallingly strict, no powder, rouge, high heels etc. for his daughters. Mother's acquaintance I have not yet made. Hildemie is very nice and speaks better English than I expected. The other daughter is older than her and paints. I don't see much of her except at meals, so I suppose she lives in her studio. The son is married and I have not met him. Hildemie has a friend staying here, who speaks very good English and is awfully nice. I have not yet made out the extent of the staff. So far there is a secretary who feeds with us, a housekeeper who doesn't, a butler and about three maids, I think, a chauffeur and then the farm hands. They have a very nice car and yesterday we were driven into Prenzlau.

The countryside is quite pretty round about, with several lakes. The garden is extensive, consisting of lawns, which are hand cut by scythe, and wonderful lilac bushes and all sorts of shrubs. This morning after family prayers on the terrace we went to watch the farm labourers dressed up in S.A. kit (Nazi) doing gym over an old mare who stood there as good as gold the whole time, while six men did all sorts of long-arm balances on her back. It is very hot to-day and we are going down to bathe. They have a pond, apparently, at the bottom of the garden. I haven't seen it yet. This morning we went for a stroll with Father round about through some corn fields. They also keep a barouche! I saw Father out in it to-day.

I don't think there is more to tell you yet. Will write again when there is some more news.

Tons of love to you, from your loving, Elizabeth.

————————

6th June 1937.

Darling Mummy,

Thank you very much for your letter and for the papers, which were extremely welcome. I'm still loving it here. Hildemie and I are great friends and I manage to make her talk English. I'm enclosing some photos. The one of Hildemie and her father is good of both, but the other one is bad of everybody. Last week we had foul weather, I think it was more or less universal. On Monday there was great excitement about the German ship being bombed, but it soon wore off. On Tuesday Hildemie and I had a riding lesson. I rode a most peculiar horse, but afterwards changed on to a three year-old which Herr Hoffman (estate manager) had just finished breaking. She is a little difficult to manage and as all other horses here are used in carriage or carts, Herr von Heyden is going to buy two new ones for Hildemie and me to ride, which is really too nice of him. On Friday we had another lesson. We are taught by the leader of the local S.A. group and as he used to be something or other in a cavalry regiment, he knows what he is about, and I'm picking up a lot of tips.

On Wednesday there is to be a 'thé dansant' at the officers' mess of the Flying corps stationed at Prenzlau. We were of the intention of going, but I think Frau von Heyden is returning that day, in which case we won't. The other day Hildemie and I beat the honey out of the honeycombs. I don't know if you know the process, but it is quite simple. Yesterday evening, Herr v. Heyden, Hildemie and I played three-handed bridge. The old boy is very keen, so maybe I'll get some more games. Saturday of next week is his birthday, for which great things are being prepared.

I would love a copy of *Horse Sense and Horsemanship of To-day* by Geoffrey Brooke if you can get it.

I got a letter from Annu the other day. She is coming here about the 1st of July. The v. Heydens do quite a lot of entertaining, nearly all their acquaintances are 'Grafs' or 'Freiherrs', all with von attached to their names, so I'm moving in high circles!

We were out watching the S.A. this morning at their usual Sunday riding and gym. This afternoon Hildemie and I are going to bathe in the Krummersee, which lies about 10 minutes walk from here on the farm, so very private and select. Hildemie is just about to give me a concert on her concertina, so I'll stop or I won't write sense.

Tons and tons of love, and to the Crolls, from your loving Elizabeth.

---

13 June 1937.

Darling Mummy,

I've no letter from you to answer this week. Yesterday was Herr von Heyden's birthday. There were great celebrations and a dinner party in the evening. The day before, Hildemie and I had helped get the best china and silver from the store and clean it up. In the morning he was presented with all his presents. In the afternoon the second daughter, Ditta, arrived, also an old friend of the v. Heydens' (a man) and a cousin (a woman). Then we had a tea party. In the evening some more guests arrived, Baron and Baronin von Buchholtz. They live in Prenzlau and are the parents of Maria, who is a great friend of Hildemie's and of whom we see a great deal. He is a very charming old man with whom I spoke English, German and Spanish alternately. After a terrific dinner, at least so it seemed because usually we only have supper, Herr von Heyden, Ditta, the other man whose name I can't remember and myself played bridge.

On Wednesday of last week Frau von Heyden returned. She is the most charming little woman, although a bit quiet.

On Friday there was great excitement in Prenzlau. A new regiment of gunners have just been transferred here into some new barracks and on Friday they marched in, or rather drove in as they are mechanised. We push-biked in in the morning to watch the proceedings and nearly collapsed in the heat.

Some time next month Hildemie is going to visit her brother and sister-in-law in East Prussia, and they want me to go too. We go by boat and the fare is only about 30 mks return. I think I could almost save it out of my pocket money. I don't yet know if we will actually stay with Hildemie's brother or if we will accompany her sister-in-law to a seaside place. Anyway it won't cost much. So far I've spent 30 mks. I've still 20 mks left out of the first cheque which I cashed at the frontier for 50 marks. I think it would be a good idea for me to go, or don't you? I had a letter from Rosy last week. I expect you were at her speech day on Friday.

I'm sorry Daddy isn't returning for so long.

Tons of love, Mumkins, from your loving Elizabeth.

19th June 1937.

Darling Mama,

Thank you so much for your letter which I got yesterday.

All last week a funny old aunt was staying here. She was easy to entertain as she slept in the morning and all the afternoon, and then went to bed at 8.30 p.m. On Wednesday we took her to Schwedt, which is a small town lying about 40 kms from here on the Oder. Hildemie and I drove with the aunt, and when we had dropped her, we went to visit a young married couple. The man is a relation of the von Heyden's, and is stationed there in a cavalry regiment. They were both very charming and invited us both to a 'Biwack' which they were going to have the following evening. A 'Biwack' is a military term for a camp. The next evening we duly turned up and there were all the soldiers with their tents, and sausages and beer and music. There was an enormous bonfire, and around it they had dug two ditches, the edge of the ditch being the seat and the ditch the footstool. There were several other officers and some girls there. We partook of the army rations of three sausages and some beer and then everyone collected around the fire and sang! Afterwards we danced. The party was broken up by rain at about half past eleven. I wish you could have heard the singing. It was too wonderful. They sang as though they were marching, leaving a pause after each line of the song and during the pause one could hear the echo. It was quite fantastic.

We had two riding lessons last week. The bloke who teaches us reminds me very much of C. Spencer! Just that type. You would laugh at the post mortem held at the supper table over the riding lesson. Father is an old soldier (incidentally was also stationed at Schwedt) and the secretary talks as though she was the only person in the world who could ride, and between them Hildemie and I are put through our paces. We haven't been bathing this week as it has been too jolly cold.

There is a lot of fruit and vegetables in the garden just now and every now and again terrific baskets full of strawberries or peas or something are brought up to be stalked or podded for preserving. To-day we are pruning the apple and pear trees.

We are making colossal plans for July. I don't know how many of them will come off. Annu also wants to come here on the 1st July, in which case, if we go, Annu may come with us, but if we don't, as we won't if Hildemie's sister-in-law comes to Germany, Annu will just stay here. Mrs Mez has invited both Hildemie and me to stay in Freiburg some time in September.

Every day we read some English. *Murder in Miami* was the first book chosen, and while Hildemie is reading, I take it down in shorthand. Send some more papers sometime, they are always welcome. The food is quite good here though a little monotonous, as when anything, i.e. asparagus, is in season, we eat it all day long! There is plenty of butter, though it is limited. This household is allowed 30 German lbs per month. Other fats, margarine, lard etc. are also limited, but it is not noticeable. The limit is to avoid waste. Some things are short, leather and rubber for instance. I sent my white shoes to be heeled, and they put black rubber on as there was no white. But such things don't disturb the comfort of everyday life.

I must wind up now or you'll find this letter censored! Sheila said that my letter to her had been opened too. I think they do it if the letter is especially fat or if there is anything such as photos enclosed. Lots and lots of love, and take Ross for a nice long walk from me.

Your very loving Elizabeth.

27th June 1937.

Darling Mummy,

All plans are fixed up for Ostpreussen (East Prussia). Annu is coming here on the 1st or 2nd July and we are all three going by boat to Pillau, which is the port to Konigsberg, on the 9th July. Hildemie and I will stay as long as Hildemie's sister-in-law wants to extend her holiday. From Pillau we go by boat to Rauschen, which is a watering place in one of the most beautiful parts of Ostpreussen, so I'm told. The journey takes about 17 hours and costs 18 mks return! We will have to put up in Rauschen at a boarding house of some sort, which I'm assured will not cost more than 4 mks per day food included. So I reckon on spending about 100 mks for a fortnight. As there is the journey by train from here to Swinemunde, which is about 10 mks return, and then the journey from Pillau to Rauschen, which costs about 3 mks. From Rauschen Hildemie and I may go to Sportwitten, where her brother and family run Frau von Heyden's family estate. You needn't send me any money as I still have 125 mks. Annu will only be a few days in Ostpreussen as she has to be back in Dresden on the 16th.

This afternoon is the S.A. Gymkhana in Prenzlau. Having watched all the training for it, it will be amusing to see what does happen this afternoon. The best horse has gone lame and the best gymnast has broken his wrist, which is a wonderful beginning!

Yesterday another girl cousin of Hildemie's turned up for the week-end. She is very nice, about 30, also rather a bright young thing and has just been to the Exhibition in Paris.

I expect you'll find this letter opened again, as it is so fat. They certainly seem to have a down on me! My clothes are very satisfactory and quite sufficient. To my horror, they only wash once a month here. However I manage to get my underclothes washed in between whiles, or else I should have nothing clean to wear. Hildemie's birthday is at the end of July. I wondered if you would buy two pairs of Richard's stockings and wash them and send them. One can't get these stockings here and she always admires mine so. I will send you her foot measurement later.

I can't say that Hildemie's English is very brilliant or that it has much improved under my tuition, but she simply won't talk English. We read every day and are getting near the end of *Murder in Miami*, and I have nearly filled a book with short-hand. I'm trying to persuade her to do some translating but so far no luck. Thank you also for the papers. Send me some more again before long. I often go to the office and either do some typing or make a general nuisance of myself. But it's quite interesting to see how everything is done.

I'm just going to send a line to Daddy. I wrote to him when I first came but haven't had a letter from him. When does he sail?

Tons of love, your loving Elizabeth.

4th July 1937.

Darlingest Mummy,

Annu arrived yesterday. There was, of course, colossal excitement. She's exactly the same as ever and it's simply topping being together again. I don't think I'll ever have another friend like her.

On Tuesday Hildemie and I were invited to a dance at Wilsikow, our hosts were the von Holzendorffs. Their estate is the other side of Pasewalk. I wore my brown check dress, which was a great success, and my dancing sandals, and slung my overcoat over my shoulders. The show began at 7.30 so we left here at 6.30 and picked up Maria von Buchholtz, a great friend of Hildemie's of whom we see a good deal, and then went on to Wilsikow. As soon as we got there we poshed up and took our boxes of chocolates and curtseyed to any grown-ups to whom we were introduced. We were then handed a bowl of various coloured hearts of paper, one of which we had to draw. Mine was half white and half blue. All the men were officers from Prenzlau, either airmen or gunners. Of course they all wore their uniform dinner jackets, which were white. The gunners had them fastened tight at the neck and the others wore them open with a tie. The gunners also wore spurs. The men also had hearts the corresponding colours to ours, and as soon as everyone was present and we had matched up, we went in to dinner. On the table were cards with the hearts painted on them instead of names. After having fetched food from the buffet, we sat down and were given champagne and a lovely 'Bowle' which is wine with fruit in it. After supper we went into the garden where a platform had been erected for dancing. All around were hung chinese lanterns and altogether it looked marvellous. We then proceeded to dance and sat out in a smallish room which led into the garden, which was lined with sofas; as it was a bit cold outside, we all sat on top of each other! The whole party went with a swing from beginning to end. No sitting about and moping. After about the third dance it began to rain! No one wanted to go indoors, so masses of brollies were produced and we all danced under umbrellas, each man having one! The rain proved to be a half-hearted drizzle and soon stopped. Then we did a 'Garten Polonaise', which means you meander through the garden with your partner. The gardens in this part of the world are all trees, lawns, paths and bushes. So they lend themselves to that kind of pastime exceptionally well. When we came in, our shoes looked as though we'd been through a swamp. Mine are still muddied up. After that the music (which was gramophone amplified over the wireless) was moved upstairs into the drawing room and we danced there until we left at 2.30 a.m. When Hildemie and I got in and let the von Heydens hear us, we crept out again and went for a swim in our birthday suits in the Krummersee with the early dawn mist rising off the water. It was a wonderful evening.

On Thursday Maria von Buchholtz and her brother Hans, who is on leave, came out here and we ate cherries. Hildemie and I had our usual riding lessons last week. We now have to ride without stirrups, which is very good exercise.

Yesterday we were showing Annu the sights of Prenzlau, in which a restaurant with a wonderful view over the lake is included. Who should we meet there but some of our good friends from Tuesday night. We were invited to partake of a drink, but it being 10 minutes to 7, we had to refuse as we have to be in to supper at 7.

Last Sunday was the gymkhana in Prenzlau. It was quite good, though we were rather disappointed with the efforts of the Alexanderhofer, as no one got a prize. I wore my home-made and the new hat, very posh! This afternoon I will don it again as we have to do our duty at a charity fête.

5th July 1937.

Darling Rosemary,

Thank you very much for your letter. Life is heavenly here. Annu is staying and next Saturday we three, Hildemie, Annu and I are going by boat from Swinemunde to Rauschen in East Prussia. (You can look it all up on the map). We may break the journey in Danzig and spend a night there. I've always wanted to see Danzig.

We are having a marvellous spell of warm weather. Tuesday of last week Hildemie and I went to a dance at a big house about three quarters of an hour's run by car from here. All the men were officers from Prenzlau, of course in uniform. It was quite the best dance I've ever been to. To-night some officers are coming here to dinner. It ought to be rather fun. In fact I'm having a marvellous time.

It's too hot to write any more Rosy, so cheerio,

Tons of love, Elizabeth.
Haus Waldeck,
Rauschen Dune,
Samland,
East Prussia.

15th July 1937.

Darlingst Mummy,

I hope you received my post card from Freie Stadt Danzig. This is the most delightful spot, and at last we are having decent weather. The journey was pretty foul as it rained practically the whole time. We have a very nice room here not far from the beach. I haven't bathed yet as I've got a cough, but if it's hot to-day I shall have a dip. To-day Annu goes – boo-hoo! On Tuesday she and I went for a lovely walk along the cliffs to a place called Neukuhnen. There we had a wonderful tea in the Kurhaus and then strolled back. It was lovely. I'm enclosing some photos which Annu took of me with Scharnhorst, the horse I ride. I think they are rather good.

We leave here on Sunday week and go by car with the von Heydens junior to Sporwitten where they live, and stay a few days there and return home on the 30th in order to be there for the 'Sommerfest' (a ball) which is being held in Prenzlau on the 31st. Last night we drank Annu's health in a very nice café here, but it got so cold that we soon went.

Tons of love, from your loving, Elizabeth.

17th July 1937.

Darling Mummy,

At last I've got your letters. They both arrived to-day, one addressed direct here and the other to Alexanderhof. Annu left here yesterday and I was very sorry to see her go, as we have been having a marvellous time together. In my last letter, which was written in rather a hurry before the others were awake, I didn't have time to give you much news.

Our journey here was most adventurous. When we got to Swinemunde, from where our boat sailed, Annu was the only one with a ticket for the boat, we had yet to get ours. When we got there, there was such a crowd and there appeared to be no more tickets for sale. A nice state of affairs, especially as our luggage was already on board. However, as there seemed no prospect of Hildemie and I getting tickets, Annu used hers to go on board and find the luggage and bring it back. So she set off and left me standing at the foot of the gangway. In the meantime Hildemie decided to go and find out if she can get any tickets and off she goes. Annu returned having rescued the luggage and gave me her ticket to give to the officer near to whom I was standing to have the date of departure altered. All this took place in a terrific crowd, where one could hardly move. About 10 minutes before the gangway was hauled up, Hildemie rushed up with two tickets, we raked our luggage together and happily boarded the ship, all very hot! We hadn't booked a cabin in advance and there were none to be had, so we did our best with a wooden deck chair and a mattress each. First we took our stuff and camped on deck. When we were well out to sea and had supped, we promenaded round to explore the ship and its passengers. In the stern a lot of Hitlerjugend and Bund Deutsche Mädchen had collected and were singing. Nearly everyone else on board collected too and we all sat singing until late into the night. We then retreated to our nest on deck and just as we were beginning to sleep peacefully, it began to pour with rain. So we had to move downstairs and none of us had a comfortable night. Everyone on board was awake at 5 a.m. as we were due in at Zopport at 7. We breakfasted and fixed various money matters and were all ready to land. Unfortunately the weather was not at its best. However as soon as we had got through customs and into the town of Zopport, our first concern was to find somewhere to sleep that night. We went first to a travel office which had a list of rooms to be let as all hotels were full. Zopport is a very fashionable seaside resort. After we had trailed around to about four different apartments, we came to rest at last in a very nice room not far from where our boat was to sail the next morning. The first thing we did was to undress, wash and get into bed. We were due to lunch with an old friend of the von Heydens' in Danzig, so we only slept for an hour and a half. When we got up we made straight for the station and were in Danzig in 20 minutes. Unfortunately by this time it was pouring with rain, so I only saw that beautiful city in the rain.

Tons of love, your loving Elizabeth.

18.7.37.

Hildemie, who had already been in Danzig, knew the way to her friend's house. We arrived there and partook of an excellent meal. The 'friend' was an old lady of 70 who had been governess to various members of the von Heyden family, including Hildemie and her sister and several cousins. After lunch she proceeded to show us Danzig and rushed about with unending energy. It is the most beautiful old town. We went back with her for tea and after tea we left. We tossed up whether we should go back to Zopport or do something in Danzig. As it was still pouring with rain, we went to a flick in Danzig, after which we caught a train back to Zopport. There we decided to have supper in the casino, which was so crowded that we had to go somewhere else. We stopped for a bit and watched the gambling, which was quite amusing. Needless to say, we did not join in, as we only had 10 marks per head. After supper we were all so sleepy that we went straight home to bed. The next morning our boat sailed at 8 a.m. Again it was pouring with rain, which was most unfortunate. We boarded the ship, which wasn't nearly so crowded as the one we were on the night before. At 12 noon we were in Pillau, where Hildemie's brother was waiting for us with his car. We all packed in and drove straight to Rauschen.

The scenery here is indescribably beautiful. The cliffs, which drop down to the beach, are sandy and thickly wooded the whole way along the coast. The beach is delightfully clean and the sand is lovely. The water is not so salt as the North Sea, and there is hardly any difference between high and low tide. The town consists mostly of cafés and photographers. We have two very nice rooms between us. One with three beds where Annu, Hildemie and I sleep and one with two beds where Tilly (née von Bismarck) and her son Botho sleep. Every morning we spend on the beach until lunch time. After lunch Annu and I used to go off alone. One afternoon we wandered along a path which went along the edge of the cliffs until we came to the next village, which was about eight kilometers from here. The village is called Neukuhsen and is Rauschen on a minor scale. There is also a military aerodrome there, so we do not miss our uniforms, of which we see so much in Prenzlau. All the other afternoons we have spent on the beach. We have breakfast and supper in our rooms. We feed mostly off stuff brought from Sporwitten and Alexanderhof. Midday we have a warm meal in one of the many cafés and tea we do without.

Bei Frau von Heyden,
Gross Sporwitten,
bei Schönbruch,
Kreis Bartenstein,
East Prussia.

Darling Mummy and Daddy,

How nice to be able to write to you both again together. I would love you to be here, it's about the quaintest place I've ever seen. The picture postcard I sent you was taken at the time when Frau von Heyden senior's parents lived here. This is where she was born and bred. The garden is completely over-grown. It is also of the park-like type so common in North Germany, but now no paths, or few, are discernible, and here and there a flower peeps from behind a mass of weeds and a hen and her chicks have taken up their abode under one of the fir trees in close proximity to the French window. The trees are wonderful, being the only plants besides the weeds which have benefitted by neglect. The house is colossal as you can imagine from the p. c., which only shows the front and one wing. More than half is shut up. Downstairs all the front rooms are in use, two reception rooms, hall used as dining room, Botho's nursery and Wichard and Tilly's bedroom. The rooms behind looking into the courtyard are not used. One is a huge dining room beautifully panelled and with fantastic furniture, another is a colossal drawing room which I haven't yet seen. Tilly has promised to show me the whole of the house when it is raining. How many bedrooms are in use I really can't say, but I should think about 12. Our room is very bright, but the wall paper is beginning to peel off and is suffering from the general shabbiness.

The household consists of: Wichard (Hildemie's brother), Tilly, Botho, a secretary, a girl who is very nice and young, an under-manager and a boy cousin who is learning farming. Wichard doesn't own this place, it belongs to his mother's family, and he is only here as manager. The staff consists of a housekeeper, also young, and three maids. It's rather fun being amongst so many young people although they seem a bit dull and serious and talk about nothing but the harvest, and the awful weather (when it rains), and the fine weather (when the sun shines). In spite of that it is most amusing. The farm buildings are huge, bigger than at Alexanderhof and the farm village is not quite so near to the house as it is in Alexanderhof, but there everything is much better looked after and much more prosperous.

Tons of love to you both and to the rest of the family, your very loving, Elizabeth.

1st August 1937.

Darling Family.

I've no letter this week to answer. I hope it is waiting for me in Alexanderhof. Hildemie is lying in bed with my cold. She had her birthday on Friday and was so rotten that she had to retire to bed, where she has been ever since. The weather has been foul.

On Tuesday Tilly showed us round the mansion. It was fascinating. Every-thing covered up with dust sheets and so gloomy. On Thursday evening the secretary and I went on our bikes to a cinema in Schönbruch. It isn't a real theatre, just an ordinary hall with a screen erected, and the only performance is on Thursdays! The film was very good, only it was cut in about 5 places and every time there was a long pause before it continued. The seating accommodation left much to be desired. Afterwards we had 5 kms to bike home, and none of us had a lamp; luckily there was a moon.

On Thursday we move from here, provided Hildemie is better, which I sincerely hope. I hope the holidays will be up to standard. Don't overdo yourselves.

Tons of love Elizabeth.

When Hildemie was in bed, I took to going for walks on my own. I had been warned not to carry a camera at all in East Prussia and I soon found out why, as across the fields some way from Sporwitten, but on their land, were built huge concrete blocks and tank traps. It was rather sinister. I could not write this information as I knew my letters were being censored.

Alexanderhof, bei Prenzlau,
Uckermark, Germany.
8th August 1937.

Darling Family,

Here we are back again in good old Alexanderhof. I only had a day to wait for your letter, which came from Sporwitten. Many thanks for it. You have a good crowd again, I notice, for the holidays. I've now got over my cough which I had in Sporwitten and was able to go to the Fliegerball last night. A fuller account will follow, now I will record events as they occurred since I last wrote.

Our last two days in Sporwitten were quite decent and Hildemie got up. She had been really rotten but I don't think that she had whooping cough. Poor little Botho got it very badly, and Tilly seemed a bit worried about him. On Wednesday morning Hildemie and I set out to gather apples in a fruit garden far enough away from the house to be extremely convenient for the village boys, so we had to pick them before they were ripe. The journey back to the house with the two sacks which we had collected was most precarious. The garden boy had come with a lively horse and a very antique gig, and as the lane was very cut up from the recent rain, we nearly capsized every time the horse broke into a canter, which was pretty frequently.

On Thursday morning we departed, and Wichard took us by car to the nearest 'station'. I put inverted commas because the place where the train stopped can hardly be thus termed, as it consisted of a wooden hut with the name painted on it. There were no tickets to be got there; we got them on the train. The train wasn't much better and came along ringing a bell! By this means of locomotion we reached Königsberg in an hour, where we changed into the train going to Pillau. The crowd wasn't too frightful and we managed comfortably to get seats. After another hour's travelling we reached Pillau, where we boarded the *Tannenberg* for the second time. It was the most heavenly day and after we had dumped our luggage, we went on deck. We arrived at Zopport at tea-time, having left Pillau at lunch-time. Luckily for us, after Zopport some cabins became disengaged and Hildemie and I managed to get a two-bunker and with a port hole and had a most comfortable night. We arrived in Swinemunde at 5.30 a.m. Friday. There we changed into the train, which landed us in Prenzlau in time for breakfast. Herr von Heyden was there to meet us. While we were still in Sporwitten, Herr von Heyden wrote very kindly offering to pay both our fares if we would travel back overland. I thought it was really very kind of him, but as we had our return tickets, we thought we might as well face the sea and really it was well worth it.

We returned here to find the house full. The family now consists of Frau and Herr von Heyden, Lisbeth, the eldest daughter and artist, an old cousin of Frau von Heyden who has come here with her companion for a rest, Frau von Arnim, the wife of the subaltern in Schwedt with whom we went to the Biwack, who was here for a portrait sitting, and the two children who arrived the day before we left for their holidays and the inevitable Frl. Harms (the secretary). They were all collected on the front doorstep to greet us. When we got inside, Hildemie's birthday table was waiting for her. She got a topping riding crop, which I very much admired, and then Herr von Heyden told me to look round the room as there was something hidden for me. Eventually, behind a cushion, what should I find but another riding crop. It's a beautiful leather one with a silver top and 'E.D. Alexanderhof Sommer 1937' engraved on it. Of course I was thrilled.

We then went in to breakfast, for which Hildemie and I had a pretty good appetite. Herr von Heyden then announced that he had another surprise for us, and when he led us through the stables, there was the sweetest little grey mare, a four year-old to go with the chestnut mare, also four years old, who was already here. We will begin riding to-morrow and I hope we will be able to ride every day. Whether Hildemie will be able to manage the grey is somewhat doubtful, but I sincerely hope so. One way and another it was quite a home-coming. As Hildemie's cough was still not quite right, it was doubtful whether she was to go to the ball given last night by the 'Prenzlauer Fliegerhorst'. However in the morning we all went to the hairdresser, and at 7 o'clock duly found ourselves mounting the steps to the Kasino, which is attached to the barracks. Frau von Heyden came with us as chaperone and had two other girls under her wing, one was Maria von Buchholtz. After we removed our cloaks, we went downstairs and everybody was assembled on the lawn behind the house, which was decorated with Chinese lanterns. I was then introduced to all the 'alte Herrschaften' and made my little curtsey, in other words all the old fogies and their daughters from the surrounding countryside. Then various officers whom we already knew and a few whom we didn't came along and after we had talked for a bit, we moved off to supper. This was on a terrace on the other side of the house, which led off from the ball-room. After supper we danced, sometimes inside and sometimes outside, where a platform had been erected in the middle of the lawn and where a second band was playing. As soon as the band inside stopped, the one outside began. Towards eleven we wandered upstairs, where there were side shows in one room, a shooting range – much excitement – and in another there was a 'Bayrisches Stüble' where we ate sausages and bretzels and drank beer. It was got up 'à la Bavaria' and was very 'gemütlich'. There we sat for hours, as outside it had begun to get chilly. Frau von Heyden had resolved to leave the scene of gaiety at 1 a.m., with which we, of course, did not agree! So at a few minutes to one, I and my partner went into the garden. Of course, after the others had waited for us, Hildemie and Maria were sent off to look for us, and of course they made a beeline for the garden where they and partners disappeared; this game continued until about 2 a.m., when we had compassion on the poor wretched Frau von Heyden, who had been trying for the last hour to get us together! She took it all as a joke and the story was expounded at the breakfast table this morning, and I think we will never hear the end of it!

I must wind up now, as the awful ordeal of a German bread and butter letter must be got over before lunch time. Tons and tons of love, and thank yo so much for 'taking it for granted' that I can go to Freiburg.

Again tons of love from your loving Elizabeth.

15th August 1937.

Darling Family.

Many thanks for Daddy's newsy letter. I hope you have all survived Hilda's holiday and that Tom and Rupert are still in existence in spite of the 3-wheeler. Anyway from all accounts the holidays seem up to the usual mark. The shoot sounds topping, especially the old boy with the hunters.

I have spent most of this week riding. The grey mare which I told you about in my last letter is simply topping. Yesterday I took a toss and am now suffering from a sore elbow, which has been bandaged in such a way that my arm is completely stiff, hence this messy letter as it is the right arm! I ride every morning before breakfast. I get up at 6 and ride until about 8.30 a.m. Hildemie wasn't allowed to ride at the beginning of the week because of the whooping cough, but on Thursday we both went out with Herr Mögelin (the Manager). Unfortunately the grey didn't like the feel of Hildemie and kicked her off twice within the first five minutes. We then all changed horses, and I mounted the grey. The young chestnut on whom I began the ride is rather bad tempered and inclined to kick. She seemed to dislike the grey mare and kicked her twice. The grey mare is now scared of all horses and is difficult to ride when there are others there. Herr von Heyden has forbidden Hildemie to ride out so I have the grey all to myself. Yesterday morning early I rode with Herr Mögelin, and the grey had still not recovered from the adventures of the day before and played up like fun and succeeded in the end in kicking me off too. Unfortunately I couldn't ride her this morning on account of my arm, but I shall probably take her out this afternoon, all being well. These two young mares are also learning to go in the cart, and we have some very exciting journeys over the fields with two bucking broncos between the shafts.

The other day Hildemie asked me to stay here over the winter and was backed up by the rest of the family. Much as I enjoy being here, my conscience wouldn't allow my stay to be thus elongated, and I really don't know how I'm going to get away from here without seeming ungrateful! As I want to go to Freiburg, I shall have to leave here at the end of August. I would go to Freiburg later, only Annu is supposed to be going into Arbeitsdienst in October, and I want to spend at least a month there. Should she not be going, I may stay here a bit longer.

Herr von Heyden went away on Friday to a funeral and won't be back until to-morrow. Luckily he didn't see me yesterday after my ride or he might have forbidden me to ride out! On Monday Herr Stroschen is coming to give us a riding lesson.

The dinner gong has just sounded, so no more. Write again soon,

Tons and tons of love, Elizabeth.

28th August 1937.

Darling Family,

Thank you so much for your letter, Mummy, which I'm sorry I haven't answered before.

Last Monday Herr and Frau von Heyden went to Sporwitten together and we were left to rule the roost! We had a grand week. I still continue to ride every morning before breakfast. Every afternoon Herr Stoschen, our riding master, came, so I rode twice. On Wednesday three officers from Prenzlau came at supper time and stayed until 12.30, when I was so tired that I could hardly keep my eyes open. We fished some wine out of Father's cellar and had a most enjoyable evening. On Thursday evening Herr von Heyden came back and Frau von Heyden arrived on Friday.

I intend to go to Freiburg on the 6th. I shall be very sorry to leave here, as they really have been too kind for words, and I've spent the most delightful summer.

I'm longing to see the new shoot. Herr Mögelin is very keen on shooting and he goes out quite often after duck. I haven't yet had the nerve to ask if I can go with him. He also has a very well trained dog of doubtful breed. There are plenty of hares here and deer, but no rabbits, or very few. The other day I saw a hen pheasant, but they are scarce as are partridges.

There's no more news for now, write to me again here.

Tons of love to you all, your loving Elizabeth.

5th September 1937.

Darling Family,

I have waited in vain this week for a letter and money, both of which I hope are on their way!

Since I last wrote, my plans have changed somewhat. I intended going to Freiburg on the 6th, to-morrow, but last week it was decided that the 'Erntefest' here was to be held on Saturday 12th, and the von Heydens insisted that I should stay over that week-end, and I simply couldn't refuse. The Erntefest is the Harvest Home, and a colossal affair. It begins at about 2.30 p.m. with side shows and children's sports and winds up with a dance in the evening which is wont to carry on into the early hours of the morning. Only the Alexanderhofer take part and any stranger is kicked out at once. There is a good deal to do as regards prizes, dressing dolls etc. and I felt that when I could really be of some use, I couldn't very well leave them to it.

Yesterday there was a 'Jagdritt' here. The German substitute for our hunting. There are very few foxes here and no hounds so two riders lead as hare and hound, one plays the huntsman in a pink coat and the rest are in the field. It was most amusing and about 30 horsemen turned up. I couldn't ride unfortunately as my beloved grey was to be ridden by our riding master, who is by way of breaking her in! And all the other horses were ridden by the various managers here. However the day before Herr Mögelin and I and three others rode over the intended stretch of land and took all the jumps, which were artificial, and that was marvellous fun. Monday week there is another 'hunt' over a neighbouring farm, to which I have been invited, so I'm afraid my journey will be postponed until the Tuesday. Annu will be furious with me.

Time Gone

All this week was spent riding, more or less. In the morning we had our lesson and in the afternoon I take Gisela (the grey), which I always refer to as mine and am most particular who rides her, out for an hour or so. A good deal of the morning is spent in the stables grooming. The groom here is chauffeur, second footman, garden help and all combined.

On Tuesday evening Hildemie and I went with Frl. Harms, Herr Mögelin and his wife, Frl Schoder, a girl staying with them, and Herr Hoffman and Herr Wacher the two under-managers, to a play in Prenzlau. It was all in 'Plattdeutsch' the dialect spoken in the North, and somewhat difficult to follow, but most amusing. We went in the family carriage, a colossal affair and ages old, with between the shafts the two chestnuts, who pulled us to Prenzlau and back at about 40 m.p.h.

To-day is Frau von Heyden's birthday and a friend, Herr von Stutterheim, who was here once before, and a niece, a very bright young thing, have come for the week-end.

Altogether it seems very difficult for me to break away from here, and I'm simply longing to go to Freiburg. However perhaps it's better that I'm not going on Monday as I've not quite recovered from whooping cough yet! It is a very long and laborious affair. Hildemie still coughs much more than I and I don't want to bring it to the Mezs. Also my money hasn't arrived. Please let me have it by next week.

Tons and tons of love to you all, your very loving Elizabeth.

18th September 1937,
Freiburg i. Brg.,
Karthauserstrasse 51.

Darling Parents,

At last I've arrived here, safe and sound. It's lovely being in Freiburg again, only unfortunately on the journey I must have caught cold, as I arrived here with the most foul cough, which I had successfully got rid of in Alexanderhof. Mrs Mez was rather afraid it was whooping cough again, so I went to the Doctor to make sure. However, he didn't think it was whooping cough, but anyway Annu and I are going up into the mountains for a few days to get rid of it.

The last days in Alexanderhof were super. The Erntefest on Saturday 11th was a colossal do. At 2.30 p.m. all the labourers and wives and children came in a procession before the house, led by a band. Herr and Frau von Heyden were standing in the porch ready to receive them, Herr Mögelin also, and the rest of the household in the background. When they had drawn up, a woman stepped forward and recited a poem to the 'Herrschaften', and then presented Herr and Frau von Heyden with the 'Erntekrone', which is a wreath made of various grains, wheat, barley etc. and very pretty. After that Herr von Heyden made a speech, and then Herr Mögelin had a poem recited to him and also received an Erntekrone, to which he replied with a speech. After that the band struck up again and we all joined in the procession, which proceeded to a field where an open-air stage had been made. Here the children danced some folk dances which were most amusing to watch. After that a play was acted by some of the village people which was very comic. After this performance we made our way to another field, where several different competitive games had been arranged for the people, or the 'Leute' as Herr von Heyden calls them. There was a shooting competition, a throwing game for the men, shovepenny, only not with money, and a dart-throwing game for the women and a climbing and a ball throwing competition for the children. Each of us, Hildemie, Frl. Harms, Herr Wacker and Herr Hoffmann (the assistant managers) and I had something to look after. There was a large assortment of prizes which Hildemie and I had bought in Prenzlau the day before. It was so arranged that nearly everybody got something. Hildemie and I had taken three hours to buy all the prizes the day before and spent 70mks and nothing we bought was over 1 mark. I had the small children to look after. It was rather a job as I wasn't at all up in their names or in the games they were wont to play. I spent most of the afternoon running after the children, who ran away from me! This went on until about 6 p.m. Luckily I got rid of the children before then and was able to have a go at the competitions myself, though not open to a prize! In the shooting I shot 26 out of a possible 36, and would have got fifth prize. At 6 we refreshed ourselves with some tea, after which we went along to see if the dancing had begun. The dance took place in a large shed where the different ploughs and farm tools are kept. At one end was a large cart, decorated with flowers, where the band sat. Next to that was a stage to dance on. At the opposite end was the bar, where beer was distributed and in front of the bar tables and benches where we sat out after dancing. A glass of beer was only given in receipt of a ticket. Each man had been given 10 tickets for beer, 1 ticket for cake, and the women 8 tickets for beer and 1 for cake. That is done in order that everyone should get a fair share and also to prevent them, to a certain extent, from getting too tight! When we got there the music had just struck up and a few pairs were dancing. We stayed for a few minutes and decided to go back and have supper and reassemble at 8.30. From then until 5 a.m. we danced solidly. Herr and Frau von Heyden stayed until about 10 p.m. At 11 cake and coffee was given out. Hildemie and I went up to the house with one of the managers and a few men and fetched the refreshments. I danced with a good many of the farm hands. Some of them were most amusing and held long political talks with me, which I took very seriously as they were nearly all tight. Herr Mögelin has to stay to the end, to see that there are no fights, so we and the two other managers stayed also. It was a most amusing evening and I think everyone enjoyed it. None of the men got disagreeably tight, thank goodness. The next day I slept until 11 a.m.

Sunday was the most mouldy weather and we spent most of the afternoon in Herr Mögelin's house planning the 'Betriebsausflug', an excursion for the workers, which was to take place on Tuesday and Wednesday of next week. Hildemie wanted to go and they all begged me to stay and go with them, and as I hadn't received any money, I thought I might as well.

Monday was also a day of excitement as there was the Jagdritt in Potslow and I was allowed to ride Gisela! In the morning I got a telegram from Cooks, whom I had telegraphed on Saturday, saying my money was at the one and only bank in Prenzlau which we hadn't telephoned and had been there for the last fortnight. As Kahn, the chauffeur and groom had had to take the horses to Potslow, Herr Mögelin had to drive the car. I really thought we wouldn't arrive whole! First of all he couldn't get it to start. The Jagd began at 3 and at 5 minutes to 3 we were being pushed out of the gates of Alexanderhof by some highly amused farm hands. We then tore through Prenzlau and out on to the road to Potslow, which wasn't exactly a very good road. However the hunt had waited for us as we were the lesser half. We being three and the hunt consisting of seven horsemen, not so many as at Alexanderhof. It was simply super. First there were three ditches with poles and then a long gallop and a very steep bank. Then through the lake with my boots in the water, followed by two poles in the middle of a field, both of which Gisela refused. There were two more jumps, then a wall, where she also refused and I descended! However I was soon up again and caught them up before the next jump. After that we climbed down into a deep lane and up the other side, then the last jump in full view of the spectators. The man who led was called the Master and wore a pink coat. On his right shoulder was pinned a fox's brush and after the last jump the signal was given for the race to begin in which everyone tries to catch the brush. We tore round and round an enormous expanse of land. Poor Gisela couldn't quite keep up with her competitors. Herr Mögelin eventually got the brush and then Halali was called. We then returned to the house and partook of a very good tea. It was a topping afternoon and everybody was frightfully nice. The next hunt is to be held to-day and the host-to-be invited me to join them and everybody seemed most distressed that I was going away.

That evening I packed, and the next day at 6 a.m. the Betriebsausflug began. There were 63 of the farm hands, and Hildemie, Herr Wacker, Herr Mögelin and me. We had the most amusing two days at Sassnitz auf Rugen. The train journey was very long from 7 a.m. to 1 p.m. But we played cards and fooled about and the time went quickly. In Stralsund we had an hour's wait and were led through the town by the gardener, who knew it. The only thing he pointed out to us was the room in which he had lain wounded during the war (WW1). When we arrived in Sassnitz we went straight to the hotel, where lunch had been arranged for us. After that they all went to the Jugendherberge (Youth Hostel) where they were to spend the night and dumped their belongings. Hildemie and I had a room in the hotel, which was very nice. We then all met again and went by boat along the coast to Stubbenhammer, where there are the most marvellous chalk cliffs rising very steeply out of the sea. We spent the afternoon there and had tea. The boat was due to sail back again at 5.30 and the two men and Hildemie and I had got a bit delayed over tea. When we got down to the quay, we saw the boat halfway out to sea without us! However, much shouting and waving attracted their attention and they returned to fetch us. When we got back to Sassnitz it was supper time. After supper everyone followed their secret hearts, and we went with the two men to a café and danced into the early hours of the morning. The next day we poked around Sassnitz and found quite a lot of interesting things down by the harbour, including a warship, which was taking part in the manoeuvres. We had an early lunch and left Sassnitz at 1 o'clock and were back in Prenzlau at 6.

That evening we celebrated my 'Abschied' with a bottle of wine and the next morning I left Alexanderhof in the old landau and two in hand. Herr Mögelin drove us in.

This afternoon Annu and I are going to St. Margen by car for a few days. Annu is going to 'Arbeitdienst' on the 2nd October so I shall probably travel then too. I'll let you know more later. I haven't visited anybody here yet, I'll do that when I've got rid of this awful cough. Very many thanks for the money, which ought to be ample. I must now pack my things.

Tons and tons of love to you all, from your very loving Elizabeth.

Freiburg i. Brg.
27th September 1937.

Darling parents,

We are now back in Freiburg again. Unfortunately we had the most foul weather and as soon as I was back here I returned to bed, which wasn't very tactful, but unavoidable. Mrs Mez had the doctor, who assured her that my cough is much better, and to-day I am up as fit as a fiddle. Mrs Mez says she won't let me go until I'm quite fit. She's writing to you so I wash my hands of all responsibility as regards my return!

The Mezs have just got a new dog, a black and white spaniel! They've had various Alsatians during the past few years, the last one being Lux, aged 10 months. As a result of the dog's playfulness, there are about 4 people in hospital at the expense of the Mezs, so when the last claimant came and required 300 marks for a broken leg, Mr Mez put his foot down, and the Alsatian has been found a new home and the spaniel has come in his stead. Annu is supposed to go to her Arbeitsdienst next Saturday, but she hasn't yet heard where she is to be stationed. Maiu has just returned from her six months, which she thoroughly enjoyed and tells the most amusing stories of her experiences! She will now be home until next May or so, when she goes to Heidelberg to study languages.

The wine harvest has begun on the Rebberg and I shall go and watch with great interest.

Tons of love to you both and don't worry about my cough because it's quite ok.

Your loving Elizabeth.

11th October 1937.

Darling Parents,

Many thanks for your letter. I spent a most enjoyable week in the Hütte with Annu and Maiu and Margarete Kanneberg. She is a lonely, backward girl and we were invited to spend a few days with her in the Kanneberg's Hütte, which is the sweetest little Schwarzwald house you can imagine. It is an old mill, and the part which was the mill is now used for storing wood and various implements. Besides the mill, it consists of two living rooms, one very nicely arranged with an 'Ofen', around which is a bench where we always used to sit. From this room there is a hatch into the kitchen, which was all electric, very modern, not like most of the Schwarzwald Hütten, which haven't even running water. Upstairs are two bedrooms with very comfortable beds. Whoever was first up cooked the breakfast. On Monday Annu and I went up by train with our bikes and the dog, laden with rucksacks. That evening we all sat in the Stübe and cracked nuts with a hammer. After tea the next day as we were doing our shopping, Annu met a soldier friend and he and two friends came to supper. There were certainly too many cooks in the kitchen that evening. As they were on manoeuvres, they couldn't stay long, but it was a most amusing evening. On Wednesday Maiu turned up with a friend from Arbeitsdienst, quite a nice girl from München, but very quiet. That evening we sat around the 'Ofenbank' and Margarete played her concertina and we all sang. On Thursday Maiu's friend departed and Maiu and I went by bike to the Feldberg. The next day Annu and I went by bike to the Tourner, also in wind and wet, and came home sopping. Maiu returned to Freiburg that day and Annu and I followed next day. We packed all our things on to our bikes, then came the dog, who was to be packed into a rucksack, and Annu was going to take him on her back, but the rucksack proved to be too small for him and after much trouble and laughter we decided to leave him with Margarete, who was coming down the next day in the car.

The rest of the family, Mr and Mrs Mez and Miss Edwards, are staying in Baden Baden, and yesterday we went to visit them. It was a good two-and-a half hour drive and Brutz drove us in the old Horsch. After lunch we went for a lovely drive through the north Black Forest to Mummelsee and the Hornisgrinde. Then we dropped the others in Baden Baden and came home.

Tons of love to you both, your very loving Elizabeth.

Annu went off to Arbeitsdienst on the 15th October, four days after I had written that letter, and I stayed on hoping I would be allowed to do the same course as Maiu. I had become very friendly with Leif Geiges, and in the absence of the twins, I used to go out with him a lot. We went for walks ending up in the Rebberghäusle. He was briefly back from a tour taking photographs, which he showed me and which he was later to publish. We kept up a correspondence until the War came. However my parents had had enough. They had decided to give up the lease of Amor Hall, and accepted Bodkin Wood's invitation to visit him in Trinidad. They wanted to see me settled before they left. My father was to take up an appointment as Secretary of the Royal Empire Society in London from Easter 1938.

So on 22nd November 1937, after much procrastination, I was journeying home. In my carriage was an American, who remarked to me: 'The trouble with this country is the little man in the big uniform!'

It was back to life's harsh realities with a vengeance. I got digs in Nevern Square. I managed to land a permanent job with an aloof, lonely and secretive individual called Mr Klingenberger. There were only two other members of staff, one a book-keeper and the other a general factotum. It was a small import-export business and he ran it from a dingy office near the Mansion House. Mr Klingenberger lived in Gloucester Road and I was often required to act as courier between office and home. I found the job neither interesting nor appealing and spent most of my time knitting. I enrolled for evening classes in journalism at the Regent Street Polytechnic. I enjoyed the novelty and interest of the work. Unfortunately I found it impossible to fit in the homework required, and I didn't manage to stay the course. My digs however were amusing, and my diary records that they were 'full of funny people'. They were mostly students. Two of my special friends there were Hans, a young Jewish refugee from Germany and an evangelising Communist, and Jimmy Hodges, a medical student from St. Mary's Hospital, Paddington, where my friend Mignonne from San Sebastian had trained as a nurse. Jimmy was a keen rugger player and took me to the matches and the Club dances. He became a steady boy friend for two years until the War split us up. I got in touch with Sheila Marshall, who had a very prestigious job in Government employ, and also with Bridget, with whom I'd shared digs when at College.

Christmas 1937 was to be our last at Amor Hall. My diary records that I met the Crolls at the Monument on Christmas Eve and that we travelled to Amor Hall together and there were 'great hilarities'. On Christmas morning I went to church at 7 a.m. and my diary records: 'We had an enormous dinner and afterwards went with Tom and Marlay for a long walk. Evening as usual and a grand beano. I got some nice presents. 26th Sunday 1937. In the afternoon Tom, Marlay and I went to Oakley and rode. In the evening there was a carol service after supper. That night I slept by the kitchen fire.

27th Monday. I went beagling with Marlay and after supper again sat before the kitchen fire and fell asleep. 28th Tuesday. I caught the 8.45 a.m. from Colchester. Tom and Marlay took me there. Worked hard all day, the first day I was alone in the office.'

Early in 1938, when my parents returned from Trinidad, my father took up his work in London and my parents moved into a flat in Kensington Church Street and I moved in with them. My life style improved greatly. They kept a foothold in Suffolk in the shape of a 3-roomed cottage at Aldringham between Thorpeness and Leiston. There we young ones would gather over week-ends and holiday periods. Jimmy could borrow a car sometimes and he drove me down there several times. Even in those days we would be stuck in traffic jams on the new Colchester by-pass, now Remembrance Avenue. Tom used to come for week-ends from Grantham, where he was apprenticed to an engineering firm. He had made friends with the Managing Director's son, George Moberley, whose family lived in Felixstowe. They would come to Suffolk together for week-ends. Often Tom would spend the time sailing with George, and once the Aldeburgh life-boat went to their assistance. George was keen on flying and persuaded Tom to learn too. He found it much more exciting than the motor bike he and some friends at Marlborough College had kept secretly in Savernake Forest in his last year at school. I remember those sunlit days when we would lie abed until Tom ran down to the Parrot and Punchbowl at Aldringham in his pyjamas for a jug of beer for breakfast.

September came and with it the Münich or Czech crisis and we all sensed war was in the air. Trenches were dug in Hyde Park and air raid shelters started to appear. I deserted my secretarial job and went off to enrol as a VAD. If there was going to be a war, I was going to be in it – nursing soldiers. I was quite ignorant of the fact that I would need four years training to become a qualified nurse eligible to join one of the Nursing Services. Nursing soldiers was simply equated in my mind with VADs of the First World War.

I reported to a Red Cross HQ in Kensington, was given an overall and a cotton square to put on my head, and told I could run errands in the building. In the evening we attended lectures on First Aid given by the Sister Tutor from St. Thomas' Hospital. Her lectures fascinated me but just as the subject was becoming interesting, she announced 'and the trained nurse will then ...' After two evenings of this I went up to her and said: 'How do I become this trained nurse?' She looked at me aghast at my ignorance: 'Four years in a training hospital – if they'll take you,' she replied. It seemed a fairly forlorn prospect, and after 14 days of excitement, and Neville Chamberlain's return from Munich with his famous piece of paper, I had no option but to return shamefacedly to Mr Klingenberger. I remembered that my namesake cousin, Elizabeth Deck from the Argentine, had come to England during the summer to start nursing at the Middlesex Hospital in Mortimer Street, W.1, so I asked her how to set about applying. I disliked intensely my secretarial work and being in the City. This might be a way out that I had never known about.

My interview with the formidable Miss D. Smith, Matron of the Middlesex Hospital, took place early in November 1938 and she told me she would put my name down for entry in September 1939. 'But I can't wait that long,' I wailed, 'if I can't come now, I can't come at all.' 'I'm sorry, Miss Deck.'

Late in November 1938 I received a letter saying an unexpected vacancy had arisen for the January 1939 Preliminary Training School at the Middlesex. I was jubilant. My parents were appalled, especially so when they discovered that the entrance fee was £10.0.0 and I was required to provide my uniform, which would cost at least £20.0.0. 'Elizabeth should earn her own living after all the expense of that secretarial college.' Not only the initial outlay faced them, but the fact that I would receive no pay until after three months work on the wards, and then only about £1.10.0 a month. Since I had not managed to save anything from my salary of £2.10.0 a week living in London, the financial prospect was bleak.

My father at this time was recovering from a heart attack he had suffered whilst gardening when they were staying in the Aldringham Cottage. My mother had to nurse him there under the primitive conditions prevailing in the cottage and in the worsening weather. As soon as I was accepted for training in January 1939, I gave my notice to Mr Klingenberger and joined my mother to help her in Suffolk. It was a bitterly cold December and a white Christmas. Everything was frozen solid and snow lay around. My mother had rigged up an old copper over a gas-ring in the kitchen with a tap for the hot water and for bathing in an old zinc bathtub. We had our baths in front of the kitchen stove. Once I filled the copper with snow, lit the gas and found in the end only a rather dirty jugful of hot water! Fires were lit in the three rooms for warmth and gas lamps lit the dark evenings. Water had to be pumped and the latrine was at the bottom of the garden and slops had to be emptied outside. It was hard, cold work. Tom and Rosemary joined us for Christmas and I received a Christmas and New Year greeting from Herr von Heyden. He invited me back in the summer. Told me that Maximilien and Scharnhorst, the carriage horses, were no longer there, but that Gisela, the grey and Helga the chestnut and Lumpi the rough-haired dachshund would be there to greet me. He did not say whether or not they still had the carriages and the horse-drawn sleigh for the winter.

When my father recovered, my parents relinquished both the London flat and the Aldringham cottage and moved to Avalon, Mill Lane, Southwold, a converted coach house facing the common. My father had had to give up his work with the Royal Empire Society.

In January 1939 I joined the Middlesex Hospital Preliminary Training School. Tom was learning to fly on an airfield near Grantham and moved into a house which he shared with George Moberley, and Rosemary was still at Felixstowe College for Girls.

Chapter Seven

Nursing and World War II 1939 – 1941

I STARTED TRAINING AT THE MIDDLESEX HOSPITAL, London W.1. in
January 1939. I moved into a room in the very comfortable, brand new
Nurses' Home in Foley Street W.1. Our rooms had built-in cupboards, wash
basin and desk, and we had the luxury of an indoor heated swimming pool.
The meals were varied and generous and of a very high standard. Our way
on and off duty lay through a basement passage connecting the hospital
with the Nurses' Home. Alternatively we could walk round from Foley Street
into Nassau Street and in through the Casualty entrance. Another way was
past the entrance to the private wing, the Woolavington, in Cleveland Street,
haunt of the criminal fraternity.

For the first three months we had concentrated lectures and were ruled
by the Sister Tutor, known to us as 'Ashpan'. 'Sweep the floor away from
you and avoid septic toes', she told us. 'Nurses never run except in case of
fire or haemorrhage'. So we learnt and very much more. We paid bi-weekly
visits to the wards, where we did two hours duty, going to medical, surgical,
men's and women's wards in rotation. I made friends with a fellow student
nurse, Elise Dunn, and we were to be life-long friends.

We wore the mauve and white striped frock of the junior probationer
nurse, and a starched white apron with bib. On duty we wore our sleeves
rolled up and held by a gathered white cuff. We wore black stockings and
black lace-up shoes of a special design to protect our feet and minimise
fatigue. On our heads we wore attractive white starched caps, which we
fixed on the crown of our heads and folded in the special approved manner
in a pleat which fell behind to our shoulders.

After three months in the Preliminary Training School, our four years of
training proper began with full-time duty in the wards and lectures from
the senior doctors of the hospital, usually at 10 a.m., which coincided with
our mornings' off duty time, and when on night duty kept us from our
beds for an extra hour or two. Our hours were long: 7.30 a.m. breakfast,

on duty punctually at 8 a.m. Off-duty time 10 a.m. – 1 p.m., having had lunch at 12.30 p.m., or 2–5 p.m., having had tea, and off duty at 9 p.m. to go to supper. It was a long ten-hour day with one full day off a week. On our days off we had to be in by 10.30 p.m., when the Nurses' Home was locked up. About once or twice a month we might be granted a late pass to midnight, when we would have to be signed in through Casualty. Coming in late without a pass needed the co-operation of the night porter to get us in unnoticed by the Night Sister in charge. The porters made a good thing out of tips from boy friends. Reporting on duty for the first time to our appointed ward, we received a 'cross sheet', on which was listed every sort of treatment that a trained nurse was expected to be able to carry out with competence. As junior probationers, we started with the simple things such as bed-making and the taking of temperature, pulse and breathing rates. The Ward Sister would arrange to test us, and having been satisfied as to our competence, would tick off the treatment and sign and date it. This went on up to the time of taking our State Finals in our third year.

The hard work took its toll and I collapsed with acute pain when on duty, and a few hours later found myself in the operating theatre having my appendix removed. I was put into one of our side wards for the first few days. I quickly discovered the truth of so much of 'Ashpan's' instructions: on the need for a gentle but firm touch and a confident manner. I experienced the skill of nurses who could lift and turn me without causing pain to an already traumatised tummy. I learnt the comfort of well adjusted pillows, the refreshing wash with water not too hot or too cold, and the gratitude to the nurse who responded to one's request for a drink or a bedpan without delay. These were lessons I learnt at first hand and I never forgot. I remember the bowl of bluebells some visitor brought me and a letter from my father addressed to Miss Elizabeth Deck, Junior. Much confusion arose in the Nurses home on account of my cousin and I having the same names.

———————

5th June 1939.

Dearest Ibbish,

We've had a fairly full week with the Spencers and Tom sleeping on the sofa in the lounge. Mummy, Alex and Tom went to Yarmouth races both days and all made a bit, luckily. C and I went one day only. On Thursday night the Bodkins came to dinner and bridge and on Friday afternoon we all went to the Suffolk Show at Saxmundham. A very fine lot of horses and cows. Geoff Rope was judging. He also showed a Suffolk horse but I don't think he won anything. Saturday afternoon, yesterday, we drove Tom to Ipswich to Alaistair Banks' birthday picnic party on the Deben by moonlight! We dropped Tom at the Banks at 5 p.m. and then went and bought a corridor carpet for the upstairs passage – a 'near white' strip. It looks very nice. This afternoon (Sunday) Helen Caulfield and cousin are coming to tea. The Hemsteds have cabled to Rupert to visit Kenya this July. He is leaving on July 6th and returning at the end of September to do another year at Malvern and then go to Cambridge.

We are much looking forward to seeing you some time in the coming week and hope you continue to make progress in spite of being in the ward. Tom is in very good form and his new house seems to be a great success. We both thought he had improved and seems to be getting quite interested in his work. No more news for the present. Let us know in good time what day you are coming and by what train and to which station.

Much love, ever your D'.

I was given a month's convalescence, which my mother managed to extend to six weeks on some pretext or other. It was beautiful June weather and my school friend Annu Mez was in England with her recently widowed mother, Mrs Mez, and her twin sister Maiu. They were on the first stage of their flight from Europe. Mrs Mez had left her three grown-up sons in Germany, and anxious to spare herself another war in Germany, had come to England to join forces with her unmarried sister, Miss Edwards, and, with the twins, had booked their passage to Australia to visit their brother, who was a clergyman and serving as a 'Bush Brother' there. They sailed on the 1st September 1939 via the Panama Canal. In the meantime Annu was staying with another aunt near Ipswich. She would drive to Southwold in the open touring Opel and we went where the spirit moved us all around the Suffolk countryside. Rupert Hemsted came to stay before leaving to fly to Kenya for the summer holidays and took me sailing on the Norfolk broads. It was sunny and idyllic, and we all knew it would not last.

Back on duty in the Middlesex Hospital, I was sent to the Childrens' Ward, 'Bernard Baron', on the 6th floor on day duty. 'We will put you on light duties, Nurse.' I loved the work there and got on well with the children. But talk was all of war, what was going to happen and when? Questions asked with a mixture of excitement, horror and uncertainty. Gas masks were issued and they started digging trenches again and erecting air raid shelters in Hyde Park. At the end of August we evacuated the ward and the two top floors of the hospital were completely vacated to allow for a direct hit. The hope was that the damage would not penetrate to the 3rd floor, where we would continue to nurse casualties and emergencies. All London Teaching Hospitals became the headquarters of a 'sector', including several hospitals outside London. Ours were the Mount Vernon Hospital, Northwood, a cancer hospital; Tindal House, an old workhouse in Aylesbury, and the newly-built hutted hospital at Stoke Mandeville near Aylesbury. To these hospitals we now evacuated our patients. We nurses went to each in rotation, returning to London after each stay in a sector hospital to catch up on lectures and exams.

My sister Rosemary had gone to Grenoble for part of her summer holiday. One by one her companions received 'come back' cables from home and Rosemary joined them in the last week of August. Late one evening that week a desperate little voice on the telephone persuaded the strict Home Sister, Helen Jones, to let her speak to me in spite of the late hour, 10.30 p.m. 'Where shall I stay the night?' she cried. I told her to come to the Hospital Casualty entrance and I would see what I could do. I met her there and we walked down into the underground passage to the Nurses Home and she bedded down in my room for the night. My cousin Michelle Croll (now Jenkins) was staying with friends in Suffolk, and at the approach of crisis, her parents wanted her with relations. My parents collected her and she joined Tom, who was on holiday in Southwold. She remembers him rushing in and bouncing on the bed in excitement at the prospect of war!

The 3rd of September was a Sunday and we were all clustered around the wireless to hear the Prime Minister, Mr Neville Chamberlain's grim announcement that we were at war with Germany. No sooner had he finished than the Air Raid alert sounded. It was horribly ominous. It was, of course, a false alarm, but we were thankful for the preparations and gazed hopefully at the tethered barrage balloons now floating above us all over London dangling their wires.

Tom applied to join the RAFVR, but they turned him down on the grounds that he was colour blind. So he joined the RASC and for the next year drove trucks all round England. Rosemary's school was evacuated from Felixstowe to Riddlesworth Hall near Thetford. Rupert returned from Kenya and joined the RAFVR. I heard no more from Germany.

The main concern in the early days of the War in the Middlesex Hospital was the drill to protect our radium 'bomb' and the radium needles inserted into patients for the treatment of cancer. The Middlesex was in the forefront of cancer research and treatment, and the radium posed a great danger in the event of its being scattered through bombardment. Sisters and Staff nurses wore red arm-bands denoting special responsibility for the radium appliances, which, in the event of an air-raid warning, had to be removed at speed from the luckless patient, put into lead lined containers, and dropped with the radium bomb down a shaft to safety far below ground.

At the Middlesex we had not only a basement, but a sub-basement and a rabbit warren of passages and cellars. Into these basement rooms were moved 2-tier bunks and later during the severe London air-raids, we went straight there from duty to our allotted bunk to sleep. Night nurses occupied them during the day to save having their rest disturbed.

In October Elise and my set were evacuated to Mount Vernon Hospital, Northwood. This cancer hospital was now enlarged with Nissen huts to take members of the Forces and air-raid casualties, but the sad terminal cancer patients lingered on in part of the original building. It was some of the saddest and most depressing nursing I ever did. Again we had the red arm-bands of those responsible for radium. We also had regular blood counts and only served a limited time on such wards.

We were housed in requisitioned private houses some distance from the hospital, and Elise Dunn and I enjoyed the novel experience of 'living out' and the respite from the strict Nurses' Home régime. Elise remembers going to sleep to my favourite record at the time, 'Hang your heart on a hickory limb', which I played on my gramophone over and over again! It was a very cold winter and we had no heating and very little hot water except in the hospital. My fur rug, a Kenyan hiarax kaross, began its wartime service as my bedsheet. We cycled on and off duty through all weathers.

Elise and I went on night duty. Three months lay ahead of us with three nights off after we had been on duty for three weeks. There were only two nurses in a ward at night with a supervising Night Sister for the whole hospital. It was a weird upside-down existence and I had the utmost difficulty in staying awake. I was the junior pro, who, after having helped settle the patients for the night, then retreated to the sluice to wash and sterilise every utensil. The sluice was that dreaded depository of dirty dressings and dirty laundry, the place to empty the slops and to put up specimens. Two hours of the early part of the night I spent in there, scrubbing and scouring and sterilising, until required by the senior nurse to relieve her for her midnight meal. I was then handed the keys to the dangerous drugs cupboard and the responsibility for all the patients, their drips and their treatments – from the skivvy to the boss. It was terrifying.

I had 'nights off' and set off for Southwold.

We were into our second year and changed our mauve and white striped frocks for blue and white striped ones. We had moved up one place in the hierarchy and now had the junior pro. under us. It didn't seem to make much difference to our pay, still only paid once a quarter and never amounting to much more than £4.0.0. after deductions of 6d per week to Hearts of Oak Friendly Society (insurance) and the cost of any thermometer we might have broken.

I made friends with Jean Kitchener, some six months my senior. She introduced me to classical music, being one of the few owners of a gramophone, and she had some lovely records. The hospital Matron, plump and autocratic, did not like the intrusion of so many young nurses in training and showed her disapproval of us. She was, however, very polite to Jean, whose haughty manner she forgave. 'For', she told a visiting dignitary, 'she's a come-down from the great Lord Kitchener'. Jean treated her thereafter with even greater disdain.

The summer had come and was hot and lovely. We raised money for the Red Cross by carrying collection boxes on our days off in full uniform. The public was unbelievably generous.

The War news was infinitely depressing. Hitler's armies had occupied the Scandinavian countries, and we lost shipping and troops in the actions off the Norwegian coast. Freddy Lewin, Field Marshal Lord Roberts' only grandson, was lost there. The Germans were sweeping through the Netherlands. The Blitzkrieg had begun. Our troops were pushed back to the Belgian beaches. Marlay Spencer was there, Tom, mercifully, still in England.

In June 1940 my father took up a teaching post at Spyway, replacing a man who had been called up. Spyway was a preparatory school run by brothers, Eric and Geoffrey Warner, in Langton Matravers near Swanage, Dorset. My parents rented a house in the village from Mrs Tod for a month and moved there from Southwold. Rosemary left Felixstowe College at Riddlesworth Hall and continued her studies for university entrance under my father's tuition. Their lease of the cottage was not renewed and my mother and Rosemary went to stay with old Kenya friends, Tim and Beryl Butler, who lived at Almer near Blandford, and my father moved into the school.

My parents had arranged to spend the summer holidays at an inn near the Spencers in Bradfield St. George, Suffolk. Their son Marlay had survived the Dunkirk evacuation and was serving on in England. They first went to Southwold to pack up Avalon and store everything in Ipswich. It was as well, as the house received bomb damage later.

In the late summer Elise and I got our first holiday and we spent it with my parents and Rosemary in the village inn at Bradfield St. George. That August the first bombs were dropped on London, and the aerial Battle of Britain began, to reach its peak late in September 1940. The Local Defence Volunteers, formed to protect hearth and home in 1939, became of vital importance as German invasion threatened. They were re-named the Home Guard.

Elise and I decided to cycle back to Northwood. The sunny summer days shone on into September and on our way in the remotest of Suffolk places we became aware of one of the many aerial dog-fights weaving their tracery in the sky above us. Suddenly from the blue came the scream of a crashing aircraft and we saw pin points which turned into parachutes with a man swaying beneath each one. We were rivetted to the spot with fright and awe, gazing at the slowly descending figures. My mind backtracked to German. What should I say if we were suddenly confronted by a German pilot? They seemed to come closer, perhaps the other two were English? Could all three be German? In the event they must have come down about a mile away and they disappeared from our view behind hedges and trees. Nevertheless we were apprehensive of the lonely road ahead and with much relief we stopped at the first village pub we came to, where all sorts of conflicting stories were already in circulation. Halfway to Northwood we spent a night in a bed-and-breakfast house. The air raid sirens sounded and the night was spent sharing a dug-out with the rest of the household. We got back to Northwood after about 80 miles, feeling very stiff and sore.

Back in Northwood it wasn't long before Elise and I were again on night duty. My father returned to Spyway for the Christmas term; Rosemary started her university career at Bedford College, London University, which had been evacuated from London to Newnham College Cambridge. My mother drifted about homeless, staying with the Butlers, Bodkin Wood and his sister Marge, and the Spencers. Tom's future changed when things got desperate after the Battle of Britain, during which his friend George Moberley was killed. Tom's renewed application to join the RAFVR was successful and in due course he found himself training at Oakington just outside Cambridge. So he and Rosemary saw quite a bit of each other at that time.

My father's letters to my mother tell the story of that Christmas term.

9th October 1940.
Spyway,
Langton Matravers.

Darlingst,

Got your letter of last Sunday today Wednesday. Grand to hear you may be here in ten days time. Like a tonic. I was beginning to feel like a monk in a monastery and not a jovial one. Am just recovering from a foul cold, a real streamer, so stayed in bed most of Saturday and Sunday. Everyone had it before me so there was no escape. We've just had the combined Swanage Prep. School sports. Spyway 2nd out of 5 schools, which wasn't bad. Also received a nice letter from Tom, giving me all his news. Acting 2nd in Command of a Company sounds most impressive. I'm sorry to hear you are going to Harrow, which seems to get a lot of bombs. (My mother's Aunt Eve, who wasn't well, lived there with Winnie Marshall). I see the Harrow School got it the other day. Sherborne village had 60 dropped in it the other day and the boys' school was hit. There was a big fight over Wareham and Weymouth yesterday in daylight. We watched it from the door of the dug-out and saw a plane come down and another burst in mid-air. The boys seem to take it very casually. Nothing fell near here. I am still getting reams of correspondence from the B.B.C. about the talk. I have at last got it fairly straight. No more news pro. tem. Hurry up and rejoin. Hope Rosie got my letter. I have not written to Beryl yet, but as you are all going anyway, no matter.

Love to you all, S.

18th November 1940.

Darlingst,

I meant to have written yesterday, but I had to struggle with the Income Tax return. Then who should turn up but Helen Atcherley. You remember, the wild woman who used to break everything up in the Hemsted household. She came to see G. Alexander, whom she used to governess in Kenya. She stayed in a room in the village for two nights. She told us a lot of things about the Alexander household. Pretty horrible and I am sorry for young Gerald if he has to go out there. She borrowed my galoshes and mack and got sopping wet every day. She'd have had my plus fours too with a little encouragement. It has been pouring ever since you left and I'm afraid you must have had a a miserable journey on Saturday, especially as you were going in the wrong direction, for me at any rate. We had a noisy night last night. A bomb on Swanage, which didn't hurt anyone and I believe a few on Bournemouth. Guns going all night. I think the Gerrys must have been pretty hard hit last week by air raids and are trying to hit back. Enclosed arrived from Alex to-day. It doesn't appeal to me. Too far away and rooms too small. If you can't find a cottage with one decent room in it, try to get something with two small rooms that we can knock into one. Geoffrey Warner was very interested in his arguments with Elizabeth and has harked back to them. I think he enjoyed them. So unusual to find anyone to stand up to him. Must wind up now, honey. All my love. I am longing for the Christmas holidays. Only 4 more weeks. Give my love to the Butlers and thank Bodkin for giving Rosemary such a treat. I enclose her card.

Ever your S.

22nd November 1940.
Spyway,
Langton Matravers.

Darlingst,

Just got your letter and the B.B.C. one. I went to the B.B.C. yesterday and saw Elspeth (Huxley) and Miss Gibbs from 12 – 3 with brief interval for lunch and then caught the 3.30 from Waterloo back to Swanage, arriving at 9 p.m. and caught the last bus back to Spyway. Elspeth was very pleasant and took down all my chat as she has to do the script. I don't know what the dialogue will be like, but they are sending me a specimen copy. Hope it isn't too 'Jack Warnerey'. However they have offered me two turns – one on the N.F.D. and the other on Kenya old and new, both I gather with Stordy and 'Bob' and 'Bill', whoever they may be, probably Canadian soldiers! Wednesday December 18th is the probable date for the first. The Warners, as usual, were charming about it and said I need not hesitate to ask for days off. Eric suddenly broached finance the other night and said he would pay me £40 for this term's work, which I thought very liberal and said so. Income Tax will have to be deducted of course. I enclose two letters from Tom and Joan (Croll).

I thank the Lord you aren't in Southampton. I am delighted to hear that you want to come to this part of the world next term. It will be grand, especially as posts seem to take longer and longer. I am going to ring you up to-morrow night. I spoke to Tim Butler on the phone on Wednesday as the B.B.C. has somehow got his address for me and rang him up. I am going over there on Sunday if the weather is all right. Tom seems all right as he is driving again. Just got a letter from E., which I enclose also. Give my love to the Bodkins. I never seem to get any time for letter writing when these B.B.C. stunts are on. Broadcasting House has been hit, but in the back part where it doesn't matter very much. The Langham has also been hit, but not badly. All my love, darling, I'm counting the days.

Ever your S.

28th November 1940.
Spyway,
Langton Matravers.

My dearest dear,

Got your letters this morning about the house and I rang up Mrs Morris and said we'd take it. She seemed very pleased and is going to let me know of any things she is short of such as towels etc. The Warners seem very pleased too, so everything in the garden is lovely. I think it is the biggest bit of luck we've had for a long time, because we shall be together again. Altogether, in spite of the War, this has been one of my good years, I consider, especially the latter part, and now Court Cottage coming along as a Christmas present – I feel more bucked than ever. About the Christmas holidays, I think, although my inclination is for Suffolk, that Dorothy's house will be more suitable on the whole. A big crowd in a pub without a lav. in the cold weather is going to be a bit trying and I think Elise and co. would enjoy Southbourne more. Besides Mrs Morris wants to see you before she goes away on January 7th and show you all the doings, and we could get here easily from Bournemouth by bus. If you want a job, you can always trot over to Studland and help Eileen Warner in the canteen. But I think you'll have your work cut out with Mrs Morris' garden, which is quite big and full of stuff. Great excitement last Sunday. A bomb fell in the middle of Spyway tennis court at 7 p.m. and another on the meadow on Guy's farm about a quarter of a mile away. I was in Swanage at the time and didn't know about it till I got back. Most of the windows in the front of the house were broken but nobody was hurt except one rabbit blown in half in Guy's field. The boys were a bit wakeful at night so I had to tell the lion and rhino stories to send them to sleep. The Warners say it didn't make as much noise as the big one which fell at Herston about 3 weeks ago. It was a small bomb, about 50lbs, they think. Must wind up now.

All my love, ever your S.

8th December 1940.
Spyway,
Langton Matravers.

Darlingst,

Got your letter of Dec. 5th yesterday with news of Rosie's move. The Balls must be odd people. Perhaps it's just as well she has left them. I have just been to Mrs Morris' to find out the shortages. I suggest you bring enough for a 4th bed, two old quilts: we can use karosses to the other beds if we want them. Plenty of bath towels but 3 or 4 face towels would be useful, also a camp mattress for the 4th bed. 3 or 4 pillow slips also, and a few dish cloths required. She is leaving us her plated spoons and forks instead of the silver. It is a very well-found little house and very warm. I think we are lucky to get it. She will be leaving about the 14th. Another bit of good news. I think I can get some petrol out of the Bristol people. I pleaded B.B.C. work in London, as I have to do 'Bob and Bill' on December 18th and again on January 1st. I shall leave here p.m. on the 16th with a suitcase, leaving my trunk here. I had a very nice letter from Nicholson the other day, saying that he was giving up his job at the M.O.I. by doctor's orders and suggesting that I apply for a job in the French section of the Imperial War Cabinet and giving me the name of a man to write to. It sounds very grand; but I expect it boils down to seeing French soldiers don't get lost in London! I'm going to follow it up as I am rather doubtful if Spyway will carry on, if air attacks increase in the spring with a possible threat of invasion. I think only one or two boys are leaving this term and two more are supposed to be coming; so I must carry on here for a bit. I will listen to 'Bob and Bill' on Wednesday. I hope Ceddie will be able to visit Southbourne. I've been offered a mattress at the B.B.C. for the night of the 18th, but I think I'll try to get out of London a little way anyhow if I can't get to Bournemouth. Give my love to the Bodkins. I am writing to him next week. Please let me know in your next letter what I owe the Balls for R's lodgings, also bills for any fees etc. that may have come in from Cambridge. It's a marvellous day and I wish you were here 'to roam the hills with me'. Everyone here, Mrs Coryton etc. all very thrilled at your coming to live here. If there is any riding kit for the girls accessible you'd better bring it, as Mrs C. is always longing for some one to ride with. Also Rosemary's School Certificate from the leather suitcase, I think, as the University people want it in connection with her Matric exemption.

All my love, ever your S.

In January 1941 my parents moved into Court Cottage, Langton Matravers. The house was at the end of a lane which ended adjacent to the school grounds. Elise and I were back on day duty at Mount Vernon.

One evening in spring a slim and bearded young Naval officer searched out Nurse Deck. I emerged somewhat startled from a patient's bedside to be told: 'My parents are playing bridge with your parents.' He had been wounded serving in a minesweeper in the North Sea. My sister Rosemary was spending her Easter vac. with our parents in Court Cottage. John Martin, for that was the N.O.'s name, was proceeding on sick leave to his parents who lived in Swanage. Later I confided to Elise: 'I bet he falls in love with Rosemary.'

Elise and my set were into our 3rd year and we got our 'strings'. These were little tapes tied in a neat bow which we put on under our starched and specially folded caps, giving the appearance that the cap was tied on. We entered our third year, our 'cross sheets' completed and our State Finals at the end. We were moved back to London for lectures and exams.

London had changed, full of gaps where buildings had once stood and friends had dispersed. Jimmy Hodges, the medical student at St. Mary's Paddington, was doing his finals and was engaged to a senior nurse there. Another friend, Hans from my 'digging days' in Nevern Square, had become an active and determined Communist. He gave me endless lectures on the subject and I started to get interested in politics. The underground stations had become the night resting place for many Londoners, who returned each night to their particular pitch. They were a merry group and sleep tended to be restricted to the early hours.

My father wrote the following letter, his last before his final, and incapacitating, illness.

Darlingst,

The position is that I have sent in my formal resignation to take effect from April 29th. The Director of the Division wants to hold it up to see whether I have changed my mind by the end of the month. But there is no chance of that happening. The urgency of the job has not yet struck me. I'll tell you why later. I am rather worried about E and will ring up Elise Dunn to-night. Excuse paper, Government offices are not so generous as they used to be.

Do come up as soon as you can, but this is only my selfishness. If you think it not worth it for 10 days or so, just stay put. I hope you've managed to fix up the cottage for next term. Will you tell Eric and ask him to excuse my not writing to him? When does next term begin?

Love to everybody, ever your S.

On 13th April 1941 my father suffered another heart attack. My mother immediately travelled to be with him. She was beside him when he suffered a stroke on 21st April 1941, from which he never fully recovered. They occupied a room on the second floor of the house in Holland Park, and shortly after his stroke they endured one of London's worst air-raids. A stick of bombs fell down the road they were in, missing the house but blowing in all the windows and wrecking the black-out. A bomber crashed on Campden Hill close by. My mother's consolation was a nun from a nearby convent, brought in to help nurse my father, reciting her Rosary and sprinkling holy water.

It was apparent that a decision about moving my father could not be made for some time and Tom and Rosemary were sent to Langton Matravers to shut up the cottage. Driving himself and Rosemary back to Cambridge in my parents' little Ford, they were hit by an Army truck which wrecked the car and sliced a gash in my sister's forehead. Only Tom's quick reaction saved them from serious injury or death. It happened not far from the Butlers at Almer near Blandford, and Rosemary was taken there to recover from her injury. I got compassionate leave to go and nurse her. Then it was that I realised my prediction was coming true. A faraway look came into my sister's eyes when she received almost daily letters from John Martin. After her accident she abandoned University and entered the Middlesex Hospital P.T.S. in September 1941, which was then at Stoke Mandeville.

My Communist friend, Hans, was trying hard to convert me to Communism. He had grown very persistent and had persuaded me in accordance with his Communistic outlook to visit his abode in one of the southern London suburbs. Hence my disappearance from the hostel that had worried my father. However, having arrived, I took fright and my father's illness brought me to my senses, but too late. My dear father had lost his speech and had a right-sided paralysis. No longer were his wise and kindly words to guide us. He was to be an invalid for eight years. He was only 58.

My mother moved him as soon as was practicable in a St. John's ambulance back to Court Cottage. She arranged with the convent to have a nun with her who would be relieved at intervals by another. Being on night duty again I used to travel to Langton Matravers for my nights off, and spent my annual holiday there helping my mother. She was able to get some golf with the Warners, and I continued to tease Geoffrey. Although my father was gaining some strength, his powers of communication were sadly limited, but he was a cheerful, co-operative and undemanding patient, and as dear to us as ever.

My worst problem on night duty was staying awake. I had no trouble sleeping during the day, but it made no difference to the struggle to keep concentration during the long night watch. Washing up after the patient's night-time drinks, I would find every cup on the floor instead of ready on the trolley for the next round. When left in charge of the ward during the senior nurses' dinner time I would walk around and around the ward in an endeavour to stay alert, only to find myself face down and sound asleep across the foot of a slumbering patient's bed! One night during my pere-grinations I was seized with panic when I found a bed empty where a very ill man, with drainage tubes on either side of him, should have been. I flew to the W.C.'s, where rumour had it patients were wont to throw themselves out of the window. Back in the ward another man, also returning to his bed, found to his surprise it was occupied. With relief I found my missing patient. I shepherded him back to his bed and reconnected his various drainage systems.

Air raids on night duty were alarming. One night when the siren sounded, lights were dimmed and the black-out checked, but the bombs fell close that night and one shattering blast blew in the high windows and tore the black-out to shreds. Some of the patients were so ill they were oblivious to anything, others remained stoically quiet and undemanding whilst we groped around with pinprick torch lights. The goldfish bowl which had been adorning the stack in the middle of the ward, shattered and we slipped on the fish slithering about on the floor. Another night a lot of fire bombs fell around the hospital and we were completely surrounded by burning build-ings. Volunteer members of the A.R.P. (Air Raid Precautions) who, in spite of a full day's work, took their turn at night watch on our hospital roof, had a busy night that night with their buckets of water and their stirrup-pumps. No ambulance could get through to us, so we in the hospital received no casualties and apart from anxiety and extra vigilance, had a relatively quiet night.

The pressure of work in the wards was intense. The London hospitals only received the most serious and urgent cases and beds had to be kept for air raid casualties. All routine surgical and medical patients were admitted direct to one of the sector hospitals. Seriously ill patients were evacuated as soon as their condition permitted. The work was thus unremitting, with every bed occupied by a seriously ill patient.

On day duty a patient who stands out in my mind was a very racey character in a yellow check waistcoat. He was a great flirt and his cheerful banter was a boost to everyone's morale. He had cancer and he had been in and out of the hospital many times and had been admitted for the final drastic surgery. His courageous spirit never deserted him and was enough, not only to pull himself through the immediate post-operative crisis, but the little man in the bed beside him as well, who underwent the same operation on the same day. He died shortly afterwards, mourned by us all and the hospital lost one of its local characters, brave and cheerful to the end. He had a wooden leg which he insisted on keeping beside his bedhead and we indulged his whim. After his death great mystery attached to this leg and Sister received the unusual instructions that it was to be placed in safe keeping in her office. We heard later that it had a secret compartment below the knee into which he used to receive stolen jewellery under a table in the Tottenham Court Road Corner House.

After our State Finals at the end of 1941 I applied to join Queen Alexandra's Imperial Military Nursing Service Reserve, (QAIMNSR). My call-up date was 1st August 1943, when I would have taken my Hospital Finals. In December 1941 Rosemary and John Martin announced their engagement. Tom had finished his flying training and was operating from an airfield in Scotland. During the summer he had been in Sussex and visited two elderly Deck aunts. They presented him with the Deck silver teapot and the silver Deck spoons and forks. These items are still cherished in the family.

Chapter Eight

Nursing and War 1942–1943

1942 WAS THE TURNING POINT OF THE WAR. My school friends, Annu and Maiu Mez, who were living with their mother and aunt in Melbourne, were both interned as enemy aliens. They were released a year or so later providing they undertook to go into hospital as nurses in training.

In February the pressure on Malta increased greatly and Rommel was threatening in the Western Desert.

In January 1942 my brother Tom was posted overseas and his letters tell of his experiences.

Sunday 1st February 1942.
P/O A.G. Deck, A.P.O. 1700.

Darling Family,

Well, here I am, very safe and very sound. I don't know when you will get this but I will send a cable to wish you a very happy birthday and God bless.

I do hope Pops is well on the road to recovery again. Now for my news.

This is not such a bad place. We are very comfortable and are fed exceedingly well. The heat at first seems terrific and one lives under the shower or in the sea.

We haven't yet started flying but hope to to-morrow. Nobody seems to exert themselves very much and if at all keen to get on and do something, one's spirits are clamped by those in charge.

I will make enquiries as to how much I can tell you in these letters and when I have the 'gen' on it I hope to make these dull epistles a little more digestible.

Much love, Tom.

Tom's light-hearted letters cheered us all up and we gathered that he was ferrying newly arrived aircraft to wherever they were needed.

In March 1942 Rosemary and John were married on John's ship in Scotland. None of us was able to be there. John had a course ashore for a few months and they took the opportunity to enjoy the time they could be together. My cousin Elizabeth Deck was married to a well-to-do medical student, Neville Southwell, and she left the Middlesex to have the first of her four children, David.

Elise and I were into our fourth year as senior nurses, working under the blue-belted staff nurses and the blue-clad Sisters with their lacey caps. Elise was sent to Stoke Mandeville and I went to Tindal House, an infinitely depressing place. I shared digs with a V.A.D., Philippa Scott (now Tooth), with whom I became very friendly and we were to remain life-long friends. Our landlady was Olive and she was very kind to us. She cossetted us with tea parties and all sorts of homely comforts.

Elise and I frequently biked to see each other and when we could get days off together, we explored the Buckinghamshire countryside on our bikes, often calling on a cousin of my father's, Herbert Norris. He lived in a dear little thatched cottage he called 'Godbegot' at Thame. He was a theatrical designer and a genealogist, who compiled much of the Deck pedigree.

Once on a summer's evening returning from a visit to Elise, I got a puncture. A passing youth offered to repair it for me. He was unkempt and slow-witted and foolishly I allowed myself to be led to a shed in a field where he said he kept his tools. No sooner were we out of sight of the road, than he attacked me. I fought like a fiend and managed to run away from him. Getting my breath back in the relative safety of the road, I saw him disappear and retrieved my punctured bike. A most frightening and unpleasant incident.

Another misfortune to befall me at Tindal House was a paratrooper patient who fell in love with me. When he was convalescent, he insisted on taking me out and I foolishly agreed to meet him. He also introduced me to his mother, obviously encouraging him in the face of her hostility to his wife. It was not long before his wife found out and complained to the Matron. I was called to account and informed in no uncertain terms that I was putting my career in jeopardy.

In May I caught measles and was carted off in an ambulance to an Isolation Hospital. In those days infectious fevers were strictly isolated and it meant a dismal few weeks cut off from the outside world. I was again reminded of what was needed in a good nurse.

Time Gone

When I was pronounced clear of infection, I went off on two weeks' convalescent leave to Langton Matravers. There I was able to give my mother a few days respite from nursing my father. A letter dated 7th July 1942 arrived for me from my godfather, Bodkin Wood.

———————

Cherry Tree,
Hacheston,
Woodbridge.

Dear Elizabeth,

I was glad to hear from you last month when you wrote from Court Cottage, 'in loco parentis', as one might say! You did well, for I think your mother is wonderful. She has had a very hard row to hoe for the past two or three years, and yet her courage has never failed. I was first and foremost a pal of Skipper, but I am proud that through knowing him I can, I think, call myself a friend of your mother's ... Have you heard more of Tom? I thought he was to ferry the new American planes across Africa from West to East, delivering them where they were wanted, but he must have been shifted to another job if he is at Karachi. And you, I hear, are busy doing your bit to set things straight and in the process, rendering yourself an irritant to those in authority. I have no doubt that they richly deserve it. The profession of nursing has battled long against abuses and silly cramping regulations.

Tom continued to write:

———————

19 May 1942
A.D.U., RAF, M.E.

Darling Family,

I am very sorry about the long silence. Just selfishness again. The last time I wrote was about three weeks ago – I am very sorry. I got your letter No.8 the other day, in which you said you had just received two letters from me. You are marvellous the way you go on and on with everyone going ill all round you. I am glad to hear Daddy is so cheerful.

Since I last wrote I have been doing quite a lot of flying and travelling. I flew an aircraft from here, the city of smells, to the country Aunt Elise visited not so very long ago, through that country down to where the Harrison-Jones of Ipswich used to live. When I had got there I had to come back by train part of the way, seven days and six nights in the train! Lovely! Never mind,

I am seeing the world. Since being back, I have been bathing at the Gezira Club every day. The other day I played some cricket and made 29! This morning I played a game of squash but it's a bit hot for that. I have been playing quite a lot of golf and hope to have a game to-morrow morning. Touch wood, I have so far kept very well. Again I am very sorry about not writing.

No more now much love Tom.

P.S. I thought I had used up all the space on this airletter but I find one more sheet still! Mac has just come in and is very 'browned off' (bored) as there is nothing to do in this city of smells at night except go to some cabaret and spend all our money! That pastime gets a bit boring as well as expensive after a bit. The European families here are not very hospitable, or anyhow don't seem to be to the R.A.F., although the pongos (Army) seem to be very well off, but then most of them are permanent fixtures round here.

No. 1.25th May 1942.
A.D.U., M.E.

Darling family,

Thanks a million for the *Picture Posts*. I received the first three the other day and hadn't seen any of them before. I'm very glad to hear about R's marriage. I got your No.9. letter telling about it to-day. Poor old E., she seems to get everything that's going. I expect she is recuperating at home by the time you get this. Make her do some work! As you see, I have numbered this letter No.1. as I don't know exactly what number it really is; so I've started again, and this time I will try to remember. Well I am still in the awful city of smells, Cairo, and have not done any work since returning from my trip through India and Ceylon, which I told you about in my last letter.

Luckily Mac is up here now so we spend most of our time together. The time is always spent at the 'front' or our 'front line', namely the Gezira Club. The weather is gradually getting hotter, and the flies are gradually becoming more numerous. I hope Daddy got my greetings telegram for his birthday, sent from Karachi. I can see that when I get home E. and I will have our time cut out to get a word in edgeways with old Pops spouting forth his views again! Keep it up. My luggage, which I hadn't seen since I first left Takoradi, has at last turned up, which is a great help, although I have had the golf clubs etc. with me the whole time. I will send you some silk stockings in the hope that you don't have to sacrifice coupons. Well, cheeribye and I hope no more bombs disturb the peace of Langton.

Much love, Tom.

No.2. 3rd June 1942.
RAF, A.D.U., M.E.

Darling Family,

I think it's about a week since I last wrote, so here we go again although I
doubt if I will be able to post this for some considerable time as I'm in the
bush! I left the dark-eyed city soon after writing my last letter and returned
to Tak. I am now on my way to, I bet you'll never guess, the good old
country of our childhood days! When they told me I nearly fell through the
floor. Anyhow, if all goes well, I hope to be there in about four more days.
I don't know of many people but there are always the Hemsteds, Sprotts and
dear old Kenton! Boy, oh boy, am I pleased! There isn't much news; the rainy
season has just started and you can't imagine what a little drop of rain does
to the country. One minute it's desert and the next it looks like England in
spring. The West Coast is very pleasant just now, although it rains pretty
frequently and it is very cool.

When I get to 'the veritable paradise', as Pops called it over the radio, I
will, I hope, try to stay there a little, 'cos I feel it ought to be rather interesting.
Well, I hope everyone is better or at least on the mend by now. Please
apologise to Lt. and Mrs Martin for my not sending them a telegram of
congratulations as yet but will do so at the first possible opportunity.

Much love. Tom.

So many of us tended to feel the utter desperation of 1942. Morale was
probably at its lowest on the home front that year. The War news was
always gloomy: the Russians retreating back into the heart of their homeland,
the Vichy French collaborating with their German conquerors and the
Japanese overrunning South East Asia and occupying many of the Pacific
Islands. And now the loss of Tobruk. We had struggled for two years with
rationing and the black-out, with air-raids and evacuation. People were
growing tired, tense and strained and there seemed to be no light at the
end of the tunnel.

For me personally it was a bad year and the depressing ambience of Tindal
House added to the sense of doom and gloom. For Tom flying the world,
and Rosemary enjoying the bliss of early married life, the gloom was probably
not quite so obvious.

Meanwhile Tom's letters continued to arrive in Court Cottage.

17 July 1942.
P/O.A.G. Deck,
RAF Heliopolis. M.E.

Darling family. Great news! I got lots of mail when I arrived in the stinking city the other day, after an absence of about a month. All told eight letters, including one from Barbara Croll (Lummis). By the time you get this, I hope you will have received my letter telling all about my Kenya trip. It is, well I maintain it is, very interesting and ought to revive many happy or unhappy memories as the case may be.

Continued at a later date when more satisfactorily equipped with pen and ink. I forgot to tell you about a race meeting I went to in the Sudan. It was very funny, no bookies, just a 1/- Tote affair and only betting on wins no places. As all the horses were local and all the jockeys too, everybody knew which horse would win! The Tote never paid out odds of greater than evens! Except on one race when a complete outsider romped home and not a soul had a bet on him. The next race they divided out the profits from that race and gave them to the winners. They paid out 4–1. I made about £1 – the first time in my life I have ever made anything! I got another batch of letters the other day. They were the first lot which were all addressed to the A.P.O. number and have just caught up with me! Anyhow, better late than never. The letters that get to me the quickest are the airgraphs, and I can easily decipher them. As you see by the address I have been posted out of A.D.U. and am now a Test pilot at the above address. There are two of us so we get quite a lot of work to do. I think June Watkins must have been posted away somewhere due to the flap, 'cos I can't contact her anywhere. Being on this job is a bit of a change 'cos one is able to settle down and get clean clothes at regular intervals and, what is more important, I am always near a fairly important postal place for sending and receiving letters instead of being in the bush. I have received all letters up to and including No. 17 except No. 14. I hope everything goes O.K. with the family and Mrs Martin.

Cheerio, much love, Tom.

20th July 1942. RAF
Heliopolis. M.E.

Darling family.

How's things? Life is still treating me fairly well, or rather very well. There isn't much news from this dump. I have been doing quite a lot of work, which is all to the good as it keeps me out of mischief. Guess what? I ran into Rupert Hemsted the other day. He was sitting in the Mess here when I walked in. He hasn't changed a bit. Very tall, but still very polite and a bit shy. He is stationed quite near here so I hope to see him soon. Got another two letters from E. She has also lost count of the numbers, so we are really as bad as each other. I sent you a pair of real silk stockings and a hand bag; give one of the two to R as a wedding present please and keep the one you want for yourself. Mac has been up in Cairo just recently so we have had one or two parties. He had rather a bad 'prang' (accident) about a fortnight ago but got away with one or two scratches. After much chasing I think I have at last run June Watkins to earth, and am going to try and see her this afternoon. We get quite good new flicks out here. I saw one yesterday with Hedy Lamarr. My gosh but she's beautiful. Another person I ran into was the MacGregor boy. They live in Southwold and I met him in Scotland when I was stationed there. No more now.

Much love, Tom.

1st August 1942.
RAF Heliopolis. M.E.

Darling parents,

How goes it? Please excuse the pencil but I am on detachment for a few days and in the desert. Very many thanks for the letters and magazines. Life here goes on much the same. I am still very fit, touch wood and thank goodness. Today I hope to be paying a visit to the land of milk and wild honey, or is it locusts? I have at last run June Watkins to earth. We have been out twice together so far and she seems very pleasant and quite good company. Rather bolshie and gets on with the job, which is a good thing! From what I can gather, she seems to be one of the only live wires among the WAAFS she works with. Rather after E's style but not so bad!!

7th August 1942.

Have just returned from the blue, where I have been doing a conversion course on to another type of aircraft. I am now living out of the mess as that is full. I have a furnished room in a flat belonging to a young couple and two small children. I took June Watkins up for a flip in an aircraft yesterday. She seemed to enjoy it quite a lot. We didn't do anything very much so she wasn't 'ick! There doesn't seem to be much else to say, except that we are still having lovely weather with the sun always shining, but then it will only be news when it doesn't shine for a day!

Much love and God Bless. Tom.

On 8th August 1942 Tom wrote to me and I received his airgraph quite quickly. An airgraph was written on a form which one could obtain and was then photographed, reduced in the printing to a print measuring 4″ × 5″ which reached the recipient. This method of communication reduced the weight and bulk of the ordinary airletter, and consequently arrived sooner. The R.A.F. had the necessary photographic technicians and equipment for the purpose.

———

P/O. A.G. Deck, RAF
Heliopolis. M.E.

Darling E,

Thanks a million for all your letters, it's been grand hearing from you. Rosy must be very much the newly married wife as I haven't heard from her as yet. True I haven't written to her, but she used to be my most regular correspondent in pre-Mrs Martin days! I can't honestly give you any more news than I give Ma, so this is in all probability second-hand news. Can you do me a favour, please? Write to my bank, Westminster, Guildhall Street, Lincoln, and ask them how my account stands, or if it's lying down and passed out! Or ask Ma to, but do it yourself if possible, 'cos I don't want Ma to know! Don't get worried but I think I'm quite a lot in credit, I hope! Well, old gal, hurry up and become a doctor so that after the war I can come and live on you! Also stop Ma from worrying about me as I am O.K.

Much love Tom.

The printed instructions on this form stated 'Write address in LARGE block letters wholly within this panel. Write the message very plainly below this line.'

The next two letters from Tom were written in increasingly dotty vein! Nevertheless they cheered us up immensely.

———

22nd August 1942.
RAF Heliopolis. M.E.

Darling Folks,

Here's your old pal Tom Deck on the air once more, and even more full of hot air this time than last! You must excuse me 'cos as yet I haven't been able to take him in hand and make him send all those cables with which he was going to add to your salvage campaign! Never fear (he and I) are still hoping! As you may have gathered by now there is no news, otherwise you wouldn't be reading the tosh written above. But still 'no noos is good noos' so cheerio no more for now.

Much love Tom 1st.

Darling parents I have taken the above Tom in hand and am now continuing as Tom 2nd, much nicer chap, tall, dark and handsome, no smoking (in the bath or in bed) no drinking (when asleep) and altogether a fine upstanding youth who loves his parents and also funnily enough those two objects which his parents graced themselves with and put the blame on the aforesaid Tom 2nd by calling his sisters as if he, poor chap, had anything to do with it. Thanks a million for all the letters and papers etc. I must mention that Miss E. Deck is mentioned in this my latest despatch for the noble way in which she is storming Tom 2nd's front with an endless and most welcome stream of interesting and mostly easily decoded photographs, although she, Miss E. Deck, herself states that she fears Tom 2nd will not be able to read the photographs on account of bad handwriting, the latest despatch from Tom 2nd on said subject states that although he will agree about the writing being atrocious, it can be and is easily decoded! As for Mrs R. Martin (late Miss R. Deck), please congratulate her on the bar she has now been awarded to her 'Order of the left hand boot'! There is only half a page more so I will give you some news. 1. ME. Very fit, healthy and flourishing. 2. WEATHER. Very fine, too fine. 3. COUNTRY. Very smelly, too smelly. 4. ACTIVITIES. Very little. Only one party per day and a few flicks. Have taken June flying twice and sailing on the Nile. It was good fun but the water is so dirty that one feels that one is sailing on a mud flat. 5. WORK. Very little, Having a slack period just now. 6. MISC. Am not living out anymore. Poor show? Yes, very poor.

Cheerio, much love, Tom.

Tom's next communication was an airgraph which was headed 'MILITARY AIRGRAPH SERVICE authorised by Egyptian Postal Administration.'

30th September 1942.106180
P/O A.G. DECK. RAF, Heliopolis.

Darling parents,

Very many thanks for all communications received. At present I am still on sick leave, now at Port Said. I returned to Helio on the 27th and hitch-hiked up here on 28th. I can't remember much about the place from previous visits.

Actually where I am staying is Port Fouad on the opposite side to Port Said. The bathing is quite nice but not a patch on that at Alex. The water isn't so clear and doesn't taste so nice! Hope my letters on Kenya arrived safely. I have received yours and in them you mention 'manners', but you don't say what kind of 'manners'. I forgot to tell you in my last letter that we had the most ginormous party on my birthday (14th September). It was the day I was let out of hospital and coincided with some of my friends' house-warming party, so we made it a combined one and jolly good it was too. I hope the bombs don't get any closer. They seem to be getting a bit too near. Well, cheeri-bye.

Much love, Tom.

Tom's next letter was forwarded from Court Cottage to Holmdale, Temple Sheen, East Sheen, London S.W.14. It was now plain that my father would be bed-ridden for the rest of his life and my mother gave up the lease of Court Cottage at Langton Matravers and took up my uncle Cedric's offer of his house Holmdale at Sheen. There she was joined by my sister, who was expecting her first baby. John Martin had gone to sea again. A cousin of my father's in the estate agency business, Gordon Cooper, was negotiating for a house for my parents in Aldeburgh, where they too lived. My parents would be able to move into the restricted coastal zone of Suffolk by virtue of the fact that in the early days of the War they had lived in Southwold, also in the restricted area.

Tom was still writing to Court Cottage:

----

17 October 1942. RAF,
Heliopolis. M.E.

Darling Ma, Pa, Baby and Pram,

The latter just means anyone who wants to be honoured by being called darling by yours truly! As I think I mentioned in my last epistle my nose is now back to the grind-stone. I'm glad my Kenya chronicles turned up safe and sound; of course looking back on my historical trip to my birthplace, I definitely feel, like most 'Poonah Wallahs', that it's not what it used to be! Since my last letter I have received a letter from Captain A.A. Banks, M.C., R.H.A. (mind you I had written him two already). The day after receiving said letter, a voice came to me across the void and through the telephone wires and the voice said it belonged to aforesaid gentleman (?), and that he was residing in hospital, just one kick in the pants from here; so what did I do? I immediately shouted, a horse, a horse, for two accas (5d.) and rode on my imaginary charger to A.A.B.'s rescue. I found him unchanged, he wasn't ill at all and making as much noise as usual. He was unable to leave his abode that day but managed to smuggle himself out next day. That afternoon he came flying with me and that night we had a party! AAB returned to hospital much too late, but who cared? Next day he was discharged and I met him and he didn't feel well, so now I think he is back in hospital! 24th October 1942. AAB has got jaundice. I have not been able to see him yet as I have been doing a hell of a lot of work. Literally I do about 50 hours flying a month, which, if you ask anyone who knows, is a lot of flying! The sun still shines down here and although it shines, it doesn't shine so hotly and soon it will be cool enough for us to run about in blue again.

Much love, Tom.

The next three communications were on airgraph.

108160 P/O A.G.
Deck,11/11/42.

Darling everyone,

Sorry for the silence I have maintained for the last ten days, but I have been very slack and selfish again. Well, how goes it? Here the Jerry is going where to I don't know, but let's hope it's hot! Now if I were to tell you I have got married, you would get a bit of a shock, well I haven't so don't have any shock at all. It's taken me ten days to think this up and I'm paid 14/6 a day for it, so you can see I'm quite well paid! Since last writing, Alastair Banks has spent three nights with me. We had some good fun. I had a night in Alexandria not long ago, and boy, oh, boy what a night! The other day I had to go up to Palestine (to be continued).

The second airgraph goes on:

I hope the first part of this epistle turns up. E's have always arrived together, so let's hope this does. Where did I finish? ... Palestine. A friend, who came up with me, and I spent a most enjoyable and luxurious night in Tel Aviv, on the coast near Jaffa. It's a grand place and if ever I get any more leave I'm going there. We brought down a lot of oranges, there are millions of them up there, but they aren't quite ripe yet, although very nice. By this time you will, I hope, be installed at Holmdale. Did anyone get the pears from that garden this summer? Poor old E. seems to be becoming all horsey again! Last night I played bridge for the first time since reaching darkest Africa and won 7/-! Much love, Tom.

25th November 1942.
P/O A.G. Deck.
RAF Heliopolis, M.E.

Darling household,

How does the new address look? I don't ha'f wish I was with you, with all the holly and mistletoe etc! I am very sorry to hear about poor old Aunt Eva. Well, things are really bright now and the War will be over in next to no time, I hope. I am still very fit. Did the last airgraph turn up complete? It was in two parts like this one. (Continuation) I think I will start to play rugger again. There are some quite good facilities for playing the game in this dump. I have been making quite a few trips to the land of milk and wild honey. It is very pleasant just now and the oranges are just coming into season, so we always bring some back with us. By the way, did I tell you that I removed my moustache? Give my love to everyone.

Much love Tom.

Tom was now promoted to Flying Officer from Pilot Officer.

---

30 December 1942.
108160 F/O A.G. Deck.
RAF Heliopolis. M.E.F.

Darling family,

Sorry I haven't written for such ages. It isn't slackness, 'cos for a change I have been doing a hell of a lot of work. Before I proceed any further in this masterpiece of literature, very many thanks for the two grand books. I have already read *The Snow Goose* about 5 or 6 times and *The Last Enemy* is now going the rounds. I sent *Snow Goose* off to Alastair; he should enjoy it. Have just received your first AirMail letter card for which many thanks. I'm thrilled about Rosy's effort, but I think Martin is all wrong and his initials ought to be C.A.A. Martin (after me). You know Uncle Tom Cobley etc. I hope you had a grand Christmas as we did here. (Continued) I was in the blue on Christmas morning but got back in time for the evening's celebrations, and boy, oh boy, what celebrations. They ceased last night, I think and hope! I have now been made rugger officer and have been playing quite a lot, once or twice a week, also quite a lot of squash. I beat the local professional the other day and won 20 accas (4/-) off him too! If the news goes on being as good as it is, we will be back for Easter, or anyhow pretty soon. Cheerio, much love, Tom.

The success of the 'Torch' landings came as a wonderful boost to everyone's morale in these beleaguered islands. At the same time news of the ferocious and bloody battles around Stalingrad signalled to us all that the tide was turning at last in favour of the Russians. Truly we felt we could see a glimmer of light at the end of the dark tunnel.

At home in Holmdale, Temple Sheen, my mother was happily anticipating receipt of one of her geese from Langton Matravers for Christmas dinner. Alas, when it arrived, it was so maggoty that all we could celebrate was its burial in the garden!

1943. The Germans were being pushed back out of Russia. In May General Alexander reported that the Tunisian campaign and all enemy resistance had ceased. In November the 'Forgotten' 14th Army under General Slim was preparing the recapture of Burma.

1943 found Elise and me back in London for our Hospital Finals. There was a new feeling of optimism in the air. In London we noticed new uniforms. Free Frenchmen and Americans in increasing numbers were pouring into the country from across the Atlantic. Men from Europe carried the names of their countries on their shoulder flashes.

Back in the wards on day duty, I found myself working under a senior Nurse Morse, another evangelising Communist. She recruited us for a start into the Socialist Medical Association, pressing then for better working conditions for nurses. She pushed a lot of Communist propaganda into our hands. It all seemed very exciting, albeit not entirely convincing. 'Second Front Now' demands were ever more strident and slogans were everywhere. Mercifully for me exams and duties gave me precious little time for playing politics. Soon my turn for night duty came round.

We always looked forward to our three nights off and although we were supposed to go to bed before going out, and similarly to be in in time to sleep before going on duty, few of us missed the whole of our four free days! We therefore experienced two periods of 24 hours without sleep twice in the short space of 96 hours. We resorted to 'Benzedrine', a proprietary amphetamine, to see us through a 12-hour stint of night duty. However it didn't seem to help me much. As I sat over the writing up of records under the shaded light at the desk in the middle of the ward, a wakeful patient would click his fingers as he saw my head droop in sleep. 'Wake up, Nurse', he would whisper. After one dreadfully busy night I came to the Ward Sister's office to give the night report to find her puce with fury.

'Not funny, Nurse Deck'. Her scorn cut me to the quick. What on earth had I done? She thrust the treatment book at me. Instead of the patient's name in the first column against the bed number was entered my own name – all down the page. I was quite shattered to see what I had done during those limbo hours under the hooded light in the middle of the ward.

One of the delights of night duty was to come back to the Nurses' Home and head straight for the swimming pool. It was always deserted at that time of day and we could plunge in stark naked. It was refreshing and served to help us stay awake for the 10 a.m. lecture!

On day duty I did a spell in the Private Wing, the Woolavington in Cleveland Street. It was very restful and elegant and a welcome respite just before my exams. My most flamboyant patient was the authoress Elinor Glyn, famous for the ditty:

> 'Would you like to sin,
>   with Elinor Glyn,
>   on a tiger skin?'

She insisted on having her own pillow cases in all shades of pastel, unusual in the days of white bed linen. She demanded that they be constantly rearranged and this task fell to me and her 'Irish Rose', a tall lanky girl from Ireland. Surveying her make-up in her little barbola mirror she would receive her visitors, usually her two elegant daughters in the splendid uniforms of high powered ladies of the Red Cross and WVS. She died later that year.

Another patient was a sad little man who fretted dreadfully whether he had cancer or not.

'They won't tell me, Nurse. If only I knew.'

The ethics of this troubled me a lot. I felt if he knew, he might at least find peace of mind. After much soul-searching and yet more questions from him, I did the unpardonable thing against doctor's orders and told him the truth. His gratitude remains with me to this day.

Back on the wards, another of my memorable patients was a young girl admitted for a straightforward appendicectomy. As I approached her bedside with the dressing trolley to prepare her for the theatre, she sighed: 'I know I'm only another patient to you, but to me I'm very important.' It reminded me of the need always to be gentle and sympathetic, no matter how busy or rushed we might be. In March I received another letter from 'Uncle' Bodkin Wood:

19th March 1943.
Cherry Tree, Hacheston,
Woodbridge, Suffolk.

Dear Elizabeth,

Whenever your Mother sends me a letter she puts in a bit of news about you and whenever I reply, I say 'yes, yes, I must write to her' and that seems to be as far as it gets. This time however, along with a phial of cream which she sent because I had mentioned how cracked my hands were, she told me you were holding down the job of acting Sister and would probably keep it till your time was up. This sounds an important job and it's very pleasant to hear you are doing so well. The nursing profession is to the fore these days and prospects seem much better. You must be very proud of Tom and his doings in Africa. Rosemary too, I hear, will soon be in the news! But, of course, your Mother is the wonder-piece of your family. Skipper must have blessed the day when he met her in what he used to describe as 'the purlieus of Kensington'. I do hope that you will be able to find a residence somewhere in this part of the world. I am torn at this moment between a desire to get away for a few days to Stortford and to Sheen and the fact that we are most definitely told that we should not travel by train except in case of necessity. I should so like a talk with you. I think you would find me much more sympathetic to your schemes for reform. It's you young people who have to shape the world and you mustn't be put off by us old fogies who bleat about getting back to normal. God forbid that we should do that. We haven't made such a striking success of things that we want to go back to the good old days.

My best love, Bodkin.

Meanwhile Tom was writing his cheery and dotty letters.

16 January 1943.

Darling everyone

All recovered I hope after a very happy Christmas. I'm afraid my letter writing has got rather out of hand as I can't remember when I last wrote. Maybe it's my memory that's going wrong! It's the flies, wogs, sun and I could go on and on, but that's what causes all the trouble in this land of sunshine and the romance of the East. Anyhow here I am quite recovered from Christmas and Noo Year. This Noo Year we had quite a to do. I took June Watkins out and I got sloshed and she remained stone cold sober! As I think I told E., June doesn't drink. Re your letter about my remark about being married, it's alright, there is no fire and at present there's only lots of water about so don't get false ideas into that sweet head of yours. So glad to hear Pops is so much better. When I get home I'm going to refresh your memory on Arabic as I have gone to the great expense of 20 accas (4/-) and bought an Arabic grammar, goodness knows why, but this country makes one do things like that.

Continued 17 January. Have just got back from a wild goose chase, only the goose in this case happens to be a game of rugger. I drove the team 83 miles to this place in a great lorry and when we got there they didn't know anything about the game! At present I am very much down in the dumps as my girl friend, an R.A.F. Sister and much the most sweet and pretty Sister in the M.E., has been posted up to the blue. She rang me last night and told me to take her out for a last and very bittersweet farewell!

Boo-hoo. Cheerio, much love. Tom.

---

29 January 1943.
F/O A.G. Deck,
RAF, Heliopolis, M.E.

Darling Ma

Many happy returns and lots of love. I will let you into a secret, you must keep this under your hat, it's concerning the news about which this letter is going to be written. Here goes, THERE ISN'T ANY NEWS! Except that we're winning the War, which of course is great news. I have had a couple of games of rugger recently, both of which we won. We're having lousy weather just recently, lots of wind and lots of sand, in fact lousy flying weather. But as there's lots of work to be done before we win, we fly and like it! Again Happy Birthday, Ma and God bless.

Much love. Tom.

9th March 1943.108160
F/O A.G. Deck. 227
Squadron, RAF, MEF.

Darling everyone.

How goes it? With me everything is just dandy. As you will see by the address I have been given the order of the boot by Helio! I managed to put up a sufficient number of blacks for the C.O. to request for my posting which, although I don't think I'm allowed to tell you what we do, is very enjoyable. I don't know when I last wrote but I have a very guilty feeling that it was in the dim and distant past. Up here we don't get many facilities for playing rugger so we have just started soft-ball. The game is really rounders with a pansy ball, bat and a lot of pansy rules! But if you mention rounders to any Canadians they will just about murder you. Anyhow it's very good fun and quite good exercise and we are definitely top dogs at the game around here. One of the squadrons we play against has a couple of O.Ms with whom I was at school, so quite a lot of reminiscing goes on. We had one hell of a party the night before I left. I took June out and she had just a little to drink, which shows she was gradually giving in! Poor show?! I have put all my clothes and all my belongings which I don't want in store with Thos. Cook and Sons in Cairo. I know you don't approve of the above firm but I wasn't able to send them back to Blighty so I thought it would be best to store it with them. We have a cinema on this 'drome (a great luxury) but the operators haven't a clue as every film or nearly every film they put on, they manage to get the reels mixed up, consequently one sees the end before the beginning etc! It turns quite a serious film into quite a good comedy! Cheerio.

Much love, Tom.

The next communication was the dreaded telegram on 10th May saying:

Immediate from Air Ministry. Regret to inform you that your son No. 108160 Flying Officer Arthur Graham Deck is reported to be interned in Neutral Territory as the result of air operations on 26th April 1943. Report states that he is uninjured. Letter confirming this telegram follows.

It needs little imagination to know the heart-sinking feeling my mother must have endured as she read the first few words, taking her back to her youth and the news of her brother Graham's death in 1915. Mercifully Rosemary was there to support her, and I was in London too. Relief came as she read on and knew that he was safe. The Air Ministry's letter of 18th May 1943 read:

Madam,

I am directed to confirm the telegram in which you were notified that your son, Flying Officer Arthur Graham Deck, Royal Air Force, is interned.

The telegraphic report received from Royal Air Force Headquarters, Middle East, states that the Beaufighter aircraft of which your son was pilot crashed into the sea near Bodrun and it has since been ascertained from Ankara that he is unhurt but interned in Turkey.

I am to enclose for your guidance a pamphlet on communications with prisoners of war.

I am, Madam,
Your obedient servant,
Director of Personal Services.

She then received the following cable from Tom:

Am fine but bored stiff hope everything ok reply Brairat Ankara. Love Tom.

To which she replied:

All well relieved at news don't get bored learn Turkish. Love Mummy.

The next letter my mother received was from an old Kenya friend.

------

c/o Mov & Tn. GHQ PAI Force
(at Iskandessen). 16.5.43.

My dear Nancy,

You will wonder why on earth you should get a letter from me after all these years. But your Tom had lunch with me yesterday at Ankara. He was looking fit and well and told me that his plane had come down near the coast of Turkey and he and his mate had swum ashore and had been interned, but hope to get out soon as refugees, or if not that way, to be exchanged. He and several other internees were lunching in the restaurant and he recognised me at the next table. I am glad he did, because I would never have remembered him, but then I don't suppose I would know my own family now, as I have not seen them for five years. He told me all about you and Skipper, and of the latter's illness. I am so sorry but Tom tells me he keeps cheerful and that you look after them all. Also the two girls are now married, or was it only one married, I forget. It was a great bit of luck seeing him as I was just off by plane to Adema and only had half an hour there. He tells me he has not written yet but has sent cables. So I said I would write and post my letter in

Cairo next Wednesday when I get there. As I said above, he looks wonderfully well and fit and cheery. They are billeted in some hotel and can go out all day on parole. They are in touch with the Air Attaché at the Embassy. I asked him if I could help in any way with money etc. but he assured me he had all he wanted. A grand lad, Nancy, and you can both be proud of him. Give my best salaams to Skipper and I hope all goes well with you all. Don't worry about Tom, he is all right. I told him he must fill in his time learning the language and not to allow himself to get soft. I don't think he will do that. You people at home have been grand through all the blitz etc. I hope you won't have anymore.

All best wishes, cheerio, yours, J. Rhodes.

This was followed by a letter from Tom:

———————

16th May 1943. Turkey.

Darling folks,

Sorry about not having written before, but as you can see I have arrived in another country! This time not on a job of work, but as an internee. An entirely new role and not a very bright one either! We got to this country by swimming and then by donkeys, buses, and every kind of transport you can think of. We eventually reached this dump of a capital. How long we will be here for, I have no idea, but the shorter the sweeter. We have been treated very well and are allowed out every day until 11.30 p.m. on parole. There are some friends and also a few allies here, all internees. Among the English is Jerry Tozer whom you may remember me mentioning, as we did all our training together. This is not going to be a very interesting letter as I don't know what we can and can't say! Anyhow I'm very fit and also very safe and sound. This little trip will add another chapter and very amusing one to my book after the War.

Much love, Tom.

P.T.O. My address is as follows:
FOR TRANSMISSION TO ANKARA.
F/O A.G. Deck, c/o Mr J.B. Hogan,
Air Ministry, A.I. King Charles Street, London SW1.

On 3rd June 1943 my mother received the following telegram from the Air Ministry:

Important from Air Ministry. Your son F/O A.G. Deck returned Egypt safe and well 1st June.

Tom wrote:

_____

12th June 1943.
F/O A.G. Deck.
227 Squadron, MEF.

Darling Folks

It's about a fortnight since I last wrote and I am very sorry about it all. As you see, I have returned to the squadron, thank goodness, and have left all the Turkish delight behind! I do hope you got my letters. Most probably all your letters to me will be stooging out to Turkey! Anyhow when we got back here there was a grand pile of letters waiting for which many thanks. Also a lot of magazines had turned up, but they are always opened by the boys, who greatly appreciate them. Glad to hear Daddy's birthday letter arrived so timely. The new house sounds grand and in a lovely position. I only wish old Adolf would throw in the sponge so I could see you and it. I can't tell you where I am but I'm nowhere near John. I am still fairly near the city of stinks. They must have improved the mail service. Sorry about the New Zealand stamps but they were the only ones available! You will be sorry to hear that Mac, the type I always knocked around town with, has bought it. He went just after my arrival in Turkey so I didn't hear about it until I got back here, when I found a cable and three rather pathetic letters from his wife Jane. She, poor girl, is very hard hit. It's grand being back here with the boys after being stuck up in the dump. Poor old Jerry is still up there. Hope you got Bill's and my photo in captivity! No more for now.

Much love. Tom.

_____

19th June 1943.
F/O A.G. Deck,
227 Squadron, M.E.F.

Darling everyone,

Thanks a million for the letters, one from Ma and one from E. They are the first I've received since I landed back in the squadron after the batch I got on arrival. It's grand to hear that Uncle Irvine has got a gong, jolly good effort. It was very nice of Wing Commander Mac. to write to you. He, as you must have realised, is my C.O., and a bloody fine type, you couldn't

123

find better. I'm sorry to hear about the hostile relations that exist between the Cedric Crolls. Aunt Elise sent me a book called *The Moon is Down*, really quite a good book and very nicely written. As you say, it is all so sad and silly. I'm glad to hear E. has got into the Q.A.'s. I don't think there is anything to choose between any of the nursing services, they are all as good as each other. I do hope E. manages to get a postponement of her calling up so as to be able to help with the move. By the time you get this, maybe I'll be an uncle. Anyhow 'on, on' (our squadron motto), Rosy. Since being back there has been quite a lot of work to do but we all thrive on it. We have quite a lot of different forms of exercise here. There is very good sea swimming and we have soccer and hockey periodically in the evenings. We have a soccer league in the squadron comprising about 8 different teams, of which one is the officers'. Needless to say we, as yet, have not won a match, but we always draw the largest crowd! Only about half the team have any idea of what one is supposed to do, so it's rather like a music hall turn. At hockey we are a bit more clueful. We don't get any rugger, for one thing the ground is too hard and the weather too hot. I hope the move goes off well, and I'm glad you're going 'home'.

Much love, Tom.

26th June 1943. 108160
F/O A.G. Deck.
227 Squadron M.E.F.

Darling folks

Things just drool on here in the same way. Haven't had a letter since the last one I told you about, but then where we're stuck at present the post ain't so good. I can only write one of these Air Mail Letter Cards a week unless I'm able to cadge one, as the issue is only one a week. Don't know what I'm going to fill all this paper up with 'cos there's nothing to write about except the dust, we've got dust instead of sand now and it's about ten times worse, and the flies. I think this place must be the headquarters of all flies. I haven't had a bath since getting back in this dump, but don't let that worry you, it's not too bad as we are able to get very good bathing every, or nearly every, day. E. better look out and get into training if she wants to keep the family swimming stakes both long distance and sprint! My poor old watch has stopped but it's not surprising since before reaching the shores of my last holiday resort, Bill and I spent two hours in the briny ocean and the old watch ticked away all the time until about a week ago! I think that effort put up the family long distance record? Can't think of any more and with Hitler back pedalling at this rate I will be shooting and sailing on the Alde at Christmas!

Much love Tom.

10th July 1943.108160.
F/O A.G. Deck,
227 Squadron, M.E.F.

Darling folks,

You lucky people, yet another letter from the fluent pen, as you were, pencil from that great fool Tom Deck! Talk about me being a bad correspondent, this is the third letter I've written without receiving any noos from the home front. Poor show! But still we have been charging round the countryside at a phenomenal rate so that it's little wonder that my colossal fan mail has not caught me up. Anyhow if the lack of mail and personal discomfort in anyway helps the invasion of Sicily, good show! Discomfort is usual in this ZYX M.E. but at present if you multiply the 'dis' of discomfort 100 times you are still far short of our present lot! Lovely moan! Well I hope to hear the great noos in the very near future that I am an uncle and that R. is a proud Ma (congrats to both J and you) and that Ma and Pa are Grandma and Grandpa! We must be growing old! Please don't worry about my wellbeing. I beg pardon, but I have dropped a brick as I received a very welcome airgraph from E. and a letter card from Aunt Elise which was very sweet of her. Re E.'s airgraph, no one need worry 'cos in my case 'no noos is good noos'. Air Ministry will let you know the minute I damage myself in the slightest way. So cheer up and if all goes on as at present, we'll have turkey together for Christmas.

Much love Tom.

21st July 1943.108160
F/O A.G. Deck,
227 Squadron, M.E.F.

Darling everyone,

Thanks a million for all the various forms of communication received in the last few days. I'm sorry about the hold up in mail from my end, but I believe they held some of the mail up before the invasion, probably through lack of facilities. Anyhow, I hope it now flows through freely. We have or rather are now settling down once more having been chasing round this ZYX desert for the last three to four weeks. God, but there are some bloody places out here!

Sorry about the language but they have got to be visited to be appreciated! Goodness knows what propaganda the Duce must have used to get his poor and stupid countrymen to come and settle out here! It's grand to be in a spot where you don't find scorpions in your bed every other night! Glad to hear you saw all or some of your old Kenya friends, I remember the name Lambert but can't place the face. Wasn't she and her husband A.D.C. Kajiado? What does Gwen Buxton look like? I remember her as being my first 'imagined' heart throb! It's funny, but also a rather degraded way of hitting the news under the heading of an interned airman! Gerry Tozer is now back in M.E. too. I hope Pops is looking up and that Mother and child are doing well. Give my love to everyone.

Much love, Tom.

My Uncle Cedric, as referred to by Tom, had met Molly Kenyon when he was stationed in Shropshire, which caused the rift between him and Aunt Elise. In July Rosemary was admitted to the Middlesex Hospital and on the 14th a daughter Penelope was born to the joy and delight of the family. I had completed my training and acquired my Hospital badge as well as my S.R.N. one, and was now entitled to wear them both. Tom wrote on 2nd August 1943.

108160 F/O A.G.
Deck, 227 Squadron, M.E.F.

Darling everybody, that includes the new arrival Penelope. A very nice name, but Pella stinks, it compares with Liza for Elizabeth! Well it's good to know Rosy was of so much use to the medical profession in that Elise could use all her experiments! I don't wonder she, Penelope, is hiccoughing after a bottle of castor oil. It's a wonder she isn't doing lots of other things too! It's grand noos and a very good show. Thanks a lot for all the various forms of noos, but I'm very sorry to hear that Uncle Ceddie is being a bit of an XYZ. Life goes on here in much the same way although lately we have been doing rather a lot of work, which is a good thing in many ways. As I probably told you, the bathing here has been rather spoilt by oil from some ship, in consequence we don't do as much swimming as usual. I had letters from both Alastair and Rupert Hemsted quite recently. Rupert has returned to M.E. and is now stationed somewhere near Cairo and Alastair is, or rather was, spending some leave in Tripoli. He was very browned off as most of his friends had been posted and a lot of new officers of whom A doesn't approve have been sent to his unit. By this time doubtless you will be installed at Aldeburgh – well anyway I hope so and I hope the place and house is as grand as it sounds. There's no noos – what again! I can't think of any trash to fill the bottom space, so bye bye.

Much love, Tom.

The house in Aldeburgh was now available for my parents and I got a month's call-up deferment on compassionate grounds to help move my invalid father and my sister with her new-born baby. I travelled to Ipswich where the furniture was stored, watched the men load it, climbed into the van with the men and set off for Fairways in the Saxmundham Road in Aldeburgh, and 'home', as Tom had put it. I saw to the unloading, lit a few fires and was ready in a few days to welcome the arrival by St. John's Ambulance of my parents, my sister and my baby niece. Having settled them in and enjoyed a few days leave, I donned my grey and red uniform and reported for duty at Copthorne Military Hospital near Shrewsbury on 1st September 1943. Elise had decided to do her midwifery. This meant she would have to stay on after her training under the 'Direction of Labour' rules to do a six-month stint on the 'district' owing to the shortage of civilian midwives. She had a very dependent widowed mother, and she felt she should not desert her, although she longed to join the QARNNSR, the Naval Nursing Service.

Chapter Nine

Queen Alexandra's Imperial Military Nursing Service (R) 1943–44

AFTER TRAINING I was accepted to serve in QAIMNS(R) and I joined in September 1943. I was posted to an ordinary Military Hospital at Copthorne outside Shrewsbury.

There I learnt the Army system and encountered for the first time one of those brave regular Q.A.'s who had served and survived during the siege of Malta. Our Matron at Copthorne was one such and it had left her with a very strange manner and a disconcerting habit of guffawing for no particular reason.

I applied for a course as Army Theatre Sister, which attracted extra pay and lasted for three months. My brother Tom's letters were continuing to arrive at home from the M.E. where he was serving:

29th August 1943.
F/O A.G. Deck,
227 Squadron, RAF., MEF.

Darling family,

Very many thanks for the airgraphs, which arrived this evening. The first batch for quite a time, not due to the lack of writing on your part, but due to affairs at this end. It's grand to hear you are all safely installed and thoroughly enjoying the new house. I had a letter from E. all about her experiences on going to join the army! Typically E! I'm sorry to hear about poor old C., hope he has quite recovered by now. By the way, the day you went for a tea picnic at Shute House and saw someone shooting, well it may interest you to know that I fly them with bombs attached!! So now you know! I don't know if the above is vital information but I don't think so. I was due for 14 days' leave on the 23rd of this month but due to this and that I only got 4 days' leave starting on the 24th and ending yesterday. Boy, oh boy, what a leave! It was spent with three other air force types at a sort of holiday resort in some mountains about 5,000 ft. up. We would get up at about 10 a.m. and walk up to another hotel, where we would have the odd noggin and talk to the various girls, the first place I've been to out here where girls outnumbered men by at least 10 to 1! In the evening dancing to at least 12 to finish off. We had some good parties! Anyhow we are now back, having had a bloody good holiday, if not much rest, and all of us very broke! I wish we could write a little more on paper, 'cos then I could go on writing till the cows come home, but it will wait until I come home.

Much love, Tom.

26th October 1943.
F/Lt!!! A.G. Deck,
please note! ME! Same add.

Darling folks,

You will please note the above and promptly dash to the nearest pub and put back a few quick ones! Well, this is the weekly Tom commentary written this week by that incredible Flight Lieutenant, Tom Deck! All's well on this front and have been charging around in a most alarming manner doing bags of work. I don't know with what I'm going to fill these wide open spaces below, 'cos we have now been stopped discussing the weather, on which subject I could write bags of nonsense, and also we are banned from discussing fruit. The reasons for the ban are that them that know are afraid you might realise we happened to be stationed outside England! I was amazed to hear that Uncle Ceddie had managed to get out of the army. Also Graham seems to be doing pretty well for himself. Did my airgraphs to the Irvine Crolls ever turn up? I sent them via you but haven't heard whether they turned up or not. The other night we had a bit of a party and, as at the end of most parties we usually return with some trophy, on this particular occasion we returned with a something great dog. It's about the size of a great dane and has attached itself to Bill Ridley, my observer, and the smallest member of the squadron, and they make a comic pair between them!

Much love Tom.

17th November 1943.
F/Lt. A.G. Deck,
227 Squadron RAF., MEF.

Darling folks,

Do you still remember it, as I'm afraid it's such an age since I last wrote. I am very fit, although I was a bit crock with a poisoned elbow, the right one, it seems to be ok now and I am back on flying. We are still doing quite a lot of work and I am thoroughly enjoying myself. Right now I am feeling a little sleepy as I was up at sparrows' whatsit this morning. Thanks a lot for your letter received the other day, do hope you manage to get Tom's house. I am extremely honoured, and you might thank Alex! Apparently the reason some of my letters have had bits and pieces cut out of them is that we have rather a clot of an Army Captain who has nothing better to do than go through our letters with a toothcomb! Hope he doesn't get hold of this, otherwise you'll never receive it! I haven't had any rugger yet, but the weather that broke seems to have mended and the ground is again becoming like concrete. We have had quite a bit of soccer and the officers' team beat all known records yesterday by winning their first match ever by the astounding score of 3–0. I had quite a few lovely Christmas cards but they all seem to have gone for a walk, and so you will not in all probability receive one, unless I come by some, by mistake on purpose! There is another O.M. on this 'drome, a type who was at school with me and who is a decent type. I'm trying to get some gen out of the various types all round me and they say that as there's not much room left, just say there's no more noos! So God bless.

Much love, Tom.

At the end of the year I was posted to a field service unit, No. 102 British General Hospital, mobilising at Ormskirk, Lancs. But before joining I got a Christmas leave and went home to Fairways. My mother and her friends had been welcoming airmen into their homes from the new huge U.S. Air Force base at Parham near Framlingham. At a party given by the Forrestier-Walkers, I met Bill Pennebaker a pilot with 390 Group flying the huge B17 bombers. My mother had invited a group of the airmen over Christmas time and Bill was again amongst the number. He subsequently called on us and I saw quite a bit of him during that leave. We kept in touch when I went off to join No. 102 B.G.H. at Ormskirk. There we took over a small civil hospital and being a 1200 bed unit, we were considerably overstaffed for the ward work, with a strength of 80 sisters.

My field experience was limited to a detachment in May 1944, when another Sister and I were sent to Bury, Lancs, for a 'War Weapons Week' to man a demonstration field hospital tented ward in the Market Place, which was one of the exhibits. The others being an obsolete artillery piece and an armoured vehicle. All three services held 'weeks' as a publicity stunt and a boost to public morale. Neither of us had the remotest idea of field nursing, but we did our best to answer questions and seem knowledgeable. However, we very soon found out that to the public we were 'Red Cross' and they insisted on giving us money – they seemed to think that was why we were there. After trying to give it back and explain who we really were, we soon gave up and put out a large washing bowl, which to our surprise was almost filled every evening. By the end of the second day we were quite embarrassed by our riches and on Wednesday morning we went to the bank and gave it to the manager with the request to hand it on to the Red Cross.

Tom wrote in the New Year:

27th Jan. and 4th Feb. 1944.
F/Lt. A.G. Deck,
RAF Station, Heliopolis, M.E.

Darling Family,

Well, as you will note by my address, I am back at the old place, and am again test piloting. This is my rest! I left the old squadron on the 20th after a very nice farewell party. We have nine pilots in this flight and they are all jolly good types and we all have a lovely time! This is particularly to wish Mummy very many happy returns of the day and have a quick one on my debt! I hope I have timed this correctly and that it turns up on the right day. I am feeling particularly sore both in body and mind this bright morning as yesterday I played my first game of rugger and had all the skin rubbed off my knees and elbows! It was a very good game against the South Africans, but we had the misfortune to lose 10–0, due mainly to the fact that they brought their own referee and two touch judges! Sore in mind 'cos having got back here at about 5.15 p.m., I was informed that I had to move out of my room to let some S/Ldr have it and that I was to move everything lock, stock and barrel and go and live under canvas once more! These base-bashers (types who have never seen the desert) get under my skin! Anyhow, enough griping. There was a sportsman's dinner the other night which developed into a very good party. Well, bye bye and have a good birthday. God bless.

Much love, Tom.

11th March 1944.
F/Lt. A.G. Deck,
RAF Heliopolis M.E.

Darling Parents,

First let me offer my humblest apologies for the umpteenth time for failing to write for so long, but then it's really you to blame for bringing me up wrongly!! At present I, along with about 40 other types, are on a 14 days' injection treatment for rabies, followed by 14 days' recuperation leave! One of the officers in the mess had a lovely Alsatian and it went nuts, and as most of the members of the mess used to play around with it, we were all being dealt with in like manner. I was invited out to dinner and dance with some people I had never met before about 10 days ago and we had a marvellous party with champagne etc. all on 'mine host', and have since been out with them twice on equally good 'dos'. They are a very wealthy drug and chemist dealer family and also very charming. I will let you have bulletins on my injections as time goes by.

Much love, Tom.

21st April 1944.
F/Lt. A.G. Deck,
166 M.U. RAF., M.E.

Darling Folks,

I have left Helio and am now at 166 M.U. as test pilot, so in future address me as above. I am very pleased to have moved as Helio was getting me down and my present location is very pleasant, made pleasanter by a very nice C.O. and officers also a lot of old squadron friends. I have been doing quite a lot of work but it all comes in rushes. Just now I am off flying for a couple of days as I have just had a sort of a cyst removed from the top eyelid of my right eye. I had it removed yesterday and tomorrow I will have the bandage removed and start flying again. Had a letter from E. the other day and she sounded considerably more contented which is a very good thing. We had a mongska (new word) party last night which ended up some time this morning. My application to join BOAC did not go through as my C.O. said he couldn't spare me!! Laughable. But still I am rather glad now as somehow I don't think I'm suited to becoming a civilian just yet.

Much love, Tom.

Queen Alexandra's Imperial Military Nursing Service

27th May 1944.
108160 F/Lt. A.G. Deck,
603 Squadron RAF., MEF.

Darling Tootsie Wootsies,

Please note that my address has changed for the seventh time since arriving in this romantic East. As you note, I am going back on ops which is a very good thing, as at the end of this tour, should take about 6 months, I will most certainly get back to beloved parents and Blighty! I am going to the squadron with my fellow test pilot from here. We have been following one another around now for quite a time, firstly meeting on 227, leaving 227 the same day joining Helio (168 M.U.), together then on to 166 M.U. together and now onto 603 Squadron together. Sort of Heavenly twins, well maybe not so much of the heavenly business. We have started a sweepstake for the date of the invasion. I plugged for 14th June and if Monty pulls his finger out and starts on that day I will pocket about £10 which will definitely be a good thing. The last few days I have been rushing around the countryside, being, or anyway trying to be, a super sleuth and investigate some thefts! Detective Deck? I don't know if I told you but some time in the near future a certain F/Lt. (Ed(ward) Powers may look you up. He was on 227 with me and is a very rough diamond – Canadian, but a jolly good type. I have had my photo taken and will send it on to you as soon as I get the prints. To-night we are having our farewell party so have a drink and think of me, as tomorrow I will be very dead!!

Much love, Tom.

Now follows my small part in the enormous enterprise of the Invasion.

In due course an order came out for us to change our traditional grey and red uniform for khaki and to be drilled by the Staff Sergeant. We unpicked our issue battledress to reshape it. This tailoring took time, and we had to cobble it together for each day's parade. The sergeant's desperate 'Swing your arms, Sister', got little response, since we knew that our garments would fall apart if we did!

U.S. Army units abounded around Liverpool and we were soon receiving invitations to their messes. They took us to shows in Liverpool as well as in their camps and supplied us with all sorts of good things we had forgotten about in wartime Britain.

On 7th July No. 4 Polish General Hospital moved in to relieve us and we were warned for stand-by on 11th July. On the 14th our valises were collected. Into these bedding rolls were packed our camp bed and chair, a canvas wash bowl, stand and bucket, and our 'Beatrix' stove as well as spare dabs and dressings we had made up and an extra change of clothes. On the 15th we paraded like pack mules with our kit-bags, fell in behind the men and were marched to the station. We clambered on to the train for our first mystery tour. Tea was served to us by the faithful and devoted WVS on Crewe station. Names of stations had been removed and we played a guessing game as to where we were. We got very excited when we recognised London, and the train rattled over succeeding junctions to emerge again in the countryside. At 4.30 p.m. we arrived at Angmering-on-Sea and the RASC transported us to our billets. These were luxurious seaside houses in Goring-on-Sea, which had been requisitioned and emptied of all contents. We were given tea and then a scramble for rooms began. Mary, Phil and I got a room for three in a pseudo-Spanish villa with rose tinted mirrors on the walls, the only reminder of more leisurely, luxurious days. We were put to peeling potatoes and podding peas for the mess and when our valises arrived, we put up our camp beds and went to sleep. The next day we took stock of our surroundings, for we had no work to do. We found the WVS canteen and several of the kind volunteers invited us into their homes, where we enjoyed the luxury of hot baths, the use of an iron, and endless cups of tea in elegant sitting rooms. In return we helped in house or garden. In the evenings the M.O.s took us to the 'Three Crowns'.

18th June 1944.
108160 F/Lt. A.G. Deck,
603 Squadron M.E.F.

Darling parents.

I'm sorry about this pen but I think it's ready for the salvage dump. It's great news about the second front. I only wish I was in it, the types must be having bags of joy. Since last writing I have been away from here twice, once to re-visit my old unit 166 M.U. The other time to a ginormous party in Alexandria. On both occasions I accompanied our C.O., Wing Commander Ronnie Lewis, and on both occasions a good time was had by all, especially at the big dance in Alex. We spent one night in Alex and returned the following evening having had a very amusing lunch with our partners of the evening before, two very lovely Irish sisters (not nurses). Ronnie Lewis left the squadron yesterday after a very good farewell party given him by the airmen. It was a great pity but we have a very nice W/Cmdr to replace him one Wing Commander Revill. I have been doing quite a lot of swimming recently. The bathing is excellent but the track to get there is b ... awful. Another form of exercise in which I have been partaking is foxhunting. The Squadron Doctor found a fox lair and so we whistle out after them most evenings, so far without luck although we put the wind up one night before last with some very close misses. It's a bit hard hitting a running fox with a rifle. Anyhow better luck next time.

Much love, Tom.

On the 19th July we were granted 24-hour passes. I caught the 10.30 from Angmering and reached Aldeburgh at 4.45 p.m. I had to catch the midnight train from Ipswich, so I rang Bill, my friend at the American Airbase at Parham, to ask him to transport me. He turned up on a borrowed tandem pushbike, and we biked the 15 miles to Wickham Market. These were the days of the flying bombs, the Vls, variously known as doodlebugs or buzz-bombs. They came at night over the Alde targeted on London. Many cut out before reaching their target and one had come down in the marshes a few nights earlier, shaking my parents' house. As we approached London, we could see the doodlebugs coming in, but because of the noise of the train, could not hear the cut-out. We gazed at them through the windows in fascinated horror. On arrival at Liverpool Street Station service people were grouping together for the journey across London to their next terminal. I joined up with a young RASC man who was also going to London Bridge Station. All the taxis had gone, the underground access was closed and we had to walk. It turned into a dash from one doorway to another as each buzz-bomb engine cut out over its target. Crossing the bridge was the worst of all. We gazed skywards from our last refuge and when we thought the sky was clear, we made a dash for it. Exhausted, I fell asleep on the train and the guard woke me up at Brighton. I was back in camp in time for breakfast. For the next three days Mary and I packed picnic lunches and went hitch-hiking around. We managed to visit my uncle in Southampton. They were having a worrying and difficult life with Southampton coming under air attack. Most nights were spent in a nasty little dug-out in the garden. On the 24th July Matron put us in the Mess on duty, and at 10 a.m. that day we got our marching orders.

We changed our money into francs and our valises were collected at

8 p.m. We slept the night on the bare floor as best we could. The next morning Reveille was at 5 a.m. and transport collected us at 7.45 a.m. and left us at the station. We spent two hours sitting on the sidings and Matron sent for the WVS van to console us with tea and buns. Eventually the train arrived and took us to Eastleigh. Transports were awaiting us there and we drove deeper and deeper into the woods until we arrived at an American transit camp.

They looked after us very well and the camp was superbly well-run. Our tents in the wood around a clearing were quite magical in the warm summer evening with the dim lights and the hum of voices. All sorts of American luxuries were available, especially in the canteen, and a film show was provided each evening. The show was in a marquee furnished with rows of poles with sacks tied on, upon which we perched. The next evening Mary went out with a boy friend who had looked her up, and left her identity card in his jeep. Matron did a round and found her absent. When she crept in under the tent flap shortly afterwards, we had to tell her the bad news.

On 28th July Reveille was at 5 a.m. and we climbed into our transports at 8 a.m. Mary was very worried about her identity card, a gross breach of security, but it was surreptitiously handed to her by one of the guards on the way out! Driving into Southampton docks, I heard a docker cry, 'Hello Joan' and there caught a glimpse of my cousin Joan looking very glamorous in the WREN uniform, white shirt, black breeches and boots on a big motor bike. She was one of the 'Don Rs' (despatch riders) and everyone in Southampton docks knew her. We finally arrived on the quayside, where we waited again before embarking on a hospital ship. It turned out to be very comfortable. We carried some senior officers as well as the Principal Matron. We had excellent meals, the weather was fine and the sea calm. We had been issued with sea sickness pills which, although never having been seasick, for some inexplicable reason I swallowed. I became so drowsy that I lay on my bunk fully clad and did not awake until 8 a.m. next morning. At 5 p.m. we sighted France and anchored off Courselles at 7 p.m. The quantity and variety of shipping was a memorable sight. Anything that floated seemed to have been pressed into use and was awaiting its turn to get alongside to unload, and then load up with returning men, sick or wounded. We spent the night on board, the ship seeming to bounce out of the water as the occasional enemy aircraft strafed the shipping concentration.

On July 29th we spent the morning on board the hospital ship, whiling away the time playing bridge with the cards I carried in my pocket. After lunch an LCT (landing craft tank) took us off, the sailors encouraging us with 'Jump, Sister, jump!' We sat on the floor as the craft chugged into the Mulberry Harbour at Arromanches and waited alongside until they dropped the rope ladder for us to clamber ashore. It was an exhilarating moment – France in wartime – D+53. The fighting troops were no longer to be seen; they were fighting their way from Caen to Falaise.

Once again we climbed into waiting transports and bumped and rattled our way down the dusty roads. In a very short time we were inches thick in dust. It clung to our eyebrows and our hair. Everywhere buildings were reduced to rubble and very few local people were to be seen. The troops hailed us with great enthusiasm. Every field and orchard was stacked full of stores, fuel dumps, vehicles or a tented camp or hospital. Men, stores, ammunition and equipment were arriving by the hour.

At last, after driving round and round what seemed like the same church, we arrived in a field full of marquees at 8.30 p.m. These were the wards of a newly arrived hospital, and the unit was not particularly welcoming when they discovered that we were to occupy them until our hospital equipment turned up. We lined up with our mess tins by an open field kitchen and had a stew supper served from a simmering cauldron. We sat on the grass in the late evening sunshine to eat it. We washed up in another cauldron of an indescribably greasy mess. I licked my precious christening spoon and fork clean. We all had our own particular little luxury which we carried with us, and these were mine. We went to bed on the hospital beds and the night was noisy. Thirty of us slept in that marquee with our tin hats over our faces. The men of our unit arrived during the night. They had had a bad journey and there was still no sign of our equipment. We lay around in the sunshine for the rest of the day writing letters home and listening to the men knocking up the latrines and the incessant buzz, and sometimes boom, of aircraft overhead.

The war situation when we arrived was as follows. Caen, 15 miles to the east of us, had finally been captured in late July after a costly and bloody tank battle. The Americans to the south-west of us had captured St. Lo in mid-July. Since D-Day 21st Army Group, commanded by General Montgomery, consisting of US 1st Army under General Bradley and British 2nd Army under General Dempsey, had lost 80,000 men, killed, wounded or taken prisoner. Each day an average of 16,000 men, 4,500 vehicles and 94,000 tons of stores moved through the Mulberry Harbour at Arromanches up to the end of August 1944. The German Divisions pitted against these Armies had been drastically reduced by casualties. Army Group B had lost 100,000 men. Panzer Lehr Division was reduced to 40 tanks and 2,200 men.

None of this did we know at the time, although rumours abounded and we were soon to see the dreadful aftermath of casualties. When we arrived, Operation Cobra was in progress. This was an encircling movement involving the US 3rd Army under General Patton and US VII Corps under General Collins, which included 2nd and 3rd Armoured Division and US 1st Inf. Division (The Big Red One), which had fought all the way from Omaha beach. Also under command was 2nd French Armoured Division under General Leclerc. They were all advancing westwards towards Argentan, pushing the main body of German defenders eastwards. To the south-east of us, and attacking the German Divisions under Generals Eberbach, Hausser and Dietrich commanded by Field Marshal Kluge, was the Canadian 1st Army under Lt. General Crerar, consisting of Canadian II Corps, British 1st Corps and Polish 1st Armoured Division, who were battling their way from Caen towards Falaise. Due south of us in Operation Bluecoat, General O'Connor's VIII Corps with XXX Corps under Lt. General Horrocks were fighting on the American flank. The fight to encircle and trap the Germans went on into the middle of August. Locked in mortal combat were the 116th, 1st SS, 9th, 10th SS and 21st Panzer Divisions, as well as the Hitler Youth Division.

Little did I know at the time of the tragic and romantic story of the Poles in the Second World War, so well described by John Keegan in *Six Armies in Normandy*. The final act of closing the Falaise pocket was left to the 1st Polish Armoured Division and the Canadian 4th Armoured Division, who all fought with outstanding gallantry. It was from these fighting units that our patients would come.

I wrote to my mother:

Queen Alexandra's Imperial Military Nursing Service

P/279445 Sister E. Deck,
102 British General Hospital, B.L.A.
July 30th 1944.

Darlingest Moma,

I think I have written to you almost every day, but by now I have completely lost all sense of time. We have been moving so much. B.L.A. stands for British Liberation Army, so you know just where I am. We had a hectic few days before we left the camp from which I visited home. Did I tell you that they took our valises off in the evening and as we didn't go until the next day, we were left high and dry with nothing to sleep on! So Mary, Phil and I spread out our gas capes and with our respirators as pillows we lay down to sleep in a huddle. We covered up with our macs, and strangely enough slept. We went that evening to the Pitt Alberts and had a really luscious bath after our hectic packings, for we were only given two hours' notice. They offered us the most wonderful bed for the night, but we felt it wouldn't be fair to the others to take advantage of the offer. It would also have been a breach of security. But it made our hearts bleed when we thought of the lovely bed and no one in it!

Next morning we pushed off to our next camp. The tents were under the trees and around a clearing. It was just too romantic at night. The Yanks had it well organised and we were treated like princesses. We also got away with a lot of dainties to help us along. We had a party one evening with some of the officers with rather disastrous results. When coming back in the dark, Phil got lost in the wood. She fell down a slit trench and became completely disorientated. Finally she walked into the Matron's tent in mistake for ours and woke the Matron up. You can imagine the schemozzle!

We had a marvellous crossing, calm and sunny – perfectly delightful. It's all so interesting and there's lots I'd love to tell you. If you see Bill again, tell him how comforting their presence is in the sky. We had a terrific welcome as we bumped over the fearful roads and were very soon under a layer of dust. Now we are in a field living in marquees. We fetch our water from two fields away in a scrounged biscuit tin and pump it ourselves. Our Girl Guiding days come in very handy and we make stick fires to heat some water and wash our socks, pants and battle bloomers. Right now I'm lying stretched out on the grass writing and the sun is beautiful. In the dim distance, the roar of artillery and near to the constant hum of traffic. Apart from that a real camping holiday. To-day we lunched sitting on the grass, little groups of us and officers laughing and chatting and the cookhouse lads doing their damnedest with the tin-openers.

God bless, darlings, and don't worry about me.
Tons of love, Elizabeth.

On the 31st July we got a lift to Bayeux in the afternoon. Most of the town seemed undamaged and was crowded with troops. There were very few local people about, but one small window in what had been the main shopping area displayed one lovely red hat. Bayeux was a great meeting place and around the town were pitched all the hospitals. The next day Phil, Hodson and I were sent to help in the theatre of No. 9 BGH. This was a Territorial Unit of 600 beds which had been mobilised at the beginning of the War. They had seen service in France in 1939/40, the Desert, Italy and now in France again. They recorded their location as 'In the Field'. The sisters were all in their 30s and 40s and most had been with the hospital since the War began. We could not have wished to get our first experience of field nursing under more splendid women. They were calm, immaculately dressed in grey cotton frocks and white gauze head squares. They had ignored the order to dress in khaki, and the hospital ran like clockwork. We felt ashamed of ourselves in our unbecoming khaki battledresses, boots and beret. The Matron received us with the greatest kindness and tolerance and we were shown to our empty tent in the Sisters' lines. When we explained that our valises had not yet arrived, we were provided with a stretcher to sleep on and drew 3 blankets each.

They worked 8-hour shifts in the theatre. I was on 8–16 hours, Hodson 16–24 hours, and Phil 24–8 hours. This gave Phil and me an hour or two off together in the evening when we used to return to 102 field to fetch our mail and clean change of clothes, which Mary organised for us. I inadvertently left a pair of black 'battle bloomers' which Mary had lent me in the jeep which gave us a lift. They were later seen flying from the aerial! For the next ten days I worked my 8-hour shift in the theatre. Ambulance convoys were coming in from the fighting towards Falaise. When one hospital filled up, the convoys were diverted to the next one. Mercifully we were too busy concentrating on our work to feel the shock of the tragedies under our eyes.

2nd August 1944.

Darlingest Moma,

We are still without a scrap of luggage, so hence this paper. We limited our hand luggage to the absolute minimum when we left one of our camps in England, after our bitter experience when we left Ormskirk and had to carry everything. Now of course we have nothing between us. I've been wearing the clothes I stand up in now for 8 days and they stink, especially after the last 24 hours when I've been on duty and sweating away like mad. Please send any tinned fruit or biscuits or home-made cakes (if well packed). We get a bit fed up with 'compo' rations, though considering everything, we are well fed. Yesterday Phil, I and another girl were loaned to another unit to help them with their work as we haven't been able to start functioning yet. We've been hard at it ever since in the theatre. You wouldn't believe what it is like. I shall be a violent pacifist after this. We work in shifts of eight hours, which gives us time to regain our wits, replace dabs and dressings, and to get a rest. We were very sorry to leave Mary behind, but we aren't far away and Phil and I managed to walk back this evening to visit them and to get the news. I have heard no War news since I've been here, so do continue to send *The Times*, now more than ever. We also went to see if our valises had arrived, as this unit can't supply us with beds. We three are together in a tent and sleeping on stretchers on the ground. Our gas capes under us keep out most of the damp. By the time I've wrapped my smelly clothes around me to keep them from being damp in the morning, I'm quite warm. The chief snag is that we are being eaten alive, I think by ants.

Everyone is so nice around here, and you stand in the road and point where you want to go and get a lift right to the door without any hesitation. Usually some dashing gallant at the wheel! Parties galore, but late nights completely taboo. Anyway it's not exactly pleasant being out after dark. I must stop now and literally stick my head in a bucket before my hair drags me away. We've had no mail delivery for 10 days, so you can imagine how we are looking forward to it.

God bless and take care of yourselves, your loving Elizabeth.

4th August 1944.

Darlingst Moma,

Just a short note to tell you I'm still going strong. I've been frantically busy in the theatre since I've been here. My shift works through the heat of the day and it's terrific. Of course the theatres are primitive and what we can do is limited. It's just like the films you see of life in a field hospital. It's what I took up nursing for, so I'm quite happy. We were thrilled yesterday to get our first mail delivery. Many, many thanks for the lovely sweets and your two letters. Morale went up one hundred percent. Must stop now. We are going to walk over to our unit. It's a lovely walk down some lanes, and very pretty. Tons of love, darlings and

God bless, from E.

5th August 1944.

Darlingest Moma,

Great excitement when I went over to the 102 field yesterday and found two more letters from you. I am still on loan and we are still working full pressure. All the units are very close to one another here, and we frequently run into old friends and acquaintances. Even if a unit is a mile or two away, one can jump in the nearest jeep or whatever happens to be passing and get a lift right where you want to go. It's all very well until the M.P.s start cutting up rough, but a smile will usually win even their wooden hearts! Our orchard is very peaceful, with a few sheep tethered just to add to the rural environment. Fancy Jimmy Cooper being out here! As soon as we get at our clothes, I'll look him up. I don't expect he's far away. One soon gets to know the whereabouts of most people.

Please can you send me some Keatings, we are being eaten to bits. My pay chit came in, and I was anticipating at least a double figure, what with field allowance etc. but all I got was £7. They haven't given me any field allowance yet, but have deducted for all the kit they issued us! Now I'm a year in, I should get a substantial rise. There is nothing to buy here, only mess expenses. The only shop in the local town is the Officers' Shop run by the RAOC. It sells clothes all right, but you have to queue for hours and usually we can't do it in the time allowed away from camp. The only thing about it is that you meet every available officer for miles around in the queue!

God Bless, tons of love from your loving E.

On 11th August we were recalled to our unit, No. 102 BGH. It was sited at Les Retailles a few miles west of Bayeux between Barbeville and Cottun. Our equipment had turned up and was being delivered to our allotted site in 'Harley Street', as the hospital area around Bayeux had become known. We got to our borrowed marquees and with our valises were taken in trucks to the hospital's site. There we joined the men of our unit, who had already pitched the Sisters' tents in a suitably remote orchard adjacent to our very large field. Phil, Mary and I moved in and set up our camp beds and our invaluable Beatrix stoves. At last we could heat our own water, which had to be fetched from two orchards away. When the hospital started working, we put out our canvas buckets for the daily fill up by the water bowser. This was for drinking and washing ourselves and our clothes. The last off duty got the least, as everyone else had topped up their own after the cows had had a drink.

At this time the controversial battle for the 'Falaise Gap' was going on some 20–25 miles south-east of us. The Americans and the Free French were encircling south towards Argentan and the British, Canadians and Poles were struggling to reach Falaise and meet the Americans and the French between Falaise and Argentan and so encircle a large German force and cut them off. It was casualties from this battle that we were to treat.

We were alerted to receive our first convoy 48 hours later. It was difficult to get anything prepared with the equipment arriving in a very haphazard fashion, for until it was unpacked, we had no boxes or containers to use for storing dressings and equipment in ward or theatre. We were unpacking crates even before our theatre marquee was pitched. However, they were up by the end of the first day. Each ward comprised two parallel marquees containing 20 beds each, connected by a cross-piece which was the entrance-cum-office, and the wards were pitched either side of the access roadway. The cross-piece housed the desk and the two primus stoves for sterilising instruments, syringes and needles. The desk was a simple trestle. Two sisters were on day duty in each ward of 40 patients assisted by orderlies. At night one sister looked after two or more wards with one orderly in each, and this would mean upwards of 50 penicillin injections three-hourly. Some nights the sister would find herself doing nothing else all night as the administration of this new drug was considered the highest priority for the soldier's recovery. As soon as a man was strong enough to be moved, he would be evacuated to England, so there was a rapid turn-over of patients.

Our first convoy arrived on August 14th and we started operating at 5 p.m. and worked until 5 a.m. I then slept until midday and started duty again at 2 p.m. and worked through until we finished the convoy. I missed the smooth running of the 9th BGH. Matron was as inexperienced in the field as we were. After one particularly distressing operation in the theatre, I paused in a tea break outside the tent amongst the discarded uniforms and dirty dressings to smoke a cigarette. I have always been a non-smoker, but a cigarette is a great soother and has a clean feel under such circumstances. Unfortunately Matron saw me and I was moved from the theatre to a ward. The pressure was less in the wards, but the heartbreak even greater. At the end of the second day amongst the evil smelling dressings, we came off duty to find our water buckets empty. Two days later I was moved back to the theatre again, where I worked for the next seven days. In the meantime

Robson and I had managed to find a woman in an adjacent farm to do our washing for us.

On 23rd August we were receiving convoys of prisoners of war. Their condition was appalling owing to the time lag in getting any initial treatment. One Pole I remember, who understood not a word of English, but spoke German. He glared at me with hate when I spoke to him in German in the hope of getting him to understand the anaesthetist's instructions.

13th August 1944.

Darlingest Moma,

Thank you so much for your frequent and very welcome letters. I have taken heed of your timely advice. But I think my secret heart usually manages to deliver some good advice whatever my actions and surroundings! Thank Goodness.

I am now back in the fold and we are hard at it. We are literally raising the hospital from the good earth and it's a truly fearful commotion. Packing cases, inventories half here, half there, primus stoves to be kept going out of doors. It's all most amazing. The tents are being erected all around us. Our field (Sisters' quarters) adjoins a farm and we are a thoroughfare for pigs, cows, bulls etc. The cows get in and drink our precious water and the pig got in and ate Matron's gas cape! And of course we have the usual livestock in the tent. The weather is heavenly.

I think I told you that Mary and I have got to know some of the many press correspondents out here. I am well acquainted with the *News Chronicle* one. He was out here yesterday evening so we get the news good and hot with all the flourishes.

I must get back to work,
tons of love darlings,
and God bless, from E.

18th August 1944.

Darlingest Moma,

Thank you very much for two letters which fetched up to-day, and *The Times* which arrive with unfailing regularity and which are very welcome. I am absolutely dead beat. We have been hectic since we arrived on our site. When we arrived here on Friday evening, we put up our beds and dug in. The next day we were told that we had to have the hospital ready to receive 300 patients the next day at noon. At that time not even enough tents were pitched to house that number. I and some others were consigned to the theatre. The equipment arrived in batches of anything and everything and took ages to sort out. Having worked like blazes, we were actually operating within 48 hours, which I think is good when one realises the terrific task involved. I was on duty all last Monday and eventually had to work all through the night as well and got to bed at 5.30 a.m. I was on again that day at 2 p.m., still operating. Because Matron found me smoking at midnight during a break we made to have some tea, I was removed from theatre and relegated to a ward. However it proved a pleasant change in atmosphere and I enjoyed trying to ease the condition of the poor laddies. Working in the wards is quite indescribable with limited water. However with the arrival of more patients, I am now back again in the hubbub and mess of the theatre.

Another snag is that my bed is giving way and is very uncomfortable. Yesterday was simply boiling and we had worked hard all day, to find, when we came off, that the water cart had broken down and there was not a drop for us to wash in. I went to bed cursing as I have never cursed before! It's not all honey and summer holiday in this job! We have no floors and it is exhausting stumbling over the molehills and irregularities of the fields. Nothing is levelled out even in the theatre and it's fearful trying to balance trollies and anaesthetic apparatus.

I'm sorry this is such a miserable epistle, but keep my letters. They'll serve as interesting, if morbid, reminders. Our tent is full of ants. They get everywhere including into our beds. We get up in the morning with the mist still around us and everything damp. The food is bully, biscuits, beans, milk, desiccated potatoes and onions (rehabilitated) and very monotonous. There is nothing fresh. By the time you get this you will probably have heard some good news of the War. Maybe we'll all be home soon, please God.

Don't get depressed, for I'm very happy when I'm not so tired and Matron isn't nagging.

Tons of love, your awful but loving daughter, Elizabeth.

P.S. Please can you get some of your women to knit some comforts for me, i.e. two pairs khaki woollen socks (to go under my boots) urgently required, also one pair khaki wool gloves.

24th August 1944.

Darlingest Moma,

I feel thoroughly ashamed of the lapse since I last wrote, but you've no conception of the pressure we've been under these past 14 days. We've got to the state when we just work and sleep, for we're dead beat when we get off duty. The girls are so pent up that in the evenings one just sits on one's bed and cries with sheer anger and fatigue. My bed has collapsed so I have to fix that before I can get to sleep. We only hope we'll get a little respite soon.

There are some funny incidents though. On passing through a ward in which out of 50 patients 4 are able to get up and about, Matron noticed two of the up-patients asleep in bed. On enquiring of the Sister why they were not helping, the girl replied: 'Oh, they're my night shift.' The other day in the theatre we had a long list of foreign names who were mostly Germans, some enemy Poles and some friendly Poles. I gave them instructions to help things along. Half way through I was confronted with a man called Yabochski. So as usual I spoke to him in German. He looked blank, so very slowly and clearly I said: 'Do you understand English?' To which he replied: 'Say, Ma'am, I'm from Canada!'

I wouldn't have believed at what cost this War is being won. I think it has had a profound effect on all of us here. The most fearful thing is the state that the Germans come in. It's ghastly and beyond my wildest conception of horror.

Larry Solon is the *News Chronicle* correspondent I've been out to dinner with on occasions. He writes quite well, I think. The Paris news is great and I think all our beaux have made tracks in that direction. Must stop now as I want to get a wink of sleep before teatime, as I shall probably be up half the night, being on call.

Thank you very much for pullover, writing paper and insect powder, all of which arrived safely. Further wants include candles, please. The weather is awful.

Tons and tons of love, darlings, E.

25th August 1944.

Darlingest Moma,

Thank you for all your lovely letters. What a tonic the mail is when it comes in! It's getting rather late so I'm afraid this is going to be a very scrappy letter. Mary and I have had 'Amami' (shampoo) night, and feel quite pure and holy. It took us the best part of the evening organising the hot water supply. Now we are enjoying what we all consider the best part of the day. There are two hurricanes burning and one candle and in one corner my stove is going strong with a saucepan of water on and in a minute or two, two of us will start to wash. We have arranged our tent with Phil's bed along one side flanked by her trunk one end and the store box the other, and the rubbish container. Across the middle of the tent a rope is stretched on which we hang our clothes. Mary's and my beds are side by side in the middle with our heads in the 'wardrobe'. In one corner a chair and trunk and the same in the other corner.

The bugler has just blown the Last Post. We do everything to the bugle here.

Tons of love, darlings, must go to sleep, your loving E.

28th August 1944.

Darlingest Moma,

Thank you, darling, for your frequent and welcome letters. How marvellous it is when the post comes in. The pressure of work continues. We have not stopped operating day or night since we started, and the problem of maintenance of stock is tremendous. Added to this we have moved three times, lock, stock and barrel, from one tent to another whilst they concreted our floors one by one. We have always carried on and never kept patients or surgeons waiting.

I have been removed from the theatre again, and it's really a great relief to get into a ward. I have ample opportunity for interpreting, and thoroughly enjoy doing anything for the lads, they are all so brave and cheerful. One thing was really rather funny. The Colonel in charge of the surgical division, in other words the head surgeon, who is very nice, came into the theatre when I was doing some rather snappy interpreting for the anaesthetist, and asked me if I was sure my name wasn't Teck instead of Deck!

We had a gin party here last night with an officer R.A. who had crashed at the Aldringham cross roads, and some of his fellow officers. I drank French wine. Our war correspondents have moved forward and we miss them very much, they were good fun.

Good night, darling, the Last Post has just blown and I must leave this peaceful pastime and wrestle with the getting-to-bed problem.

Tons and tons of love, E.

7th September 1944.

Darlingest Moma,

Thank you again for all your welcome letters. I'm glad to hear the swallows are being so considerate and affording you ample opportunities for nature study. Since my letters seem to entertain all Aldeburgh, keep the more interesting ones. They may come in handy for my memoirs!

Now another era is over and I am on night duty. For the last week I have been working in the P.O.W. ward. It was like old times and I found my German growing more fluent each day. One of my patients was a cuckoo clock maker from near my old haunts, so we had long and lengthy reminiscences. The fact of my being in contact with these people again has brought home to me so forcibly the utter futility of this whole struggle and makes me feel quite depressed about the post-War era.

I have been out to one or two parties this last week. Somehow one never seems to meet any very inspiring people. Most in a place like this seem to forget their principles entirely, and everything seems so superficial and unreal. I suppose that's bound to be in a battle zone. I'm glad to be on night duty and away from the racket of the day, when everywhere you go, Matron dogs your footsteps and grouses about some triviality. It's been lousy weather lately and we are sinking into a nice muddy apathy. You'd laugh to see me stumbling around the wards at night with a hurricane lamp in one hand and a box of pills or a dressing tray in the other. Of course we never can see a thing, and the floor is so fearfully uneven. I wear my battledress and boots and gaiters. It's quite a problem keeping warm, especially when the rain pours in at all corners and makes great lakes on the tarpaulin floor. I have a very good orderly with me, who gets the primus going and brews up the necessary quantity of tea every now and then. We live in fear and trembling of the beastly thing exploding and setting fire to the tent. It has done this already once in here, but the men are quick on the uptake, the only snag being that they put it out with the drinking water, which meant that the ward went thirsty for 24 hours until the next delivery!

Things are changing very quickly around here, and there are now almost as many civilians to the square mile as soldiery. But I don't get any opportunity to progress with my French. I will try and get down to it whilst I'm on night duty.

Phil and Mary have moved out of my tent and it has been turned into a night nurses' abode. The girl in with me now is a priceless creature from Lancashire. She never stops talking, which is rather trying, but she is very amusing and very full of her own importance. Have just interrupted this epistle to have my midnight meal. The orderly fetches it for me in my billy cans. By the time it reaches me it is stone cold, so we cook it up again on the old oil stove. When I want to go to the lav, I have a cross country journey to make, which takes ten minutes and involves climbing through two very muddy and slippery ditches. Usually we just sit down by the hedge, but it's full moon just now, and that practise must cease forthwith until the moon is more obliging and tactful.

It's very difficult to keep my feet warm. Can you please persuade your knitters to get down to at least 2 pairs of socks. These are really urgent. Can you conceal in your next parcel a few sweets? You needn't declare them. All we get in that way is vitaminised chocolate and it's absolutely lousy stuff.

I'm looking after 100 patients at night. They are a mixed bunch, including Canadians, Britishers, Poles, Czechs and French, not to mention the inevitable P.O.W.s. So it's a real Tower of Babel. Must stop now and start on my round. It's raining and I must endeavour not to fall over guy ropes nor slip in the slush outside the door.

Tons and tons of love, darlings, and God bless, your loving E.

17th September 1944.

Darlingest Moma,

Thank you so much for your letters. I think the most peculiar correspondent I met was Austin Hatton of the *Evening News*. He was one of the first into Paris. We haven't seen any of them for ages. I expect by now they're nearly into Germany. I'm so glad to hear Rosy fetched up safely. But I take a dim view of the remarks in your last letter about me writing to her before I left about you. Somebody's got to look after you for me when I'm away. I'm glad you'll have Rosy for M.M.'s birth (William). There'll be a bit of an upheaval at Fairways, I should think. You'd better book Elise as midwife.

Life goes on here much as usual. I seem to sleep most of the time. The most uncomfortable part of life nowadays is coming off duty in the morning to a beastly damp tent and damp bed, neither having been lived in during the night. Otherwise I love it, and am getting well versed in the art of keeping warm in the early hours. I have two nights off in front of me. I'll write and tell you how I spend them.

We've quietened down considerably now, which is a blessing and most girls are managing to fit in days off. Bayeux has turned into a wonderful shopping centre. Lots of stuff, especially cosmetics, have been released from Paris, which has been a wonderful city all the way through apparently.

There's really very little to write about. My patients keep me very entertained. I told you probably that I have a Czech in the ward who speaks nine languages. He told me to get a book called *The Loom of Languages* by Frederick Bodmer. Do you think you could get it for me?

No more now, tons and tons of love, E.

By August 25th Matron got around to drawing up an off-duty roster, and Mary, Phil and I hiked into Bayeux on our first half-day off. It had changed a lot since our first visit at the end of July. Shops had opened, French gendarmes were on point duty, and most of the military traffic had moved away towards Paris and Brussels. Paris had been liberated on August 25th and Brussels on September 3rd 1944. Bayeux was now a local leave centre. One warm sunny morning Mary, Phil and I went to swim in a nearby river. Unfortunately some of the soldiers on the bank would not believe that Mary could not swim and threw her in. I tried out my life-saving knowledge, but found I was not strong enough to overcome her struggles, and although within a few feet of the bank, we both went down together. Fortunately Phil got the soldiers to pull us out in time, but it was a close-run thing.

We now had much more time to accept some of the many invitations we received.

On the 20th September 1944 I was writing again to my mother.

———————

Darlingest Moma,

Thank you so much for the lovely parcel of warms. Just what I need. The weather is very variable and some nights aren't so bad, but what it will be like later on goodness only knows.

Our orchards are giving us all claustrophobia and we long to be on the move again, but of course anything can happen at any time. I've just had two nights off.

The first evening I went with a gunner called Charles to the garrison cinema. The first film I've seen since I've been here, so that was a pleasant change. The following day Mary had a half-day so we packed up a picnic and went for a hike. We didn't get as far as we had hoped, but managed to reach Caen. We sat on a bit of raised ground overlooking the town and it was like picnicking in a vast graveyard, so desolate is the scene. This morning I tried to go shopping, but I stayed too long in bed and the shops were all closed for lunch when I arrived.

We have slackened off a lot now, so I expect I shall spend a peaceful night. We still have a dog's life from the Matron but everyone adopts an air of indifference and tries not to let everything get them down. We only pray it will all soon be over.

Lots of love, darlings, take care of yourselves, your loving, Elizabeth.

———————

22nd September 1944.

Darlingest Moma,

I was very stunned when the news of Tom arrived to-day. I only keep thanking my lucky stars that he's posted missing, for at best there's a wide margin of hope. Thank God, too, that Rosy is at home. I only wish to goodness I could be with you. Please, please darling send for me if things are too overwhelming, for that's what I'm here for. I just keep praying that some decent news will turn up soon. If he is a P.O.W. and do-as-you-would-be-done-by is anything to go by, he should have good treatment after my efforts here. Anyway, we can hope, and that's something to be thankful for. He'll have a string of adventures to add to his already hefty pile. I'm keeping back one photo of him and sending you the rest. I had such awful premonitions about him when the photos arrived here. Isn't it peculiar?

I'm enclosing a letter to Nanny Wilkinson thanking her for the gloves. Re your question, I would like the wool made into khaki socks please. I do hope Tat and Irvine have turned up, or Rosy is back or something. Do get someone to stay with you, darling.

To-day Mary and Phil had days off, so I didn't go to bed, but went out with them. We went first to St. Lo, then Lessay, Valognes, Carentan, Isigny and home. You can't imagine how fearfully the War has hit that part. St. Lo is just rubble and nothing habitable. While walking down a street, we paused and there was stony silence. It was uncanny. The rural scene is disfigured by broken trees, shattered branches, thrown up earth and craters.

When I got back, your letter was awaiting me and poor old Mary and Phil got the brunt of it. Thank goodness they were there. Did Tom tell you that he had a new observer F/O LaRoy Heide, DFC, a Canadian? Bear up, darling, and don't give up hope. Please write all about yourself, and don't think about it too much.

Take care of yourselves, your loving E.

25th September 1944.

Darlingst Moma,

You can't picture the excitement this evening in our tent when Phil marched in with your letter saying Tom was interned again. We immediately opened our Naafi spirit ration and drank to Viva everything! The whole camp seems so interested in Tom's welfare, he's quite a notorious figure. It's a marvellous relief and I shan't need to worry half so much about you either!

Thank you so much for the parcel of socks and enclosures. Very, very welcome. I'm so glad Rosy is with you for a bit. She writes to me saying John's got leave and it's the first they've had since Christmas. The Navy are the only people who get leave from this theatre, since our leave ban which was imposed in April. Everyone out here, RAF, Navy, all wear khaki. I bet Tom's in Turkey again. I wonder when you'll hear from him. I like the idea of the postmaster bringing you the wire, he'll be tapping all your messages and using a softening up process when the news is bad.

No more now, darlings, take care of yourselves, all love, Elizabeth.

Time Gone

On the 4th October 1944 Tom was writing again in his carefree manner!
4th October 1944. S/Ldr or, to give the full title, **Squadron Leader A.G. Deck, 603 Squadron, RAF., MEF**.

Darling parents.

I am sorry I had to be posted missing but when one sort of disappears, the Air Ministry has to do the informing act. Anyway I hope they told you as soon as they knew I was O.K. I arrived back here yesterday after three rather hectic nights in Cairo followed by an even more hectic night here! As you doubtless know, I ended up in that frightful country Turkey once more! We had rather a boring time but were quite comfortable. As you see by the address, I am now a S/Ldr. Amazing isn't it? By the way I hope that £100 was put to your credit as I have had no reply to my letter from my bank, so let me know if you have got it or not. I am very fit and roaring to go.

No more news at present. Much love, Tom.

9th November 1944.
S/Ldr. A.G. Deck, RAF., MEF.

Darling Mop and Pop,

Many thanks for the letters. I don't remember when I last wrote, but I hope it wasn't too long ago? Life goes on in these sandy wastes in much the usual manner. We are doing practically no work so spend our time training and playing games. Swimming is out now, as it's too cold, but we are playing soccer and soft ball. We had a very good rain storm the other day and night and had a game of football the next day. It was a very good mud match and we won by 7 mud pies to 2 mud pies! Our sheep is going great guns and should be ready nice and fat by Christmas! You will most probably remember MacClure, a friend of mine who bought it in Malta, well I think I told you his wife Jane got married again and now has a small son. Well anyway I had a letter from her the other day and she is bored stiff. She lives in some little village in Sussex. I'm sorry to hear that those something flying bombs are troubling you. I only hope none start dropping around Aldeburgh. I'm sorry this is such a dull effort of a letter but there's an even greater shortage of noos than ever before.

Much love, Tom.

After Tom's description of his latest adventure, I was writing home again.

27th September 1944.

Darlingest Moma,

My letters seem to take an awful long time to reach you. Yours come here in about 4 days on average.

To-morrow I have got a night off again to coincide with Mary's day off. So we will probably hit the trail, which is quite out of order of course. In the evening we are going to dinner at an American officers' mess, so we are all looking forward to a good feed. The food here isn't bad, but terribly monotonous. I simply can't look a dehydrated potato in the face now. We never get any fresh vegetables, all either dehydrated or canned. I've written to Elise to get me some multivite, for when the apples have ceased to fall on our tents, we won't get any vitamins at all. I left my tin hat too close to the tent flap and it filled with rain water on top of my collection of apples. During a noisy night I automatically reached out for it to put over my face and got a drenching and a bombardment of apples! We never see butter, and jam and marmalade are in short supply. Milk is all canned. We get bacon, beefsteak pudding all out of a tins as well as tinned spotted dog and 'duff'. The bread is foul and all white. Occasionally we get some real meat, which is probably frozen. We can never get a meal out in restaurants, though I think Paris and a few places west will provide such luxuries. The people here seem to be far from starving and I believe from what I hear that there is plenty of food in Paris and all the towns.

I hope to get into Bayeux and send R. a cosmetic parcel for her birthday. There are the most lovely cosmetics available and cheaper than in England. What amazes me about the goods in the shops here is the good taste in the design. Although the material of which a thing is made may be very inferior, the way it is made is always tasteful and therefore doesn't look so shoddy as the corresponding type of thing in England now. Some of the materials and clothes are really lovely, but not available to us of course. The hats are wonderful, the most fantastic designs and so truly French. Nearly all the women and girls one sees are wearing some really smashing hat to make up for what they lack in the rest of their wardrobes now. I can well understand a Yankee who said to me in Liverpool, what a real treat it would be to see a smartly dressed woman again! I must say the girls here knock spots off our girls for dress. The men and boys, of course, wear the familiar knickerbocker and black beret rigout.

The other day an American nurse came over to see us, whom we knew in Liverpool. We had an amusing time comparing notes. We went together to watch a baseball game, which their hospital was playing against one of the Canadian hospitals near us. It was fun and we met more U.S. nurses and some of the Canadian girls.

Must wind up now, I'm afraid I'm doing a very lazy night duty. All my patients are convalescent and sleep like tops. I get wrapped up in my G.I. greatcoat and my fur rug and with my legs and feet in the 'oven' (under the table), I manage to sleep pretty soundly too. Always from 2.30 a.m. after the Night Sister's round, until about 6 a.m. when I slowly come to in time to wake the men! That's one thing about the Army – hard work never lasts for long. Though I don't doubt it will start again soon for us.

Good-night, darlings, and take care of yourselves,
tons and tons of love, E.

P.S. R. might have recognised a doodlebug when she saw it! I take a dim view of that. Some people don't know there's a Waaaaar on!

On 29th September we started closing down some of the wards. A fortnight later we packed it all up. In the meantime, at the beginning of October, I was still on night duty, now looking after five wards. I was particularly angry one night to come on duty to find several 'S.I.'s and 'D.I.'s (seriously ill and dangerously ill) patients scattered between the 5 wards and only 3 orderlies. I had as well two men with typhoid who required an orderly to themselves as part of the isolation precautions. The man who was eventually sent was quite incapable of any nursing procedures and I complained bitterly and loudly to the duty M.O. and was in full cry as the Colonel happened to do a round. 'I was fascinated' was his only comment when I later apologised for my outburst. I got my orderlies and the offending Davies was taken off nursing duties altogether. That night two p. o. w. officers escaped from the officers' ward, where poor Hodson was in charge. She took the rap but no one bothered much.

11th October 1944, Wednesday.

Darlingest Moma,

You must be thinking I'm dead and gone by now, as it's such ages since I last wrote. I wrote to Alex the fateful letter about the Matron about a week or two ago, when things were pretty desperate here, never dreaming that she would pass it on to another QAIMNS, even if it were her sister. I was quite shattered when I heard she had sent it on. As things are panning out, I don't think we can possibly be keeping Matron for long, as she has been getting into hot water with all the M.O.s and the C.O. But it's wicked for us, for we get the brunt of all her temper when she has had a row with the Colonel.

I'm on day duty again now and I've been out to dinner or dances every evening since I came off night duty on Saturday, hence no letters. I expect you'll hear from Tom, for it takes a while for letters to fetch up. I hope they send him home. His operational time must soon be up again, as he started in February, didn't he? I wish this b ... War was over. I hope to goodness the F2s don't land on top of you.

The Naafi have built a marvellous club out here for us, it is quite near and we can get in to enjoy tea by a fire and get some Naafi cakes! We also have dances there on a real wooden floor instead of waltzing over concrete or tarpaulin.

I can't send you any coupons for the wool as all our coupons were taken in before we left and needless to say, I had none.

I'm on duty nursing two typhoid patients who are terribly ill. They are asleep just now, so I'm taking the opportunity of the lull. It's pouring with rain and the wind is blowing, and every now and again an accumulation of water on the tent roof empties itself through the nearest inlet onto the tarpaulin floor and rivers are coming in from everywhere. The mud is becoming famous. I now wear real soldiers' boots, black issued ones. At least they keep the rain and the damp out.

Tons of love, darlings, your ever loving Elizabeth

15th October 1944.

Darlingest Moma,

Many thanks for two lovely parcels and several lovely letters. The parcels arrived safely, though the book looked as though it had had a ducking. However it's quite legible and it's lovely to have it. Many, many thanks. I hope it wasn't too expensive. The other parcel arrived safely and didn't appear to have suffered the same fate as the book. The hidden treasure is very much appreciated by the gang. The candles are lighting the darkness now and having a whale of a time going out in turn as there is a fearful gale blowing and the tent will take off any minute now. It's been pouring with rain and we are now an inch deep in mud everywhere except just inside our tents, and several inches deeper in some places, such as the mess entrance and the gateways. Luckily the officers' shop had a supply of gum boots in so we have all invested in a pair. You'd laugh to see my latest pair of slippers, clogs with basket tops and lined with bunny rabbit. Just the job to keep my feet warm and well away from the damp.

Mary and I had a wonderful shopping day in Bayeux and bought up masses of cosmetics. We ran into the man who accompanied me from Liverpool Street station to London Bridge station the night of my 24-hour leave, when we dodged the doodles. He recognised me. We had a wonderful party that night, three M.O.s and Mary and Phil and I went to the Lion d'Or to have dinner. We had to supply the food. Phil had had five chickens given her by an American, which was the origin of the whole show as we didn't know how to get rid of them! We produced some army rations, i.e. tinned salmon and sausage meat, sugar and coffee. What those cooks did to it all we just don't know, but it was the most marvellous dinner I have eaten for ages. We had champagne, red wine and calvados as well. Afterwards we waltzed over a tarpaulin floor at a dance given by one of our fellow hospitals.

The Naafi has just opened the 'Q.A. Club', the most popular resort in Normandy. We danced there last night and it was great fun. What's so nice is that one invariably meets people there whom one has been longing to visit and never managed. I met two girls I trained with there last night.

Must stop now and write to Tom. Don't send any more parcels for a while until I let you know again, but carry on with letters and papers.

Good-night, darlings, and take great care of yourselves, tons of love. E.

On 11th October 1944 we were told we were being pulled back to England, that we would have leave and then move to Antwerp when they were ready for us. On the 13th October we evacuated all our patients. I got my two typhoid patients ready and promised to write to their parents if I got back to the U.K. first. The next day we cleaned and sterilised, packed and handed in all the equipment and the men started taking down the tents. Everything literally collapsed around us. We stayed in our mess lines for another 12 days. One night I slept through all the excitement when two of our sergeants pulled down Matron's tent in the middle of the night. We all felt she had had it coming to her for some time!

We gave a big farewell party in our farmer's barn, decorated with old man's beard and autumn berries. We had all sorts of food in tins, some from our American friends. We got 12 eggs and borrowed the farmhouse saucepan. We had a wonderful fire in a room up above the barn, the only lighting being the fire and a hurricane lamp. About 14 of us cooked eggs, spam, sausages and bread over the enormous log fire. The floor was tiled and it swayed ominously, but it held while we sang and danced the night away.

We were on six hours' notice to move and on 25th October, with terrible hangovers, we packed up in the dark and the pouring rain and, with our valises, were collected and transported to a château near the sea. Once again we lived with mirrors on the walls.

29th October 1944.

Darlingest Moma,

Many thanks for two letters and two bundles of papers, very welcome, which arrived to-day. Our mail has been held up a bit, but not for long. Fancy Charles Deck being married! Who to – the girl who followed him home from the Argentine? And how did Aunt Vi get home? Had a long letter from Rosy, who seems to be a lady of leisure these days.

Well, we are now out of our last mud patch and into another. They got us out of bed at 6 a.m. in the dark to pack our valises and be ready to move off at 9 a.m. It was raining and you can imagine what it's like packing up bedding, taking down chairs, camp beds and packing them surrounded by mud and the shouting Matron. All this palaver to move us about two miles down the road into a château. After standing about in the muddy smelly farmyard, watching our valises getting muddier and muddier, we eventually piled into several three-ton trucks and skidded and swore and arrived at about 11 a.m. We then rapidly distributed ourselves into the available rooms, pulled our valises to pieces again, plus mud, put up our beds and got into them again. There was no lunch for us, so we went to sleep until 6 p.m., when the miserable cookhouse staff managed to cough up the inevitable bully beef and bread and tea! Then out to a party in the evening.

The evening before we had had a smashing barn party, which really was a lark. The place we are now in is, or was, a smashing place. Rather smaller than most and, like all the châteaux around here, almost a replica of Alexanderhof. They have some lovely stables and breed race horses. Madame lives here in the house and organises the breeding and Monsieur trains them somewhere near Paris. I love the stables and do my best in appalling French. Six of us, Mary, Phil and I and Elsa Watts and two other very nice girls live downstairs in what was presumably the salon. It has two lovely wall mirrors facing each other. The mural decorations being very dainty panels with pictures painted on to the walls of Victorian ladies and gents sitting under trees with Versailles in the background. There are also two lovely built-in cupboards with shelves and a fireplace which burns merrily without smoking and keeps us busy all day (when we're not out) fetching in kuni (firewood). We have a debi with water always on the hob, very efficient hot water system. The drainage is non-existent and the slops, I very much regret to say, go out through the window. (You don't know what dreadful habits you'll have to cure me of when I come home). The snags are that there are practically no window panes in. The doorways have no doors and the one curtain cutting us off from the hall-cum-reception room is wholly inadequate, and men, visitors and otherwise, are perpetually walking in when we are washing or in the nude! The other snag is the smell. We've eliminated everything visible and come to the conclusion that there must be a dead German in the wall somewhere. Some of the floor boards have come in very handy for firewood and we've investigated the gaps for smells without success. Our life is spent sleeping, keeping clean (or an apology for it) and going to parties, which happen every night. We are longing to get moving and get some work to do. This transit life is bad for us all.

Must stop, am going out again, this time to stoke up with tea and buns at the QA Club. Dorothy Wilson, who was with me at Ormskirk, is in the next field. I have just heard from Annu that Maiu is engaged to an Aussie airman.

Tons of love, darlings, from your loving awful daughter, Elizabeth.

On 2nd November, after another 10 days of idleness, spent mostly at the QA Club in Bayeux, we packed up once again, spent another night on the floor, but this time in front of a good fire for it was very cold, and on the 3rd were taken in ambulances to Arromanches, where we boarded a very uncomfortable cross-Channel ferry at 10 a.m. There was no accommodation for us, but Elsa and I made ourselves warm on a bench on deck. We disembarked the next day at 2 p.m. and were welcomed by the ever-willing WVS with a good hot stew on the docks. There was nothing we needed more, cold and hungry as we were.

At 3 p.m. on 4th November we started another mystery tour. Mary, Phil, Elsa and I got a compartment to ourselves on the train taking the whole unit. It was midday the next day before we arrived in Peebles. It was Sunday and snow lay around. We scrambled out on to Peebles station to the utter dismay of the station master. No one expected us. A duty officer arrived and said we would have to march three miles to a hutted camp which was empty and locked up. It was the only accommodation they had for so many and he would send the Quarter Master to take the inventory and unlock it for us. For once our dumpty little Assistant Matron from Aberdeen, nicknamed 'the haybag', put her small foot down and we sheltered in the station, brewing up on our 'tommy cookers' and mess tins, whilst a truck was found to ferry us in relays to this deserted camp. The QM was ferreted out from his Sunday rest and proceeded laboriously to check the inventory: 'Stoves, coke-fuelled, 1. WC pans 1.' and so on through all the huts. It was 10 p.m. before we sorted out our valises dumped in a heap in the snow in the dark. Mary was delighted to find herself in Scotland – halfway to her home in Wick. She fortified us with whisky mac – we put up our beds and went to sleep. The water was frozen solid in the morning, but we were proceeding on leave and it didn't matter any more.

Our week's leave was soon up. It was wonderful to be home again, to see my parents and enjoy home comforts, somewhat blighted by the wretched doodle-bombs which came over every night.

———————

Strathcathro E.M.S. Hospital,
Brechin, Angus, Scotland.
1st December 1944.

Darlingest Mom,

I was delighted to get your letter this morning. Having had no mail for a week, I felt very much the forgotten hero! What a stimulus mail is! It gives one the most lost feeling not to get any.

Well Scotland is a marvellous place. My first love is Peebles and reminds me very much of the Black Forest. I even went scouting up through the pine woods one afternoon and up to the summit. It was lovely. Just the place for a holiday. And the swift-flowing rivers everywhere, so fresh and clean. I'm enchanted by Edinburgh and can quite see why the Lanes choose to live there. The silhouette of Princes Street is lovely in the mist. We spent one afternoon with the Yanks up at the castle. It was grand and a marvellous view. They had come up from Liverpool. We had a grand trip from Edinburgh to Montrose over the Bridges of Forth and Tay. The latter really marvellous. Yesterday Mary, Phil and I had a day off. We got off duty at 3 pm the day before, so we took a bus to Aberdeen. When we got there it was just getting dark, so we set to find some accommodation for the night. We looked for an officers' club and after much enquiring, we arrived at the Lady MacRoberts hostel. There we received a rather cold reception from the good lady, who said she didn't take in girls. Three RAF officers were highly amused by the whole proceedings. The good woman eventually fixed a place for us by phone and gave us the address. Off we set, hadn't got 100 yards when we found we'd forgotten the exact address. However we arrived where we thought she said, to find we were at the wrong house. So we tried a few alternatives. Finally we gave up and phoned the good woman from one of the wrong houses. All this took about half an hour. We eventually arrived in a nice house and a very nice woman who did us very well and seemed pleased to see us. We went dancing in the evening with some officers of the Arnhem crowd. They were good fun. Next day we got tea and toast in bed at 10 a.m. and a smashing Scottish breakfast at 11.30. Then she rooked us 7/6 a head. I was rather surprised that she charged us anything. But it certainly was very comfortable, electric blanket etc. to warm our beds. We then viewed Aberdeen through the mist. I should imagine it's lovely in the sunshine, but looks rather formidable through the mists. It is a lovely shopping centre. The weather deteriorated and we ended at a flick. The first evening we had here we went to a hop in Brechin and met some of the local RAF. On the strength of which we went to a party on the airfield the next night. When we're not out, we enjoy the baths! But we're very unsettled here and looking forward to getting something definite to do. The wards are very slack. Most of the patients were wounded in Normandy and now one sees them at a far advanced stage of their treatment, unlike our former efforts on their behalf. This is an enormous hospital built in the grounds of a very stately home. This afternoon we three went for a marvellous bike ride around here. The patients are very sweet to us and hail us like long-lost friends even though they've never seen us before. All of which is very tedious for the poor civil nurses. Anyway they all have good words for the Normandy QA's.

Can you spare any of your sweet coupons? There are some wonderful varieties up here. Must pack up now. Take care of yourselves and write again soon.

Tons and tons of love, your loving E.

We had been only a fortnight at Strathcathro when we were recalled to our unit in Peebles. This news came when we were on our hitch-hiking week-end. We had decided to cross the Highlands from Perth to Inverness. Our friends had told us that there was practically no traffic, and so it turned out to be. However we got a lift from a Pole recently out of the German Army, then from a chauffeur in a private car, followed by a Count who had been visiting his son nursed in Peebles by one of our unit in the Hydro. Our final ride was in a Royal Navy truck going through to Campbelltown and he took us to Crianlarich. We went to the station and telephoned to Mary for news, and she told us that we must return immediately as we had been recalled. It was Saturday afternoon and the Skye Express had not yet gone through. The station master invited us into his office and we watched the deer on the hills through his binoculars until he put us on the train to Glasgow. From there to Edinburgh, where we spent the night, and on Sunday made our way back to Strathcathro. We got a lift in a truck, but it blew two tyres near Cupar, Angus and we had to walk. The only car to pass us was a staff car with three Generals. They very kindly stopped, but could only offer one of us a lift, so we thanked them but said we would stay together. We plodded along in the gathering gloom until across the snow we saw a light. It was a farm house. The farmer welcomed us in and invited us to join in a wonderful Scottish tea whilst he rang the hospital to ask them to send transport to pick us up in Brechin, which we reached by bus. We said farewell to the friendly hospital and reached Edinburgh, where we ran into several of our unit with tales of 14 days' embarkation leave and tropical kit. On arrival in Peebles we were met by the welcome news that Matron had been posted and Haybag, the Assistant Matron, informed us that the unit was going to India and that we were to proceed on fourteen days' embarkation leave.

I was home again on the 14th December 1944. Elise came to spend Christmas with us, and Rosemary was able to leave her family for a couple of days to join us. I had already been over to the Parham U.S. Air Base several times, and on 23rd December Bill came over with Harwood Rhodes to have supper with us. Elise and I went to Parham for their parties on Christmas Eve, Boxing Day and New Year's Eve. In between time Elise and I acted as beaters for old Burmingham's shoot and brought home some welcome game birds for the pot. Before leaving home, I arranged that my mother would have a few days' break from nursing my father, and join me in Scotland before we left for India.

On New Year's Day 1945 Elise returned to her duties and in the afternoon Bill came over. We picked our way over the minefields to Slaughden Quay and said good-bye at 10 p.m. I caught the night train and from London joined many of the unit returning to Peebles.

I got a room in Peebles for my mother, and booked tickets for the *Dancing Years*, then on in Edinburgh. I met her on 5th January off the train, and after lunch we did some sight-seeing. She was keen to see the Usher Hall, associating it with her grandmother on the Croll side. The next two days were spent viewing Melrose Abbey and on the Sunday we went by bus to Queen's Ferry and saw the Forth Bridge. In the evening I invited Mary, Phil and Elsa to supper. We spent the Monday night in Edinburgh, went to the theatre and did some shopping in Jenners the next day. After a film we had supper, bade farewell, and my mother caught the night train home. The next day, 10th January, I took over duties from Elsa, when a wire arrived to announce that Tom was back from the Middle East. Overwhelmed with excitement, I rushed off to the C.O., who granted me another 4 days leave, and once again I caught the night train south after ringing Bill to give him the news. He came over the next afternoon, and Tom arrived the following day at lunch time. What excitement and what a reunion! My mother heaved a sigh of relief that we were both back home safely, only to disperse in the very near future; Tom to fly Meteors from a Scottish airfield, and me to India.

We spent the week-end catching up with all our news, swapping stories, going through Tom's photograph albums and hearing all his adventures. He gave us a silken parachute for his three female relatives to turn into underclothes. On Sunday we bade farewell to our mother and father and I accompanied Tom to Ipswich, where I met Bill, and we had an hour and a half together before I left again for Peebles. There a letter awaited me from Elise to say she was engaged to Harwood Rhodes, whom she had met in our house when Bill brought him over for supper just before Christmas. She wrote, 'Bill is nuts about you'. I wasn't sure about this, and he had never told me so!

19th January 1945.
102 British General Hospital,
Peebles.

Darlingest Mom,

Many thanks for the cigs and the photos and your letter. I meant to send a wire to-day to send off the b.bs but will do so first thing to-morrow so that you can post them in the afternoon and maybe I'll get them on Monday. There's a frightful lot of chat going on and I can't concentrate at all. You'll be pleased to hear that my greatcoat has fetched up at last. It's really smashing and looks the tops. Such a change after that other awful affair. But I must say it did keep me warm. Our new matron has arrived. At least the one who is to accompany us. She is a very dignified and efficient person. A great change. She is horrified at the camp and has already moved 20 of us out of the worst hut to the Hydro, and I think will move more of us soon. Also she got us coupons the first day. So it just shows! Maybe our luck is in. Have now quite recovered from vaccination etc. and cold is gradually subsiding. We all went to Edinburgh to have a last money-spending orgy yesterday. In the evening we went to the officers club and I phoned Bill. He said he hoped soon to get over and see you and meet Tom. Maybe he has made it by now. He seems most anxious to meet Tom, who I hope won't be rude to him! After all this we went off to catch the 8.30 bus to Peebles. We waited and waited in the most bitter weather I have yet experienced here. It had been sleeting and a frightful wind got up, which blew us right out of St. Andrew's Square. After waiting an hour, we were told that the buses could not get through and that we wouldn't be able to get back. So the usual excursion to the RTO and a search for beds for the night. We tried the YWCA, which was most unsatisfactory. Eventually the officers' club turned up trumps and put us up most comfortably, bath and all. Another stranded episode! By the time we caught the first train in the morning, we had collected some MOs and some men and quite a few more sisters. Today we have been pottering around Peebles. Ran into John Brown and Mrs and a few other MOs, also two naval officers whom we had chatted to the night before at the officers' club in Edinburgh. So on the strength of all this, we had a ginormous party at the Green Tree, whence I have just returned. I've just had a hanky washing session which sobered me up before letter writing. (Drunken daughter – AWFUL –) Not so bad though really! I've just had long consultations with the Matron re bathing and washing facilities, when I had to go to her hut to draw water, as our one tap is frozen again. She really is very nice. The poor old Haybag is in a frightful state, having to account for past inefficiencies.

No more. Tons and tons of love, Elizabeth.

After a week of injections and general preparations for departure, we embarked on 23rd January 1945. So an eventful year came to its close and new horizons stretched before us.

Chapter Ten

2. A.I.I.M.N.S.R. India – 1945

O N JANUARY 20th 1945 we were warned for embarkation on the 23rd. Reveille on 24th was at 5 a.m. and we walked to breakfast by the light of the men's burning straw palliasses, which lit up the snowy scene. We embarked at Glasgow docks at midday and lunched on board. Mary, Phil, Elsa and I were in a 4-berth cabin. The ship was comfortable but crowded, the public rooms cramped but we were well waited on.

New sounds awoke us, the running feet of the matelots, the throb of the engines, and the tireless and noisy tannoy. We were moving down the Clyde. We anchored off Gourock and Elsa gazed for four days at her home in Dunoon. We slipped out of the river on 28th January 1945 bound for India. We quickly adjusted to life on board ship, once the majority got over their sea sickness.

Letters home to my parents and to my friend Elise Dunn (now Rhodes) tell the story. (Edited).

Darlingest Mom, Pops and family,

The first few days out, 50 per cent were laid low. Poor old Phil was quite out for the count, also Elsa, Mary not quite so bad and I managed to keep on my feet all the time, so acted as nurse. I eventually cured Phil on ginger pop and the Yanks' glucose sweets, the ones I got from Parham Air Base in my Christmas box! The first day they were so ill I spent the afternoon playing bridge. The ship gave a heave and I and my chair completely overturned, plus ash-trays, cards, glasses and all, amidst shrieks of girlish giggles.

Mary's and my sessions at the bridge table usually draw a crowd of onlookers, so we have met masses of people whom we now play with. We have one session daily with two Majors who are very good players and have taught us a lot. We have four or five others with whom we play and we also take on two of our M.O.s, which is usually a most hilarious game. Last night I played with a man named MacCrae, who came over from the Argentine with Harold Deck in 1940. I've also played with the Assistant Matron and some of the senior officers.

The first few days we were on board it was bitterly cold, so we acquired a length of rope and started a communal skipping session. A few people looked at us in blank amazement from under their caps and scarves and coat collars. In a short time we'd collected about 30 people bobbing in and out of the skipping rope! Skipping is now one of the highlights of the morning programme. So we got to know a lot more of the boys on board. I have never been at such close quarters with so many eligible young men in all my life. My footsteps are now dogged by a willowy Captain we call Digger. He is very kind and pukka but not really my type. I play chess with him. He doesn't play bridge so I can escape him on that score. Now he has written an ode on bridge. Reminds me of your wartime trip and 'The Sisal's the Devil'! Lately another has joined Digger trailing me, a man in the Suffolk Regiment. However, the four of us keep very much together in the vain hope that by keeping the men on the move they won't become too persistent. Any undesirables we get rid of by flying a distress signal to our dental officer, Ivor by name. He has been with us all through, is married, and is an awfully nice bloke. We've got to know him very well over these many months. He is quite a comedian and has rescued us on many occasions! Life is very noisy and very crowded, but we have got used to it now. Thank goodness there are no liverish old people to be disapproving and constantly requesting silence. This being an unknown luxury on board a troopship. We have singsongs in the evenings sometimes, and last night we had a priceless session with 10 people playing pounce patience. It was a riot. My idea, as usual!

I have started to learn Chinese and Elsa has decided to join me. There is a Chinese girl M.O. on board, so I hope to ask for her assistance over the difficult pronunciation. Just beside me now is a Swahili class going on. A rather nice looking middle-aged Major has been studying it religiously every day. His name is Phipps and he lives in Angmering. He has stayed with Queenie Gorringe in Kenya, so we have long chats and I gave him the Hemsteds' name. You may hear a spectator's view of our antics on board ship. He was heard to say, 'The ship rocks when that girl laughs'.

It is getting much warmer now and we spend most afternoons basking on A Deck to the tune of a squeaky gramophone. Very languid and pleasing. To-night we sneaked up on A Deck with a gramophone and danced. It was devastatingly romantic under the stars and the ship's lights. But the sticky deck, the dim music, the sway of the ship and one's endeavour to keep in rhythm make it a very tiring exercise. This was unofficial, but now it's official and we dance most evenings. Great fun is deck tennis, and we nearly fall overboard in our excitement. A few of Tom's late 'friends' are on board, with very musical comedy uniforms.

Thank you for teaching me bridge and languages. I've not been stuck yet and I think I can enjoy so much more than those less fortunate than I. Our post arrangements have been rather vague, and I've been writing short letters to post en route and this chronicle to post on disembarkation.

Tons and tons of love, darlings, Elizabeth.

The first draft was posted off on the 24th and the four of us were handed our warrants to Sialkot in the Punjab. We left with several other groups posted to different stations in the north of India. The men of the unit all went to Bangalore and were eventually disbanded.

We travelled as a group as far as Delhi. We were quite unprepared for life on the sub-continent, where a whole new world opened before our eyes. I had memories of Kenya, so different in every respect, but I viewed India in the light of those memories. The first astonishment was the sheer density of population. They were everywhere, lying in the streets and on the station platforms, squatting against the walls or in every doorway, perching on any ledge, clambering on to the train, sitting on the roof, or hanging perilously to the steps and running boards. Even in the countryside, where there was cultivation, the fields and roads were a constant stream of people and animals, bullocks, buffalo, donkeys, camels, sheep and goats, mules and horses. At every stop we quickly learnt to close the outside wooden shutters of the carriage windows against the onslaught of humanity, and the persistent endeavours of the vendors quickly sensing greensticks. We found the heat and dust very trying and woke up with sore throats. The fine red sandy dust of India was in everything and covered everything.

Our mess was in a nice old bungalow with its own large garden, a bearer, cook, sweeper, mali and other hangers on, and a tonga and tonga wallah to take us on and off duty. The Matron was another veteran from Malta and even more deranged than the Matron at Copthorne. Three Sisters from the 24th were already there. The hospital was on the outskirts of the cantonment and consisted of the main building, built in the old style with thick walls, high ceilings and a surrounding arcaded verandah, and another similar building, which was the Families Hospital. There were only nine patients, but a very sick Nursing Sister in the Families ward, and there I found myself on night duty two days after arrival.

Our lifestyle changed completely. We quickly learnt to enjoy our new comforts and opportunities to the full. The bearer, in the manner of his kind, summoned the derzi, the dhobie and various other trades people who were not slow to take advantage of new arrivals. I got my racket restrung and we went to the Club to play tennis every day. We very soon got caught up in Club life such as it was in Sialkot. Shopping in the bazaar and in the City was a never ending fascination, and after the shortages and rationing in Europe was a veritable Aladdin's cave. Not only new sights but new sounds assailed our ears. The raucous bird cry, the swish of the bundles of twigs sweeping inside and out, the constant hubbub and clatter of the bazaars, the clip clop of the tonga ponies and the drivers' cries to the sleepy bullocks yoked to the rumbling carts, and the evening sounds of bands, pipes and drums from a mess dinner night. We were lulled to sleep at night by the bubbling of the chowkidar's hookah on the verandah guarding us, and woken by the early morning bugle call from the troops' lines.

Anxiety was mounting about Sister Taylor, who was getting worse. The Brigadier came round and there was trouble for 'Rigor Mortis', our dozy chief M.O., and for poor stupid old Miss Webster, the Matron. After several nights' hard work and anxiety I was able to report on the 13th March that she had come through the crisis. My diary does not record her illness, but I think it must have been typhoid.

Our daily round now, as well as playing tennis and going to parties, included bicycling round the cantonment and lessons in Urdu from a munshi the bearer had brought along. My letters home describe our daily life.

P/279445 Sister E.A. Deck,
102 British General Hospital
attached British Military Hospital,
Sialkot, Punjab.
4th March 1945.

My darlingest Family,

As far as I can remember, my last letter was journey and nothing else. I have written to Marley, though I don't suppose I'll see him, as we're about as far from anywhere as we can be here. I've also written to Noel Tyrer.

This is a real outpost, very flat and just a series of bungalows and troops' lines, like any old station anywhere. There's also a bazaar and native quarters. Our mess is a very pleasant house, and we have several bearers between us. Phil and mine being called Hassan! Shades of the old days in Kenya. The house is surrounded by a verandah, one storey high and very high rooms, all whitewashed. We come into the dining room from the front verandah and the drawing room is connected by a folding door and leads out on to the back verandah and garden, now a bit dried up but nevertheless full of flowers and vegetables. The roof is quite flat. The mess is just like a private house and there are only eight of us altogether, so it's quite like family life. A very pleasant change and happy atmosphere to start off in. The dining room table is always polished and laid with dainty mats and nice glassware and crockery. The food is superb. I must say the cooks are excellent. Eggs practically every morning for breakfast, all and every sort of vegetable, cauliflower, spinach, carrots with our beef, mutton or chicken. Sweets usually consist of fruit, banana trifles, lemon meringue tarts, fruit salad, fruit toffee baskets and so on. I'm sorry if I make your mouth water. Oh – and cream and butter galore, also the most delicious marmalade! Apparently we can send quite frequent parcels, so as soon as I can get down town, I will get some marmalade, butter and sugar to send you. Let me know if you want dried fruit as well. Tea, I imagine, you don't want.

Phil and I share a room. It leads off the dining room and has French windows on to the front verandah and another on to the side verandah. Off it is our dressing room and off that again the bathroom. This consists of a bricked area with a gutter on which stands our zinc hip bath and two commodes, so Phil and I sit one on each and grin at each other! Hassan organises the sweeper and bath water is produced and pots emptied at the appropriate times. The boys' quarters are just behind the house, just as in the Nairobi houses. We have our own tonga, a sort of four-seater dog-cart with two wheels, the seats being back to back, and a dear little piebald pony to pull it. The tonga wallah is a cheerful bloke, and we are always driven on duty and off duty by tonga. The alternative form of locomotion in Sialkot is a bicycle. Unfortunately the bicycle duka has run out of bikes to hire, so we just depend on the tonga. The hospital is a nice airy building about a quarter of an hour's walk from our mess. There are two buildings, one the Military Hospital and the other the Families Hospital. At present I am on night duty in the Families Hospital. We only do a fortnight at a time, so it won't take long to go by. The first day we arrived we were free all day. So we unpacked immediately and changed into mufti, which we always wear off duty. My regret is that I haven't more warm clothes. I am sitting now with a jersey and my greatcoat on beside a fire. It was very hot, however, when we first arrived. It seems so incredible – instead of coming to the War, we seem to have come right away from it.

I'm going to buy some cotton material and get an evening skirt made, and just have a few chiffon blouses to alternate with it. The derzi copies frocks out of any magazine or any drawing one likes to give him, and makes the garment inside a week, an ordinary length frock for Rs 1. - (1/6d), and an evening frock for about Rs. 6.!! It's absolutely incredible.

The second day here we trailed on duty to find practically nothing to do.

That evening the girls already here had very kindly organised partners to take us to a dance that was on. However, having promised myself a week of early nights, I stuck to my guns and retired to bed early. Phil and Mary and Elsa gallantly staggered out much against their wishes, and said the partners were frightful. To-day, our third day here, Elsa, Phil and I went to the Club to play tennis. The courts are grand and we found a box of balls in the mess. There are two markers (pros) both Indians, very good players, whom one can play with for four annas (4d) a time (16 annas to the rupee). We soon met some of the officers stationed here. One very nice chap, who is secretary of the tennis. He was very struck with Elsa's play. She is championship standard and has a very graceful style. Even I hope to improve with the practise I hope to get. I got my racket restrung in a day. It's incredible how quickly one can get things done here. I should imagine one can get more comfort here for less money, than anywhere, and still the people grumble about 'wartime' conditions. It makes us hoot with mirth.

Can you please send me a few magazines like *Vogue* as soon as you can, so that I can choose some frock designs, also *The Times*. It will be most welcome, and any other interesting periodical. Wondering how Rosy is and Tom. Can you share this letter with them?

Tons of love, E.

March 10th, 1945.

Darlings,

We are all aching for mail, having had none since the day we landed now nearly three weeks ago. I'm longing to hear how Rosy is. (She was expecting William). How do you all fit in now she is with you?

I am still on night duty and will be for another week. There isn't much for us to do except that just now I am looking after a QA who is very ill and doesn't seem to have any desire to pull through. It is very depressing.

We all laughed over a remark in Alex's letter to you, which you forwarded to me, namely that in India I would meet real men and forget the gumchewers! I wish you could see the 'real' men. You can tell Alex by far the most interesting people out here are the Indians. I always laboured under the illusion that they were comparable to the African. Nothing of course could be further from the truth. Although the percentage of illiteracy may look high, I'm sure there must be as many well-educated Indians in India as there are Britons in Britain. It's staggering how intelligent the average Indian – not necessarily high class – seems to be. All the small children can be seen in the streets coming back from school with their slates covered in Urdu script. I have the feeling perpetually that there are invisible sign posts everywhere – for Indians only.

What also amazed me is to what extent British and Indian officers associate together. Nearly every mess seems to have one or two at least Indian officers. At dances one always meets them with their wives. In fact our best surgeons here are Sikhs, who seem to be the nicest of the Indians that I have met so far.

Tons of love to you all, your loving, E.

13th March 1945.

Darlingest Moma and family,

Still we wait in hope for some mail. Obviously all mail addressed to the A.P.O. number will be delayed, but with any luck we will get a reply to our letters from here shortly. I have a few snaps to enclose this time, hence an envelope. I'm still on night duty, but Phil is now on with me. I have only seven more nights to go. Yesterday we had a marvellous day. Three majors stationed up here were going on their monthly joyride and invited three of us to go with them. At 9 a.m. they rolled up in a very comfortable truck. A converted 15 cwt, to be precise, with an open roof. There were six of us altogether. We drove to the frontier town of Jammu, and from there it was a marvellous climb up and down the most hair-raising roads, right into the Himalayas towards the Banihal Pass. The scenery was fantastically beautiful. At first very jagged, grotesque landscape with tropical vegetation, low stumpy trees and cactus plants. As we got higher, it became more wooded, and the mountains more superb, and in the distance the snow-capped peaks. From practically no feet sea level, we got to 7,000 in about 100 miles. It was steep climbing, and the hazards in no way lessened by jay-walking coolies and porters, bullocks, goats and buffalo with no road sense whatever. There is a variety of water buffalo very common in use here as bullocks. Eventually we reached the snow line and the fir trees, and one might well have been in Switzerland for the grandeur of the view. On top of the particular pass we reached we found a wooden chalet, which looked for all the world as if it had been transplanted from the Schwarzwald. We picnicked on the snow, or rather on a patch of ground which was clear, just beside a snowdrift. We looked through the firs to a most wonderful scene of ragged snow-capped peaks in the distance. I think if ever I get any leave, I shall have to spend it in the Kashmir mountains.

We left our 7000 ft pass 100 miles from home, at 4 p.m. and, believe it or not, arrived on the doorstep at 8 p.m., just in time to go on night duty. We had stopped for three quarters of an hour for tea at a Dak Bungalow, after the worst part of the road had been successfully negotiated. Going back in the evening was really beautiful, with the evening sun setting the rocks aglow.

On arriving back we had the misfortune to drive up to the doorstep as the

Matron walked in from the Hospital. She gave us a rocket for being out all day, but it was well worth it.

Tons and tons of love, Elizabeth.

On 22nd March Ivor Edwards-Stuart was admitted and we were summoned to Miss Webster's office.

'We have admitted a very awkward and difficult senior officer,' she announced. 'You will see to his treatment in the most formal and professional manner, and you are not to stop and gossip.' The reason for this was that the last time he was in hospital he had written a lengthy complaint in the complaints book! Her remarks were quite enough to ensure that we quickly made his acquaintance and stopped to gossip for as long as he wished. I sensed an immediate attraction to this highly intelligent individual with a refreshing wit.

Chapter Eleven

Courtship and Engagement

FROM THE DAY THAT IVOR EDWARDS-STUART WAS ADMITTED to B.M.H. on 22nd March 1945, I was surprised to find myself fêted and entertained by officers from the Frontier Force Regiment. The main body-guard – for that was what it turned out to be – consisted of Ronnie Webb, an Australian, Chris Miles-Thomas, who had just arrived in the Centre after leave from a job as Indian Air Force liaison officer, and fat bumbling Johnnie Johnson. They seized on every off-duty moment I had, and we played bridge, tennis and went riding. Miss Webster was furious, and my relationship with her became ever more strained. Chris recalls waiting for me in our sitting room under the watchful eye of Miss Bates, and Johnny asking innocently: 'Organising the flowers, Matron?'

Ivor's orderly, Main Gul, arrived daily to see to his needs and always kept a well-stocked drink cupboard for him to entertain his visitors and us. I was soon confiding to my diary how strongly I was attracted to him.

On 2nd April, my 27th birthday, I gave a big party in the mess. As Ivor was still in hospital, Ronnie and I carried him some of the cheer by bike to his hospital bed. He was discharged on 5th April and from then on my body-guard gave way to him, and I was seldom without his company. On the 6th I succumbed to the prevailing bug. We had all suffered minor bouts since arriving in India, but never serious enough to put us to bed for more than a day. By the 9th, after a hot milk and brandy, Ivor's special cure, I staggered back on duty.

18th March 1945.

Darlingest Mom,

Your letter of March 3rd was the last to arrive. Phil and I are coming off duty together, which is very nice as it gives us our nights off together too. Last Thursday Phil and I had been invited to a dinner and dance at the Club. So we asked the old girl if she'd mind if we were off until midnight, providing someone would stand in for us. She didn't seem to mind, so we did. It was a grand party and we did the Cinderella act at midnight. Our partners took us home, waited whilst we cast our ball gowns for grey gingham, and then escorted us on duty!

I think I told you of the calamity with my evening skirt, which the derzi made short! Well he arrived just before the party with a marvellous evening skirt, the same transformed. Today Sydney called for me at 10 a.m. mounted on a very nice looking chestnut polo pony called George, and his syce brought round Rufus, a beautiful chestnut, for me. We went out riding the whole morning. Rufus belongs to one of Sydney's brother officers, who is going to sell him. There is a system here, whereby officers can buy Army horses for Rs100. - (£7.10.0), and sell them only to people in the Army. It's a fixed rate and the Army can call on the horses if they are needed. Rufus is an absolute dream and a real ladies' horse. He is not a very good jumper, and has a nasty habit in the stable of biting you. Phil and I can go shares on his upkeep which comes to Rs. 100. - a month, if someone will buy him.

Phil and I have a munshi to teach us Urdu. I am getting on fine and can make myself understood, but can't understand much yet.

Tons of love, Elizabeth.

4th April 1945 (edited).

Darlings,

I'm longing for some mail. There's been another hold-up, so none came to-day. I had a marvellous birthday party. It was a wow! There were the four of us, Matron, the girl who was so ill, Helen, and her sister and one of the other QAs. We had invited the daughter of one of the Colonels and another Colonel and his wife, two boy friends of Phil's, one of Mary's and eight others, being various people who have taken me out, twenty-two guests and two gatecrashers. We started off at 8.30 p.m. when Vic, Sydney and Randall arrived with Vic's gramophone and records. We fixed this up at the verandah end of the drawing room so that it could be heard on the verandah and drawing room too, which we cleared for dancing. The bar, buffet and seats were in the adjoining dining room. At 9 p.m. people began arriving and the bearers handed round the cocktail which Mary and I had mixed with an incredible nonchalance! Gin, vermouth, rum, orange juice and ice! It went down well. At 10 p.m. we dug into the cold buffet supper. Vic is the most wonderful pianist and he played most of the evening, syncopated music. Warsaw concerto and so on. We had laid a treasure hunt, with the clues done in verse, and we put up advertisements pinned on the wall for people to guess when they had nothing better to do. After we were well fed, Vic sat down to the piano and Elsa and Randall sang. We turned the lights low and it was very 'gemütlich'. After that the gramophone brightened us up and we danced until 3 a.m. The chief snag was the lack of girls. Having invited all our friends, each of us found ourselves trying not to tread on someone's toes – very tricky. I think everyone enjoyed it. I certainly did. The Matron had a hang-over the next day, which was a very bad thing. We'd had a lot of opposition from her and she hasn't the remotest idea of entertaining. However, we persuaded her to return some of the hospitality we have received from the various Colonels' wives with a dinner party! The cake was a scream. It was done in chocolate and silver bobbles, depicting mountains, packs of cards, tonga whip, bicycle and tennis racket.

I expect Rosy is causing some sensation. Good luck and God bless and for God's sake do the sterilising properly.

Tons and tons of love. E.

12th April, 1945.

Darling Moma and family,

Still wondering how Rosy is doing. Today I got notification from the bank that Rs. 100 was waiting for me, so off I went to collect it before they changed their minds. I think it was a marvellous idea of Tom's and a lovely birthday present and it certainly was very welcome. I have now been able to buy Rufus, and am having dealings about his stabling. As I have had so many rows already with Matron, I simply daren't ask her if I could stable a horse in our perfectly good stables. I called on the Colonel's wife who lives next door, and she is going to look out for somewhere nearby so that I can keep an eye on the syce.

Phil has been very difficult to deal with lately. The trouble is she doesn't like my current boy friend. He is a temporary Lieutenant-Colonel in the Frontier Force Regiment aged 30, and has been out here 11 years. His name is Ivor and he was in the Burma Retreat. We play bridge mostly. It poured with rain yesterday and every roof leaked, but I didn't mind getting wet – it's the first real rain we've had.

By now rumours were circulating in the station about our romance and Matron became ever more hostile. The conflict of my own emotions and the varying and abundant advice given by everyone around me threw me into total confusion. On the 10th April a TAB jab put me to bed for the day, for which I was thankful. I decided that whatever happened, I should not make any decision until the War ended. When Ivor proposed on the 14th, I didn't know what to do. It was what I wanted, but dare I make such a decision in the face of so much advice to wait? Ten days later I was off sick again. It was getting very hot, over 100 degrees Fahrenheit in the shade in the day-time. Elsa, Phil and I were constantly going off sick for a day or two at a time. The heat, the unaccustomed climate, as well as our hectic off-duty life was telling on us.

15th April 1945,

My darling Elise,

I was so thrilled to get your two letters written from Fairways. Thank goodness you turfed old John out. Fancy bringing a septic throat near Rosemary at such a time. I nearly had kittens when Ma's letter reached me, a day ahead of yours, saying John was in the house with septic throat and R. nursing him. I had visions of her having the baby and puerperal sepsis and God knows what. I prayed that you'd arrive on the scene and you did. I was so thrilled to get an EFM saying son born both well. What a lot of excitement there is in our small circle these days!

Your wedding day will be drawing nearer and nearer by the time you get this if it is up to date. Maybe you are already Mrs Rhodes. How odd I shall have to address you differently. Well now for my news.

In my last letter I think I wrote at great length about Ivor, and the scandal in Sialkot and Phil ticking me off. The next day I was still feeling lousy and spent the day in bed. I was woken up by a telegram which read 'I love you. Suggest strong allied counter-offensive, marry me. I love you, Ivor'. I gaped at this incredible message and tore it up. The following morning a most apologetic chit from Ivor by his bearer to say he had asked his pal Ronnie (a very lively Australian) to go out and send me a wire, as he, Ivor, was not allowed by me to visit our mess or send his Frontier Force orderly along. I had asked him not to come, and to restrict the number of chits he sends by his orderly in view of his extreme unpopularity in the mess here. Apparently Ronnie and Johnny in leg-pulling mood had sent me this message! Ivor of course was furious with them. I thought it all rather funny. As I had been so seedy, I had decided that I would be in bed each night by 11 p.m. and have rigidly adhered to this timetable. I have been down to tea with Ivor on several occasions at his bungalow, and last night as I missed dinner in my own mess, went back with him for dinner. Last night was too much for him and he proposed. I said 'no' very firmly, but I'm afraid I am very fond of him and will get more so. I shall have the opportunity of seeing so much of him that it will stay on a 'no' basis for a good long time. I have a horrible feeling I might marry him in the end though. What is so astounding in this place is that as soon as one is seen or known to be friendly with some man, immediately invitations flow in for 'you and Ivor'! To-night we are going out to dinner with a very nice couple. The man is in Ivor's regiment. We are playing bridge.

I often wonder so much what the family would think of Ivor. He is small, about the size of Bill, fair, blue-eyes and very skinny. He has a quiet rather nervous manner. Very much the old school tie and regular Army type, though he has some pretty progressive ideas, especially in politics. Rides a lot, of course, and has incidentally loaned me his breeches. He is a Major, but at the moment is doing 2nd in command, so has been a Lieutenant-Colonel for the past three months. He is awaiting a posting on active service in Burma. I haven't mentioned as much as this to the family yet, only about my current boy friend Ivor, who has lent me his breeches. As usual, you are my first confidante. I'd tell Ma only she gets so het up and worried I'd rather know Ivor a lot better than I do before I write at great length about him to her. It may all die a natural death. I tell you because I know you like to be kept up to date with my 'affaires de coeur'. I really have fallen again this time. With Bill I have a great feeling of fondness and respect, but not that funny breathtaking sensation which makes you lose your head. I thought I'd grown out of such childish ailments, but there it is. Ivor is terribly bossy and most people are scared stiff of him. But he is always helping his junior officers out of difficulties, although very strict with them. As regards Bill, I fondly imagined that writing to each other, we'd get to know each other better, but that is a fallacy. Writing letters is only of use in maintaining whatever contact one has at that stage achieved, but is never any good at furthering a friendship. I see this only too clearly in Elsa's romance. She met Derek on board ship, under what are not natural conditions. They decided to get married the night before they left for their various destinations. Next time they meet will be at the altar. I think it's a bit too much of a rush. I'm going to try to persuade her to take 10 days casual leave and go and see Derek in Calcutta. At least that will break their next meeting at the altar.

Well, Elise, my love, be a good wife. I don't think I can possibly give you any words of wisdom in your great undertaking. It's to you I'll have to come for advice. Write and tell me everything. What a rigmarole I've written now, you'll be getting very bored.

All love, Elizabeth.

22nd April 1945.

Darlingest Mom,

Thank you very much for another parachute bra, posted on the 28th February, which arrived the other day. Also *The Times* of 26th, 27th Feb. and *Illustrated London News*, *New Review*, and *Picture Post*. All very much appreciated by everyone. In fact they're the most recent illustrated papers in Sialkot, I think. Do keep up with *The Times*. You've no idea how marvellous it is to get them. I sent off a wire to Elise Rhodes yesterday, which I hope arrives on her wedding day.

Life here jogs along more peacefully on the whole. I suppose as I spend most of my spare time at Bungalow 94, where Ivor and his gang hang out, I'm away from the uneasy atmosphere of the mess. They are building a few jumps in their compound. As I've got Rufus' saddlery from them, I school him there quite a bit. They've a decent patch of ground with fewer holes than most compounds. I'm enclosing a photo of Ivor. I can't imagine what you'd think of him. He drinks like a fish except for a month a year, when he goes on the waggon. He has lived most of his life in Australia. He went to Sydney University before going to Sandhurst. He is clever, though I wouldn't say intellectual in the usual sense of the word. His chief interest seems to be Military History and his room is lined with books, mostly history. He was Mentioned in Despatches in Burma in 1942. He is very sophisticated really and loves entertaining. We have terrific arguments and rows, both suffering from the same sort of superiority complex. He thinks he will be posted back to his old battalion in Burma in the near future. In fact a posting came through whilst he was in hospital. He speaks and writes Urdu and Pushto and is rather like Tom in his attitude to authorities and fairly pushes people around. He is very serious about me, which makes me laugh quite a lot, much to his exasperation. His great friend Ronnie is going to Madras to be married next month. I rather think they've got marrying on the brain. The third of the gang in Bungalow 94 is Johnny Johnson, who is married to a girl who trained at the Middlesex and came out here as a regular QA in 1938. Ivor has been in the Royal 3rd Sikhs Frontier Force for 11 years, though his family is naval, as far as I can gather. If you want any more details, Elise has a lot of gen. I'm sure, and certainly hope, that you'll be seeing lots of her in the near future. Don't get worried, I won't dash off and get married in a hurry or even engaged, but I thought you'd like to know what's going on. Phil, Elsa and I are all going to Lahore at Ivor's invitation, so they must be deciding that Ivor and his gang aren't so bad after all. Personally I find them good fun. They are terribly snobbish and critical of the other funnies in Sialkot, which is probably what antagonises Phil and Co. so much. At least that's what I put it down to.

Well darlings, don't let this shatter you too much. I suppose the blow will fall soon or late, and I know you like to know what's cooking in the same way that I do. I'm not, repeat, not, engaged to Ivor, although the subject has been broached on occasions only to meet a very flat refusal from me. However the fact that I fell heavily – my secret still – and still go about with him, rather belies my words. Time alone will tell.

Don't worry, darling, I promise I won't do anything in a hurry, in spite of postings to the front. Probably not even get engaged. It's all very difficult so far from home.

Do write soon, darlings, your very loving, Elizabeth.

On 30th April I was posted with Mary to the Indian Military Hospital, where there was a smallpox outbreak. We had had further vaccination on arrival in Sialkot which had taken very well, in spite of repeated vaccinations on board ship which had shown no reaction. It was a relief to have something new to think about and a break from Miss Bates' snide nagging.

The I.M.H. presented a scene such as I had never dreamed of. Hundreds of sick men crowded into wards, some on the floor with the very minimum of comfort. Nursing as we had practised it was out of the question. We could only attend to the administration of drugs and to some of the more complex dressings and treatments. Otherwise they were fed and cared for by orderlies, comrades or relations. The traffic in and out of the wards resembled a railway station. Sick men lay everywhere in the smallpox ward, where we administered drugs for the relief of fever and pain and gave sips of water. We felt despair at our inability to do more to relieve their suffering, which they accepted with patience and resignation. Mary and I were bewildered and shaken by the experience. Three days later I was on the sick list again and back in the cool of the Families ward, and the tender mercies of the Ayah. Ivor visited me and calmed me down and on the 3rd of May we got engaged, to the delight of the Regiment and my friends. I was in a whirl of happiness, excitement and indecision. Mercifully Ivor took over.

4th May 1945.

Darlingest Moma,

I have not yet received any stirring reply to my letter of Sunday before last with the long tale about Ivor. I can well imagine your reaction, darling, and am scared stiff of it. I am going to get engaged to Ivor. I've held out on him up to now, but I knew from the beginning that I'd marry him in the end, and it's just so damn silly saying what you don't mean. We spend all our spare time together, in fact it's just awful when we aren't together, so it really is time we got weaving on something. Nobody knows in Sialkot except Ronnie,

Ivor's great friend; in fact we only decided last night that we'd better get going so I'm writing to you straight away, as I know, like myself, you like to have your finger on the pulse of things. I just can't imagine what you'd make of him. He's as bolshy as I am, and as I told Elise, is quite well versed in 'How to Tame the Shrew'. He has little to recommend him except that he's a darling to me.

What a letter to have to write on Pop's birthday! Thank goodness Rosy is with you. I really am so sorry to have to inflict you with another s-i-l, but I suppose it would have come sooner or later. The extraordinary thing is that he's an Englishman, better perhaps than a German. Doubtless he will cough up some relatives for you to view to soothe your troubled conscience. His mother is in Australia, his father died when he was five and he has no brothers or sisters.

I'm dreading announcing it in Sialkot, but I think it is a foregone conclusion, anyway with most people. I hope you don't think the 'men' have gone to my head, or have any other peculiar notions. Since I've been in the Army, there have always been so many men around, that that complex hardly worries me. It's just that as soon as I met him I knew something was brewing, and we're now so fond of each other and peaceful and happy in each other's company, that there is no other way out. And he isn't the first that's proposed to me out here!

I wish I could put on my seven-league boots and tell you instead of having to resort to this inadequate medium. At least I know it won't take too long to reach you. Please don't feel unhappy, darlings, and give Pops a real birthday kiss,

from your loving, awful daughter, Elizabeth.

7th May 1945.

Darlingest Moma,

By every mail I await your reply to my letter about Ivor. How I wish I were at home and not such miles and miles away.

Last Friday evening Ronnie had a big party laid on to celebrate his departure. He has gone to Madras to get married. On Thursday evening, when we decided we would get engaged, we told Ronnie straight away, but told him to keep it quiet. The following day Ivor told his Colonel and I told Elsa, who was very pleased. She was feeling very depressed and cheered up more than she has for a long time. As Mary was leaving for Dalhousie that evening, Elsa said we couldn't leave her in the dark, so Elsa told Mary. Then of course the cat was out of the bag, so at the party that evening we told everyone. It was a marvellous evening and everyone was simply wonderful. Poor old Miss

Bates, the Matron, was shaken to the core. She hates Ivor about as much as she hates me. 94 Bungalow went in for celebrating in a big way. Ronnie has now gone, so Chris and Johnnie are left to hold our hands.

Now, of course, the question of when we shall get married arises. This is the awful problem. Ivor is posted to Burma and his posting hasn't been cancelled, so as things are at the moment, he is due to leave here four days after 1st June. I am liable to be posted at any time which makes things very difficult. Naturally we want to get married and enjoy our time together in Sialkot, and also some leave together. We should wait, I know, but it does seem so useless and such a waste of time. Because it will be difficult for me to get leave when I want it if I'm single, I'm applying for special marriage leave to-day and so is Ivor and we are hoping to get married on the 19th of this month in Lahore.

As regards finances, we live on Ivor's pay. He has a few savings in England, also a house in Southsea, which presumably will realise something some time. Otherwise love, love, love! This is a frightful letter to write. I'm going to wire Elise today to tell her to contact you and break it gently. Also Ivor is wiring a cousin of his, Doreen, so you and she must get together. Will write again to-night, but want this to catch the morning's post. I wish I could tell you instead of having to write.

All love darlings, E.

8th May 1945.

Darlingest Moma,

To-day a wire speeds off to tell you that Ivor and I are getting married on 19th. I'm simply shaking all over at your awful sunken feeling on receiving the news. I do hope you can contact Doreen, as she will tell you about Ivor and at least be a member of his family for you to meet. Darling, he's quite one of us, lives the same crazy way, and bullies me unmercifully. He is very determined. Our tastes coincide all round in the people we like. He's not charming to meet, but has a heart of gold and the right ideas.

Please give me your blessing. I know it's indecently quick, but he goes to Burma on June 7th approximately. Can you please insert this announcement in *The Times*, if possible before the 19th.

'The engagement is announced and the marriage will shortly take place between Major Ivor A.J. Edwards-Stuart, The Frontier Force Regiment, son of the late Lieutenant C.C.A. Stuart R.N. and Mrs G.K. Stuart, of Neutral Bay, Australia and Elizabeth A. LeMesurier elder daughter of Mr and Mrs S.F. Deck of Aldeburgh, Suffolk.'

I will write again to-night. Please bless us, we are so happy together. If only I'd been sensible and made up my mind sooner, we would not have had this rush. There's nothing shady about the hurry, it's just that we won't have any time together otherwise.

All love, E.

8th May 1945 – V.E. Day.

Darlingest Family and Moma in particular.

By the time this reaches you, you will all be milling around in frantic circles at the awful daughter's latest effort. I am terribly, terribly sorry to spring it all so desperately suddenly on you all. Although I swore I wouldn't get married whether Ivor went to Burma or not, when it comes to the point it is so damn silly waiting, especially with both of us in the services and our futures so shatteringly vague. I kick myself now for not having got engaged sooner, for it was so obvious that we would in the end. Then we would have had more time to get ready and let you know.

I just can't tell you what a whirl I've been living in lately. Ivor does most of the arranging, thank goodness, and now most evenings are a procession of having drinks here and drinks there, though there are not many people left for me to meet in Sialkot. I am meeting Ivor's men, V.C.O.'s and goodness knows who, all in the Regiment. All with no decent clothes! Johnny Johnson and Chris are fixing all the wedding bunderbast. We are getting married in Lahore by the Archdeacon in the Cathedral at 6 p.m. and catch the 9 p.m. to Simla. There we hope to stay in the Cecil Hotel if we can get in. Ivor has two batches of relatives in Simla. I'm getting my leave from 17th, and we all go down on the night train to Lahore, Johnny, Chris, Mari (another Sister) and Elsa.

I'm going to spend my V-Day off in Lahore trying to get some clothes from a woman Molly Sawday has told me about. It depends on what I can get, whether I am married in uniform or in mufti. What a pair of daughters' weddings we will have had! Anyway, no expense, Moma darling! After the honeymoon we come back to the Mountview Hotel here, where one lives very comfortably, until Ivor is posted.

Life is really marvellous, darlings, so please be happy about it. There's so much I want to tell you, but I have to write in such a hurry. I am just off to listen to Churchill's speech, due through at 7.30 p.m.

We are very busy in the hospital. We work the same hours as in England, one day off a month and two half days a week and the temperature 100F for the past fortnight. I'm feeling fine, Ivor soon bullied me out of my 'heat exhaustion' and 'tummy'! He got browned off coming to see me in hospital.

The Victory must be so exciting at home, but hopelessly remote here. In fact for us the War only begins now.

Tons and tons of love, darlings.
Gosh I pray you'll not be too upset,
your loving, E.

9th May 1945.

Darlingest Moma,

Have just got your letter in answer to mine about Ivor. I can't tell you how worried I've been about having to wire you so suddenly and do everything in such a rush. Darling, I hope you will understand how awful it would be to wait. Ivor turned down a Staff College course a little time back so that he could go back on active service. A thing I think he now regrets. He is definitely posted as from beginning of June, when he will be boarded category A again. Although the end of the War out here seems imminent, there will probably be a lot of campaigning still and people like Ivor will have to serve. Then again, neither of us having our homes here, it would be frightful spending our leave together unmarried, because I was going to have leave at the end of this month anyway. We haven't done anything foolish which would have necessitated a quick wedding – this only occurred to me the other day as being a thought which might cross your mind, especially after my theories about sleeping with the man one is to marry before marrying him – so have no worries there. We don't suffer from lack of self-control. It is extraordinary how one is attracted to a person really. Ivor is quite unlike any boy friend I've had hitherto. Although we argue and disagree about little things, fundamentally we have the same ideas and tastes. Funnily enough, he is very pro-Russian, which is very out of keeping with the rest of him. He certainly is the world's worst snob, you two should get in a huddle. It is very difficult indeed to convey a person's character through the post. He has certainly sown his wild oats as a bachelor. He has a hell of a lot of personality and we just talk the same unspoken language. What more can I say? The more we're together, the deeper grows our affection. He is 30–31 on 11th June.

Our trip to Simla will be another epic, dog, bearer and all. Ivor has a pet of a dachshund called Gretel. The bearer is a Pathan from the North West Frontier Province and, like all his kind, wears his hair in a long bob parted in the middle! His name is Main Gul. Ivor gets Rs 1300. a month and Rs. 250. marriage allowance when we marry, less income tax, of course. So we shouldn't do badly and can save my pittance. If we both go on active service, we will be even better off. I apologise for this fearfully disjointed letter. I'll make him finish his letter to you so you may know something of him. He has been worried stiff over the letter he intends to write to you and Pops. It is damn difficult.

All love, darlings, E.

14th and 16th May 1945 (edited).

Darlingest Moma,

Your letter of 6th May has just fetched up. I am expecting a wire from you any minute in answer to the one I sent off last Monday. Darling, I know you will think: 'why don't they wait?', but when it comes to it, what is the point? We are so happy and do want to get what time we can together. I'm scared stiff I'll be posted even before my leave comes through. It's been a hectic 10 days since we got engaged and Ivor and I will be complete wrecks by the time we get to Simla. Last night we entertained six of Ivor's V.C.O.s. None could speak English and my Urdu is not exactly conversational yet. However I managed to follow the gist of the chat and butted in pretty often. We also have to visit various Indian officers with wives, but not the ones in purdah.

To-morrow we go to Lahore to get me some clothes, and also to see the Archdeacon and fix the wedding. Johnny and Chris have been marvellous and laid on everything. We have got accommodation in Simla and intend staying there until the end of May and then go on to Kulu, which is supposed to be very beautiful. We shall have to take most of our food and our bedding rolls. We're simply longing to get to the hills out of this inferno. Ivor is looking ill, as he didn't go away for his sick leave, as he should have done, on account of me. But some weeks in the hills should do us both all the good in the world.

Ivor, of course, doesn't want me on active service, naturally enough. I think the answer is to get cracking on a family pretty soon. We both want to and the chances of us being able to enjoy much of the first two years of married life together are pretty slender.

Great excitement yesterday when Ivor's pay arrears rolled in, just upwards of 200 pounds. I haven't got an engagement ring yet. There's nothing worth having in Lahore, so we're waiting until we can find something worth buying. A regimental brooch is on the way, gold set with diamonds. I haven't seen it yet.

The dress situation is still acute. Elsa and I and Ivor and another of his officers went by truck to Lahore. We went to the Gown House. They are making me a turquoise blue wedding frock. Plain top, gathered skirt from hip level, and three-quarter length sleeves. I also bought a white evening dress, a green linen everyday frock, and a navy blue linen coat and skirt with all round pleats. The hat business was most amusing. The place recommended to us had moved to Simla for the hot weather, so we ended up in the bazaar and eventually found something which I can fix up with veiling. We also visited the Archdeacon in the Cathedral, who was very charming and helpful. It was terribly hot and we were completely exhausted. Coming back, we drove into a terrific dust storm and could hardly see three feet in front of us. I am writing on duty and have just been interrupted.

You must forgive these letters of the last few days, but life has been unbelievably hectic. It's all so terribly exciting and hardly seems true. I hope Pops took the news ok. I'm so happy, please be happy with me. Write to me in Simla: Mrs Ivor Edwards-Stuart, c/o Mrs Grant, Grand Hotel, Simla. That is Ivor's cousin. I can't remember where we are to stay.

All love E.

18th May 1945.

Darlingest Moma,

Poor Miss Deck – only 24 hours to go. I've never wanted you here so much in all my life. I suppose one always feels homesick before one gets married, whether at home or not. I do wish you had been able to know Ivor beforehand too, though with all his faults, I think you will like him. He is hopelessly outspoken and terrible with people he doesn't like, worse than me! I think at one stage he was quite worried about my family – like you! However I gave him your letters to read, also Tom's, which quite set his mind at rest. I know the rush of our wedding will upset you, but under these conditions it would have been hopeless to wait. There is no doubt at all to me that Ivor is the man for me. He certainly can deal with me, which I don't think has happened to me before. I've always done the dealing.

I still have no wire from you. I suppose there's been delay with the mail owing to the V. Day and the holidays. That would happen just now. Our engagement announcement appeared in the *Statesman* yesterday. I only hope *The Times* makes it.

Wedding presents are coming in from the locals, mostly furniture so far, some silver ashtrays, and two silver napkin rings, and a cheque of Rs. 50. from the Colonel.

Darling, please don't worry, I'm terribly happy and excited underneath everything. Miss Bates is perfectly beastly, but Elsa has been a great help and a grand friend. She comes down with me to-night to Lahore and will look after me.

All love, darlings, and do write, your loving, E.

There was an unfortunate mix-up with my letters and cables home. I had cabled and written to Elise that I was getting married and asked her to console my parents. She, of course, got the news before they did, although the letters went in the same post and the cables on the same day.

Not wishing to invite the whole station to our wedding, we slipped off to Lahore, complete with body-guard, Chris, Johnny and one or two others, whom Ivor posted to sit on the sidings outside Elsa's and my carriage in Wazirabad station whilst we waited to be hooked up to the Frontier Mail in the early hours. He was still unsure of me and feared I might escape. The rest of the wedding party was Dougie Cairns, Hardy, David Plim, Ken Came and Gordon Williamson. Elsa came as my bridesmaid and Ivor's orderly, Main Gul, and the dachshund Gretel, completed the party.

Part Two

The Husband

Chapter Twelve

The Story of a Youth in Australia.
His Forebears, Childhood and
Training – 1784–1934

IVOR ARTHUR JAMES STUART, (later Edwards-Stuart) was born on 11th June 1914 in Sydney, N.S.W. in mid-winter. His mother Gladys was the third child of Tudor Vaughan Howell Thomas and Isabella Caroline Grant. Isabella came of an interesting Indian Army family and was the youngest daughter of General Charles Grant and Frances Eliza, née Roberts, whose father was General Sir Abraham Roberts. Her mother was his first wife, Frances Isabella, née Ricketts. Ivor was to write his biography, *A John Company General, The Life of Sir Abraham Roberts*, in later years. Ivor's great-grandmother Eliza was half-sister to the famous Victorian Field Marshal, of whom Kipling wrote his famous poem, 'Our Bobs'. He was known in the family as 'Uncle Fred'. He and his sister Harriet were the children of Sir Abraham and his second wife, the widow Isabella Maxwell.

Eliza married General Charles Grant, Bengal Artillery. His father was Robert Grant of Ballindalloch and Speyside. His mother was Elizabeth Farquharson. Her parents were William and Leonora Farquharson. In the family possession are portraits of Robert and Elizabeth Grant and of her parents William and Leonora Farquharson and of Sir Abraham Roberts, as well as two portraits of earlier ancestors, Sofia Poyntz-Ricketts (née Watts) and her mother the Begum Johnson, whose biography was also written by Ivor, *The Calcutta of the Begum Johnson*. Sofia was the grandmother of Frances Isabella Ricketts, the mother of Eliza, Maria and George Roberts.

Eliza Roberts and her sister Maria were married on the same day, in the evening of 20th October 1842, Eliza to Charles Grant and Maria to William Maconochie Wellwood. As with all service families, they were constantly on the move and the Indian climate took its toll on Eliza's health. Their first-born son Robert died in infancy and Eliza penned a sad little poem to him which is so evocative of the tragic lives the young mothers in India endured. (See *A John Company General, the Life of Sir Abraham Roberts*, page 218).

General Grant's illustrious career in the Bengal Horse Artillery involved him in many campaigns, including the 1st Burma War and the 1st Afghan War under his future father-in-law, Abraham Roberts. A year after his marriage in 1843 he was on the march again in the Gwalior campaign. He was subsequently wounded in the Battle of Sobroan in the 1st Sikh War. At the Battle of Chilianwala in the 2nd Sikh War Charles Grant's quick thinking saved the day, and he was awarded the C.B. Later he was stationed in Lahore, where sadly Eliza died in 1853, giving birth to twin boys who were still-born. She was only 32. The griefstricken father sent their three little girls, Fanny Maria, Charlotte and Isabella, to England to be looked after by Eliza's half-sister, Harriet Roberts. General Grant retired in 1859. He was awarded a knighthood, but refused it on the grounds it would increase his expenses. He settled in Cheltenham, where he devoted his life to bringing up his three daughters. He furnished his house with many things brought back from India, and all his belongings were divided up between his three daughters, and many of these remain with the family.

Ivor's father died when he was five years old. His mother Gladys' immediate reaction to Claude's death was to return to England from Australia. However, a very good friend of Claude's, a Paymaster Commander in the Royal Australian Navy, strongly advised her to accept the offer of an Australian war widow's pension, as opposed to a Royal Navy one. This proved to be very wise financial advice as the Australian pension was tax free and subject to periodic increases, whereas the English one was neither. Gladys wisely accepted this advice and she proved to have a remarkably astute financial instinct. She built on the legacy of property which Claude had left her. After his death she converted Holt Avenue into two flats, enabling her to let one. She built up a little business making chocolates which she sold to David Jones and other superior stores in Sydney.

Ivor remembers his early days there and the good smell of home-made confectionary. He remembers his 6th birthday party and the good things laid before his small friends. He left Redlands School and went to the local public (council) school and from there to Knox College, where he joined

Donald Airlie Warden, known as Mick, Neta Perkins' much younger brother. When Knox was sold and moved, he stayed with its successor St. Leonard's School, where he proved to be an apt and intelligent pupil. He took part in athletics and won a prize, a glass vase, and an academic prize in the form of an inscribed medal. Early on he joined the Boy Scout Movement and started as a member of the 1st Mosman Cub Pack.

In 1924 Gladys decided once again to try her luck in England. She sailed with Ivor, aged 10, via South Africa, and Ivor's photos trace their journey. She lived again with her mother Isabella, who became devoted to her young grandson.

It became clear to Gladys that she was much better off financially in Australia, and so on the 4th January 1927 she and Ivor set sail from London in S.S. *Largs Bay*.

Back in Sydney, Gladys and Ivor returned to the Wycombe Road back flat and Ivor resumed his studies at St. Leonard's. He joined the 1st Cremorne Scouts and at the end of 1928 went with the NSW contingent to the All-Australia Corroboree in Western Australia. He travelled with his friends and the many Scouts attending the Corroboree by train across the Nullabor plain. Many are the photos he brought back after a three-week camp. One of his friends was 'Tiger' Moore, and his sister Nell was Ivor's first girl friend. In October of 1929 he represented the school in the Associated Grammar School Athletics and ran in the 100, 200 yds and the relay, and in December of that year he was off again to an All-Australia Corroboree at Lake Illawara. In January 1930 he became Acting Cubmaster of the 1st Mosman Pack. He was not yet 16 and at the same time was a Patrol Leader in the 1st Cremorne Scout Troop. One of Ivor's fellow pupils was a Murdoch, and Ivor was able to get a holiday job in their store in Sydney.

Ivor's success in running both his Cub Pack and his Patrol brought him to the attention of Mr MacAlister, the Scout Training Camp Chief at Pennant Hills. MacAlister had a Rover Crew, which he drew from the various Troops in and around Sydney, who helped with the administration of the Training Camp. He introduced eight selected juniors to help the Rover Crew, of whom Ivor was one. The Rover Crew was divided into 4 Patrols and one patrol was on duty each week-end and on the 5th week-end was held a general crew reunion. As well as Scout Training, the Rover Crew built the log cabins and the open-air chapel, where years later Ivor's son was to be christened. Ivor made many life-long friends amongst the Rover Crew, including the youngest of the Croll cousins, Darcy, much younger brother of Raleigh's. When General Sir Robert Baden-Powell, founder of the Boy Scout Movement, visited Australia, he was so impressed by the work done at Pennant Hills Training Camp, that he granted them the privilege of calling themselves the Baden-Powell Rovers.

Mr MacAlister, who lived with his sister at the camp, was an enormous help and support to Ivor and became a substitute father to him in his teenage years. In 1931 Ivor passed his matriculation and joined Sydney University. His subjects were History, English and Anthropology in his first year and in his second year he studied Japanese History and Philosophy, in which subject he gained a higher distinction. Ivor did not join the Sydney University Regiment with his friend Ken Mosher, but continued instead with his Scouting. He passed his Wood Badge in August 1931 and in October was presented to the Chief Scout, the Governor of New South Wales, Sir Philip Game.

From an early age, and especially after staying with his grandmother Isabella, Ivor had had the ambition to join the Indian Army. Gladys' stories of her forebears and her brother Ivor's exploits in that famous body of men in that fabulous country had fired his imagination. Aunt Violet's constant reminders of the three Generals and one Field Marshal in the family added to his ambition. The three Generals were General Charles Grant, Ivor's great grandfather; General George Roberts, his great uncle and Eliza's brother. Aunt Violet said he always referred to himself as the General Roberts of the Royal Descent, as he traced his ancestry back to Catharine Swynford, 3rd wife of John of Gaunt, 4th son of Edward III. The third was General Sir Abraham Roberts, his great great grandfather; and the Field Marshal was Lord Roberts of Kandahar, Great Uncle Fred.

But how to afford the fees at Sandhurst, and the long journey to England? Ivor couldn't ask this of his widowed mother. While still at school, therefore, he applied for a King's Cadetship which, if he were successful, would assure him a free education at R.M.C. and an initial allowance for the costly uniform. Early in 1932 he was interviewed for the King's Cadetship by the Governor-General, Lord Stonehaven, and was subsequently granted this award. The next problem was to get an introduction to a shipping company who might be persuaded to employ him on a ship sailing for England. A friend of Gladys', a Mr Klippel, said he could find him a passage as an Assistant Purser. Before leaving Sydney University he gained a credit in Oriental History, and was also made a full member of the Baden-Powell Rover Crew.

On the 17th May 1932 he bade farewell to his mother and his friends and sailed from Sydney in S.S. *Port Denison*, not, alas, as Assistant Purser, but as ship's general dogsbody. The old boatswain and his friend the ship's carpenter took pity on this very youthful 17 year-old and when Ivor went ashore in Townsville on a Scout undertaking in full uniform, they made quite sure he came to no harm or ridicule from the baser members of the ship's company. In Wyndham they spent several days whilst meat was loaded at night and hides by day, causing a memorable stench in the tropical heat.

On arriving in England, Ivor went to London and reported in to the Boy Scout Association Headquarters, where he had an introduction to Sir Alfred Pickford.

Before leaving Sydney, Ivor had been given an introduction to Admiral Thesiger by Mr MacAlister and this he now took up and was duly invited to stay with the Admiral at Liphook in August. He was somewhat surprised and alarmed to find that after arrival, the maid had unpacked his suitcase and arranged all his belongings for him. The Admiral took Ivor to meet his friends the Baden-Powells, who lived nearby at Pax Hill, and there he discovered that their son Peter was also joining R.M.C. Sandhurst at the same time as himself. Lady B-P therefore invited Ivor to spend the night with them before joining and said she would drive them both to Sandhurst. Ivor and Peter entered Sandhurst on 2nd September 1932.

Chapter Thirteen

The Soldier, Frontier Force Regiment – Indian Army 1934–41

IVOR ENTERED THE ROYAL MILITARY COLLEGE, Sandhurst and was placed in No 4 Company of Old College. Like all Gentlemen Cadets, he learnt the hard way under Guards Drill Instructors. He was to become great friends with the B-Ps, who were most impressed by his Scouting record, and many of his early leaves from Sandhurst were spent with them. During the summer vacation Ivor had invited an Australian scouting friend to stay with his grandmother in Southsea, and the two of them went off to the World Jamboree in Budapest in 1933. There they found a use for Latin as being the only lingua franca amongst so many diverse nationalities. Ivor's scouting had stood him in good stead. He had continued his athletics at Sandhurst and represented the R.M.C. against Oxford University. He contracted german measles in the intermediate term and was sent to Aldershot Isolation Hospital. The Army Medical authorities viewed this complaint as likely to have serious effects on the heart if strenuous exercise was undertaken, and for this reason anyone contracting it was taken off all strenuous exercise for several months. He was disappointed to find that he could no longer take part in any athletics.

At the end of Ivor's first year at Sandhurst he was invited to tea with his grandmother's cousin Aileen, Countess Roberts, Field Marshal Lord Roberts' elder daughter. Subsequent to this invitation, Ivor was interested to note that his Company Commander at dinner deigned to engage him in conversation. 'I hear from my friend the Countess Roberts ...' etc. Hitherto he had steadfastly ignored Ivor's existence. Ivor passed out of R.M.C. Sandhurst on 1st December 1933. His position was high enough in the exam. list to ensure him a place in the Indian Army. He was gazetted 2nd Lieutenant, Unattached List Indian Army (ULIA), as from 1st February 1934. In January 1934 he stayed with the Baden-Powells again and went to tea once more with his cousin Aileen at her home, 'The Camp' at Englemere, Ascot. She had been invited to visit the 3rd Bn. (Sikhs) Frontier Force Regiment in 1924, as two of her father's orderlies in the 2nd Afghan War had been from that battalion, then known as the 3rd Sikhs, and Lord Roberts had previously been Commander of the Punjab Frontier Force. The 3rd Sikhs was the battalion which Ivor had always wanted to join. Aileen was in a position to write a recommendation to the Commanding Officer on Ivor's behalf, and this she did.

Meanwhile, Gladys had travelled from Sydney to be in England whilst Ivor was at Sandhurst and she moved in with her mother and sister in Southsea. Before attending Ivor's passing out parade, one of her friends had given her a sword belonging to a man called Anderson and this, with a little silver matchstick holder, was presented to Ivor. Gladys stayed on with her mother after Ivor left for India as Isabella's health was failing and she died in 1935. Gladys, Violet and their brothers sorted out the will and with their share the two sisters bought adjacent semi-detached houses in Grove Road, Southsea. Gladys let hers and returned to her flat in Wycombe Road, Neutral Bay NSW. She now had two houses and a flat all let, bringing in rent, as well as her R.A.N. pension. Ivor augmented this with a monthly allowance as soon as his pay slips began to come in.

Ivor sailed away to his new life in S.S. *Nevasa* on 16th February 1934. On board with him were his companions from Sandhurst who were joining the Indian Army, amongst whom was James 'Tough' Fairweather. He was hoping to join the 4th Gurkhas. Also on board were reinforcements of British troops travelling to India to do their tour of duty with their various regiments. The British Army in India was quite distinct and different from the Indian Army. The former came under the War Office in London, whereas the Indian Army was under the direct control of the Indian Government and the India Office in London. Similarly the Indian Civil Service (the 'Heaven Born') was separate and distinct from the Civil Service in Britain. Both Indian Army and the ICS recruited only from the top of all exam lists. The British Army in India consisted of British Regiments consigned to Regimental tours of duty of 12 years. Their officers and men did tours of three, five, or seven years. The Indian Army, on the other hand, recruited its men, and in the 1930s increasingly its officers, in India. The Indian Officers did their training at R.M.C. Sandhurst, where they joined the select body of men from Britain and the Commonwealth who had chosen the Indian Army as their career. Later the Indian Military Academy was established in India.

Ivor and his friends arrived in Bombay on 9th March 1934. All the young officers destined for the Indian Army were on the Unattached List, and had to serve their first year with a British Regiment. Ivor, James Fairweather and two others were posted to the Highland Light Infantry, then stationed in Peshawar. As was the custom, the regiment had sent four servants to meet them in Bombay. These men were Poonchies from the small state of Poonch adjacent to Kashmir. The HLI was then serving its year of duty in Razmak in Waziristan on the Frontier, and because their tour had been extended, they had not yet returned to Peshawar, so the four young officers had to spend a month with the Welch Regiment in Rawalpindi until the H.L.I. returned. They arrived in 'Pindi on 11th March 1934.

The first thing Ivor did was to settle down to learning Urdu, and on the 9th April they were on their way by train to Peshawar to join the H.L.I. Charles Campbell, Ivor's cousin and grandson of Isabella's eldest sister Fanny Maria, whom Ivor stayed with during his visit to England in 1926–7, joined the train at Nowshera, and they all dined that night in the Peshawar Club. Charles Campbell was serving in the Guides Infantry Frontier Force, and was stationed at Marden.

Ivor and 'Tough' Fairweather (so called on account of his prowess at boxing) found themselves under the command of Lt. Colonel G.G.F.F. Greville, an imaginative and outstanding commander of the 2nd Battalion H.L.I. They had been stationed in Razmak, Waziristan and their record had been so good that the battalion had its customary year-long tour extended by six months, which accounted for their delayed return to Peshawar. They had acquired the nickname on the Frontier of 'Guy Greville's Frontier Force'. However back in the flesh pots of Peshawar, their impeccable record gave way to 53 Courts Martial in 12 months. This was the year in which Ivor, James and the others served with them. These young officers had an unusually exacting experience of peacetime soldiering under the eagle eye of the R.S.M.

During the next six weeks Ivor met Brigadier (later F.M. Auchinleck), a man for whom he had the greatest respect and affection.

The rigours of Indian life were borne in on these young officers when one of their number died suddenly in Rawalpindi. Six weeks after arriving in Peshawar, Ivor succumbed to sandfly fever. However, in spite of minimal treatment, he recovered sufficiently in a fortnight to visit Kohat, where the 3rd Bn (Sikhs) 12th Frontier Force Regiment was stationed, and where he was called for interview. He met the Commanding Officer, Lt. Colonel Macartney, Captain Geoff Vosper and Lt. Peter Higham. The next day he met the Brigade Commander, Brigadier Scott, whose son was two years later so tragically shot and killed in the Shahur Tangi ambush when he was on his way to join the Regiment. Ivor visited the lines of the sepoys or jewans (Indian private soldiers), and the Frontier Force Chapel (St. Augustine's Church). By the end of the second day he was informed by Colonel Macartney that they would accept him into the Regiment. A happy young man returned to Peshawar knowing he was to serve in the Punjab Frontier Force (Piffers), of which his illustrious uncle had been Commandant.

Ivor's last ceremony with the H.L.I. was on the 8th March, when the regiment celebrated Assaye Day by Trooping the Colour.

The great day came on 21st March 1935 when Ivor joined the battalion of his choice, the 3rd Bn. (Sikhs) 12th Frontier Force Regiment, then commanded by Colonel Harry Finnis. Ivor had had to leave his servant with the H.L.I. and he now had to engage another from the recommended list supplied by the battalion. He had the good fortune to inherit a man, Taj Mohammed, commonly known as Albert. Albert was a great character. He had been a 3rd Sikh Mess servant when the Battalion was stationed in Calcutta. The story went that the Mess ran into financial difficulties and Albert and a fellow Mess servant, Frankie, took on extra work at night, reputedly as chuckers out at a brothel, and paid their earnings over to help the Mess out of its difficulties. Albert was a man of infinite resource.

In the next weeks Ivor took a riding course with Probyn's Horse. He visited the Kohat Rifle Factory in the tribal territory beside the road between Kohat and Peshawar, then housed in one shed.

In the Jubilee Birthday Honours of 1935 the 3rd 12th FFR was designated 3rd Royal Bn (Sikhs), and after Independence, the Pakistan Army still refers to it as the 3rd Royal. Life in the Nicholson lines in Kohat went on at a leisurely pace, with training, games and athletics, as well as language study. The young officers were entertained by the married officers and got to know their wives and families. Ivor passed his Urdu exams and was getting on with Pushto. In August he was on leave again, and went to stay with James Fairweather with the 4th Gurkhas in Bakloh, a hill station, and followed that with another training camp for his Scouters at Takhiya. In October the Hindu Festival of Dassehra is celebrated. In the previous year he had been invited to join the celebrations of the 1/7th Rajputs in Peshawar, but now in Kohat it was celebrated in the 3/12th Indian Officers Club, where the Officers' and the Indian Officers' (V.C.O.s) swords were blessed. M.T. malaria caught up with him in October and he went on the sick list. Ivor records extracts from his confidential report for 1935: 'A very keen and intelligent young officer who has worked hard and made distinct progress. He has initiative and common sense and has displayed powers of command and leadership well up to the average. He has taken a great interest in his men and their games and has shown tact in his dealings with all ranks.' (G.G.F. Greville commanding 2 HLI). 'An officer who, if he goes on as he has started, should do very well.' (C.J. Auchinleck, commanding Peshawar Brigade.)

On January 17th 1936 the Battalion left Kohat for Wana in Waziristan and Frontier duties. The training and life style of this non-family station was recorded by Ivor on his ciné camera and is now on video tape with a commentary.

The 3rd Royal Sikhs were now moved to Wana in South Waziristan. The journey was to take the Battalion eight days. They travelled complete with mules and regimental chargers, weapons and ammunition, field telephones, tentage, mess equipment, servants, and personal baggage, although no wireless. Their signalling was done by heliograph and flags. The Brigade Signal Section provided such wireless communication as was then available. The sets were generally unreliable and very bulky, being carried on mules or in trucks. They spent two days in Manzai, unloading the train and reloading for the march to Wana. They left Manzai on 21st January and their first night halt was at Chagmalai. On this march were the Colonel, Paul Meade, Major Arthur Cumming (later VC) and Subalterns Higham, Reford and Ivor. The next day they reached Sarwakai, which was a base for the South Waziristan Scouts and there they spent the second night. Their next two stops at approximately 15-mile intervals were at Dargai Oba and Karib Kot and on 25th the 3rd Sikhs marched into Wana. Stationed in Waziristan at this time were two Brigade Groups, one at Razmak and the other at Wana, also two groups of Scouts, the South Waziristan Scouts and the Tochi Scouts, who came under the jurisdiction of the Political Agents of South and North Waziristan. These were also locally recruited khassadars, tribesmen who joined with their own weapons. So there was a graduated response to tribal outrages, first Khassadars, secondly Scouts and lastly Razmak and Wana Columns. Accommodation at the Wana Camp consisted of tents for the sepoys (jewans) and Wana huts for the officers. These were made of mud walls and a tented roof, and were considered a safe form of housing in earthquake-prone areas. The basic facilities consisted of the water tower and electricity generating equipment. Sanitation was in the hands of the Madras Sappers and Miners.

The young officers soon settled down to camp routine and training. Pickets were posted on a rock in the camp named Gibraltar picket, which provided a good overall view of the surrounding area. Ivor's first experience of going out on column was on 16th March to Tiarza. For entertainment, the officers depended a lot on horse shows, point-to-point racing, polo and drag hunting with the Wana Pack. There was also golf, tennis and swimming in the Mess swimming bath. Regimental recreation consisted of competitions and gymkhanas, athletics and hockey.

Ivor took his first local leave from Wana in April and ran another Scout Training Camp at Takhiya. He had bought a ciné camera and this camp appears on the film. As mentioned earlier, these films have been transferred to video tape. After the camp he visited the Regimental Centre at Sialkot for the first time. Leave was generous and very necessary from the non-family Frontier stations, and the allowance was three short leaves of ten days each, and long leave of three months each year, as well as an eight-month leave every three years to enable officers to visit their homeland. For this purpose the Government opened a 'passage account', into which they paid sufficient money to allow for four first-class passages to England during their service.

After Ivor's leave, the Battalion was out on column again chasing after Abdulla Jan, a renowned bandit from Afghanistan. After this excitement, Ivor visited Razmak to attend the District Promotion Course. Whilst there, he attended the races and was able to take part in one of them. Whilst the battalion was in Wana, it was decided to upgrade the barracks with permanent buildings. A unit of Bengal Sappers and Miners was drafted in to help with this work and battalions took it in turn to make the concrete blocks. In October they moved into their new quarters.

Ivor left Wana to take his first long leave of three months from India and sailed from Bombay on the *Strathaird* for Sydney on 5th November 1936.

On the boat he met Betty Armstrong travelling home with her mother to New Zealand. By the end of the trip they were officially engaged, and they decided that Ivor would visit her family on his next long leave. They kept up a correspondence for the next year. Ivor arrived in Sydney on 26th November and was greeted with joy by his mother, as she had not seen him since he waved her good-bye in England early in 1934. The first part of his leave he spent renewing old friendships in Sydney, and after Christmas he and his mother drove to Adelaide to stay with their cousins the Wellwoods (their respective great-grandmothers were Eliza and Maria Grant). As his leave was only for three months, it did not allow time for a visit to Betty in New Zealand and he sailed back to Bombay from Adelaide in the *Narkanda*. Ivor was an excellent bridge player and on board he made up a four with Lady Cynthia Colville and Algy Heber-Percy, ADC to the Governor-General of New Zealand. They arrived in Bombay on 30th January 1937 and by chance on the train north to Delhi Ivor came across the Baden-Powells attending a Jamboree in Delhi. Ivor joined them and spent a night with the English contingent there before continuing his journey back to Wana. He records his 1936 confidential report, which reads as follows: 'This officer is very keen and active. He is full of confidence and quick on the up-take. He is cheerful and of temperate habits. With more experience he should prove a valuable asset to the Battalion.' (P.A. Meade, Cmdg. 3rd Sikhs).

He wasn't long in the station before being sent on a PT course in Rawalpindi, and on that journey too, he bumped into the B-Ps. In Rawalpindi at the time was the 3rd Sikh Subedar, Major Gurdial Singh, who was being fitted for his uniform as one of King George VI's Orderly Officers, for which task he had been selected. Colonel Meade was also there and he and Ivor went along to make sure everything was done correctly. It was also on this visit that Ivor met Eric Goddard for the first time. Eric was then commanding the 4th/15th Punjabis. On his way back to Wana he was put in command of the escort to the convoy proceeding from Manzai to Wana. A fortnight later Ivor was travelling the road again, this time on his way to the three-month PT course at Kasauli. He left Wana in an armoured car and passing through the Shahur Tangi, he noticed tribesmen on the surrounding hills who should not have been there. He reported this to HQ in Manzai on his arrival there, and having done so proceeded on his way to

Kasauli. Three days later George Scott, travelling to join the 3rd Sikhs in Wana, was killed in an ambush by the same tribesmen whom Ivor had spotted in the hills and whose presence he had reported to the HQ. It happened nevertheless.

At the end of his course, much of which Ivor had filmed for use later in training, he travelled back through Lahore where he ran into R.A.K. (Stinger) Sangster of his battalion, and they breakfasted and lunched to-gether at the Punjab Club. The journey back to Wana this time was in a staff car from Dera Ismail Khan to Manzai and thence by B.T. (Brigade Transport) aircraft to Wana. The road had been closed after the Shahur Tangi massacre. This time he was to stay in Wana until his next long leave. Things had settled down a bit and everyone was able to concentrate more on their recreational activities. Ivor ran the PT courses and organised the athletic events, in which he took part, on one occasion winning the 100 and 220 yard-sprints. Once again these young officers were reminded of India's treacherous climate when another of their comrades died in D.I.K., Captain Kenneth 'Swallow' Swales. September turned out to be an exciting month. Out on Road Protection Duties, they were fired upon and the camp suffered heavy sniping on 28th September. On Column on the 29th Ivor records:

'At 11 a.m. C Company was sent out on Mobile Column. The Battalion followed up an hour later and took up a position near Tiarza. But nothing happened until withdrawal. I was with 'C' Coy and we did the right flank guard and were fired on from close range all the way back. We suffered no casualties.'

'A' Coy went out to protect the Sappers and Miners working on the Inzar-Narai road, and they had to fire on snipers. When the C-in-C visited, it was necessary for them to turn out on road protection duties again. As well as their active service, Ivor was working hard at his language exams, and he passed his oral Pushto in October. He also received a written commendation from the Brigadier for his work on the PT course for the Brigade. The unsettled state of affairs through September culminated in the battle of Inzar Narai. This was undertaken in conjunction with the Brigade from Razmak, where the Rajputana Rifles were serving, and who suffered two casualties in this action. They were all supported by the Crossley Armoured Cars from Razmak.

On 24th November 1937 Ivor flew out of Wana to Kohat on his long leave of eight months. From Kohat he drove to Peshawar, where he stayed with Colonel Eric Goddard. Soon he was on the Frontier Mail for Bombay and embarked on the *Mooltan* for Sydney. On this trip he met a young married woman called Pat, who was visiting her parents who lived in Adelaide, where she disembarked and Ivor went on to Sydney.

Soon he was off again to see his new girl friend Pat in Adelaide, accompanied by his mother, who wanted to attend the Australian Tennis Championships, and they stayed there with the Wellwood cousins.

In New Zealand Betty's family inveigled him into giving talks to local societies on the North West Frontier of India, and he moved all over the country with Betty, visiting her friends and relations. However, he didn't take to the family and broke off the engagement. Back in Sydney he was taking another girl friend to the 400 Club.

At the end of June he sailed on *Nieuw Holland* to Singapore via the East Indies. His photographs illustrate his visits to the islands of Macassar, Bali, Sourabaya, Samarang, Batavia and Singapore, where he stayed with Charles Howell, an Innes Noad cousin. This trip is recorded on his films. He arrived back in Bombay on 22nd July 1938 and was greeted again by Pat.

During Ivor's absence on leave, his Regiment had moved from Wana to the Princely State of Baroda. Although the Princely States were independent of the British Government of India, they often invited Indian Army Regiments to be stationed in their territory. The officers of the 3rd/12th FFR became acquainted with the ruler, the Gaikwar of Baroda, and he was entertained in their mess. Ivor was appointed Acting Adjutant a week after his return and took over from Peter Higham. Doris and Arthur Cumming were in the station with their son Ian during the school holidays and Ivor was often their guest, not only at the house, but also on private expeditions. Doris was an accomplished pianist and her dearest possession was her father's wedding gift, her baby grand piano. Little did Ivor anticipate that she would bequeath it to him for his grandchildren many years later.

In September 1938 Ivor was posted to take over as Adjutant of two Indian Territorial units, the 11th Madras Battalion and the 14th Coorg Battalion. So off he went to Bangalore. En route he stopped in Poona with Dinah, the very amusing and unconventional wife of Gladys' much younger cousin Frank Grant, the youngest son of Ivor's Great Aunt Fanny

Maria Grant of Bedford. Ivor was very fond of Dinah and they went to the races in Poona together. Arrived in Bangalore, Ivor bought his first car, a 1927 Ford, and in November he met and fell in love with a married woman called Dot. This affair went on until he returned to his regiment in Baroda 10 months later. But he did some work too, and earned the following confidential report from his C.O., Lt. Colonel Miller-Hallet: 'A quick and accurate worker who proved his adaptability and powers of organisation in dealing with entirely new conditions and different ideas owing to a change of Commandant. His powers of command and personality were well shown in the way he influenced P.T. throughout the Battalion with improving materials and instructors. Self-reliant and a good judge of men, the Battalion owes a great deal to the work put in, both during and subsequent to training in preparation for next year, by him. Strictly sober in his habits, his manner to his superiors and inferiors in rank was good.' His report from his own Battalion C.O., Lt. Colonel Paul Meade, reads as follows: 'While with the Battalion, his work has been satisfactory. He is keen and alert and is not afraid to express his views. His manner in dealing with all ranks is good and he is of strictly temperate habits.'

Back in Baroda in May 1939 he took and passed his promotion exam. Once again he was Acting Adjutant until the Second World War was declared on 3rd September 1939, when he was recalled to the 11th Madras Regiment.

His work now involved raising the Battalion to war-time strength, and that task completed, organising the Battalion for Railway Security. As Bangalore was too far south for the stretch of track that they were responsible for, the regiment moved at the end of September to Aurungabad. These duties meant much travelling up and down the lines and general reconnoitring. They guarded the first part of the main line from Bombay to Delhi and to Calcutta, as well as the many branch lines off it. Ivor was amused to learn that his nick-name in the battalion was the 'Green Chilli', which was explained as being very sweet and pleasant, but hot! He took the opportunity of visiting the famous Ajunta and Ellora Caves and other antiquities in this part of India. But his main anxiety was to get back to the 3rd Sikhs and to serve with them on active service. To this end he petitioned the C.O. and General Heath commanding 5th Indian Division, but his efforts, although approved by higher authority, proved in vain. When he heard in March 1940 that his application to join the regiment had been cancelled, it came as a great blow to his morale. He put his heart into his Madras regiment and continued to work with dedication and competence.

In May 1940 Ivor moved the Battalion HQ to Deolali, from where it was easy to get to Poona to see Dinah and Frank Grant and attend the races there. Once, after a bad day with the horses, he was playing equally unsuccessfully with a fruit machine when he was interrupted. He turned to find the Gaekwar of Baroda who murmured that he had one token left, so would Ivor mind if he used it? In went the token and out came the jackpot!

In May 1940 Ivor was strongly recommended by his C.O. for a War Course at the Staff College, Quetta. Wishing still to be an active war-time regimental soldier, he turned this offer down. In August 1940 he went to Bombay to say goodbye to the 3rd Sikhs, embarking for service in Eritrea. His main recreation at this time was losing money at the Poona Races. He did not have much luck and was forced to sell his ciné-camera and his car.

At the beginning of 1941 Ivor heard from England of the death of his step-grandfather, Rear Admiral James Stuart R.N. It had been his father's wish to return to his proper surname of Edwards on the death of his step-father. Ivor therefore felt it incumbent upon him now to fulfil his father's wish. He accordingly took the advice of his C.O., Lt. Colonel Miller-Hallett, that to change his name in the middle of a War would result in considerable bureaucratic confusion and possible loss of his name from the lists. He therefore advised adding the name of Edwards to Stuart. Ivor took this advice and through the Residency Orders, Hyderabad, Deccan dated 15th February 1941 he became known as Ivor A.J. Edwards-Stuart from 4th February 1941.

His duties now included escorting Italian prisoners of war who had begun arriving in India, and the Battalion moved to the P.O.W. camp at Jallahali. In April he again tried to get a posting back to the 3rd Sikhs, but was sent instead to the 4th Sikhs back on the Frontier. The Battalion was stationed in Damdil, part of Raz. Col. (Razmak Column) and were constantly on punitive duties, destroying villages and guarding roads, which had to be kept open under guard. These were known as 'Road Open Days'. Considerable unrest was being stirred up by the Germans and their agents in Afghanistan. Serving with the Battalion at this time were Sam Manekshaw and Rathy Sawnhey and with them Ivor was able to make up a very good bridge four. Amongst their various actions against tribesmen, Ivor once found himself in command of the Battalion. They were relieved in October by 7th Kashmir Infantry and they left the Frontier for Wah near Rawalpindi.

Chapter Fourteen

With the 4th Sikhs F.F.R. in Burma 1941–42

O N 1ST NOVEMBER 1941 the 4th 12th (Sikhs) F.F.R. received orders for mobilisation and they left the N.W. Frontier for Wah near Rawalpindi. Ivor's own story follows, written up from diaries and from notes kept on the back of maps in Burma. This account has been lodged in the National Army Museum. Use was made of it by Jimmy Lunt in writing his account of the Burma campaign 1942, *The Retreat from Burma 1941–42*, published by Collins in 1986.

Now follows Ivor's personal account of his part in this campaign.

With the 4th Sikhs F.F.R. in Burma, 1941–42.

Having spent the first year of the War with a Territorial Battalion, and during this time having seen the 3rd Sikhs depart for the Middle East, my posting to the 4th Sikhs in Waziristan in June 1941 was a great disappointment. However, at the conclusion of the Upper Tochi Operations we were again sent back to Wah and rejoined 16 Indian Infantry Brigade under Brigadier Gattie. This was part of the 7th Division commanded by Major-General Wakeley, famous in hunting circles.

On 1st November 1941 we received our orders for mobilisation and equipment poured in on us. In the meantime Brigadier Gattie was promoted Major-General and Brigadier Jones took over 16 Brigade, which then consisted of ourselves (4/12/FFR), 1/9th Jats and 1/7th Gurkhas.

At length on 1st December we left Wah for Calcutta. The trip across India took four days and was by the normal route via Rawalpindi, Amritsar, Ambala, Bareilly, Lucknow, Benares, Patna, Asansol and on to Diamond Harbour. The officers present with the Battalion were as follows:

Commanding: Lt. Colonel W.D. (Donny) Edwards.

2nd in Command: Major R.A.K. (Stinger) Sangster.

Adjutant: Captain Ataqur (Turk) Rahman.

Quarter Master: 2/Lieut. Ata Mohd.

Motor Transport Officer: 2/Lieut. J. Boyd.

Subedar Major: Subedar Major Sukh Ram.

Jemedar Adjutant: Jemedar Abdur Rahman:

Jemedar Q.M.: Jemedar Gurbachan Singh.

Intelligence Officer: Jemedar Fazal Dad.

HQ Company: Captain Ivor A.J. Edwards-Stuart, 2/Lieut. M.P. Warshaw, 2/Lieut. J. Bowerman, Subedar Tikka Khan, Subedar Rangin Khan, Jemedar Promodh Singh, Jemedar Balshlaver Singh.

A Company (Sikhs): Captain Sam Manekshaw, Subedar Balwant Singh, Jemedar Didar Singh, Jemedar Kartar Singh.

B Company (Dogras): Captain D.B. Wallace, Subedar Sundar Singh, Jemedar Prem Singh, Jemedar Tulsi Ram.

C Company (Punjabi Musselmans 'P.Ms'): 2/Lieut. Peter Stewart, Subedar Sukhar Khan, Jemedar Allah Yar Khan, Jemedar Sultan Ahmed.

D Company (Pathans): 2/Lieut. W. Hunter, Subedar Qalander Khan, Jemedar Din Mohd, Jemedar Islam Bahadur.

Although the stay in Calcutta was short, we managed a visit to the Bengal Club and had a very good dinner at Firpo's.

Early in the morning of 6th December 1941 we set sail in the S.S. *Karoo* and had as escort H.M.S. *Exeter* of River Plate fame and later to be lost in the Java Sea. On the outbreak of war with Japan on that same day, she sped off into the blue and left us wondering whether a 3″ mortar or an Anti-Tank Rifle was the best protection against submarines. However, the trip passed off uneventfully and the morning of 9th December saw us in the Rangoon River.

As a unit we were lodged in the local jail and very early on, the G.O.C. Burma, General MacLeod, paid us a visit.

On the evening of 10th December 1941 we left Rangoon in two trains, arriving in Mandalay the following morning. (See Map 1 in the manuscript). In Mandalay we spent a very pleasant three weeks. The War had not yet affected this part of Burma and the Upper Burma Club and the race meetings flourished as normal. Training in jungle warfare was carried out in a half-hearted manner, much against the will of us junior officers, who felt now was the time to learn. We were to pay the cost of this later. Instead all officers were told they should ride motor bikes and I did a hair-raising practice run to Maymyo. On December 23rd we had our first Air Raid Alert, but no bombs were dropped and the aircraft remained unidentified. We had difficulty getting permission from the civilian race committee to remove the wooden railings round the race course in order to have a field of fire for our machine guns, it being assumed that the race course was the most likely place for Japanese paratroops to land. Every machine gun post, therefore, had to be provided with an axe to chop down the fence and railings in the event of a Japanese attack. We were also not allowed to put an observation post on Pagoda Hill, the only prominent high feature.

Both Christmas and the New Year passed off in the normal manner, but at last came the orders to move – on 4th January 1942 – to Tennasserim in the very south of Burma bordering Malaya, which now appeared the threatened area.

At this stage of the War there were only two Indian Infantry Brigades in Burma, 13 and 16 Indian Infantry Brigades and 1 and 2 Burma Brigades. The latter, composed of Burmese, had to be stiffened up with Indian units as the Burmese proved not over-anxious to fight.

We left Mandalay early on 7th morning and arrived at Martaban before dawn the following day. As this place had been bombed a few days previously, absolute chaos reigned and we took the whole day to get across the Salween to Moulmein. On arrival, the 4/12th Sikhs FFR were ordered to join 2nd Burma Brigade commanded by Brigadier Bourke, whilst the remainder of 16 Brigade with a Battalion of Burma Rifles went off to Kawkareik. Besides ourselves, the 7th and 8th Burma Rifles were in Moulmein and 3rd and 6th Burma Rifles at Tavoy and Mergui also came under command. We only spent one day in Moulmein and on the night of the 9th January the 4th Sikhs left Moulmein for Ye, where we arrived early next morning. I was

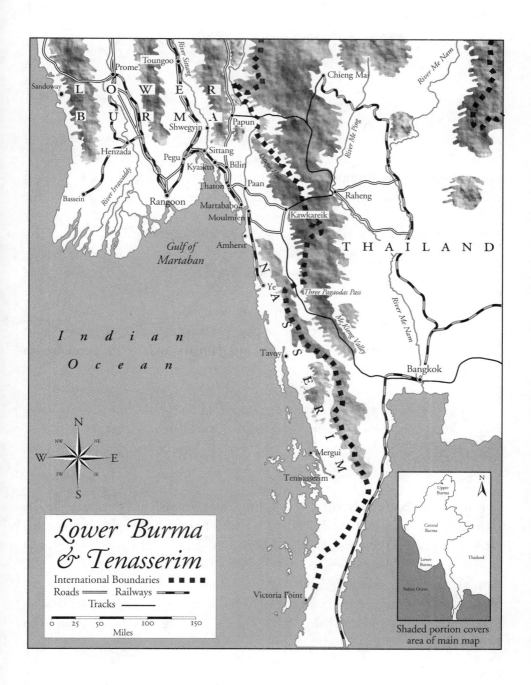

Lower Burma
& Tenasserim

International Boundaries ■ ■ ■ ■
Roads ══ Railways ▬▬▬
Tracks ▬▬▬

0   25   50   100   150
           Miles

Shaded portion covers
area of main map

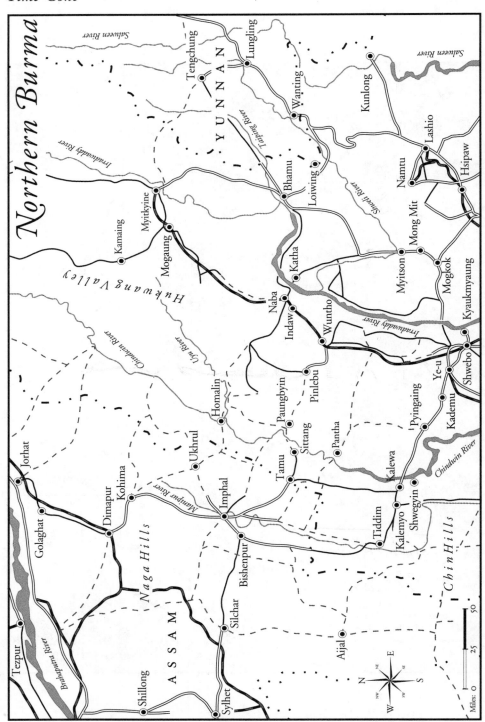

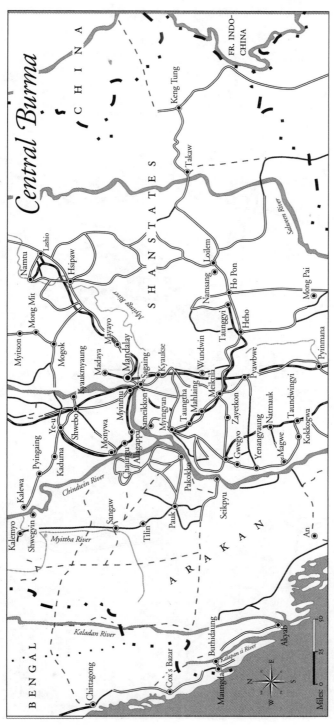

Central Burma

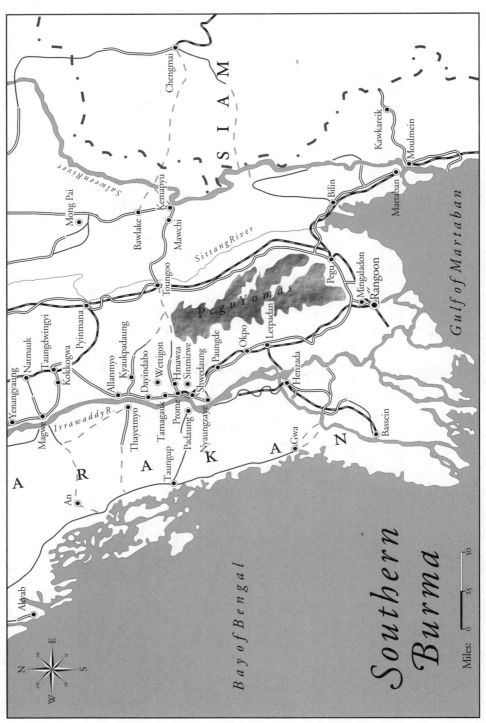

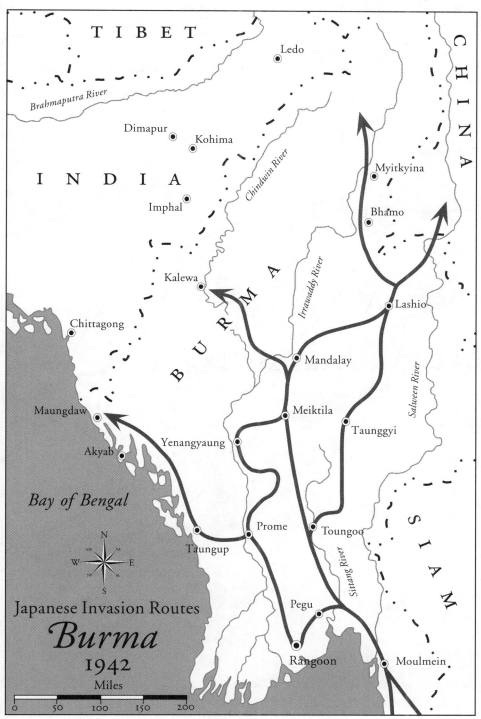

TIBET

Ledo

Brahmaputra River

Dimapur

Kohima

CHINA

INDIA

Chindwin River

Myitkyina

Imphal

Bhamo

Kalewa

B U R M A

Irrawaddy River

Lashio

Chittagong

Mandalay

Salween River

Maungdaw

Meiktila

Yenangyaung

Taunggyi

Akyab

Bay of Bengal

N
NW   NE
W   E
SW   SE
S

Prome

Toungoo

SIAM

Taungup

Sittang River

Japanese Invasion Routes

Burma

1942

Pegu

Miles

Rangoon

Moulmein

0   50   100   150   200

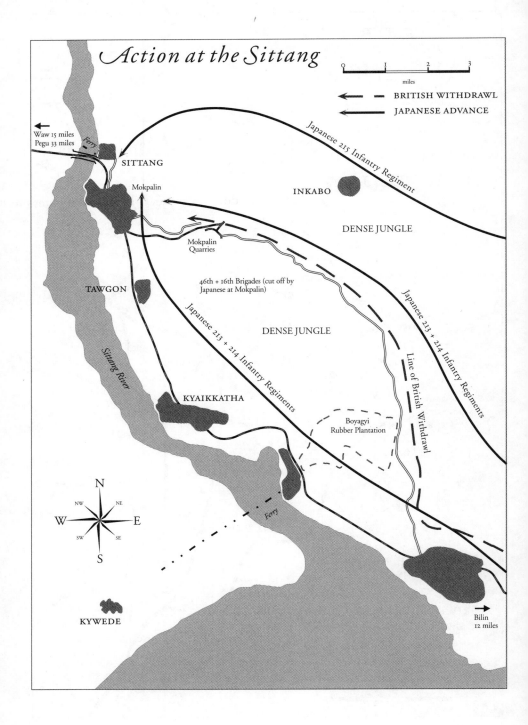

Action at the Sittang

miles

← – – BRITISH WITHDRAWL
← JAPANESE ADVANCE

Japanese 215 Infantry Regiment

Waw 15 miles
Pegu 33 miles

Ferry

SITTANG

Mokpalin

INKABO

DENSE JUNGLE

Mokpalin
Quarries

TAWGON

46th + 16th Brigades (cut off by
Japanese at Mokpalin)

Japanese 213 + 214 Infantry Regiments

DENSE JUNGLE

Line of British Withdrawl

Japanese 213 + 214 Infantry Regiments

Sittang River

KYAIKKATHA

Boyagyi
Rubber Plantation

N
NW NE
W E
SW SE
S

Ferry

Bilin
12 miles

KYWEDE

now again given command of 'D' Coy. with Bill Hunter as Company Officer. At Ye again absolute chaos reigned, as the only method of getting across the river was by sampans, of which only a few were available and each one carried only about eight men or an equal weight of stores. It actually took over two full days to get the Battalion across the river. (The strength of the Battalion numbered between 800 and 900 men.)

At this point in Ivor's narrative I again refer to General Smythe's account of his problems in the hope of giving the reader an overall view of what Ivor and his men were up against.

General Smythe's report after his inspection on 10th January 1942 points out that with an area 800 miles from Mergui to Papum, his forces were impossibly stretched. He describes the garrison at Mergui defending the airfield as a hostage to fortune. It was miraculously rescued by sea under the noses of the Japanese some days later. The garrison at Tavoy, an hour's flight north from Mergui but closer to Japanese HQ in Bangkok, Siam, was equally a hostage to fortune, and General Smythe explains that all he could do was to offer the Commanding Officer, Colonel Cotton, advice as how best to use his small force. Five days later Tavoy garrison was in contact with the Japanese and on 19th Jan. 1942 the remnants of them were struggling back the 150 miles to Moulmein.

Ivor's account continues:

'On the 11th I went on to Kaleinaung about 100 miles further on with 'D' Coy. Kaleinaung had a well appointed Dak bungalow overlooking a river, from where we could see miles and miles of thick jungle extending to the Thai border. It was only on the day after our arrival here that we got the first reports of the Japanese advance along the road to Tavoy. The day after that Wallace arrived with 'B' Coy. and Major Sangster took over command of the detachment. In the meantime we carried out extensive patrolling, including a motor patrol to Tavoy.

I myself took a motor patrol down to Tavoy on the 17th and saw the Area Commander, Colonel Cotton. At that time it looked as if we were temporarily holding the Japs, but even then the Burmese troops did not appear reliable. The following day the news from Tavoy was very bad and evacuees were passing through Kaleinaung all night. No more messages were received except one which afterwards proved to have come from Japanese sources. This was on the 19th January – the day that Tavoy fell – and it was obvious that they had got hold of our cipher code.

Evacuees and fleeing Burman troops continued to pour through Kaleinaung all through the 20th January, and about midnight a report was received of some British officers down the road who could walk no further. As soon as possible I collected some men for escort and went out and collected Colonel Cotton and several of his officers – all in a very bad way. As there was now no point in staying in Kaleinaung, which could easily be by-passed by the Japanese, we withdrew the same evening to Ye to rejoin the Battalion. As we drove down the road, Stinger Sangster driving, I noticed Japanese in the forests on either side of the road. Near Ye I said to Stinger, 'Don't look now, but we are passing through some Japanese.' It was a Division, possibly the 55th, and they did not want to make themselves known to us, hoping they had remained unseen. En route we destroyed three bridges at milestones 28, 42 and 59 from Tavoy.

On the 22nd January '42, according to orders, the whole Battalion withdrew to Moulmein. On arrival there we heard that 16 Brigade had been attacked, beaten up, and were withdrawing. (For interesting descriptions and details of this and other actions see *The Longest Retreat* by Tim Carew.) Incidentally, before leaving Mandalay, Lieutenant-General Hutton had been appointed General Officer Commanding, Burma, not a very bright choice. He was an outstanding staff officer, but had never had command of troops in battle.

The days in Moulmein were spent digging and wiring to make our position on the ridge as strong as possible. However on 26th January I was called away to Kyaikto to join 17 Division as Liaison Officer for 2 Brigade. Major General Smythe was the Divisional Commander. I left Moulmein the same day and from Martaban one could see the glow of fires in Moulmein started by the looters. I arrived at Kyaikto the following day and reported to 17 Div.

On 28th January I again returned to Moulmein with Generals Hutton and Smythe on a visit of inspection. On the way we visited the newly arrived

46 Indian Infantry Brigade commanded by Brigadier R.J. Ekin, a Piffer, and consisting of 7/10 Baluch; 5/17 Dogras; and 3/7 Gurkhas. We also saw 16 Brigade at Thaton. The K.O.Y.L.I. were later to join 46 Brigade and the Duke of Wellington's Regiment 16 Brigade.

On arrival at Moulmein, I learnt that 'A' Coy. was out on a show and had contacted the Japs the previous evening. The remainder of the Battalion was just due to move out. Their object was firstly to contact Major Bourke with a company of 1/7 Gurkhas, who had been cut off at Kawkareik, and if possible also beat up the Japs. I joined them, having sent the General, whom I couldn't contact, a chit to say I had done so. We were rather late setting off and when we met Sam Manekshaw near Mudon, we found he had lost contact and by that time it was too late to go on, so we settled down for the night. The following morning, 29th January, we moved out and went to Tagundaing, where we managed to contact Major Bourke. As he seemed quite confident and there were obviously no Japs in that neighbourhood, we then withdrew to Moulmein, leaving 'D' Coy. with Bill Hunter at Mudon to see Bourke through. Shortly after dawn on the morning of the 30th January we woke up in Moulmein to the sound of continuous small arms and mortar fire with the occasional burst of gun fire. The Japs had commenced their attack. All we had in Moulmein at the time were the 7th and 8th Burma Rifles, much under strength; the remnants of the 3rd and 6th Burma Rifles and the 4th Sikhs, less 'D' Coy. and one Mountain Battery (John Hume), in support.

The battle raged all day and as night fell the advantage was obviously with us, although the Japanese forces were increasing and without reinforcements we could not hope to hold Moulmein for very long. During the day Brigadier Ekin had arrived to take over command of the defence – a most unjustified insult to Brigadier Bourke, a capable and confident soldier. Jimmy Green of the 59th F.F. Rifles also arrived as Brigade Major. In the morning a few stragglers arrived from 'D' Coy. with the story of a night attack which had forced them to withdraw. It was learnt later that fortunately they had very light casualties.

During the night the Japs reinforced their attacking troops and managed to force a position on the left of the ridge. We had learnt a valuable lesson on the challenging of sentries. At one place the Japanese gave the correct pass-word, entered the area, and began firing in the direction of their own troops. Having thus re-assured the garrison, mainly gunners, they then turned upon them and massacred all except one. The situation was obviously deteriorating and early in the morning, before dawn, Brigadier Ekin gave the orders for the withdrawal. The 4th Sikhs were to act as rear-guard to the force. On the whole the withdrawal was carried out very successfully, the Japs not following up too closely. The only difficulty we had was with 'C' Coy., Peter Stewart. As the telephone broke down, I was sent up to arrange for his withdrawal. The situation I found serious and the first thing I knew was a bullet through the radiator of my truck. The situation was now that the Japs were around the flank of 'C' Coy. and in fact we were engaged in house-to-house fighting along the ridge road, and on the left the Japs were actually in the houses on the Moulmein side. However we eventually managed to get the Company out without many casualties.

Fortunately the Japs did not follow us up too closely once we had got clear of the ridge, and we were able to board the last ferry without any further casualties. The trip across the Salween (1 mile) was far from pleasant as the Japs had mounted a couple of infantry guns on the ridge and we were shelled the whole way across. Fortunately only near misses were registered, although several other vessels were hit. The tragedy of the whole show was that owing to the danger of losing all we had on board, we could not stop to pick up survivors of other boats. Many must have been drowned.

On arrival at Martaban the Japs kept up the shelling but little damage was caused although a direct hit was registered on a troop train. I joined Brigadier Bourke and Jimmy Green and went with them to Thaton – HQ 16 Brigade. Later that evening Jimmy and I returned to Martaban to clear the remaining troop trains and we did not arrive in Kyaikto until the early morning of the 1st February 1942. That evening I went to Rangoon to try to replace stores etc. that we had lost at Moulmein. I collected a lot of blankets and other necessary items as well as some whisky. Stinger Sangster went sick the same day so I became 2nd in command and an Acting Major. Just before I left Kyaikto, Bill Hunter arrived in with 'D' Coy., who had had some pretty grim experiences. Both he and Subedar Qalandar Khan got a Mention in Despatches for their part in the isolated action.

I returned to Kyaikto on 3rd February from Rangoon and three days later, on the 6th February, General Wavell visited us. On the 10th I finally succeeded in getting away from HQ 17 Div. and handed over to Bill Hunter my job as Liaison Officer and returned to the Battalion. Shortly after this, 2 Brigade moved further north and we became Divisional troops and later joined 46 Brigade under Brigadier Ekin. The latter had returned to Kyaikto after the battles of Duinzeik, Pa-an and Martaban, in which the Brigade had been pretty badly shattered, but had fought most gallantly against very heavy opposition. In fairness to Brigadier Ekin, it must be added that the dispositions of his Brigade were forced upon him against his own better judgement.

The situation was now that 16 and 48 Brigades were holding a position along the Bilin River. On the 18th February we received information that it was thought that the Japs were trying to outflank the position and we were ordered to clear the left flank of the forward areas. We embussed at about 2000 hrs and were taken down to the 71 MS near Alugale. From there we set off at 0100 hrs along the jungle track to Alugyi. We arrived at the track junction just south of Alugyi at dawn and turned right towards Paingdawe. As the jungle was thick and every inch on either side of the track had to be cleared, the going was terribly slow and it took us about 4 hours to reach Paingdawe. We halted there for a while. By 1400 hrs we had reached the bottom of the slopes of the hill feature NE of Paingdawe. I was then ordered to take 'C' and 'D' Coys. (2/Lt. Peter Stewart and Subedar Qalandar Khan) and clear the hill.

The attack commenced at about 1500 hrs. On arrival at the bottom of the hill, it was found that it was impossible to ascend it except in single file owing to the thickness of the bamboo. Even then we had to cut every inch of the way with dahs. We had almost got to the top of the hill without incident when we reached a small clearing. Jemedar Allah Yar Khan, who had moved over to the left, reported that he thought some enemy were ahead of him. Suddenly all hell seemed to be let loose in the form of mortars and machine guns. We suffered heavily. During the next few minutes, owing to the thickness of the jungle, contact was lost with the two rear platoons of 'D' Coy. and a platoon of 'C' Coy., neither of which took any further part in the battle. Peter and I with two platoons got in an attack which drove the Japs out of their forward positions. We had been suffering casualties the whole time and now had very few men left. Already I had lost two valuable N.C.O.'s in Havildars Ghulam Hussein and Wakil Shah and the only remaining N.C.O. of the platoon was seriously wounded. We made three more attempts to cross a small gap, but each time were driven back with heavy losses. The enemy remained unseen in the jungle. Peter now attempted to get round the right flank but all that happened was that I eventually lost contact with him. I now only had four men left and Subedar Qalandar Khan. He went off to contact Peter. As he was disappearing into the jungle, I suddenly saw about thirty Japs approaching him from a flank. I shouted and we took up fire position to cover him back. He failed to heed my warning and went straight for them. I saw no more and we could do nothing. Shortly after this, I decided it was useless to continue. Having evacuated all wounded, I withdrew back to the Battalion with my small party. Peter Stewart with his men had also withdrawn. We spent the night on the Bilin River with 16 Brigade. Continuous firing went on all night and the Japs made several attempts to penetrate the position without avail. For this show Peter received an MC; Subedar Qalander Khan a posthumous IOM; Jemedar Allah Yar Khan IDSM and the following were Mentioned in Despatches: myself, Subedar Sukhru Khan and Naik Makhmad Din Shah. I had actually put both these latter in for IDSM. (Ivor too was recommended for MC).

On the morning of the 20th February the whole force broke off contact and withdrew to Kyaikto. Of the two rear platoons of 'D' Coy. who disappeared on the ridge above Bilin, the Pathan Orakzais drifted in. I put the Platoon Commander under close arrest and as this caused restlessness amongst the Orakzais, I instructed my orderly/gunman, Ghanum Gul, to put my camp bed in their lines and said I would sleep there that night, which I did. (Officers at that time went into battle armed only with a revolver. For that reason they always had a gunman who was probably also their orderly. Later officers were armed with sten guns when available.) Early on the 21st February the Japs made an attack on the Division and owing to the hasty way the troops had been pushed into position by night, panic and confusion reigned until daylight. That morning the Division again withdrew to Mokpalin, whilst we went straight back in MT to take up a position on the bridgehead for the Sittang River. We were bombed and machine gunned the whole way and progress was slow. Bombing us, besides the Japanese, were the Indian Air Force. This unpleasant attack from our friends stopped when one of the pilots who had transferred to the IAF Naranjan Prasad, recognised his battalion and reported the faulty bomb-line to HQ. Our wireless sets were extremely temperamental when we had any and communication and identification extremely difficult in the terrain in which we were fighting. Gurkhas, Burmese and Japanese all looked rather alike and mistaken identity was inevitable in the general confusion. We didn't actually arrive at the bridge until late in the evening and we went into reserve, intending to take over the forward line at first light.

The Japs meanwhile had done a wide outflanking move and came in behind the remainder of the Division and attacked the bridgehead. The Burmans in front panicked and ran and we had to push in a sudden counter attack with 'A' Coy. (Sikhs) under Sam Manekshaw and 'B' Coy. (Dogras) under Wallace. This managed to retrieve the position, although we suffered heavily and Manekshaw was among those wounded. He later received an MC for this action. Brigadier Hugh-Jones later came and took over command of this area. In the afternoon very heavy artillery fire caused us to evacuate the bridgehead but we re-occupied it again at nightfall.

As the only news of the rest of the Division was that it had been cut to pieces (inaccurate as it later proved), it was decided to cut our losses and withdraw. We did so at about 03.30 hrs. At a conference on the bridge with Brigadier Hugh-Jones, Joe Lentaigne (C.O. 1st/4th Gurkha Rifles), Donny Edward (C.O. 4th/12th F.F.R.) and me as 2nd in command, it was apparent we could hold out no longer and we therefore decided that the bridge must be blown. It was, at 5.30 a.m.

We then occupied a position on the western bank of the river. Sitting on the banks of the Sittang with Turk Rahman, some shells fell close. I recognised them as coming from John Hume's Mountain Gun on the other side of the river. I knew it was his from serving with him on the Frontier. It was later learnt that Bill Hunter was missing from the previous day's operation. He had last been seen trying to get through with a message. At about 9.00 hrs that morning (23rd) some of our troops suddenly appeared on the east bank of the river. The numbers gradually increased and masses of men began to swim the river. Most of them succeeded in getting across, but once again many must have been drowned and all equipment was lost.

That evening, 23rd February, we did a long and weary march withdrawal to Pegu 30 miles away, where we arrived the following morning and joined 48 Brigade at Kale Camp. We didn't remain with them long and on the 26th again returned to 16 Brigade. Two days later we moved to Hlegu, another 30 miles on. On the 2nd of March General Wavell again visited us and we learnt with pleasure that General Alexander had taken over Burma Army and Brigadier Cowan had taken over 17 Division. I encountered a Sergeant of the Duke of Wellington's who carried a sackful of primed grenades. He assured me that it was only the last one that was dangerous. He said, 'Now we'll win, Sir'. I wished I could share his confidence.

On the 3rd March I went to Rangoon for the last time. It had become a dreary city of silence. Not a Burman was to be seen and all around were signs of previous looting and rioting. On the 6th March I took a patrol out to Kya-in-aste and on my return was greeted with the announcement that I was now commanding the Battalion as Donny Edward had taken over 63 Brigade. This Brigade had only just arrived and had lost two Battalion Commanders and two Adjutants killed and the Brigadier and the Brigade Major and the third C.O. wounded in an ambush. I managed to reinforce our Battalion by collecting up some of the Baluchi and Jat regiments who had got lost in the confusion. (Years later, at an Indian Army Reunion, a man introduced himself to Ivor as one of the Baluchis with him in Burma. 'I will always remember you in those days, you always looked so cheerful').

The general situation was now far from pleasant. 48 Brigade (Gurkhas) were in Pegu with a strong road block south of them and the Japs pressing from the north. 16 Brigade were at Hlegu and 63 Brigade at Taukkyan with another road block north of them on the Prome Road. 46 Brigade by this time had ceased to exist. Rangoon had been evacuated and the sky was black with smoke.

On the morning of 8th March we moved to Atukkyan to assist 63 Brigade in forcing the road block whilst 48 Brigade were given the task of breaking out of Pegu, which they eventually did after a very hard fight. We were bombed and machine-gunned most of the day, but had no really hard fighting although the Japs got in amongst us several times with their mortars and light machine guns. General Alexander happened to be on the Rangoon side of the road block. He sent for me as C.O. of the 4th Sikhs and said:

'I have just arrived in Burma and I don't intend to be put in the bag to-day. I want you, when I give the order, to take your Battalion round the left flank of the road block.' Fortunately before the order came, 63 Brigade broke through the road block. I later discovered that the Japanese Commander, sticking rigidly to his orders to take Rangoon as a priority, had sent his main force around his right flank, namely on our left, thus reducing the road block. Fortunately as 63 Brigade had broken through, I was not ordered by General Alexander to advance, otherwise I would have met the main Japanese force head on. Instead we picketed the road to Hmawbi and then did a long cross-country move by night. The following morning we moved by M.T. to Taikkyi and thence by train to Keikia.

The long and dreary withdrawal to Prome now began. Day after day we were bombed and machine-gunned from the air but other than normal patrol activities, had no major clash with the Japs. On the 13th we moved north of Tharrawaddy and thence by train to Okpo. We only stayed there for two days and on the 15th moved to Thegaw and took up a position in the Myauk-chung area. The Colonel returned on the 18th and on the 20th we withdrew to Zigon. We stayed in Zigon for six days and on the 26th left by rail and route march and arrived in Paungdale, east of Prome, on the morning of the 27th March. While we were at Zigon, General Slim became Corps Commander of 17 Division (16, 48 and 63 Brigades) and BurDiv (1 and 2 Burma Brigades and 13 Brigade).

The 7th Armoured Brigade had arrived in Burma before the evacuation of Rangoon, and was doing extraordinarily good work with very part-worn tanks. Air support was now nil. It was the intention to concentrate Burma Corps in the Prome area, but this was not successfully accomplished. On 28th March I was sent out with a carrier patrol from the Duke of Wellington's to contact 5 Burma Rifles, who were coming across country from Toungoo. We met them at Pauntan.

Early the following morning, 29th March, we received orders to move south from Paungdale through Prome and secure Shwedaung and Modaing in order to see some British troops through who had been fighting further south. Two or three miles south of Prome we were met by a Liaison Officer who informed us that not very far from where we were, a police detachment had been fired on and that we would have to clear carefully all the scrub on both sides of the road. We debussed and moved slowly forward. We had got through the scrub and on towards a small village through which the road ran when we were met with heavy fire. A fierce battle began and 'C' and 'D' Coys. attacked the village. They made a certain amount of progress but could not clear the village and suffered quite a lot of casualties. However they attacked again and I went over to command 'D' Coy. By this attack and by firing the village at the same time, we managed to clear it after a stiff fight and were well rewarded. Three M.Gs., a dozen L.M.Gs and about a hundred rifles were captured. The enemy, a mixed force of Thakins (Burmese traitors) and Japanese, had suffered heavily. We alone captured 97 Thakins, and the rest of the battalion had been killed to a man. This was the first time we had met the Thakins and they fought well until discovered, but after that cringed for mercy.

Having reorganised, we pushed on to Shwedaung, where we contacted the main Japanese force (later estimated to be an infantry regiment), which was holding the road block. Shwedaung was a large village surrounded by jungle. One flank of the enemy rested on the Irrawaddy and the other in the foothills of the Pegu Yomas. A three-company attack, 'C' Coy. on the left, 'D' Coy. in the centre and 'B' Coy. on the right, was pushed in, but although 'B' Coy. made a certain amount of progress and got into the edge of the village, the attack came to a standstill and Wallace and Jemedar Tulsi Ram were wounded. We made several more attempts to get in but 'B' Coy. kept on losing heavily and we eventually had to relieve them with 'A' Coy. At one point I was confronted by a Thakin. He raised his rifle, I aimed my revolver at him, fired and missed. I started to laugh, knowing what a rotten shot I was with a pistol, but Ghanam Gul, quick as a flash, raised his rifle over my shoulder and shot him dead. Almost immediately Jack Boyd and Jemedar Kartar Singh were killed, but the Company held their position in the jungle and accounted for many Japs, although they themselves were unable to make any headway. Before nightfall the 56th F.F. Rifles arrived to our assistance but it was too late to do anything and we withdrew into a box for the night. We had suffered over sixty casualties. Offensive patrolling continued all night and many clashes occurred.

Early on the 30th March both Battalions had another crack at clearing Shwedaung, but again we were driven back. The main trouble was that we had a great expanse of paddy to cross, with its little banks and ditches, before we reached the jungle, and the Japs had received strong reinforcements during the night. It was later estimated that the Japs were about 5000 strong (against our 1500). The British offensive from the south had also failed and there were now five road blocks in the village itself. At one point the Colonel was sitting by the roadside and I was standing behind him. Suddenly he asked: 'Why did you kick my backside?' To which I replied: 'Sir, I did not kick you. I think a Jap bullet has just hit you, as I can see blood on your shorts.' Sure enough a bullet had ripped through his clothing and grazed his buttocks.

At about 1500 hours we made our final attack. I was now commanding the Battalion. We went in astride the road and this time managed to clear quite a large amount of the village, including the first road block, without too many casualties. As we had not gone very wide, mortars and snipers kept at us the whole time but most of the transport and troops were able to get through from the south. During this time the Japs were very persistent in their dive bombing, but although we were not dug in, they caused very little damage.

At about 1700 hours the order to withdraw came through and we plodded sixteen miles along the road to Pauktaw, N.E. of Prome. The troops' morale was high for although we had had our casualties and had not been completely successful, we had hit the Japs a damn good crack and the troops knew it.

We had one day's rest in Pauktaw and on the night 1st–2nd April the Japs launched their offensive on Prome. Throughout the night there was heavy mortar and MG fire and some very stiff fighting, but the odds against us were too much and another withdrawal became a certainty. We were the last to withdraw and our positions were pounded by mortars and artillery before we got the orders to move. The troops were grand and put up a first-class show. If the Japs had but known, only one weak Battalion had been facing a regimental group (equal to a strong brigade) for over twelve hours. We had a long march of 18 miles that day and as usual the Jap Air Force were with us the whole way. At one stage we learnt that a Jap column was six hours ahead of us on a parallel road. We learnt from captured orders that our forced march had taken them by surprise, as they had not expected us to cover such a distance after so much continuous fighting.

Another long withdrawal had now started, marked by no major clashes, but only by sweaty marches, continuous patrolling and incessant Jap air activity. Ywataung, Allanmyo, Mogaung and Nyaungbintha – we saw them all en route to Taungdwingyi, where we arrived at last on the 8th April – a total withdrawal from Prome of 130 miles.

Many hours were spent digging and wiring Taungdwingyi, but in the end to no avail. Although in a fierce battle in the centre of the Corps the Japs were driven back and suffered heavy casualties, in the end, owing to considerations on other parts of the front, we again had to withdraw. We went by Myothit and Natmauk. We stayed in Natmauk for about a week to see 17 Division through, and we were engaged with the Japs on the road towards Monywa. When clearing this road block, some Cameronians were sent to support us. I was standing next to one of their men who was well-armed with a 2″ mortar while he waited for his sergeant to catch up with him and I saw him shot with a sniper's bullet between the eyes. He fell and for some moments looked as though he were asleep. Then I had the extraordinary and overwhelming spiritual revelation that I was aware of the moment this man's soul left his body, for he then looked quite dead.

On the 23rd we again moved and took up positions at Ywarrum, Mahlaung and Ondaw, but our halt was at the Ava Bridge over the Irrawaddy. Whilst holding the bridgehead, we were supported by a unit of the Chinese Army. But they melted away in the night leaving our flank unprotected. During the next few days we spent guarding the bridgehead at Sagaing, we were very heavily bombed by the Japs but eventually the 17th Division came through and once again we got clean away. It was in this area that we first faced the refugee problem. A continuous stream were coming through the whole time and cholera and smallpox were rife. Owing to the number of deaths on the road and the heat, the stench was indescribable. We had to dig trenches for the dead, and cover them in.

On the 24th April we again moved back via Nyaungin, Sadaung, Ye-u, until after a hair-raising 28-hour drive through teak forests we at last arrived on May 3rd at Shwegyn on the banks of the Chindwin. We had to abandon most of our remaining stores here and then crossed over in ferries, a two-hour trip to Kalewa. We were then sent off to Kalemyo to protect the flank of Burma Corps against a suspected Jap move up the Gangaw Valley. At

Kalemyo was a large monastery and I took some men with me to make sure the Japanese were not already in residence pretending to be Buddhist monks. I ordered a strip search of all the monks, but finding them bone fide, I apologised and left them. On 10th May I recced Imbaung, where Burma Army HQ had been and there found a very frightened little dachshund bitch. Ghanum Gul fetched her out of the bushes and we found she had been wounded by a bomb splinter. We dressed her wound and wrapped her in a first field dressing and she stayed with me for the rest of my march out of Burma. She was quick to jump into a slit trench when the need arose, lying beside me if I was fortunate enough to be in a car or a truck, or trotting alongside me on the march. She slept in my blanket and we kept each other warm, and Ghanum Gul fetched titbits to feed her from the cooks. I called her Susan. The Japs bombed us again, but the suspected Jap move turned out to be Burma Brigade coming up the road.

On the 13th May 1942 the final move was made and we moved slowly up the Tamu Valley via Inbaung, Yasagyo, Kanpet the 90 miles to Tamu. There it was very cold and I cradled Susan inside my jacket to keep her warm. I took the forward unit on by truck into Imphal, where we arrived on 20th May. No one expected to see us and certainly not in the numbers which finally struggled into Imphal. 17th Division came in marching, heads held high, each man with his rifle, even if his boots, if any, were worn out and his clothing ragged. A Regiment from the State of Kashmir were mightily impressed by our soldierly bearing after five months of a fighting retreat.

Of the officers of the 4th Sikhs who started out from Calcutta in December 1941, we returned with Lieut. Colonel Donny Edward, Major Ivor Stuart, Captains Turk Rahman, Wallace and Stewart, Lieutenants Warshaw, Bowerman, and Ata Mohammed, and about half the Battalion strength, namely 400 VCOs and men.

The campaign was now over and considering that it had been a continuous withdrawal of about 1200 miles, morale was exceedingly high. On the whole, after the Battle of Rangoon, Burma Army had given a good account of themselves whenever they had met the Japanese and it was only lack of supplies, communications and troops that led to this withdrawal. The 17th Division fully avenged themselves at the Battle of the Pegu Yomas in 1945.

After arriving at Imphal, the men of Burma Corps were dismayed to find that Imphal was so poorly garrisoned that they were to have to stay to reinforce it. Ivor remained with the 4th Sikhs in Imphal, being one of the fittest. After the five long months of incredible hardship and uncertainty, the first imperative for the Battalion was to get the sick and wounded evacuated and the others away on leave. One Sikh Naik had returned on leave to his village and was telling the assembled villagers of his adventures in Burma. His grandfather asked him what had happened to Pegu.

'We lost it', answered his grandson.

'When my father was in the 4th Sikhs in the 2nd Burma War in 1853 they won Pegu,' said his grandfather. 'Now you go straight back and don't come home until you've recaptured it'. Such was his stern instruction to the young Naik. The boy returned to the Battalion and did not venture home on leave again until 17th Division recaptured Pegu in 1945. A triumphant warrior was able to return to his village with his head held high.

The Battalion eventually moved to Ranchi in September 1942. Ivor was granted three months' leave, and left for Calcutta on 23rd July 1942 with his orderly/gunman Ghanum Gul and Susan the dachshund. In Calcutta he bought all the back numbers of the newspapers which carried accounts of the War, and the War in Burma in particular, and these he pasted into the beginning of his account of the retreat, which he wrote up from the notes he had made on the back of his maps. It is from this manuscript and its maps that the foregoing account has been taken.

He travelled to Poona and spent his leave there with his cousins Dinah and Frank Grant. They had been looking after Ivor's beloved red setter Simon, to whom he now introduced Susan, the dachshund.

At the end of his leave Ivor was posted to the 8th/12th FFR and the parting of the ways now came for Ivor and Ghanum Gul, who had so faithfully shadowed Ivor throughout the retreat and had saved his life in Shwedaung. Ghanum Gul returned to the 4th Sikhs. During his leave Ivor had renewed his application to return to the 3rd Sikhs, part of 8th Army. But one of his erstwhile comrades had just finished the Staff College course, so he was posted back to the 3rd Sikhs and Ivor sent to the 8th/12th.

Ivor joined the 8/12th at St. Thomas' Mount, Madras. Dennis Slattery was 2nd in Command to Colonel John Redding, so Ivor came in over Dennis' head, which was not a popular move. The task of the Battalion was to train for the recapture of Burma as part of 19 Division and officers with experience in Burma were invaluable. Ivor now moved all over Southern India, reconnoitring and on endless divisional exercises. Sadly he had to put down his red setter at the end of the year, but he still had Susan.

In 1943 Ivor became the anchor man for the 8th/12th, which suffered a succession of commanding officers coming and going. In February Geoff (Jam) Vosper arrived to command and went sick, so Ivor commanded until Victor Wainwright appeared in April as temporary C.O., only to disappear shortly afterwards. So Ivor was again in command until Colonel Jerrard arrived in June. The result of this was that Ivor never succeeded in doing three consecutive months in command, which would have given him war substantive promotion to Major.

In July Ivor took leave and went to Kashmir, where he found himself in the same hotel as his 2nd cousin, Marjorie Barber, sister of Charles Campbell. She was married to Philip Barber of 10th Baluch Regiment. They had one daughter Pamela who was at school in England being looked after by her grandmother Hilda, the only married daughter of Fanny Maria Grant, Isabella's eldest sister.

Back with the 8th/12th and after a long and tedious day without a driver, Ivor crashed his jeep and his beloved Susan, the dachshund, was killed.

1944 dawned badly for Ivor. In January he contracted tick typhus. Knowing he had a high fever, he dosed himself with aspirin, crawled under his mosquito net, lit a cigarette and fell asleep. He woke to find his bed alight and himself badly burnt on the left side of his neck and over his shoulder. He was admitted to No. 38 British General Hospital in Bangalore, and treated with triple dye, the then modern treatment for severe burns. The M.O. mistook the high fever for an infected wound, in spite of Ivor's protestations that he never went septic. He explained that he had had a high fever, which was the reason for the burn in the first place. However the doctor insisted on the triple dye being stripped from the burn, an agonisingly painful procedure, only to find a clean wound without sign of infection. They finally diagnosed tick or scrub typhus. He was fortunate to survive this deadly disease, one of the few who did in those days. He stayed in hospital having treatment and eventually skin grafts. He endured one operation a month for the next three months. He was eventually discharged on 14th May 1944.

He went to Simla to convalesce, where Frank Grant was now stationed. Ivor had travelled with a Maharani who had several dachshunds, and she told Ivor how splendidly they protected her from snakes and scorpions. He eventually acquired another dachshund to replace Susan and called her Gretel. Another of his encounters on his travels was with a Gurkha officer who had also been at the Battle of the Sittang. In discussing the fog and confusion of that action, they reluctantly came to the conclusion that at one point they must have been fighting each other.

Ivor's next posting was to the Regimental Training Centre at Sialkot at the special request of Colonel John Redding, who was commanding there. Ivor was not enthusiastic, wanting as ever to get back to the battle fronts. He was declared fit in July for promotion and for command. Amongst his assorted duties at this time, one was to close the Piffer Mess in Kohat, where John Furness was stationed as Staff Captain. In August, back in Sialkot, he was given command of Specialist Battalion, which included the Boys' Company, akin to the British Junior Leaders Regiments. Ivor was back on the familiar and favorite ground of youth training, of which he had had so much experience in the Boy Scout Movement.

In January 1945 he was Acting Second-in-Command and at the end of the month was promoted temporary Lieutenant-Colonel and War Substantive Major. In February he went on a pre-staff College course of one week in Agra, and he was able to visit the ancient monuments there of great beauty and antiquity.

It had not been a happy or fulfilling year for him, and he found himself drinking ever more heavily, a temptation never far away in the heat and the monotony. But change was around the corner. On 22nd March 1945 he was admitted to the British Military Hospital in Sialkot and his diary records: 'Met Elizabeth.'

᎒᎒ Part Three ᎒᎒

Marriage and Travel Home

Chapter Fifteen

The Young Married Couple
Marriage – India 1945

IVOR'S AND MY WEDDING PARTY arrived in Lahore on 19th May 1945 and went straight to Falettis, where rooms had been booked. The temperature was 104F. After breakfast and a wash I went off to collect my wedding dress.

We were married in the heavenly cool of Lahore Cathedral at 6 p.m. Elsa, who had a lovely voice, sang for us.

We had four weeks leave and we went to Simla to meet Ivor's cousins, Frank and Dinah Grant, and Marjorie and Philip Barber. Simla was unbelievably beautiful and I welcomed the cool fresh mountain air. We had a lovely room looking out on to the mountains in a comfortable hotel. I found I had a gentle, considerate and kind lover. We were very happy and content and did not think too much about the future and the separation that would inevitably come.

We had not been a week in Simla on our honeymoon when I received warning of a posting for field service. Ivor immediately composed telegrams to Sialkot and to HQ Delhi to the effect that I was now married and no longer eligible for field service. Having ascertained the movements of the Dak runner, we set off for Narkanda by car to the Dak bungalow there. By returning on foot, we would be able to keep ahead of him and so complete our honeymoon without further official communication being able to reach us.

I wrote home:

24th May 1945,

My darlingest Moma,

I can't tell you how upset I was when by the 19th I had had no reply to my wire. However the only Sister left on duty at B.M.H. that day had instructions to phone through to Faletti's in Lahore if any cable arrived. Imagine the sinking feeling I got when your and Elise's cables came. Yours saying 'Elise only informed' and I realised with horror that Elise had taken you the news. By now I hope my long and lengthy wire has reached you. I did long for a word from you before I got married. I can't describe to you how homesick I have felt. However that misery is now over, Ivor having bullied me out of it. Ivor has just read up to this full stop, and decided that I hadn't even told you that we are married! Well, we are, thank God, and life is marvellous. I'm not going into ecstasies over anything, for you know and have lived it all yourself.

Now for some real news. The last few days before the wedding were really awful, and I was as miserable as could be, no mail, wondering whether I was sane, wondering what and when I was going to pack. Flat spin was the description. However, after the Colonel's party on Thursday evening and receiving the blessing of Ivor's regiment, we got ready to leave Sialkot on Friday. Elsa came with me, and six of Ivor's brother officers, one having already gone on. A wire came from George Sawday, who was to have given me away, to say he couldn't make it, so we had to swop round the best man, and Johnnie gave me away, by virtue of being a married man, and Chris became best man.

We arrived in Lahore at 6.30 a.m. and the cavalcade made its way to Faletti's hotel, where we had rooms booked for us. Elsa and I bathed and changed, had breakfast and were whisked off to the hairdresser. After that to the Gown House where my frock was being made, They had turned up trumps and had everything practically ready for me. The wedding frock looked tops. After the fitting I was whisked off to interview the Archdeacon. He was very nice and we kissed the Bible and signed forms and surveyed the scene inside the Cathedral. We decided, with Elsa's help, on the music. The Archdeacon warned Ivor that if he, the Archdeacon, was late, to get hold of him at the golf club!

After this we all congregated at Faletti's for lunch. All our guests had had a pretty busy time organising everything from train accommodation to drink and flowers. After lunch Elsa and I left the party and had a rest. Strangely enough I slept. At five to six Johnnie turned up and of course I wasn't ready. The flowers, white carnations, had arrived and in true Indian fashion, were all wrong. So I had to sit down and pick two posies to bits and make them into a spray. My face streamed with sweat when I tried to make up, and when Johnnie came I hadn't even my frock on. However we made the Cathedral in a be-garlanded car. The service was beautiful and most inspiring and the Cathedral was a haven of coolness after the heat outside. We had one hymn, 'The King of Love my Shepherd is', which Elsa and the Archdeacon rendered between them. The ring nearly didn't go on and got stuck on my knuckle, but I suppose this always happens! Johnnie gave me away with the wrong hand, probably due to the fact that coming down the aisle with him, I nearly broke his little finger in agitation. Afterwards we all stood and had photos taken. I felt like a Cheshire cat. Ivor and I climbed into the flower-bedecked car and felt rather like the baboos on a day out. We had a quiet (?) reception in a room to ourselves. One of the others had managed to get some hock. I swallowed two glasses right off. Then I was called to the phone. This was Mari ringing from Sialkot with your wire. Had I not been well-sustained by good wine and the relief of the wedding being over, I think I would have passed right out. Ivor presented me with the most lovely pearl necklace. Of course my first reaction was to bite the pearls, much to Johnnie's horror. Ivor is used to the way I accept presents! They are really lovely. I haven't got an engagement ring yet, Ivor wants to wait until he can get a decent one. I then changed and at 8.30 we piled into a car and took off for the station. There we found a very comfortable compartment which took us through the night to Kalka. A taxi, organised by Frank Grant, met us and we drove the 60 miles from Kalka to Simla through increasingly inspiring scenery. Now we are perched on one hilltop and look across at another hilltop with most of Simla clustering up its slope. It is lovely at night when everything is lit up. As no cars, except those of the Viceroy, the Governor of the Punjab and the C-in-C, are allowed on the one road in Simla, the taxis have to park at the bottom of the town. Here one is met by a conglomeration of rickshaws and coolies. We were also met by Dinah Grant. We then piled into a rickshaw each and watched a procession of coolies set off with our valises and baggage balanced precariously on their shoulders. The rickshaws here are one-seaters only, drawn by four coolies. Ivor and I are very popular with the rickshaw wallahs, being very light weights! We were then dragged up the most terrific slopes. I was terrified the coolies would cave in and I would fall backwards down the hill.

After lunch we buzzed off in the rain, completely enclosed in our rickshaws, to our present abode. We have a lovely room, dressing room and bathroom. Very big and comfortable. Main Gul, Ivor's orderly, is most intrigued by the new arrangement.

Please forgive me for the shocks and all the sleepless nights you must have had on my account. But I'm happy darling, so please be happy with me.

All love and please write a nice letter soon,
your loving, but awful daughter, Elizabeth.

Time Gone

Darlingest Moma,

On arrival back yesterday from a trek, a marvellous batch of mail from home awaited us. I can't tell you how much it cheered me up to hear from you at last and to hear that you were happy about me. I imagine the letters I wrote you during the fortnight before I was married were completely haywire and that you must have thought I was quite off my rocker. Yesterday Ivor was like a dog with two tails and an 'I told you so' expression on his face, having had to console me on the absence of mail for the past 14 days.

My last letter from Simla told you of the wedding and the week's activities. The next day a chit came from Sialkot warning me to stand by for an immediate posting for field service. You just can't imagine Ivor's wrath. We sent telegrams all over the place and thanked God we had made the wedding safely. I must say I wasn't expecting it, but Ivor said he was amazed I got to the wedding without an intervening posting. Poor old Elsa, whose wedding is on the 12th June, all in white and being married from the house of one of the Colonels, has been posted miles into the blue. Ivor then ascertained the movements of the Dak runner, booked a car and we hastily packed a bedding roll, and a well-stocked tiffin basket and took ourselves, Main Gul and Gretel up to Narkanda (10,000 ft), 40 miles from Simla on the road to Tibet. It was very wild and beautiful and Tibet lay 150 miles on. We planned to stay there for 3 or 4 days and then walk back, staying each night in a Dak bungalow, on that stretch of road, these being approximately 11 miles apart. Dinah said she would forward any official telegrams.

We fed ourselves and lived in the Dak bungalow. We cooked everything in my two mess cans over a log fire. We got up at about 11 a.m. having lain in bed with the door open looking over the tree tops and the gambolling monkeys to the most marvellous view of the snow-capped ranges. We than had a bath in the tin tub, lit the fire and got down to the eggs and coffee. By this time it was about 2 p.m. I had three weeks of *Times* with us and Ivor finished your attempts at the cross word! He came to the conclusion your average is three words! It was a very nice feeling sitting up there in our mountain solitude finishing the cross word you had started months ago. So go on sending *The Times* whatever you do. At about three we started to scramble up or down hill. The people one saw on the road were fascinating. Tibetan types and lovely women, looking very like gypsies and all sorts of travellers, coolies with a variety of loads, mule caravans and people on horseback. We used to find the most lovely big fir cones too with which we eked out the kuni (firewood). Ivor is also working very hard at my rotten Urdu. When we came in we sat and rested and then contemplated our second meal of the day. We opened a tin of something, sardines or meat, and Ivor and Gretel ate half each approximately, as I don't like tinned meat. We must have lived on love for those four days, for apart from one and a half dozen eggs and two packets of biscuits, we had accounted for hardly any of it, and Gretel ate most of that.

For our safari back Main Gul organised a mule for our baggage. On our first day's journey we went off before Main Gul. We had an eleven-mile walk to the next Dak bungalow at Matiana, through gorgeous scenery. About three miles out an almighty thunderstorm overtook us and before we had found a shelter we were drenched, so we had to keep walking to keep warm. I was wearing a pair of Ivor's grey flannels and carrying a blue and white parasol to keep off the sun. But it did quite well as an umbrella. Gretel got drenched and whined for the last mile. It was torrential rain. We arrived at the Dak bungalow frozen and wet. They got a fire going within about five minutes and we stripped and Ivor wrapped me and himself up in the curtains. Main Gul arrived about two hours later feeling pretty browned off, and we decided in future he could go on ahead. We had a superb tea and a very good dinner thanks to an efficient khansama running the bungalow.

From Matiana we had another 11-mile walk to Thaog. This was a very pleasant walk too. Unfortunately Gretel, on one of her hunting expeditions, mistook a bit of grass at the road's edge for firm ground and fell over a 200 ft. cliff. She rolled along with loose stones and rocks for another 200ft approximately. We thought she must certainly be dead. I watched Ivor's skill in the mountain country as he ran down the precipitous slope to pick her up. He took about half an hour to reach her and we were amazed that she had no broken bones, only a very bruised eye and mouth and ear, and considerable shock. He climbed back with her in his arms and we carried her to Thaog. The Thaog bungalow wasn't so efficient so we cooked again in the old mess cans. We doctored Gretel and put her to bed. We sent Main Gul on in front and put Gretel, the dachshund, up on the mule to save her walking. We stopped for tea at Fagu Dak bungalow, which must have one of the finest views of any place. Miles and miles of hills bounded by vast snow capped mountains. From there we walked another six miles to Wildflower Hall, where we are now staying. We are here by the grace of God and Ivor's personality, as when we arrived we found Main Gul and the luggage and the mule and Gretel all piled up at the entrance. Main Gul had been told that there was no accommodation.

This is a heavenly spot – a honeymooners' dream. The amusing thing about it is that before coming to Simla the one place Ivor was not going to take me to was Wildflower Hall. It is renowned as a place to visit from Simla on a Sunday. It is a hotel right up on a pine covered hillside, commanding marvellous views from various parts of a beautifully laid out garden full of roses and English flowers. Walks through the pine woods in all directions.

We have a sitting room, bedroom, dressing room and two bathrooms (tin tub and thunderbox), which comprises half a log cabin, literally on the tip top of the hill about five minutes walk from the hotel. The food is superb as is the service.

Tons and tons of love darlings, from m. w. Ibbish.

6th June 1945.

Darlingest Mom,

Another lovely letter from you yesterday awaiting us at Dinah's. You certainly seem to be organising everyone in Aldeburgh, surrounded by friends as usual. I also had a long and lengthy letter from Elise and a charming one from poor old Bill. I am surprised he took it so badly. I'm glad he's been promoted and is on a special job and has gone back to the States. Amongst Ivor's letters was one from his Uncle Ivor, father of Doreen. He was anxious to have your address so will probably contact you. Also you may hear from his mother. Our engagement was in the Sydney papers and I wonder if Aunt Mabel saw it.

Last night we went to a smashing dance in Simla. We had a very spooky journey back in the rickshaw, 6 miles up the wild mountain-side at 4 a.m. pushed by six coolies. We are just off for a short walk over the top of the hill to a place where we can get tea.

Tons and tons of love, darlings, E.

15th and 22nd June 1945 (edited)

Darlingest Moma,

I'm afraid it's simply ages since I wrote. There is so much to tell you and so little time to turn round, that I don't know where to begin.

First of all, how marvellous Tom getting the DSO. As you say, how does he do it? Needless to say, I haven't heard from him, too busy with Jane I imagine! I was tickled to bits to hear of her and your description of it all in your letter. I hope she will be able to cope with him. He certainly needs some handling. Fancy him going to Germany – the north somewhere, I expect.

We descended from the glorious heights on Sunday, to what is a literal hell. We lunched with Dinah and Frank and left by car from Simla at 4.30 p.m. We had a marvellous drive down, but just before Kalka the hot air met us coming up from the plains. It was like driving into an oven. At Wazirabad we found Mary Mackay in the next-door compartment, so we climbed in with her and exchanged all sorts of news. She had been posted to the hills and back again to the plains at Lahore and was very fed up. She was on her way to Elsa's wedding. We arrived at the worst time of day, 3 p.m., and the temperature 111F in the shade. We went straight to the Mountview Hotel, which is the only place we can be together. We have a sitting room, bedroom, two dressing rooms and two bathrooms, which with food costs us approximately £7. a week for the two of us. It is very handy and pleasant and just like a flat. We are upstairs and have a very spacious verandah back and front. We are right at the end of the block so have it all to ourselves and no one coming past.

I might say that from the word go Miss Bates, the Matron, has been as unhelpful as is possible both to Elsa and myself. You remarked in your letter you were glad she had been helpful. What I wrote was hopeless, beastly and spiteful with it. She failed to advise me on the correct way to apply for marriage leave, a concession granted to all QA's, so I had to take war leave, as also did Elsa. This means we are done out of an extra month's leave. I did however get the information that my active service posting was cancelled and that I could stay in Sialkot for the next three months. The object of Ivor's and my visit was to get this marriage leave application put in and in the meantime get 10 days' station leave. Matron went off the deep-end, refused point blank to sign the leave application which the C.O. had sanctioned, refused information about the marriage leave and put me on night duty! You can imagine we feel pretty sick about it all, especially as Ivor is likely to go off within the next three weeks. Ivor is absolutely livid, as it means I never see him except during his siesta. He goes on parade before I come off duty, and is on parade again at 5 p.m. and I go on duty before he comes home! In spite of two Sisters volunteering to do my night duty, she wouldn't take me off. Ivor comes up to the hospital most nights.

Many many thanks for the clothes, which arrived very well. I love the coat and so does Ivor. I tried it on with the sweat streaming off me. All the papers, *Times* especially, are very much appreciated by both of us. The parachute pants are lovely. Have you made me a petticoat, the one thing I could do with? The old nightie you made and hate was my honeymoon nightie after all, and the active service pyjamas have been bequeathed to Ivor!
How lovely to have so many of your friends in Aldeburgh. My love to them all.

Tons and tons of love, darlings, E.

Last time I wrote I was sick in quarters and after two days an ultimatum arrived from the C.O. to say 'warded or duty'. Apparently Matron had created the most awful row because I had not been admitted to hospital. So in desperation on Saturday morning I sat in Ivor's office and rang up the Principal Matron in Delhi. She was a bit staggered, but listened to my tale of woe, but we were cut off. So I wired her and then wrote an apologetic letter. I stuck night duty for another four nights. My fortnight was up on Wednesday, but Matron put me on for another four! However, luckily at 23.30 hours a telegram arrived from the principal Matron saying 28 days leave without pay granted. Brimming over with delight, the next day I waltzed into the hospital and said good-bye. Now they just can't be too nice to me. Poor old Ivor had just about had it with his dormouse wife. We are still awaiting news of his immediate future. At present the 'normal channels' are sitting on his board papers. Long may it last. We've certainly been inundated with parties since my leave started.

We have now more or less fixed up all our kit and stored it. There is a very good furniture maker here, and we are getting a few odd things made in anticipation of getting our own bungalow and to save us the expense of always hiring furniture, which one has to do out here. This old boy also has a very nice writing desk which I want to get, but we are humming and haaing about the price.

The heat has been terrific. 24th June registered the peak temperature 120F in the shade. That night it didn't drop lower than 100F at any time in the night. But a few days later it was relieved by the rains. And did they come! Now it's rather like living in a hot house, the temperature being about 90 – 100F and very, very humid. We have about two or three very sticky and uncomfortable days, then down comes the rain again and everything in the garden is lovely. One is perpetually soaked in sweat, and the thing to do is take everything off and lie or sit under a fan which keeps you dry, and then it is quite pleasant. The trouble is it simply wrecks your clothes and you can't wear anything for more than 4 – 6 hours without changing and sending it to the dhobie. We eat packets of salt and drink gallons of water, lime juice, and orange and lemon juice. Most people in the station have prickly heat in varying degrees of intensity. Thank goodness both Ivor and I have kept quite free so far, Ivor having a very sound method of avoiding it, which certainly has worked so far.

How is Pops these days? How marvellous it must be to be able to get him out in the car. I was thrilled to hear about Jane. Is she still driving for the Red Cross?

Must stop, as I have 1000s of letters to write. The day is very much interrupted by the fact that we go to bed in the afternoon 2 – 6 p.m. Ivor gets up for his evening parade at 5.30 p.m. and we never have dinner until 9.30 p.m. or 10 p.m. and bed again about midnight or 1 a.m. Then Ivor's morning parade at 6.30 a.m. I stay in bed until he returns for breakfast 8.30-ish. So really there is only the morning to do things.

Tons and tons of love and longing for more letters from you,
your loving Elizabeth.

10th July 1945.

Darlingest Moma,

Your letter of 29th June has just arrived, the first for over a fortnight. We've enjoyed a marvellous 10 days of peace and normal existence together, when the dreaded posting came in for Ivor. He goes off to-morrow. Our plans at present are for me to go with him as far as possible and then on to Patsy for the remainder of my leave. I have to be back here by 27th, so it will only be a week with them at most. We are going to see the Principal Matron in Delhi to find out what's what about my release. I expect I shall have August in Sialkot anyway. It's absolutely grim, the thought of Ivor going away, and being here without him will be hell. But at least it is his Regimental Centre and one is in touch with what is going on. This is a very scrappy note written amongst the awful muddle and desolation of packing up!

Must stop darlings, lots of lovely letters have just come in, I will answer next time.

In great haste, E.

26th July 1945.
c/o 12 F.F.R. Centre, Sialkot.

Darlingest Mom,

I'm sending off a wire to you to-day, because I think you might have given me up for lost. Please forgive this terrible lapse, but we've been on the move for the last 14 days. Now I feel for poor Rosy. It's incredible how all the silly ideas I had about husbands and wives being separated and how good it was for them, simply vanish into thin air now that it applies to me. I feel just like a fish out of water now that Ivor has gone, it's quite awful. However it's the same old story, we've been lucky to have had the time we did together. Coming back here where I'm so used to him being around has been made worse by having to move back into the Sisters' Mess.

Terrible news awaited me and even now I can hardly grasp it. Poor Elsa died of infantile paralysis on July 18th, just five weeks after her wedding day. I think it is too pathetic and it makes me quite sick inside when I think of poor Derek. We left here for Calcutta on the Wednesday evening. Elsa was on night duty that night, and the following day had dreadful backache, so reported sick. On the Saturday she lost the power of her legs and on Wednesday morning at 1 a.m. she died in the iron lung, six days after she went off sick. Poor Derek was at sea at the time and didn't get the news until he got to Colombo. He flew straight here and arrived the Sunday after she died. I think it is all so frightful and terrible for her parents too. You can imagine, I miss her very much, we had so much in common, especially now. Thank goodness I went with Ivor to Calcutta. It was well worthwhile, as his transport was delayed for a week. We had a most successful day in Delhi as he wrote and told you. It's awful feeling he has gone into that filthy fighting again, and they are wading around up to their necks in mud after the monsoon. We are all very depressed about the War out here. Repatriation and release has upset everything and of course equipment is just as short, in fact a week ago they even cut the mens' cigarette ration. I think people at home forget we still have our men fighting on the worst front of the whole War, and many of them P.O.W. still. Whilst we were in Calcutta there were literally hundreds of officers detained, waiting to go to the front for lack of shipping and aircraft. Now Labour has got in we might as well bury our heads in the sand. It makes one very fed up with the home Government.

I have moved back into the Sisters' Mess with Main Gul and Gretel, so I'm an object of suspicion on the part of the other servants, and I'm afraid envy on the part of the Sisters. The only redeeming feature being the fact that Matron is on leave. 27th July. Main Gul went to the Centre to-day and collected all the mail. One from you dated 18th July. Many thanks. I'll send you a list of things I want. Also a letter from you to Ivor. Do write to him occasionally in the jungle: 8th 12th FFR, SEAC.

I had a letter from Mrs Stuart to-day who said Aunt Mabel had rung her up and had lunch with her. She told my m-i-l that I was her favourite niece!

Tons of love, your loving E.

1st **August** 1945.

Darlingest Moma,

A lovely batch of mail arrived yesterday. Yours of 2nd, 14th and 22nd July. Also one to Ivor acknowledging his letter from Delhi. Nearly a week has gone by again since I wrote to you and barely 10 days since I said good-bye to Ivor. I had two letters from Calcutta and two lots of lovely silk material which he bought the day before he left. Now I have to wait for mail.

I am now quite recovered and am on duty. Another Sister turned up the other day, which makes another pair of hands, so we're not too hard pressed. It's no fun this weather, when you don't even have time to breathe. There is a very nice Sister acting in charge. She is an Australian and she has been in the Desert and Italy. She is a very good sort, but a bit humble! I have lots to do each day. Phil has now left and I have all Elsa's things to see to. I have to get them packed up and insured.

The thunder has just started up. It's such a welcome sound for as soon as the rain comes, it cools off beautifully. Gretel the dachshund is a grand companion. She's a priceless dog, full of character. I always take her up to the hospital, and I think I shall soon be acquiring the name of Jane too! Gretel gets the funny looks of Fritz in the cartoon.

I'm gradually getting round to writing all my letters, and there's always so much to tell Ivor. I get all the mail to deal with, everything that comes in, financial or otherwise, and just send the chits on to Ivor, which may interest him. I always send your letters on, as he particularly requested me to. He loves the news from Aldeburgh, even though he doesn't know anyone you talk about. Your description of Jane's mother was very amusing. I still haven't had a word from Tom. Don't worry about sending things when coupons are at such a premium. I was hoping more things would be available, but I suppose that won't be yet awhile. I would like the rest of my clothes that are wearable. I really cannot remember what I've got.

By the way, Ivor's other names are Arthur James – quite Deckish! I think I told you we called on old Macfarlane and he kept talking about Alfred Deck and all the other Decks. There seem to be a whole bunch of them out here. When we were in Calcutta Alfred had just gone up to a hill station to a niece's wedding. I don't know who that could be? Mrs Stuart, Ivor's mother, wrote about some Decks out there too.

Tons of love my darlings, and keep writing often, your loving E.

When Ivor's posting came through to the 9th/12th in Burma I went with him to Calcutta. It was teeming with troops in transit and the Grand Hotel was the RTS's HQ and the general meeting place. We met many friends, and we dined and danced to 'our' tune, 'Always', then the vogue. I returned to Sialkot with Main Gul and Gretel, and Ivor flew off to North Burma with some Americans on the first leg of his journey to join his unit. I fell ill on the train on the second night with a high fever. Main Gul was marvellous and kept me plied with cool drinks. At Wazirabad, where I had requested to be met by an ambulance from Sialkot, I had a long hot wait for the connecting train. Main Gul shepherded me to the Ladies room where he left me in the care of an elderly English missionary. She laid me on the bare earth floor and cooled my brow. She was calm and kind. On arrival in Sialkot, where there was still no ambulance to meet me, the news of Elsa's death from poliomyelitis was a deep and devastating sorrow. I went straight to bed in the Families Hospital and spent a lonely and miserable time. Ivor had arranged that Main Gul should be available to help me if I needed it and he was a tower of strength, keeping the ayahs up to their work and making sure I had all I needed. When I was better, I had the unhappy task of packing up Elsa's things and tending her grave. On our return to Sialkot in 1980 we searched everywhere in two cemeteries for Elsa's grave but could find no trace of it. The newer of the two cemeteries had been very badly vandalised. I was now to become the fortunate recipient of a wonderful batch of love letters from Ivor in Burma. The intense heat of June had given way to a damp sticky atmosphere, but the thermometer was still around 100F and the weather, if possible, was even more trying. Tempers were getting very tetchy and everyone was becoming slightly demented. I went on night duty. Even at night the heat was intense, the temperature seldom dropping more than 10 degrees Fahrenheit. To add to our discomfort, we had to wear khaki drill slacks with boots and gaiters and long-sleeved bush shirts as protection against mosquitos. I took Gretel on duty with me. She was an alert little dog and a good protection against surprise snakes or scorpions, for she would always do a tour of the wainscoting on entering a room. She justified her existence by killing a scorpion for me, and later on day duty, in killing a rat under the nose of a disapproving inspecting C.O. All manner of life went on in the old flues and nooks and crannies in the walls of the old buildings.

One of my patients at this time was a WAC (I) girl, (Women's Auxiliary Corps – India). She told me her mother lived in Sialkot City and she was stationed in Lahore. She had a very difficult time there as her male relatives, brothers and cousins, disapproved violently of her joining the Women's Forces and coming out of purdah. She was seldom able to leave the barracks as they would lie in wait for her. I marvelled at the courage of this tiny, attractive and dignified girl, who blessed the custom of purdah in so far as it enabled her to move about unrecognised in the all enveloping garment. In it she went off in the tonga to see her mother. She became one of the anonymous mass until she had to emerge again in uniform in Lahore and run the gauntlet of her male relatives.

4th August 1945.

Darlingest Moma and Pops and family.

Some more *Times* fetched up the other day and I saw Charles Deck reported killed. What a terrible thing. I knew you said he was missing, but there was such hope so near the end of the war. What agony that poor boy suffered. He knew he wouldn't come through alive. Also all sorts of people I know engaged and married.

Great excitement – three letters from Ivor. Poor darling, he arrived only to be told that his posting was cancelled, so he is mucking around between Division and Army HQ trying to find out his new assignment.

To-night I'm going to a party with Ronnie Webb and his wife. He is a pet and one of the old 94 bungalow brigade. She is a most peculiar girl, and because she is going to have a baby, she is dashing off home to South India to her parents and leaving Ronnie high and dry. Most odd. Heaven and earth wouldn't induce me to go away from Ivor if I could possibly be with him. Another friend of Ivor's in the station has his mother staying here, Mrs Slattery. I think she comes down to keep an eye on him. His father has an interesting job, some sort of advisory resident in one of the Indian States.

There are three new Sisters here now. Phil has gone to Kasauli near Simla, so I'm the only survivor of the famous quartette. Mary is in Lahore and I hope to see her sometime. As the Sisters are new and know no-one, I thought it behoved me to have a party for them. So they were thrilled when I suggested it, so here I go again. My Urdu really started coming into its own under Ivor's tuition, but my education is rather left in the lurch now. I can speak more than anyone else in the hospital and consequently get far more respect from the Indian servants than the others.

Very worrying news from Australia. Ivor's mother is very ill. She had a motor smash a few months ago and has some latent head injury which gives her dizziness and headaches. He'll be terribly worried.

Tons of love, darlings, E.

11th August 1945.

Darlingest Moma and family,

No news from anyone since a letter from Rosy a few days back. What terrific news, first the atom bomb, then Japan's request for armistice. We are anxiously waiting for each news bulletin to hear whether or not the Allies will accept their offer of unconditional surrender, with its stipulation about the Mikado. We're all keyed up to celebrate in a big way, but it won't be the same with Ivor still away.

We had the party for the new Sisters on Friday night, and it was a great success, but after I left to go on night duty at midnight it rather fizzled out (with apologies for the trumpet). But they really are a hopeless bunch at a party – no conversation at all. I had them all paired off as I thought fit and introduced them accordingly and told them where the other had been etc. so that they had some conversation to start on. But I had to go round to each guest in turn and help the conversation along. The only other live spark was the elderly Australian, who is an absolute gem, Miss Donohue. Several of Ivor's friends came, three especially, Ron, Dennis Slattery and Roy are very good and take me to the Club and invite me to their parties. Just to pass the time away. But it's horrid entertaining without a husband. I miss Ivor very much.

Fixing up Elsa's affairs had taken a great deal of my time. I now have everything safely settled. Phil had left everything only half done and that not properly. It has been very sticky again the last few days and one's clothes get drenched in the space of 10 minutes. I am on night duty again, but as there is very little to do, I just get undressed and go to bed most comfortably in the Families Hospital. I get up for a bath in the morning when the ayah calls me with a cup of tea! I then do a round and go off duty. I'm very fond of the ayahs, they are pets. One of them presented me with a nest of bangles, which she put on my arm and I now can't get off.

Tons of love, darling to you all, your loving daughter, E.

15th August 1945.
VICTORY DAY!

Darlingest Moma and family,

Many, many thanks for your two letters, August 1st and 4th. I'm sorry my telegram was misleading, but viva saves a word and I knew you couldn't have had any mail for ages. Viva was anything but descriptive of my mood when I returned. Of course I wrote to Mrs Watt. Phil, who looked after Elsa the whole time, wrote details of everything. It's so ghastly I still can't really register it all, although I go regularly to her grave and look after it for Derek. I have had two lovely flowering shrubs planted at the foot, one a sort of laburnum and the other hibiscus, the most beautiful flower, I think. I have one on my desk on night duty under the light. I have also got three huge debbies dug in, which I keep filled with water and fresh flowers. The cemetery is a very beautiful place, like an oasis in the middle of the bleak plains, with lovely trees, shrubs and in full view of the hills, snowcapped and lovely in the cool days, but obscured during the hot weather by dust and atmosphere. It was awful the other day when a chit arrived addressed to Elsa, and I had to break the news to this chap who had been away. I have dealt with all her kit, done all the packing and arrangements for Derek, and dealt with all the Army red tape.

The last letter I got from Ivor was dated 8th August and he was fed up as he had had no mail from me, which I've been sending to the Battalion he was to have joined. We're hoping against hope that he'll get the Staff College – perhaps in December.

Our acting Matron, Miss Donoghue, a grand person, an Australian, pinched two bottles of champagne from the Hospital stores to-day and we had a V. dinner by ourselves in the mess! The awful old Webster comes back next week – boohoo.

I gather Tom is in for the regular R.A.F. That is something you never contemplated, all your children in the regular services! And well represented. Your wild and woolly daughter married to a rigid disciplinarian. Ivor heard about Elsa from Jimmy Davidson, whom we met in Calcutta and whom Ivor has since contacted in Burma. Jimmy came out on the boat with us and is Derek's best friend. He was to have been best man at the wedding, but was in hospital at the time. There has been a pandemic of infantile paralysis and out here, a particularly virulent type. Some say she got it in Kashmir, but personally I think she got it in Lahore, where there has been a big casualty roll from it. Luckily she is the only case we have had in Sialkot.

My little dog Gretel is an absolute darling. She is grand at night and I lose all my spookiness. She comes into the hospital and literally goes round every nook and cranny. The Ayah is always tickled to bits, and calls it the inspection and says 'much duty for Gretel'! She certainly works harder than I do, for when I have finished my letters, I get undressed and go to bed. Only two nights have I had to stay up at B.M.H. on account of patients not being so well.

How lovely for Pops getting his joy rides. Tons of love to you all, E.

———————

18th August 1945.

My darlingest Moma,

To-day your two letters dated 9th have arrived. I'm so sorry you're all so worried about Tom's impending marriage. I can well imagine the type Jane is, and I quite agree with you that they both seem too young. A man like Tom needs to be absolutely fed up with bachelor life before he will ever settle down. Once he reaches that state, and always providing he meets a girl he can really fall for, he would make an excellent husband. That type always do – viz. Ivor! But as Ivor says, you've got to live out your bachelor days to the full and the man must do the chasing – not the girl. It will be Jane who will regret it, because if she isn't a satisfactory wife, Tom will just leave her to stew in her own juice and lead his separate life, which in the end is worse for the girl than for the man. Also I think you're stepping off on the wrong foot when you decide not to have any children. But Tom will probably grow out of that. It will all come right in the end, so don't let it worry you. I think you should make it quite clear to them both and especially Jane, that you don't intend to support them. Tom's future seems precarious enough as it is for himself, let alone plus a wife.

   Ivor has great hopes of getting to the Staff College now that things seem to be packing in. But I don't really feel that we're through with this Jap business somehow. It all seems highly unsatisfactory so far, and Ivor says that's rather the sentiment of the men at the front, relieved as they are at the news. They feel the Japs haven't had a knock-out blow yet.

Tons of love to you all, your loving E.

Ivor wrote to me from Rangoon as follows:

Great excitement to-day was caused by the much awaited arrival of the Japanese for the surrender. They arrived in by air and then came down from the airstrip in a long procession of M.Ps, Japanese, station wagons, trucks and powerful staff cars. They passed our front gate as we were playing bridge on the upstairs verandah, so we got quite a good view of the whole cavalcade. I expect they have already been in conference but we haven't heard any news of the discussion so far.

Ivor at this time was part of a pool of prospective commanding officers for Operation Zipper, which was to move into Malaya to clear out the Japanese. An operation in which Army Command was expecting extremely high casualties, so the relief was enormous when the Japanese surrendered. Events had come full circle for Ivor, as he was in at the beginning when the Japanese invaded Burma.

4th September 1945.

Darlingest Moma and family,

Terrific news. I was awoken yesterday morning with a telegram from Ivor from Calcutta saying he was returning and arriving Wednesday afternoon. This morning I had just arrived on duty when a phone call came through from him in Delhi. He gets the night train, so he has the day to spend there and is going to see the Principal Matron to get them to speed on my release. We've got our original room in the Mountview Hotel again, which is a very nice one, but I hope we won't need to be there longer than a fortnight at the most, as it's going to be so awful for Ivor being on leave and me working.

Quite the wrong way round, and he does loathe it so much. I must stay on duty this week-end, as there will be no one in the daytime bar Miss Webster. But when Van comes back on Sunday, I think I'll tell them they've got to let me go.

It will be marvellous to get out of this heat. Up to 100F again. The minimum temperature for August was 70F night time. This hot weather has been very long according to everyone. I've been working very hard this week, in fact the day before yesterday I was on all day from 8 – 8 pm with just two breaks for meals. We have a most charming new C.O. who has been P.O.W. in Germany since Dunkirk. He is certainly a new broom and is pulling the place together marvellously. The whole place has gone to seed, and our C.Os have been worse than useless and of course poor old Matron is dippy.

I'm so terribly excited I don't know whether I'm coming or going.

In great haste, darlings, tons and tons of love, E.

When Ivor returned from Burma on 5th September I had just had the news that I was to have treatment for amoebic dysentery. Although I had no symptoms, tests had shown that I had the amoebic cysts. The treatment was over a period of 31 days. Ivor saw the M.O. with a view to getting me transferred for treatment to the B.M.H. in Dalhousie in the hills. All this was agreed and then something upset the whole arrangement and I was told I could not travel. Ivor was furious. The Staff Captain from the Station HQ came to tell Ivor he was harbouring a deserter and that I was to have my treatment in Sialkot. Ivor replied that he was only looking after his wife and that if they wished to pursue this course he, Ivor, would take it up with higher authority, so we left Sialkot as planned and appealed over their heads to the D.D.M.S. in Lahore, who confirmed that Ivor was right to take me to Dalhousie.

In Lahore we met the Slatterys again, and Mrs Slattery insisted on sending her Rolls Royce to take me to the station. It was a great relief to reach the blessed coolness of the hills again. We booked into Stiffles Hotel and I was admitted to the hospital for treatment.

19th September 1945

Darlingest Moma,

Maybe when you get this you will already have had Ivor's chapter of accidents. But in case the mails are haywire and you get this first, I'll give you the gen.

We had a marvellous week in Sialkot, back in our old room in the Mountview Hotel, the main snag being that I was on duty. I had had a report back from the laboratory about a week previously that I have the amoebic dysentery bug. This was an absolute fluke and very fortunate that it was found so soon, as I have had no symptoms whatever, and have been as fit as a fiddle since my fever bout in July. It was when I was in hospital after I came back from Calcutta, that the M.O. said I must send a specimen for investigation. He thought it would be a good idea in view of my many attacks during the summer. This report came back positive for gardia, which is a bug allied to the amoeba, but not so devastating in its ultimate effects. He then said that as I was fit, I was to take a course of mepacrine and after that another specimen to see if it had cleared up. So it was in this other specimen, taken at the end of August, that the amoebic cysts appeared. So really I am very lucky to have this advance information, and nip the beastly thing in the bud. The anti-amoebic course is now 31 days, a very comprehensive and thorough affair. It is a practically certain cure when caught so early as mine, unlike Marlay's case, when the patient is probably racked with the disease before he ever reported sick. Then trouble does start. Poor old Ivor, it was beastly sort of news to greet him with on his return on leave. With these hospitals, once in, it's all your life is worth to get out again. So hence our battle in Sialkot. The M.O. did let me down, as I only went into Sialkot Hospital on the under-standing that he would transfer me to the hills, as a) I couldn't stand the heat during a strenuous treatment, having had the whole summer on the plains, and b) I couldn't stand Miss Webster. Both reasons he heartily agreed with. The rest of the story Ivor has told you. How we walked out on him to interview the A.D.M.S. in Lahore. He, of course, was charming, sympa-thised, and telephoned to Dalhousie, where we were greeted as something rather special. We are progressing very well with this treatment, the worst of which comes at the beginning, six injections of emetine, one a day, overlapping with 11 enemas of special solution, which has to be retained. Today I finish my last emetine injection. I had two emetines in Sialkot, consequently felt pretty lousy during all our journeyings, added to the excitement of Ivor being back. But he was marvellous, quite the best nurse I have ever had. He put me to bed after we had seen the A.D.M.S, organised everything, did the packing and unpacking. When we got to Pathankot, the railhead for Dalhousie, he put me in the Dak bungalow, blanket-bathed me and fed me. I would never have got here otherwise.

When we got up to Dalhousie at about 8.30 p.m. after a lovely drive along a terrifying mountain road, we were ushered into an empty room in our hotel. This hotel runs two places in Dalhousie, 'the lower' and 'the upper'. The rooms prepared for us were in the upper, and as this involved another 15 minutes up the steepest of hills, Ivor decided to bed me down in the nearest available, as I had to be shipped to hospital in any case the next day. You should have seen that room. It reminded me of one of the beach cottages in Thorpeness, with a glazed-in verandah, and everything with the air of 'for the summer only'. We got a fire going and the luggage strewn all over the place, and the dog and me feeling like nothing on earth on the bed. It rather reminded me of a scene out of the *Constant Nymph.*

The hospital, as is the nature of all Military Hospitals, is about as inaccessible as it possibly could be, and is a 40-minute walk from our hotel. About 30 minutes downhill and 40 minutes up. There is no transport and the only thing is to walk. I have a room to myself, and our plan is for me to stay in hospital until the enemas are over, and then the rest of the treatment is swallowing pills each day. Our task now is to persuade everyone concerned here to let me go up to the hotel, stay in bed completely, let Ivor look after me and see I swallow my pills. The Colonel in charge here is a nasty old man and I think we've got a tough proposition ahead.

It's absolutely marvellous to be able to sleep under something again and feel the comfort of blankets and a warm bed, and the peace without the constant whining of the fans, and the joy of being cool and dry, instead of saturated with sweat ten minutes after one has changed one's clothes. It certainly was an experience, but I hope I never have to spend so long on the plains in summertime again. Here we are having the tail end of the monsoon and it is still raining and very misty, very like England! In about ten days' time it should be really lovely.

Ivor has spent every day down here with me from 2–11 p.m. in defiance of the visiting hours. The time went all too quickly when he was here, although in hospital time can never go too quickly. So my 16 days in hospital have gone by. We whiled away the time by giving each other language lessons. Ivor is a very good teacher and I think it is a thing he could take up when he retires. My Urdu is progressing slowly but surely, mostly I lack opportunity for conversation, although Ivor makes me speak correctly to Main Gul, who, being a Pushto speaker, speaks a very clear Urdu. Ivor has taught me the alphabet and I can now read the script slowly and write it a little. Then I give him German lessons.

Ivor is very interested in his ancestors, so do get copies for me of both Deck and LeMesurier trees please. I do hope we will be able to see old Herbert Norris when we come home. I don't know who the authority is on the LeMesuriers now old Aunt Eva is dead.

I had mentioned to the M.O. in charge of Families that I wanted to go out as soon as my enemas were finished, and she said that was all right provided I returned to hospital to have the EBI pills. When one takes these, one has to stay in bed and do nothing, as they are rather strong, and the next day she was posted. Ivor said I must find out one way or the other what was to happen to me, so I braved the Colonel. The dear old man said, 'Yes, why not, but come back for the EMI.' As my release papers had not come in, when Ivor arrived he asked the Colonel if he might phone Sialkot to find out if they were there. The C.O. Sialkot said my papers had come in and that he had sent them direct to me. This is marvellous news, and no-one else can sit on them if they are not signed. We are so thrilled.

So glad, darlings, that you have the phone and the car, such boons.

Tons and tons of love, E.

13th October 1945.

Darlingest Moma,

Your letter of 27th September fetched up the other day. I'm so glad Tom and Jane's visit went off o. k. and that things aren't as bad as they seem. I think Tom would be far better off with a regular commission in the RAF. I can't see Jane being very happy in Basra amidst the oil pipes, the heat and the desert.

I'm now finished with the treatment, and am up and about again. Ivor really has been marvellous, looks after me, washes the undies, makes the coffee, takes the dogs out (we are looking after one of the Slattery's dachshunds) and generally does all the chores.

We are going off to-morrow to Khajiar (pronounced like Kadjiado without the 'do'). This is one of the beauty spots around here and is the staging camp between here and Chamba. We are staying there until Wednesday and then going on into Chamba. The Slatterys have very kindly arranged for us to stay in the Rajah's summer house, which will be more pleasant than the Dak Bungalow. The point about it which Mrs Slattery seemed to think most in its favour, is the fact that it has wired in doors, as leopards abound and she's frightened we might lose Gretel. Gretel will have to come nearly all the way either on the lead or in my dandy on account of leopards. We will be quite a cavalcade. Two pack mules, one of the Rajah's horses for Ivor and Mrs Slattery's dandy for me and several orderlies and the Slattery's dog in his dandy! The Rajah's horse reminds me of 'All the King's Horses and all the King's men'! It's the pottiest little state and should be very amusing. Nibby, one of the Slattery's dachshunds, had to be left in Dalhousie to be treated by a vet as he had been bitten by a wild cat. As they had gone away, we took compassion on him and had him here.

Mrs Stuart has sent us a lovely tea table cloth and table mats which she had crocheted. I'm longing to see it all.

God bless you, and tons of love, Elizabeth.

21st October 1945.

Darlingest Moma,

The last letter I got from you was dated 2nd October, but as our mail is being held up now, owing to our movements I don't expect to hear any more until we reach Lahore.

We left Dalhousie in fine form. I was carried in Mrs Slattery's dandy. This is a terrible affair which looks like a canoe on two poles and is carried on the shoulders of four coolies. Apart from the awful sensation of being carried, it is damned uncomfortable. In the end I rode the pony and Ivor walked. It's most precarious riding as the paths are often no wider than 2 or 3 feet with a sheer drop down on one side and steep rocks on the other. But it is very beautiful. We halted for three nights at Khajiar at a heavenly spot, which could have been in the Black Forest. We had the Rajah's summer house to ourselves, and it is most comfortable. The journey on here was a replica of the previous one from Dalhousie to Khajiar, only the last two miles were so steep that I trusted myself to neither dandy nor horse and chose to pick my way down behind Ivor. It was very, very tiring. We dropped 2000 feet in two miles.

Chamba town lies in the valley of the Ravi River, one of the five rivers of the Punjab. The valley is very narrow with steep hills coming down to the river bed. It is about 3000 feet above sea level. There are no other Europeans here. The Slatterys have a lovely house and from the garden we look down a cliff into the river, which is very rocky and flows very swiftly. There is a constant roar from the rushing torrent and it reminds me of the sound of the sea.

Mrs Slattery has us in fits of laughter over the State and all its doings, and the goings-on in the Palace and the way the Rajmata treats the poor little Rani. (N.B. So ably described many years later by Molly Kaye in her story, *The Far Pavilions*).

Yesterday Ivor and I accompanied Mr Slattery to the Rajah's bear shoot. We all met on the common at 8 a.m. The Rajah and a cousin of his, the Maharajkumar of some State between Delhi and Calcutta, and various hangers-on. We walked out of town, as the road was very steep and the horses were led down behind us. All the syces were dolled up in green and red livery. When we got across the swing bridge at the bottom, we mounted. The road at first was along the river and flat. After three miles we began to climb and for about six miles we scrambled up the most incredible paths. I never would have believed I had the nerve to ride a horse along such tracks. Eventually we arrived near the summit of the valley. We could see the beaters, members of the State Forces, lining the hill tops. The various guns were relegated to their stands or machans. Ivor and I perched on a rock, whence we had a wonderful view up and down the valley. After much bugle blowing and shouting the beaters started off, complete with drums and pipes. We waited for about one and a half to two hours whilst they gradually beat the hill slopes into the valley immediately below us. They made an amazing row and hurled huge boulders down into the thickets too close for them to beat. As they began to emerge into the clearing below us, the Rajah gave up hope of a bear appearing and he unloaded his rifle, as did Ivor and the Maharajkumar. Of course, at this crucial point a superb black bear emerged. Ivor rapidly loaded and so did the others. The best shot was gone. The guns below us got several shots in and finally the Maharajkumar killed him with an excellent shot at very long range. I was very sorry for the poor bear. It was a pretty poor way of getting rid of him really.

After this we sat down in the shade beside a stream and had a very good lunch. Curry and a lovely pillau and cold chicken. Afterwards, feeling more like going to sleep than anything else, we scrambled further down the valley and took up our stands again. They drew blank until right at the end when we had a few quite exciting moments, but the bear very cleverly got away. We then had a welcome cup of tea. The Rajah would have gone on until it was too dark to see, but Mr Slattery managed to persuade him that as there was four miles of dreadfully steep downhill track it would be better to cover it before it was quite dark. We walked all the way down as fast as we could. Ivor set the pace and fast it was. I scrambled along after him and we outstripped the others, making the flat in about an hour, by which time it was pitch dark. There was a lovely moon, but it was behind the hill. We rode in by the light of several hurricane lamps. It was a grand day. Ivor and I are probably going out again after birds, pheasants and partridge. The weather is perfect, just like hot English summer weather. It gets dark early because of the mountains. As the Rajah is going to Amritsar to buy horses, the Slatterys are going to Lahore about the same time as we are.

Ivor has secured the Staff College, and we are really thrilled to be able to make some definite plans at last.

Tons and tons of love, E.

4th November 1945.

My darlingest Moma,

Now for a detailed and consecutive account of our doings. We thoroughly enjoyed staying with the Slatterys. They had some really marvellous carpets. Gretel, unfortunately, christened one, luckily one of the not so valuable ones. As she's a dachs, and they are dachshund lovers, she got away with it. Mrs Slattery and I were going to the palace to see the Rani, but unfortunately the day we were going it poured with rain, and as Mrs Slattery has not been very well with jaundice, she didn't go out, and the next day we left. We were going to trek three days to Pathankot, but the rain had turned to snow on the higher ground and the road was not considered very safe, so we came back the way we went and stopped again for the night at Khajiar. We rode the whole way and made it in good time. Khajiar had had some snow and the next day, when we went on into Dalhousie over the pass, the snow was at least 6' deep and the road consequently very slippery. I can tell you that after about 6 miles of riding under those conditions and along a very narrow track with a very steep drop down, I couldn't take it and walked the rest of the way. But it was very beautiful and difficult to believe one wasn't in Europe. We arrived in Dalhousie and put up at the Slatterys' house there. The next day they both arrived in, and the following day we all motored down to Lahore in the Slatterys' Rolls-Royce. It was a marvellous journey in the open car. We left at 9 a.m. and arrived at Pathankot for lunch. We had tea with some friends of theirs in Amritsar, and finally arrived in Lahore at 6 p.m. Mrs Slattery had told us where to get pots and pans, so we went straight off that evening to one shop and bought our dekchis (nest of Indian saucepans without handles), and other kitchen stuff and our dining room knives. The whole lot cost us Rs. 250. - Then we rushed back, had a bath and read our mail, which took about one and a half hours. I had a letter from Tom dated 18th September which gave me no news at all and said nothing about Jane except that they married in 'one hell of a rush'.

We are off to Kohat to-morrow and I'll write to you again from there. We hear wonderful reports of Quetta, so are really looking forward to it.

Thanks again a million for everything, tons of love, Elizabeth.

Ivor had written to his old bearer, Taj Mohammed, commonly known as Albert, who had joined the Additional Police in Kohat, to say he was bringing his bride to visit Kohat. Albert was employed as bearer-cum-driver to the Police Commissioner, then an Indian. Albert arranged to meet us in the official car and that the Police Commissioner would entertain us to morning tea. Accordingly we were met at the station and driven to the bungalow, where we were introduced. Albert disappeared to the kitchen and emerged with a tray of tea and dainty accompaniments. Thereafter he collected us again and brought along his young son to see us. He then arranged a car to take us through the Tribal Territory to Peshawar. We bade him a fond farewell and hoped very much that we might be able to employ him again some time in the future. Ivor showed me the rifle factory in the Tribal Territory, where all manner of weapons were expertly copied in very primitive conditions, and later from Peshawar we visited the Khyber Pass.

29th November 1945. Sialkot.

Darling Elise,

We have nearly come to the end of a really wonderful leave, and as usual I have managed to see some more of the world. I think I last wrote to you from Chamba. From there we went to Lahore, then to Rawalpindi and then overnight to Kohat. There we were really on the North West Frontier, the most romantic frontier in the world. Ivor, who was stationed there before the War, says it is just the same. I heard all about the Frontier Force, as the place is steeped in Frontier Force traditions, and always has had one of its battalions stationed there. From there we motored through the Kohat Pass to Peshawar, through Tribal Territory which is outside British India. There every man always carries his rifle, and every house is built with a high wall enclosure and a watch tower and houses several families. A village consists of several of these fortified houses. But they are a marvellous people, charming in spite of their ruthlessness and lawlessness. The country is brown, barren and rocky. Peshawar is superb, a marvellous bazaar with all kinds of furs and some marvellous carpets. It is quite fascinating, but unfortunately we are broke. We got permission to go into the City, the native part of the place to visit the Thieves Bazaar, where, if one has been robbed, one may be lucky enough to buy back one's belongings. The rest of the place is the cantonment area where the Europeans live. We had a grand evening at the Club there, a dinner dance and Ivor seemed to know nearly everyone. From Peshawar we returned to Sialkot to pack up our kit and try to get some servants to take to Quetta. We have had a hectic ten days here. There are always so many people here that we know, and friends of Ivor's passing through the Centre whom he hasn't seen for ages. So every evening has been either dancing at the Club, or bridge or dinner parties. To-day Ivor has gone to Lahore in an Army truck to send all our kit off, 11 trunks and about 15 packing cases. Thank God it all goes at Government expense. We have had a lot of furniture hand-made here by a famous old firm. It is priceless to walk down the bazaar and see your dining room chairs in the middle of the road being worked at! But they turn out marvellous stuff and very cheap, considering it is all hand-made, and comes to pieces for packing purposes. So you can imagine, we're longing to see it in all its glory in our own bungalow. We are having frightful difficulty over servants. They want so much pay and then expect a staff of six or seven in a small bungalow for two people. We still have a week here and live in hopes that we will at least have a cook and a sweeper, the two essentials, as we can take an orderly from the Centre. Ivor is entitled to one, as he comes to the Staff College from SEAC. The weather is very pleasant here now. Hot English summer weather and cold nights. Now the heat haze has gone, one has a marvellous view of the snowcapped Himalayan peaks. They look superb and sometimes seem just to float between heaven and earth. I go down to the ranges in the mornings to learn how to handle a rifle and revolver reasonably efficiently. We look forward to some fun here soon! I was thrilled today when the first instalment of winter clothes arrived from home. In Quetta the maximum temperature in the winter is 40F and the minimum about 40F below zero. So I'm in for some extremes of temperature this year. I can't tell you how marvellous it is to be out of the Army. But you too must appreciate the break from nursing. What a drudge! But we had some fun in spite of it all. Ivor hates nursing and nurses, and has never quite got over the shock of marrying one. I do get mad when I'm not even allowed to tell people I was in France! The highspot of my career! You see I'm truly browbeaten, the Shrew is Tamed. But I get my own back, and life is full of laughs and we love it. I hear a good deal from Rosemary, and have had several from John, who is milling around in the China Seas somewhere.

Well, old dear, tons of love and don't let Douglas get too boisterous.
Your loving E. (N.B. The child turned out to be Carol).

2nd December 1945

Darlingest Moma,

We have now at last managed to settle something in the way of servants. We have collected a very nice sweeper, who we're hoping won't rat at the last minute. So far he comes up every day and cleans Gretel. Just to give him something to do, since we have employed him from the first of the month. For bearer and khitmagar (waiter) we now have Main Gul, who stays with us as orderly, and thus substitutes for bearer. The other man is a friend of Main Gul's and they come from the same village.

He has served with Ivor in the 4th Sikhs when they walked out of Burma. Main Gul was in the Western Desert and Italy, so they both wear a string of medal ribbons. Makhmad Salim has been an orderly off and on during his career and actually asked if he could come to us as he is taking his release. Neither of them has a clue about housework or serving at table, but they're sound loyal men, which is what matters most these days. The cook we're not quite so happy about. He has been cooking for friends of ours here, but they are not so particular as we are and I'm afraid he has had things a bit too much his own way. But he seems cheery and is quite a good cook and very economical apparently, which is the chief thing. I'm afraid the fact that he is a Christian has rather prejudiced us, as there is usually some murky reason for them being so! We're not really worried, so long as the house servants are reliable. We'll probably have to get a 'masalchi' (washer-upper) in Quetta, as Main Gul and Makhmad Salim are far too superior for that.

The furniture is getting on fine and we see the bedstead sitting in the middle of the road when we walk down the bazaar. It is a low double bed, divan type in shape, but with Indian bed webbing for the hot weather. We also have four very nice tub chairs, which will do for bridge and we are getting two low bedside tables to go beside the passion waggon! A very nice drink cabinet is in the making to Ivor's design. We also have a frameless long wall mirror, two bridge tables, two folding deal tables, a standard lamp, and our Queen Anne dining table and chairs, which are not ready yet.

Must fly as we're going down the bazaar.

Tons and tons of love from us both, E.

We finally set off for Quetta, where we arrived in the middle of December. Our journey took us along the Indus to Rohri where the railway crosses the river. The railway line to Quetta is one of the great Victorian engineering feats. It crosses the wide Indus over an iron bridge, then across the desert through Sibi, one of the hottest places on earth, until it reaches the steep climb up through the many tunnels needed to take it through the rocky, forbidding mountain range, until it finally coasts down onto the 5,000 ft plateau to Quetta. This was the route taken by Ivor's great grandfather Abraham Roberts 106 years earlier, when he led his brigade in the 1st Afghan War.

In Quetta a new chapter in our lives began.

Chapter Sixteen

Quetta and Motherhood –
Australia 1946

W E HAD NOW ENJOYED A WONDERFUL HONEYMOON, a mercifully
short separation, a joyful reunion, my release from Army service, and
a lovely two months' leave visiting Chamba State and the N.W.F.P.

The time had come for us to set up our first household.

Quetta was reached by rail over a track which constituted one of the
engineering feats of the Victorians, climbing up steep gradients, through
numerous tunnels and over deep gorges. It followed the route across the
Sind desert and up through the Bolan Pass into the wide valley where Quetta
lay high above sea level. It was the same route which Ivor's great-grandfather,
Abraham Roberts, had followed with his Brigade on his way to the First
Afghan War in 1839.

Staff College,
40 Austin Road, Quetta, Baluchistan.
15th December 1946.

My darlingest Moma,

I'm afraid my last letter was written ages ago, but being on the move for five
days takes a big hole out of the intervening time. We had a fearful journey.
The first stage from Sialkot to Lahore was bad because our accommodation
wasn't reserved and we had to get out in the middle of the night and change
and hang about for hours. We had piles of kit, three servants and a dog, so
you can imagine what it was like. In Lahore we visited dentist and hairdresser
and then didn't move from the hotel in order not to spend money! We left
on Sunday night for Quetta. We travelled on the slow train, as firstly it saved
us another night in Lahore, and secondly it arrived at a more suitable time
of day, namely 1 p.m. instead of 5.30 p.m. We were met very satisfactorily
and whisked off to the Staff College Mess for lunch, and then driven to our
bungalow. There the helpfulness ended. I have never seen a house in such a

state of filth and dilapidation. I could have wept, especially after two nights and a day in the filthiest train, it was almost too much, especially as there was no prospect of a bath! Four cold taps are the sum total of the sanitary arrangements, and the garden is non-existent, just a lot of pebbles like a shingle beach, with wisps of straw, old tins and junk lying about.

We are surrounded by hills which look exactly like the ones at Aden. The cantonment is very dry, pebbly and sandy, and such few trees as exist have no leaves now, and there isn't a blade of grass. A howling icy gale whistles continuously through the pass, and it's very cold. Fuel is strictly rationed and all extra firewood has to be bought now as all the roads are blocked next month and the wood carts can't get through. There are running streams beside the roads, but only in the Staff College area. To add to our difficulties, we are four miles from the bazaar. It is a fearful grind back on a bike, all up hill and against this dreadful wind.

We had only two very inferior mats to put on our stone floors when we arrived, and it seemed then that we should never get the house warm. We have now managed to hire four more at the price of Rs. 16. - a month (about 25/-). The furniture supplied by M.E.S. (Military Equipment Services) is in the last stages of decay and is quite frightful. In the town they charge Rs. 2. a piece a month to hire stuff. So you see prices are exorbitant. Food is expensive, decent drink unobtainable and all other commodities either unobtainable or very expensive. So it's no pleasure resort. The only compensation seems to be the very exhilarating air and continuous sunshine.

The authorities at the Staff College seem very unhelpful and very much on the defensive. This course is more than 70 percent regular officers and the others are prospective regulars. As the instructors, in many instances, are of the same seniority or only a very little senior to the students, their attitude is understandable. One of the senior instructors, now a Lieutenant-Colonel, is a man who was Brigade Major to the Brigade Ivor was in in Burma. They were then both Majors, and Ivor told him in Burma that he (Ivor) thought he (the Lt.-Colonel.) was tactically unsound and that he hadn't a clue as to how to run a staff office! We feel this is a good beginning, as the bloke is now to lecture to Ivor on these subjects! It's all really rather funny. The students are grand and needless to say Ivor has met umpteen old friends. With the house in its present shattering state, we have had people in and out. Our chief bugbear is the fact that our kit hasn't yet arrived. There is so much in it that we desperately need. We have now started feeding at home and are trying out the cook. A bit shattering on occasions, but he has possibilities. We had to borrow some crockery from our next door neighbours, Jane and Ken Bright, and we can't hire any here. We are wondering why everyone raves about Quetta – perhaps it is pleasanter on the summer course? We are not joining the Club as we simply can't afford to, and we know too many people to be able to stay out of parties.

Tons and tons of love from us both, and a happy Christmas,
from your loving E.

28th December 1945.

Every day I have been waiting for a letter, but so far no luck. Your last was dated 25th November, which is now nearly a month old.

We are getting quite settled in, and do manage to thaw out in our little room in front of the fire. It really is bitter and we had our first fall of snow two days ago. It wasn't very much and the sun has now melted it all away, but there is plenty lying on the surrounding hills, which makes them look very pretty but reduces the temperature considerably. It is terribly dry, and for that reason there is no pretty frost, as there is no dew to be frosted.

I'm getting to know the other wives gradually. There are some very nice girls here, and I have made friends with one called Bunty Baxter. She's a bit out of the ordinary and we get on very well. The house also is beginning to look a bit more habitable. We have one small room at the back where we can get a really good fug up. In it we have our desks and two armchairs and my sewing box and a lot of books plus family photographs and various junk. Adjoining is the dressing room, which has two chests of drawers and two wardrobes. Off that again our bedroom, which is very large and cold. That leads into the sitting room on one side and the spare bedroom on the other. Both very large and draughty. The dining room is off the sitting room and spare room. We keep a fire in there always, as it is impossible to sit still at meals otherwise. Off the dining room are the pantries and kitchen.

Ivor's course has started. Apparently the lecture rooms are bitterly cold and he comes back frozen. Last night the Staff College Mess gave a party for the marrieds to meet the bachelors, and for the various instructors' wives and other ancient inhabitants to have a good look at the new entry.

I do hope you all had a happy Christmas and that it wasn't a white one like ours. We had a very good party on Christmas Eve. We started off in a bachelor's quarter, where about 10 or more people collected, and after drinks and eats we migrated to the Club. There we danced until the early hours and it was all most hilarious. They really are a grand crowd here and we have some good fun. When we awoke next morning, the place was covered in snow again and a real white Christmas, which I'm certain no one dreamt of! On Christmas Eve before lunch we had quite a collection of people in to drinks. On Christmas Day two of the bachelors, Peter Stewart, who walked out of Burma with Ivor, and one of the British service people, Pat Dorman, collected us to go to church. It was just like the village church at home on Christmas morning. Only the building is earthquake proof and consequently looks like a piece of meccano. Afterwards we drifted to the Club and listened to the band and eventually arrived home for lunch with two extra mouths.

Tons and tons of love, your loving, E.

————————

3rd January 1946

Darlingest Moma,

It seems ages again since I wrote or heard from you. Never have I cursed Christmas so much. We seemed to be constantly running out of things, bread, potatoes, coal etc. I was far too worried to enjoy myself much. Thank goodness it is all over and I hope next year we shall be more organised and able to be more Christmassy. The house looks a bit more presentable, though no warmer.

We had plenty of parties, drinks and dances. We went to a terrific party on New Year's Eve, which was good fun. We went on to the Club to see the New Year in. I have been looking after Bunty's three year-old, Angela, for the last two mornings as Bunty had to go into hospital for a few days just over the New Year, which was rather bad luck.

Since I last wrote, Peter Stewart, a great friend of Ivor's, has moved into our spare room as a p.g. It does help to keep the house warm, and he pays his messing money to us instead of to the mess. It all helps and the fuel allowance is very welcome. He's a nice lad and very easy in the house. There always seem to be people coming in and out and the days are very hectic and I never manage to catch up with myself.

Ivor has a considerable amount of very dull work to do these days, and I must stop and do some typing. Tons of love to you all and do write soon. I hope you aren't as cold as we are.

Your very loving, E.

We had been allocated one of the pre-earthquake bungalows, the old original ones which had survived the devastating earthquake of 1935. We called ours 'Wits End'. It was near the end of the road and beyond lay the rocky, barren plain, criss-crossed by old water courses and large well-like holes reaching down to the ancient underground karezes which carried the snow water from the foothills to the Hanna Lake. This acted as a reservoir. The heights of Murdhur rose from the plain and dominated our view.

On the opposite side of the road lived a newly commissioned Indian officer whose name was Das, the same as our sweeper. This led to some embarrassment early on on two counts. Firstly, whenever we called our sweeper to his duties, Lieutenant Das would pop out of his front door. Secondly, because his original application for commission had been turned down by Ivor when he was serving with the Madras Regiment in 1939/40.

In the garden at the back of the house were two Wana huts, supposedly for our use at night in case of earthquake. I mistook them for the servants' quarters and that is where they moved in. There were three categories of houses at the Staff College then: the ones like ours, which were allocated to couples without children, the war-time hutted accommodation allocated to couples with one child, and the modern earthquake-proof houses allocated to couples with two or more children. Because most of the Indian officers had the largest families, they were, on the whole, the occupants of these quarters. Unfortunately some of the wives were unaccustomed to such homes and had little notion of how to live in them. On account of the cold, some of them tended to live and cook in one room, which was not usually the kitchen, to the detriment of the parquet floors.

In our bungalow I had had to have a thorough cleaning up operation before we could settle in, which included washing off the betel-nut stain on the wainscoting left by the previous occupants. Our kitchen was of the usual Indian pattern, with a fire in a hole surrounded by a spacious hob. Somehow Indian cooks managed to produce fantastic meals on this unpromising arrangement. The khansama (cook) did the marketing, and having arranged with me the day's menus, the meals would appear on the table at whatever time the Sahib decided to eat. I was in no position to tell him how to cook anything, as apart from my short instruction on invalid cookery in my Preliminary Training School days at the Middlesex Hospital, and any tips I had gleaned from Mrs Slattery's excellent and efficient household, I had absolutely no idea how to produce even one course of a meal!

Our bungalow had the usual bathroom arrangement of zinc bath and thunderbox (commode), and a drain running through a hole in the outside wall to the garden, where the bathwater was tipped and used to water the plants. It also had an outside door for the sweeper's access. As well as attending to the commode, his duty was to heat the bath-water, and carry it in in a square kerosene tin with a wooden handle slotted in at the top. The bath-water was heated in a metal drum with a funnel through the middle into which Das fed the wood chippings, which he lit to produce the heat for the water. This Heath Robinson affair was placed outside the door to the bathroom. Since the house faced south, the back premises were on the north side of the house, and this is where the icy wind blowing down the Khojak Pass froze everything in its path. Das sat patiently and philosophically chipping wood and feeding the heater, wrapped up in a thick blanket and squatting in the lee of the water heater. How he ever got any hot water for the baths I shall never know. The freezing wind blew into the bathroom every time he opened the door. It blew up the drain and through every crevice. I eventually arranged a good fire in the bedroom and had the bath brought in there.

The air was so dry in Quetta that one had to use oil in the bath to prevent one's skin cracking. An empty can of tinned food filled with water in summer would evaporate within a few minutes, and the laundry was dry as soon as one had finished hanging up a line. There was a tale current amongst the Army wives that due to the exhilarating air – or was it the water – fertility was particularly high, to the terror of those who did not wish to conceive and the happy expectation of those who did, which included us. Sure enough, after a couple of months, I found myself pregnant. On 17th April I suffered a threatened abortion. A dose of morphia and a week in bed settled things and I was warned that I should rest a lot. So I would stay in bed for breakfast and rest in the afternoon. I continued to take Ivor's notes and type them back for him.

On this, the first post-war course, there was a high percentage of Indian officers, some newly commissioned, because of the speeding up of the Indianisation of the Indian Army. So we entertained a number of Indian couples to dinner and of course mixed with them as usual at the mess parties and other private dinner parties. Entertaining them at home did not meet with the approval of Gretel, who would sit under the table growling until banished in disgrace to the bedroom! Makhmud Salim was his usual chatty self, greeting our guests as his very special friends. He complained to Ivor that he had difficulty understanding the Memsahib.

'Oh, that's easy,' explained Ivor, 'when she says 'lao' (bring) you take it away, and when she says 'lejao' (take it away), you bring it. Main Gul understands her perfectly.

'Thik hai, (o.k.), Sahib', was his simple reply and off he went happy.

In April the men went off on a five-day exercise and I moved in with

Bunty in her Braithwaite Road house, one of the modern ones. Our p. g. Peter had borrowed my beloved riding crop given me at Alexanderhof in 1937, and he had broken it in half. I asked him how he managed that, and he told me he had used it to whack his servant. I was horrified and was quite pleased to see the back of him for a few days.

With the spring, gardening began and I tried to persuade the Staff College mali to allow me a little extra water on my patch for my lettuces. He had control of the water channels which came from the Staff College up the hill and we were one of the bottom houses. So the water had mostly evaporated or soaked away long before it reached us. As the weather grew warmer, we took picnics to Hanna Lake. It was very low at this time, awaiting an earth tremor, so I was told, to open up the water courses.

By May the weather in Quetta was warming up, gone the cold wind and instead dust and blazing sun, but still cold at night. The temperature in 24 hours could swing from 100F during the day to 60F at night, a wide variation. On the first Sunday in May, Wallace Chisholm came with a station wagon and with Peter, Bunty and Pat Dorman and our dogs we took a picnic to Urak, a charming fertile valley with a stream running through terraces cultivated with vines and fruit trees. In a lagoon the dogs played and frisked, and we cooked our lunch over an open fire. Peasant women appeared in their crimson dresses, the bodices embroidered in black or navy, and a small boy presented me with a bunch of roses. It was a lovely day out and a welcome change from the barren surroundings in which we lived.

On 18th May Ivor booked us into the Dak bungalow in the juniper forests of Ziarat at 11,000 ft. It was cool and fragrant and we celebrated our first wedding anniversary with Peter and Pat Dorman and our assorted dogs. As well as Gretel, we had now acquired a spaniel puppy we called Ross, and Peter had another of the same litter called Wink. During the last week of May Chris Miles-Thomas turned up to spend a week of his leave from the Scinde Rifles with us. I took him to the Club swimming pool most days. Ivor got off duty early one day and we all went down to the bazaar and later back to the Club to cool off in the pool and have lunch. We entertained his Colonel and wife and several of our friends to dinner, and it was a week of parties.

The six-month course came to an end in the middle of June and Ivor started getting our furniture back into its crates. There were numerous farewell parties and at a buffet supper given by one of the Directing Staff I recorded in my diary: 'Wonderful supper, but dreary party, 33 percent drunks, 33 percent religion, 33 percent Indian.' We packed up our kitchen and fed in the Mess for the last few days in Quetta. All our belongings were consigned to Cox and Kings in Bombay for storage. Ivor had applied for overseas leave and was taking me to Australia to meet his mother. So there was no staff posting for him and he was sent on temporary duty to HQ Southern Command in Bangalore, five days and five nights away in the train.

We boarded the train on 20th June 1946 with Pat Dorman's two bull terriers and our two dogs, Gretel and Ross, with Main Gul and Makhmud Salim in attendance. After an up-and-down sort of journey, on the whole reasonably comfortable, we arrived in Bangalore at 7 a.m. We put up at Lavender's Hotel and Ivor reported in to Southern Command.

As usual we were quickly swept up into the local social life, dances at the Bangalore United Services Club and drinks with friends, including Wallace Chisholm, who had been posted to a staff job in Bangalore and was to be married on the 8th July. We were invited to lunch with Lieutenant-General Rob Lockhart, then commanding Southern Command. Ivor knew him as he was also a Piffer. Shortly after our arrival, Ivor had been told that we could not expect a passage to Australia before mid-August, by which time I would not be allowed to embark. Shipping companies would not allow a pregnant woman on board within three months of delivery. Ivor cancelled his leave and applied for a staff job in Bangalore. The next day we got notice to leave for Bombay as we had been granted a passage, so plans went into reverse.

On our last day I had to present myself to the doctor for a check before embarking. My pregnancy, I fooled myself, was not too noticeable, but a very alert Indian woman doctor, with barely a glance at me, said 'How many months?' I got on board with only three weeks to spare. We had a farewell lunch with Ken and Jane Bright and were joined by Bliz Reford from the 3rd Sikhs, whom we had missed in Kalyan. In the hotel we had met the Stebbings, who were also travelling to Sydney, so we joined them in a taxi to the docks. Tired and excited, I settled into a comfortable cabin to rest. We sailed on S.S. *Madura* of the B.I. Line on 15th July 1946.

My brother Tom, now married to Jane (née Devereux), had applied for a regular commission in the RAF. However, on the grounds of his colour blindness, this application was turned down, which almost broke his heart. He then applied for a job as trainee manager on a rubber plantation in Malaya. This application was successful and he was writing again to our parents:

3rd June 1946,
On the Boat.

Darling parents,

Just a note to thank you very much for all the lovely holidays and here's to the next time. I am very fit and very red! The boat is packed full, about three-quarters civilian and the rest troops. Men outnumber women by about 4 to 3. The people on board are a queer mixture, the large majority very much 'half-Sir!' I am in a cabin (pre-war 4-berth) with eleven others. Luckily I was first in and chose the middle bunk near the port-hole, a godsend. We sleep in tiers of three and Jack Moss, the other RAF type going out with me, is above me. Food is good. Actually it's a b ... scandal to think that we have to pay £107 for this kind of berth, and everyone is the same or worse, men, women and children, Labour Government ahoy! It is a dry boat, no alcohol, and the old planters bind a bit about not getting their 'stingers' (a whisky and soda). Our cabin is composed of mostly elderly planters who, to start with, took rather a dim view of Jack and me, as they thought we were civil servants (apparently very taboo). But when they saw us learning Tamil and discovered we were going planting, a big thaw out took place and we are now accepted! Agar is on the boat and I chat to him periodically. Most of our time is taken up with learning Tamil or reading and in the evening we go to the flicks every third night and the odd bridge and parlour game occupies our other time. Jack and I entered for the bridge competition and we've just met our opponents, two rather ancient women! So keep your fingers crossed. We are due to arrive in P. Said tonight. Whether we will be allowed ashore or not I don't know.

Love to you both and to Dorothy and Gordon. God Bless, Tom.

Ivor's and my first day on board S.S. *Madura* was spent taking stock of our fellow travellers and we were not greatly impressed. We went with the Stebbings to the Captain's table for meals. This, as it turned out, was not a good move. We soon found some bridge players, as well as a couple who were anxious to learn, and to whom Ivor gave lessons throughout the journey.

Two days later we dropped anchor off Cochin. The ship lay off shore for five days whilst cashew nuts from East Africa were unloaded for shelling, and another consignment of shelled nuts loaded, or so I was told. On our first evening in Cochin we went ashore with two friends in a rowing boat to this enchanting, lush and watery beauty spot. We walked to the hotel for a meal and were rowed back in the middle of the night. The next day we went ashore again and visited the bazaar and lunched in the very nice Club. Our trip the next day was in a launch to see the harbour and the Royal Indian Naval Base at Ernaculum. On 23rd July we weighed anchor and sailed round Cape Cormorin to one of the most southerly places on India's east coast, Tuticorin. Again we anchored off shore and watched fascinated the heavily laden barges sailing out, and our own primitive methods of unloading. The next day brought us to Colombo, where we were to spend another three days. Ivor had a friend from wartime days in Sialkot, Ken Youngman, who was back in Colombo with his tea company. We arranged to dine with him on our last evening and in the meantime booked into the Mount Lavinia Hotel for a good night's rest. Mount Lavinia was a paradise outside Colombo on the seashore, cool and peaceful and in a beautiful tropical setting, with the palm trees reaching down to the beach. There we enjoyed some good food and a stroll along the beach in the evening. On our final day we returned to Colombo and lunched at the Galle Face Hotel and in the evening Ken Youngman entertained us and presented us with a bottle of whisky for the long, lonely sea voyage ahead.

On 23rd July we sailed for Fremantle, 13 days away. Mostly it was boring and sometimes very stormy. I walked my two miles round the deck each day and bridge filled most of the rest of the time. We became friendly with Ivor's bridge pupils, Nan and Peter. The Captain was a dour man with his family in England, and he could see no reason why his passengers should not be subjected to the rigours of English rationing. The food reflected this. One evening steak was on the menu. Ivor, in a loud voice when served, demanded of the steward: 'Take it away and bring me one like the Captain's!' For the rest of the journey the Captain fed in his cabin and we got a much improved menu. Because of the meagre nourishment, Ivor had arranged early on that I should have a special tea brought to me in our cabin consisting of a boiled egg and a glass of reconstituted milk. We celebrated our imminent arrival in Fremantle with a dance on board. We tied up the next day – Australia at last.

It was bliss to get ashore and we walked to the bus stop and took the bus to Perth. The shops were stunning. I yearned for some fresh milk, and Ivor treated me to a milk shake. We lunched with some of our fellow passengers and revelled in the wonderful food. For me the first taste after war-time England and India. It rained and I was reminded of England. We were back on board in time to sail for Melbourne, another five days away.

On 15th August we had a farewell drink with the Stebbings, Clynes and Colonel Brand, as we had decided to disembark in Melbourne and go by train to Sydney, sparing ourselves another week on board. We spent the day in Melbourne visiting the Liaison Mission and going to the theatre to see *Blithe Spirit.* We caught the train for Sydney at 6.30 p.m. and arrived in Sydney at 9.50 a.m. on Saturday 17th August 1946, eleven weeks before the baby was due.

130 Wycombe Road, Neutral Bay,
Sydney, N.S.W. 22nd August 1946.

Darlingest Moma,

We arrived off Melbourne on Thursday evening, 15th July, and tied up and disembarked on Friday morning after nearly five weeks of the damned *Madura.* I got my hair done and Ivor went to the Liaison Mission to report in and try to get some news. I was very impressed with Melbourne, as I am with Sydney. The shops are too marvellous and the food – well we just can't eat it yet, everything is too nourishing and good, after the awful Indian stuff. The fruit is quite beyond my wildest dreams and everything has such a wonderful flavour. Everyone is so friendly everywhere. We caught the evening train from Melbourne after ringing up Ivor's mother. The train journey was very uncomfortable as owing to the coal strikes, all the sleepers had been taken off, and we also had to change in the middle of the night on to the different gauge. We arrived in Sydney at 10 a.m. and I was getting very dithery at meeting my m-i-l, so I lagged behind Ivor and hung around the luggage. He completely missed his mother on the platform; in nine years they had both altered tremendously. However it wasn't long before all the threads were picked up. My m-i-l asked me to call her Tilly. She is charming, a small person with boundless energy, and she nips around the house before I can turn round. She has been tremendously excited and all teed up to meet me. Now we are all beginning to sort ourselves out after the rush of the first few days and we get on very well. She has made the most wonderful woollies for the baby, everything in white, which I like best. She has made a lovely shawl and cot rugs. She has also got a wicker cot and mattress, and has had all sorts of things put into the flat for my convenience, such as an extra hot water geyser in the kitchen. Needless to say, I am getting hopelessly spoilt. She has laid on a doctor and, with the greatest difficulty, got me a bed in a very good hospital. So she has been marvellous. Her car has been done up. It's a dream of a little bus – a Standard 4-seater with folding hood, ideal for out here and does about 40 miles to the gallon. We have all sorts of trips planned, but first we are getting our clothes fixed and the baby's things all in order. We are also having a little rest from roaming after being on the move since June. On Saturday we spent the day eating and clearing away and talking. In the afternoon we drove up to Pennant Hills, about 12 miles, to the Scout Training Camp, which is always Ivor's first port of call. It is a marvellous spot in the bush on a sloping hillside. There is an open-air chapel and log cabins which Ivor helped to build in his Scouting days.

On Monday we went into town to the big shops. We took the ferry across the harbour. It is quite beautiful and we landed in the centre of the city where the ferries tie up. Ivor had gone in early and Tilly and I followed on as I went to see the Doctor in the morning to stake my claim and say I had arrived. A very charming and efficient woman doctor, who was very sympathetic and said: 'You have had a terrible time travelling and on top of that meeting a new mother-in-law.' However, I think she soon realised that I was enjoying life and didn't waste any more sympathy on me! She gave me a thorough overhaul, said the babe was in a good position and that everything should be ok. She told me what to eat and what not to eat and we got on very well. Ivor and I are going to the hospital one morning this week to make our bow. They do appreciate friendliness and one certainly gets it back a thousandfold.

We had a marvellous time looking at the shops, buying odd things for the baby and for ourselves, having first collected our clothing and food coupons. Ivor gets his food coupons from the Army people in Melbourne, but his clothing ones he has to get here. He only gets 24. Pyjamas and shirts are the same coupon value as at home, but socks and handkerchiefs are coupon free, and anything of pure wool is coupon free. Cotton goods are all rationed and expensive in coupons. Food rationing is very liberal, though people here complain about it, but by English standards it's luxurious – 6ozs of butter per person per week, 2lbs of meat per person per week. Ham, bacon, sausages, fish and stewing steak are all coupon free. There is milk ad lib, but no cream unless you buy it in the country. We had a roast chicken which I thought was a turkey by Indian standards. Tea is not so easy, only 2 ozs per person per week, but we'll get some sent from India. There is an awful cigarette shortage, which doesn't affect me but hits Ivor and his mother rather hard.

To get back to our shopping spree in town, Ivor had been scouting around and was determined to buy me an engagement ring. So we ended up minus a lot of money and plus the most heavenly ring. A small but really beautiful solitaire diamond in white gold and a plain claw setting. The diamond glitters the most lovely colours. I then collected my coupons. I get 195 for myself and the babe, which is generous, and extra butter coupons, which gives me a pound a week.

We had lots of mail awaiting us from home and from India. Ivor heard from the Colonel of the Seaforths, whom his Uncle Ivor had contacted for him, and the Colonel was very hopeful about his getting into that regiment.

I must stop this rigmarole. Impressions of Sydney: very pretty girls and all so well dressed and turned out, beautiful blue skies and Mediterranean blue water. The city and suburbs built on hilly country sloping down to the sea. There are lots of lovely gardens and everything is very clean. The buses and post offices look just like the ones in England.

With tons and tons of love from us all, Elizabeth.

My mother-in-law's flat was the back part of a large bungalow on the main road from Neutral Bay to the ferries which plied to and fro across the harbour to Circular Quay in the heart of the city. The front flat of the bungalow was let and was the most attractive part of the house. The back flat appeared to me to be a bit cramped, and our bedroom, right beside the entrance, was filled with a large bed and a large blown up photograph of Ivor's father Claude. Across the narrow passage which ended in Tilly's bedroom was the living room, beyond which was the kitchen. The bathroom and lav were reached by a covered way across the backyard. Ivor's mother was slightly taken aback by my utter uselessness in the kitchen. It was my first experience of life without servants and somewhat of a culture shock. The Sydney suburbs were a rash of brick bungalows with corrugated iron roofs, although relieved by some beautiful trees and gardens full of flowering shrubs and colourful blooms. The flowers and vegetables all looked like prize winners at an horticultural show. I recalled my father's reaction when he visited his sister Aunt Mabel in 1934 – 'where every prospect pleases and only man is vile.'

The first few days passed in a euphoria of new sounds, the raucous bird cry, the rattle of the eucalypts in the breeze and the rumble of the trams up and down the road from Neutral Bay to the ferries. The fabulous beauty of Sydney harbour, with its busy sea lanes and its little wooded coves with bobbing sailing boats moored in their shelter, entranced me. All this enhanced by the wonderful sunny weather. When we went to the City, taking the ferry from Neutral Bay, I thought it was the most wonderful way to travel to work in the City, and from Circular Quay to walk up the hill to one's office. We had already driven over the 'Bridge', which dominated the harbour without competition then from the Opera House, which was to come years later. Ivor in his youth had walked across the bridge on the day it was opened.

During the following week the *Madura* arrived in Sydney and we went to the docks to retrieve our heavy luggage, some of which had to go into bond to avoid paying customs duty. Ivor kept his medal collection, which he was able to catalogue during this leave. His service revolver was confiscated to be returned to him outside territorial waters when he sailed for India. Having dealt with these matters, Ivor went off to camp that week and left me and Tilly sewing shirts with Peg Perkins' assistance. When he returned, he and I went into town again and met Sam Manekshaw who had served with Ivor in Burma and was wounded at the Battle of the Sittang Bridge. He had a job as liaison officer and was not finding the Australians particularly welcoming. We also met Ivor's old Scouting friend, Kenny Mosher, at the Australia.

Our second week-end in Sydney found us at the races, which we thoroughly enjoyed. On the Sunday Ivor borrowed Tilly's car and took me to Pennant Hills Scout camp, where I gave a lecture at the invitation of Mr MacAlister. Afterwards we went to tea with the Dicksons, an elderly couple who had befriended Ivor in his youth, and who lived in a lovely house with a beautiful garden at Castle Hill.

By now I had taken to going for walks by myself and exploring the surrounding area, particularly Balmoral and the beach there, which I loved. Tilly started taking us for drives to the local beauty spots like Manly Beach and Forest Hill. Ivor invited his godson Philip Badham to stay and he accompanied us on some of these outings. The highlight of that particular week was the RAF Ball we attended, where, to my surprise and amusement, debutantes were presented. As the weeks went by, Ivor and I were going ever more frequently to our refuge at Pennant Hills. We would spend the night there and sit on the verandah in the moonlight and watch the opossums. Mr MacAlister had asked me to organise the camp hospital for him and this I was glad to do. We also went to stay with Ken Mosher and his wife Imelda. Ken had been a prisoner of the Japanese and one of the few to survive their treatment in Borneo. Don Wall's book, *Sandakan, the Last March*, describes this disgraceful episode. Ken had been on that death march, but when the officers were separated from their men in 8 Div., he was sent to Kuching. Ken and Imelda had just had their first child and seeing life with a baby depressed me beyond words. It was as well that my mind was taken off the matter by Tilly's plan to visit Jenolan for a couple of nights. We drove into the lovely Blue Mountains and visited the cave with the fossilised skeleton of an Aborigine. The success of that trip to the Blue Mountains set Tilly planning a more ambitious tour to Melbourne and back by the coast road in Victoria.

On 28th September we went off on our marathon journey in the little Standard. We spent the first night in Goulburn, where we stayed in a simple but clean pub for 12/- each including our meals. On the second day, through wind and rain, a rear wheel of the car became loose. However, by driving slowly and carefully we reached Canberra and put her in a garage for repairs. We stayed in the Civic Hotel. Canberra was an extraordinary place. Like so many of the new capital cities being built at that time, it was mainly wide streets with newly planted trees, large Government buildings and empty plots for future housing. The huge Australian War Memorial stood dominating the empty scene. We had intended making a visit to my old school friend Maiu Mez, now Sams, who lived in Wagga Wagga, but owing to the delay caused by the car breaking down, we had to put it off and proceeded instead through Yass to Reedy Creek. The bridge there was under repair and our troublesome rear wheel locked again. We were lucky to be near a house, whence we phoned for a breakdown van. We sat by the roadside from 4–8.30 p.m. until the van arrived. It then failed to start, and between us we blocked the bridge until a passing Buick towed us both out of the way. We got going again but not for long. Eventually it was decided I should take a lift back to Yass, where I arrived at 10.30 p.m. I found rooms in the Club House Hotel and Tilly and Ivor arrived half an hour later having been towed in by a lorry.

A garage fixed the car for us the next day and we set off through the lovely country to Gundagai, and reached Warrgaratta after having tea in Albany. We stayed in the Commercial Hotel, an old country inn reminiscent of the wild west and pioneers. It was very cold and there was no hot water.

We had arranged to meet my cousin, Aunt Mabel's daughter the Reverend Deaconess Sheila Payne, in Benalla, where we lunched with her. I recognised a strong likeness to my Grimsey cousins, Aunt Amy's daughters. We went on our way after lunch and had a picnic tea by the lovely Goulburn River, and then drove on to Melbourne.

On the first day of our return journey we lunched with Valentine Soul, a dear old man, in a delightfully Victorian household a few miles out of Melbourne. We had a splendid meal served on a lovely dinner service. Our journey now took us through delightful countryside, alternately pasture and bush, to Warragul, where we found a comfortable pub and spent a congenial evening round the fire with striking railway workers. On then to Haunted Hill, after which we drove through true Australian bush and arrived at Lakes Entrance, a lovely seaside place with very pretty lakes. As usual we were confronted with our last evening meal punctually at 6 p.m. This was having an increasingly depressing effect on Ivor and made the evenings seem interminable. The next day's drive was through huge gum trees and tree ferns and a very large snake crossed our path. In the very hilly country we stopped outside Cabbage Tree for a break and beyond Bell Bird for lunch. After crossing Cann River, we arrived in Genoa. This was a delightful place with a very nice pub run by friendly people and a glorious log fire to cheer us. I went for a walk after supper (tea) in the moonlight across the river. We made a diversion the next day to visit Gipsy Point and Malacoolar, very beautiful small fishing villages in loch-like country, then on to Eden, another lovely seaside place. The weather was warm and sunny and we had a pleasant bush picnic and the good fortune to find a very comfortable hotel, the Grand, in Bega.

The next day's drive was slow and over very bad corrugated roads. The scenery, on the other hand, was lovely, forest, hills and sea with dunes and inlets and lochs and a charming fishing village at Bermagui. It ended at the Monarch Hotel at Moruga, but another dreary evening, and as my diary records: 'good old Australian nothing to do.'

We were getting near home now, for which I was thankful, as I was beginning to feel very uncomfortable squashed up in the little car bouncing over the rough roads. We crossed Bateman's Bay by ferry and called on Mick Warden, Mrs Perkin's brother, in Milton, where he farmed the family property. We skirted Jervis Bay, the Royal Australian Navy base, and spent the night in the Prince of Wales Hotel in Nowra, a flamboyant red plush establishment and endured another dull evening. My old school friend Annu Mez, now Edwards, had married a week after us and spent her early married life in Nowra. Unfortunately they had recently left for England, so we missed them. From Nowra we detoured to Cambewarra Mountain with its wonderful views, then through Kangaroo Valley to the Fitzroy Falls, finally calling on Ivor's friends the Moshers before getting home.

1st November 1946.

Darlingest Moma,

A letter from you dated 27th October just arrived to-night. So glad to hear Barbara has the daughter she wanted.

I am now sitting like a time bomb! The only consolation being that I can hear it ticking and I think it will go off literally any minute! You needn't worry about my dates being out, I'm not as clueless as all that. For my sake I hope our wire reaches you before this letter.

Tons of love, your loving, E.

3rd November 1946.

Darlingest Moma,

Now I'm a proud Mama! Can you believe it? I hope you got the cable in good time. I wrote you on Friday evening last only 10 hours before Antony was born! In my wildest moments I never anticipated everything being over so quickly. On Friday I had vague pains, all very low in the tum and nothing in the back, and for that reason I didn't take them very seriously and was quite prepared to sit until Monday before anything happened. I had a bath as usual before going to bed that night. It was a little hotter than usual and it must have started the works. As soon as I got to bed, the same pains came thick and fast and it looked as though Ivor was going to have a disturbed night. So at 11.30 Tilly rang the doctor and hospital and we drove to the nursing home. There was only one nurse on duty and she not a midwife. However, my pains seemed to have departed and I felt a complete fraud. Ivor dumped the bags and went home meaning to ring at 9 a.m. and expecting to be told to wait until the evening. I had the time-honoured enema and was put in the labour ward to sleep, which I did in between pains until about 2.30 a.m., when I got a pushing pain and had to push willy nilly. After the second of these and accompanying stretching, I thought I should be landed with the baby any minute. It was about 3 a.m. and the solitary nurse was doing the other babies, so I was all by myself. However I shouted for her and convinced her that anything might happen at any minute and she agreed to fetch the Matron. Matron arrived in her dressing gown, took one look at me and clapped a mask over my face, after I'd had one more push. After that I knew nothing until I woke up at about 5.15 a.m. with Antony alive and kicking! He was born a few minutes before 5 a.m. He is ginger and has a perfect skin, an inheritance from Ivor, I feel. He appears to have Ivor's nose and forehead, but wide-spaced eyes which will doubtless be blue, gold eyelashes and brows, perfect ears, in fact not bad. I wish you could see him. It's all very thrilling although I still feel remarkably un-maternal! Ivor was very cool, calm and collected and slept until Matron rang him at 5.30 a.m., when he would have gone to sleep again only his mother wouldn't let him. I don't know how I managed to get off so lightly. We have now decided to have all four children in quick succession and get the baby stage over in one fell swoop!

Tons of love, your loving E.

P.S. Ivor has just arrived with your cable. Many thanks. did you get ours before Antony was born?

12th November 1946.

Darlingest Moma,

At last the nighties have arrived, so they are not too late after all. Thank you darling, very much, I do hope they didn't entail too much sacrifice of coupons. The cot cover too will be most useful. Your letter, written on Antony's birthday, has also arrived. I too was thrilled to think you knew so soon. Antony is very well. He was circumcised yesterday and doesn't seem to have turned a hair. He feeds marvellously, which is a relief. If he keeps this up, he won't be much trouble. Mother of course is far more nuisance! I have had a lot of trouble with my breasts. They seem to be settling down at last, thank God, and there's pints of milk. My other worry at the moment is that I can't even stand on my legs! The Doctor said yesterday that I could start getting up. My legs have been very sore and very stiff and getting very weak. I've kept doing exercises and made Ivor massage me once or twice. However I suppose they'll get better. I probably told you I had a lot of cramp before Antony was born and also whilst he was being born, so maybe that is something to do with it. I hope to get out of this hospital on Thursday, the day after to-morrow.

Tons of love and many thanks, E.

23rd November 1946.

Darlingest Mom,

Your letter of 13th November arrived the other day. I'm glad you're off on another little jaunt and hope the 'W.W.' ('Wild Women', East African Women's Association) weren't too wild. Your little pink cot cover is an absolute boon. The weather here is quite impossible. It's freezing one minute and boiling the next! I never know how to dress Antony a) to keep him warm b) to keep him cool! The pink cover seems to be the answer at the moment and he lives in it. The nighties will do when he is 4 – 6 months old. Everything I have is much too big still, however he'll grow into them. He is doing very well and his only trouble seems to be acute constipation – like Mother! I weighed him yesterday for the first time since leaving hospital and he is now 6lbs 11ozs, having put on his scheduled 6ozs very nicely. I also went to see the Doctor as directed, and she was perfectly satisfied. He sleeps very well and yells very well. I regret to say I don't hear him at night, although he is in our bedroom! Both Ivor and I sleep through it. I wake at 5 a.m. partly from physical discomfort and partly habit, always to find A. awake. His waking hour seems to be 4.30 a.m., which isn't bad really.

On Thursday we christened him. It was a terrific day. I think I told you of all the trouble we had over a C of E parson. In the end Raleigh Croll rang up to say he could get us a Presbyterian. So we said 'o. k'. He was a very nice man and conducted a very simple and pleasant service. It was a gorgeous afternoon. Ivor and I borrowed Darcy Croll's ramshackle old car and drove up to the camp at Pennant Hills before lunch. We lunched there and I fed Antony and dressed him up in the family christening robe, in which he looked rather sweet, with the frills and furbelows. When all the guests arrived in various cars, Antony had just finished getting his wind up and lay in his basket looking perfectly angelic whilst everyone inspected him. We then all trailed down to the open air chapel, which involved some minor mountaineering, and the ceremony was held. Afterwards we came back to the log cabin verandah, where we had some champagne and the top layer of the christening cake. The whole thing went off with a terrific swing. All the guests prior to arriving at the camp collected at Tilly's, where she met them and organised them into the cars. A very amusing incident was when Raleigh, who was giving the parson a lift, said he had more room in his car. Tilly turned to Michael Stuart in fun and said: 'you'll go, won't you?' knowing Michael would say 'not bl … likely.' Then Aunt Mabel chirped up and said 'I'll go – I'm a church worker!'

Antony is a pukka tough and has a terrific hand-grip and a strong kick.

Must stop, tons of love, E.

Time Gone

Later I wrote to my friend Elise:

We spent our leave under rather trying circumstances. Ivor hates being at home with his mother for any length of time. As he is the only child, naturally he is the be-all and end-all of his mother's existence. She is a delightful person, but she is old now and has had a terribly hard life and I don't think she ever got over the shock of Ivor getting married and the fact that he is no longer entirely hers. Not that he really was before as he's fearfully independent, but she could think he was. As a result you can understand that she had a very natural subconscious resentment of me. I think she likes me well enough, but there just was always an atmosphere. I tried hard but I couldn't rise above it, and the prospect of having to stay in Australia and let Ivor go home without me was more than I could stand. It was hard for poor Ivor too, as he loathed being at home all the time but hadn't the heart to break away as he felt his mother would be so heartbroken, quite rightly. However, before we knew of his date of sailing, and while I was still in hospital, Ivor managed to get a small flat about 120 miles from Sydney at Bundanoon, right out in the bush. We were to go there a week after I came out of hospital without his mother. I think he fixed it up in desperation, as I got so depressed in hospital, I used to spend my life weeping! I think he told his mother I wouldn't live with her when he went, but I don't know where I should have gone with the child. The week after I came out of hospital, when Antony was 3 weeks old, we weighed him and he was gaining beautifully – just as he should. The day before we were due to leave for Bundanoon, the phone went when I was in the flat by myself and it was the Liaison Mission people to say that Ivor was to sail on December 7th. It was then 26th November. My heart dropped into my boots and it was then I think that the damage was done to my milk supply, for when we returned from Bundanoon, Antony had lost 2ozs on his previous weighing. Ivor and I had talked and talked over our plans, and decided that as the boat was going to Colombo and not any Indian port, I might as well come with him. It meant that my passage would be paid, whereas if I stayed in Australia, we would have to pay it all ourselves. When we had decided that I should travel with Ivor, we rang his mother and told her to come up and join us, as we would both be leaving. It was only fair for her to see as much of us as she could. We were to sail on the Saturday, and on the Monday we returned to Sydney. It was on the Tuesday that I discovered Antony had lost weight. You can't picture the flap I was in (or can you?) I was in the throes of ringing up doctors and baby clinics when Ivor, who was in town fixing the passage and 1001 things, rang up to tell me that our heavy kit had to be ready to load the very next day! At that stage I hadn't even got a cabin trunk, let alone done any packing. However I was far too worried about Antony and his underfeeding to worry about packing. That afternoon I spent test-feeding at the clinic, the end result being bottles, teats, glaxo etc. and I was furious. How I got through the Tuesday, Wednesday and Thursday before we embarked on Friday I don't yet know. I still look pale and pink-eyed and quite washed out as a result. What with Antony and his feeding racket, umpteen people in to say good-bye, packing, packing, packing. It was a nightmare.

At last we got on board to find Ivor in one dormitory and self and Antony in another both on D. Deck and so aft that we were on top of the propellers. Talk about travelling steerage! There was only one other girl with a 15-month old baby and a QA Matron. The latter, with Ivor's assistance, washed the nappies for me. She was grand! In Melbourne we had one more frantic day, when my old German friends, the Mezs, turned up to meet us. It was marvellous seeing them again and Ivor liked them awfully. Antony had a bad day and ended up by being parked on the floor of the ladies cloakroom on two cushions in charge of the attendant in one of Melbourne's poshest hotels, where we had dinner with our friends. Needless to say he roared his head off in justifiable indignation.

As ever, yours, Elizabeth.

A month before Antony was born, Tom was writing to our parents again:

2nd October 1946.

Gadek. Malaya.

Darling parents,It's the awfully ungrateful son again, and darlings, I'm sorry but the last two to three weeks have been a bit of a resettlement campaign! I went down to Singapore on the 11th of last month as I heard the boat was due in on the 12th. I motored down with another type from up here, we got down at about 7 p.m. and found out that the boat was not due in until the 13th, so I parked myself on Gwen Lane and spent two very enjoyable nights with them. I like Frank a lot, a very sound type. The boat was due in at 10 then 11 then 12, bags of panic. Eventually I got down there at 12.15, just after it docked, but no civilians were allowed on or off before 2, so after a quick look at all the faces leaning overboard, of which Janie's wasn't one, the type I came down with in the car and I went off and had a few drinks to encourage us! We got back at about 2.15 only to discover that the ticket he had (I hadn't got one) wouldn't allow us on board, but just at that moment I espied my love, back view, so I gave a yelp and she turned round and completely failed to recognise me! Anyway, after proving my identity and being introduced to the boy friend, also ex-RAF, who had been a bit of a hero and got her and most of her luggage off the boat, we departed for the Raffles Hotel where Frank had managed to wangle us a room. It's a shocking dump. At 4.30 approx. we met the boy friend again, David Shanon, and a rather big party ensued ending in Jane and I having one of our mad fights and she rushing round Singapore by herself in a rickshaw and me trying to get the police out to look for her! After a couple of very hectic days, during which time we decided to separate on numerous occasions, we eventually got on to a train and arrived in Tampin at 5.00 a.m. on Monday morning!

More apologies from your awful son for not writing more often and for not posting this before now. To-day (8th) another of Begg Roberts' managers has come up to live with us for some time. His estate is in Java and he cannot go to it until the trouble quietens down in that part of the world, so the only place he can come to is here, where he will probably take over from me until his departure, a bit of a blow but he seems quite pleasant and it may all be a blessing in disguise. Anyway we are keeping our fingers crossed to that effect.

Much love Tom.

The gap in Tom's letter had been used by Jane to say that she hoped to take up welfare work and was learning to ride the motor bike, so that she could go off into the blue with her English-Malay dictionary and bottles of DDT and Dettol on the back!

Having embarked on R.M.S. *Orbita*, we found that conditions on board were bad. Because of her reputation and in spite of a long queue of people waiting to move overseas from Australia after the War, they could not fill her. Hence our abrupt summons to sail, as all service people at the end of their leave or posting were rounded up to take passage in her. The decks with cabins remained unoccupied. Antony's accommodation was a net hammock attached to the safety rail of my bunk. Mercifully I had insisted, against much opposition from the shipping people in Sydney, on bringing Antony's wicker pram with me. So I was able to put him in it on deck, tied to a handrail and well protected by mosquito netting, where he was able to lie and kick or sleep in peace. One unfortunate girl with a Chinese baby had to carry him with her everywhere, as she had left cot and pram behind as instructed.

There was a dreadful atmosphere on board, aggravated by the fact that the ship was still 'dry', although by this time British shipping had reverted to its usual 'wet' state after the War. All ships went dry during the War to conform to American requirements. My life was governed by Antony's complex feeding arrangements, which took up a lot of time. The stewardess was very helpful over the feeding bottles as I had no facility for sterilising or for boiling water, and because of the very limited time that fresh water was available for washing, the QA Matron helped Ivor with the nappies. There was only one sitting for meals and dinner was at 7 p.m. I seldom managed to arrive in time and the stewards refused to serve me any course that I had missed. I lived on puddings and cheese. The final straw came when a member of the crew discovered a stowaway on board. Orders were given for every passenger to be mustered on deck at 5 a.m. Having just got to sleep, I was furious at being rudely awakened and told, 'Get on deck and take your baby with you.' Ivor and his dormitory companions were equally angry at this unwarranted disturbance, and furious signals went off to HQ Singapore loud with complaint at our treatment on one of His Majesty's hired transports. The Australian doctors had refused to vaccinate Antony against smallpox at such a young age, so I got the ship's doctor to do it for me. Ivor became very friendly with this Irishman and he let us move into his empty sick-bay and get away from the dormitories. After we left Fremantle, Ivor at last got possession of his revolver, and we had a whip-round to pay for the stowaway's passage. My mother later sent me a newspaper cutting of a report of this woman's arrival in Liverpool.

As we were calling at Singapore, I had written to Tom, hoping that he and Jane might be able to meet us in Singapore, but we had such a short stay there that it was not worth their while making the journey from up country.

A letter from Tom to our parents had given his latest news.

19th November 1946.
Gadek Rubber Estate,
Tampin, Negri Sembilan.

Darlings,

I expect you have completely given me or rather us, up for lost. I haven't the vaguest idea when I last wrote, but feel it is probably many moons ago. In fact I have an awful feeling that the last letter I got from you two days ago referred to my last letter to you dated 25th October. Well, anyway I will assume so and try to give you the highlights since then. What grand news about E. She wrote me a reply to my letter, which I got about two and a half months ago, and in which she asked me to get her some elastic, which I did, and I've still got it. I am a shocker! Jane and I are glad to hear about Gordon's eye. He must be a different person after such awful suspense. The main item of news is that Jane is going to be a mother, me a father and you two grandpop and mop once more. We reckon the ETA is about 1st July. It's a boy! We've proved that by using a gold ring suspended from a piece of cotton, if held over my hand it goes round in circles, if over Jane's hand, up and down, if over Jane's tum round and round in circles – q.e.d! It's either going to be called Julian or Jeremy. Which do you like the best, or hate the least? After that bombshell, we will pass on to other items of news. We got an enormous lorry for the estate t'other day. It had to be collected from a place 90 odd miles away. I was going to fetch it on the motor bike and Janie decided to come too, so we set off very early in the morning and after travelling about 50 miles, we stopped for breakfast and I left Janie there, quite a nice 'rest house', and went on and collected the lorry and picked her up on the way back. So we now have transport for getting around. Life goes on in much the same way as usual. I play rugger every Saturday and sometimes on Wednesday. Janie always comes with me and she watches and talks to various persons on the touch line and in the evening we adjourn to the club for dinner, dance and party. Miller, the bloke who is here until Java is open once more, has now moved into the big house, so we are once more on our own in our house. He is away just now having gone to Kuala L. for the races last Saturday. We expect him back to-night. He is quite pleasant and very harmless and much better than Allan, who doesn't need to visit whilst he (Miller) is here, a godsend. Next Saturday there is the return match v. Selangor the (K.L.) people and a very good party should be had afterwards. And November 30th is St. Andrew's night, which, as nearly every other person is a Scot, is a 'right royal affair'. During the week things are usually fairly quiet, although we either have someone in or go out about three nights out of six. No more for now. I will get Janie to add a few words. Much love, and I'm sorry I can't be there to discuss the MCC tour with Pops. I still reckon we'll win even after the display v. All Australian XI.

Much love from us both and God bless, Tom.

The next day Jane wrote that she was 'preggers' and that they were quite blasé about it, but it was relieving the boredom. She goes on to say that after much ring-swinging they had decided that it would be a boy, but not to worry too much about the name Jeremy as it's bound to be a girl, and that she doesn't mind what sex it is. She also wrote that Tommy was reckoned the third best rugger player, and is in the Negri Semblam team.

When we reached Singapore, Ivor went ashore with the ship's doctor to buy some drink. They had quite a party ashore and by the time the ship was due to sail, there was no sign of them. I became increasingly anxious and decided the only thing to do was to stand at the top of the gangway with Antony in my arms and prevent the crew from raising it. At the last possible moment Ivor and the doctor appeared on the quayside, a bit the worse for wear. Ivor's only justification was to say: 'Ship can't sail without the Doctor.'

Our next port of call was Colombo and we were back on the sub-continent. It was Christmas 1946. A New Year was about to dawn in new places for the three of us.

Chapter Seventeen

Last Days in India – Ceylon, Bengal,
Madras and Home 1947

BY THE TIME WE ARRIVED IN COLOMBO, I had decided that I would disembark with Ivor, regardless of where he might be posted. At least Antony and I would be on the same continent. I wrote to my friend Elise:

Colombo is one of those maddening harbours where the ship anchors off shore and one has to land from a gangway onto a pontoon and thence into a launch or rowing boat. The day we disembarked, there was a fearful swell in the harbour and poor old Ivor got his toe crushed taking Antony from me. I was on the gangway and he was on the pontoon which was bouncing about like a cork, and his toe got crushed between the gangway and the pontoon.

In spite of this Ivor stood his ground and took Antony in his arms. He reported into the local Army authorities to find that no posting order awaited him. They had to signal to Delhi HQ for orders, but no instructions arrived before the ship sailed on to England. My letter to Elise continues:

We were completely shattered by Ivor's posting orders. He is back with a battalion doing internal security duties in Dacca in Eastern Bengal (now Bangladesh), a non-family station and in one of the worst riot areas. We thought at least he would get a staff job, but he has gone back to regimental soldiering, which is an awful strain nowadays in the Indian Army. We had two sticky days in the heat of Colombo. Ivor had looked up an old friend who had served in the F.F. in the war, Ken Youngman, now back in his job with a tea company. As neither Ivor nor I wanted to keep Antony in the heat of Colombo, Ken suggested I stay in the Bandarawela Hotel in the highlands in the centre of the tea plantations. Ivor managed to get 24 hours leave to take us to Bandarawela before leaving on New Year's Day for his week-long train journey to Dacca.

This is a wonderful place – beautiful hill scenery in the midst of tea plantations, with a cool climate, although very wet just now because of the monsoon. The hotel is very pleasant and homelike. Any evening that I feel like it, there's always a gang of people in the bar and everyone knows everyone else and it's all very friendly. So I couldn't be in a better spot and it's notoriously healthy for children. Of course I flap like an old hen over Antony. I must stop now and feed him. I expect Carol is getting enormous. It will be her first birthday by the time this arrives. I got a very nice letter from old Bill P. He does write in such a quaint style! Love to Harwood and tons to you, old friend. Write again c/o Grindlay's Bank, Colombo, as I might move from here.

As ever, Elizabeth.

16th February 1947.
Hotel Bandarawela,
Ceylon.

My dearest Elise,

Life is hell without Ivor, as you can imagine. He is in a basha camp (grass huts) several miles out of Dacca and there is only one other British officer in the battalion, an old friend, Ronnie Webb, and his wife and baby girl. Dacca has only about 20 Europeans now so life is terribly dreary for him. Not knowing what is going to happen or when is rather getting us both down. I can't join him as it's a non-family station, otherwise I should have been with him by now – riots or no.

Antony is flourishing here and has put on nearly three pounds since we arrived six weeks ago. He is at the sweet cooing age and lies and gurgles to himself for hours on end. He never cries. I loathe not having Ivor to enjoy him too.

Write soon, love, E.

I reported in to the M.O. at Diyatalawa and also got my NAAFI card for rations from the shop there. Kind people would give me a lift to the camp and I took Antony to be weighed. I met several of the tea planters in the hotel bar and was invited to their beautiful homes with fabulous gardens. One in particular I remember called Ballagalla Ella and some very kind people called Grant. One garden looked over an escarpment into the jungle hundreds of feet below, where one could see elephants in the clearings.

Ivor in the meantime had been sorting out the 8/12th F.F.R. He wrote that he hoped I could join him when he had arranged joint messing with Ronnie and Pat Webb. They had the only concreted kitchen area other than the messes. The basha camp lived under the perpetual fear of fire. Everything was very dry and the train sparks and the local youth, who liked to throw fire brands into the camp, caused Ivor to have a whole company on fire picket. Ivor took himself off to Sialkot, the Regimental Centre, with some of his problems. He stopped off in Delhi and saw Wallace Chisholm, who then had a staff job at HQ. Ivor was angling for a staff appointment, and as General Rob Lockhart, commanding Southern Command, was due to visit Delhi, he hoped his request would receive favourable consideration. Wallace had already handed Gretel back, and Ivor took her with him on this trip so that she should not be abandoned again so soon. When he got back from Dacca, he got permission for me to join him. I got his letter on 10th March 1947 saying 'Get to Calcutta'.

I rang Mackinnon Mackenzie for news of shipping and with the request for a passage as soon as possible. Our old friend S.S. *Madura* was due in on 16th March. On the 16th I got a message to say there was a phone call coming through for me and to stand by. It finally came at 11 p.m., Ivor speaking from Dacca and wanting to know when I was coming. My diary records 'The whole hotel listened in!' He had been trying to connect to the hotel for about a week, but his signallers continually put him through to Shillong in Assam instead of Ceylon! I rang Cooks the next morning and they told me they had booked me a passage on the *Madura*, which was sailing on the 20th. I got Antony's food ready, packed, and my friends drove me to the station to catch the overnight train to Colombo. There I was met by Cooks who said that the *Madura* wasn't sailing until Saturday 22nd March, but that I could embark. Helen Oldfield was in Colombo and we lunched together at the hotel and she looked after Antony while I went to the docks to see the luggage through. We had a nice comfortable cabin, and the crew, who had known me on the way to Australia, were delighted to see me and the baby I had produced! The ship was not full on its last leg to Calcutta, and with a few others I sat at the Captain's table. It was a different and much nicer man than the one we had known on the way out.

We arrived off the Hooghly River at 5 p.m. on the 26th March and picked up the pilot. We anchored in the river at 11 p.m. At midday we started moving up the river again and arrived at Garden Reach at 6 p.m. I fed Antony early. The poor child was covered in mosquito bites from the last night in the river, as well as suffering from prickly heat. He was not at his best to greet his father, who was coming to Calcutta to meet us. I was in my bath when the stewardess called me out to tell me that Ivor had come aboard with the police in their launch. It was 27th March 1947. We spent the rest of the evening celebrating and consuming the remains of my Naafi whisky ration. The ship eventually docked the next day at 6 p.m. but we were unable to go ashore because of the curfew. Poor Antony had to spend another night in the humid heat amidst the swarms of mosquitos. One of Ivor's fellow officers, Lieutenant Nand Lal, was waiting to help us at Sealdar station, and again Ivor was unable to contact him because of the curfew. We eventually disembarked on the 29th at 11 a.m. and got a taxi to the Grand Hotel, still the same old R.T.O's transit camp.

It was very hot and Ivor discovered he could not get an armed escort to take us through the rioting areas of the adjoining Muslim/Hindu quarters. Escorts were reserved for British service personnel only; Indian Army had to make their own way. The Sikh taxi drivers would not go off the main roads, nor take us through the Muslim area, so we had to fall back on the decrepit horse-drawn carriages of the Muslims, commonly known as 'tikka gharis'. We put Antony in his carry cot on the seat behind the driver, whilst Ivor and I sat, eyes on stalks, on the seat facing the way we were going. At every intersection of the narrow alleyways through which we trundled, we looked for signs of rioting crowds, for we stood no chance should we inadvertently run into one. The road was too narrow to turn in and the poor old horse could barely manage a trot. It was my most terrifying experience. As we approached the main road we saw a lot of patrol cars, ambulances and fire engines. My diary records 'Things looked sticky'. As we reached the entrance to Sealdar station, I saw a posse of Indian police squatting on their blankets and I stumbled thankfully from the ticka ghari with Antony in my arms to join them – safe again. Ivor went off to find a room for us to spend the day until the train left for Dacca at 11 p.m.

We arrived at Goalunda Ghat at 6 a.m., where we were to pick up the river steamer to take us up the Brahmaputra to Narayanganj, the riverside halt for Dacca and our camp at Tezgaon. It was a beautiful 12-hour trip upstream through the watery countryside, where the villages clustered on the mounds which rose above the flat plain. Ivor had become friendly with a Major Bowers in the Assam Rifles and his wife Dulcie, who were stationed in Dacca. They very kindly sent their car to meet us and take us to the camp.

The first news to greet Ivor on his arrival back in camp was a posting as GSO II, Madras Area. The realisation struck us that we had spent all that money on a ten-day journey, only to have to retrace our steps almost the whole way back again! At least the next journey would be at Government expense.

On 31st May 1947 and my first full day in camp, the Battalion's 6th anniversary celebrations were the order of the day. First on the programme was a 'pagal' gymkhana, or crazy gymkhana, and we watched it at 8.30 a.m. I then turned to the task of settling into some sort of routine in our grass hut. Because of the perpetual fire risk, Antony's carricot had all essential documents, money and valuables under his mattress, with him on top of it all and Gretel on a lead fastened to the cot handle. This arrangement enabled me to pick him up cot and all and dash for the door. Ivor had fixed up some pretty curtains from cloth woven in the local jail. Some of this durable weave is still doing duty after 50 years. The hot water supply was a simple matter of filling the ubiquitous kerosene cans with water at dawn and standing them in the sun. In this way hot water would be available from about 10 a.m. onwards for the washing.

The day's celebrations ended with a 'bara khana' for the jewans and I was invited to taste each of the dishes. I met all the V.C.Os and afterwards we were entertained by the Khattack dancing, and the very spectacular sword dance. The following day the Colonel was entertaining the local dignitaries from Dacca and he asked me to receive the guests. I spent the morning in the officers' mess arranging the flowers and helping to organise the party. The camp lights failed that evening so it was difficult to get dressed in time. I met the Nawab of Dacca and his wife the Begum, a very petite and attractive woman. We spent a most amusing evening.

My duty the next day was to present the prizes following the inter-Company football competition. This was also early in the morning, and before lunch there was a mess party and I was asked to cut the cake. In the evening we were guests at the Commissioner's house in Dacca, and later went on to a party at the Club, where I met again most of our guests from the previous evening. In three short days I had met most of the Battalion and all the important residents of Dacca, both British and Indian.

The Battalion was on internal security duties and this involved helping the police to control the endemic rioting in Dacca, now exacerbated by the uncertainty of the immediate future of the sub-continent. Rumours abounded, and policy making was going ahead furiously in the government circles throughout the country. No one knew quite what lay ahead. The Colonel informed Ivor that he was going on a course and Ivor would be required to command the battalion until he returned. Our move to Madras was therefore postponed. So we settled down to a few weeks of new routine. Pat, her baby Patsy and her ayah, spent most of their mornings with us. We ate together in Pat's basha, just down the road. Almost every day we enjoyed visits from friends and brother officers. There was no time to be bored. The first week-end I was there Ronnie went off on a pig shoot, and Ivor organised a truck for Pat and me to go to the races. We loaded up the two babies, the ayah and the dog and set off for the Club. We left the ayah there with the babies whilst Pat and I walked over to the race course to watch the very unpredictable Dacca Races. One peculiarity of the race course was a little temple surrounded by trees and bushes in the middle of it. One never quite knew in which order the horses and riders would emerge from behind this object! When the races were over we spent the evening in the Club meeting all our friends and fellow race-goers. This became a regular Saturday outing and was always much enjoyed. Many evenings we were invited out to parties given by our friends in Dacca, and we always took the children with us. Although I had no ayah, our orderly was most anxious to help care for Antony and finally prevailed upon me to let him feed him sometimes. Ivor invited the V.C.Os to a tea party and Antony was the centre of attraction. He played his part well, but found the Sikh's beards a bit daunting.

We were invited to the Palace. I wrote to my mother:

I must tell you about my visit to the Palace in Dacca. Ivor had warned me what to expect. He couldn't come down the morning I went with Ronnie and Pat, but had been before to a meal. The Begum is a spritely, vivacious and petite person, very dainty, and one wonders how she manages to get out of the Palace looking smart and clean. It is an enormous building in complete disrepair. Washed clothing is put out to dry on the terrace steps. The lawns, which in former days swept down to the river, are just dust, stray pie-dogs and dirty children running around. The staircases in the palace feel as though they will give under you. The Begum is officially in purda as they are Muslims, so she showed us her quarters first, where she lives in a room adjoining her 'son'. This man is her step-son actually and several years older than she, I should think. He has a bed, but the old Nawab sleeps on two mattresses on the floor. We were then shown the Durbar hall and the banqueting hall, both choc-a-bloc with all sorts of incongruous pieces of furniture including crystal chairs, all looking a bit tired and moth-eaten. Her little dog followed us everywhere and managed to make at least one mess in every room, which didn't seem to worry the Begum at all and probably accounted for the strange and unpleasant smell. Finally she took us up to her own private look-out tower. From there we looked down on all sorts of shacks surrounding the palace in which live the 'family' – in all upwards of 500! On returning to her quarters through the palace, we passed the Nawab and step-son holding a conference – all in dhoties and pyjama jackets and unshaven, squatting on their chairs. Ivor afterwards told me that they were probably holding a Muslim League meeting! The step-son, when he appears in Dacca, is always immacu-lately dressed, which one would never credit, having seen him at home. Dacca, in keeping with its palace, is equally dilapidated.

The next two days were occupied with packing and farewell parties. We departed on 16th April. Once again the Bowers put their car at our disposal. The VCOs lined up to say good-bye, and each one garlanded Ivor. Antony and I got two garlands each. We lunched with the Commissioner at Narayanganj before boarding the river steamer at 1.45 p.m. After a very pleasant cruise downstream, we reached Goalundaghat at 11 p.m. and were glad to lose the company of a rather aggressive MLA supporter (Muslim League). East Bengal was soon to become East Pakistan and later on Bangladesh.

We travelled through the night on the train to Calcutta, where we arrived at 6 a.m. Jemedar Sher Shah took our kit for us in a 'ticka ghari', and we managed to get a taxi to take us to Howrah Station. There was still a curfew in force and trouble in Calcutta, but we had an uneventful drive to the station, spent the day in a retiring room and caught the 6 p.m. to Madras. We had two nights and a day on the train with the baby and Gretel, but no orderly to see to our needs. I managed to get hot water by going up to the engine driver with a can, which enabled me to warm up Antony's feeds.

I had brought my own boiled water ready bottled with which to mix the feeds. By the end of the third day's travelling Antony was getting a bit restless, but he was very good under the circumstances. He was nearly six months old.

We arrived in Madras at 10 a.m. on 19th April 1947 and were met at the station, which we had hardly dared hope for. We were taken to Mackay's Gardens.

Our life in Mackay's Gardens lacked all privacy. So we used to sit out on the lawn under the stars in the evenings in order to converse without being overheard. We were rather a trial to our neighbours, as Antony was inclined to be noisy during the afternoon siesta, while at night Gretel gave tongue as she sought out the bandicoots which infested the place. I once watched her as she killed one leaping from the verandah and caught it in mid-air! Ivor looked up old friends in Madras, the Killicks. I explained we needed a bearer and Binty sent a very nice old man round to see us. We were delighted with him.

We were constantly searching for a bungalow or flat to escape the discomforts of Mackay's Gardens. On one of Ivor's visits to the housing authorities he discovered that they were very short of clerks. Having one surplus to establishment he made a deal – clerk in return for the next vacant accommodation. By the end of May we moved into an empty flat in Khadar Nawaz Khan Road. This was a modern building with indoor plumbing, a new experience for us. The sapper in the flat below us had installed a pumping arrangement from the well in the garden to the tank on the roof, and so long as he and his family were in residence this worked well. The old man got hold of a cook for us, and he and the chokra (boy) now looked after our needs. They borrowed the necessary kitchen equipment and we took crockery and cutlery on loan from Mackay's Gardens. There was no point in getting all our luggage from Bombay when it was now quite obvious that we would not be long in India. We sent for some of our smaller items to make life a bit more comfortable and hired a bed, a table and two chairs. Spartan it was, but at least we had a home of our own again. Our sapper neighbours were soon to go back to U.K. and we inherited all manner of useful items that they no longer wanted.

In May the 4/12th F.F. came through Madras and Ivor and I went to the docks to meet them. They stayed in the transit camp for a week and we had several parties with Ivor's old friends. Also in May Ivor got the devastating news that he had not been accepted for British service in the Seaforth Highlanders. It was a bitter blow and he now got down to thinking of other jobs in which he might have a chance. He wrote off to the Colonial office and decided to take a correspondence course in law. Our future looked so uncertain and the terms for staying on in India were not attractive. They were for a 3-year contract only and British officers could only apply for regiments in the country in which they were then serving, in Ivor's case India. As his regiment would go to Pakistan, this held no attraction to him. When Ivor saw General Eric Goddard, who had taken over command from General Rob Lockhart, Eric advised Ivor to apply for the R.A.F. Regiment, who were then looking for experienced officers.

It was all very sad and depressing for us, not helped by the hot and humid weather, which was very wearing on the temper. Both Antony and I were suffering from prickly heat. It was now 107F during the day with 70 percent humidity. Nevertheless in June we were organised enough to hold a small party for Ivor's birthday, and soon after an old friend of Ivor's turned up, Edward Walker. He was about to be married to Linda, a FANY, a very vivacious and amusing woman. We were asked to be witnesses at the ceremony in their hotel bedroom! They moved into Mackay's Gardens and Linda would come to take Antony and me to Elliot's beach in her ramshackle car. These were lovely outings. Antony loved the beach and I thoroughly enjoyed the bathing when the surf was not too strong. Our other haunts were the Adyar Club, the Gymkhana Club and the Connemara Hotel.

From home I got the news which my mother had received by cable from Malaya that Tom and Jane had a baby daughter, Nicola, born on 11th July 1947.

In mid-July the sapper and his family below us went back to England and an Indian family moved in complete with cow and chickens, in which Gretel took great interest. The first we knew of them was when we returned with some friends to our flat and found our new neighbour fixing up his wireless aerial on our verandah!

As July turned into August, the weather became cooler as the monsoon broke. Ivor was busy organising the Independence Day Parade for Madras. The sub-continent was to split between India and Pakistan, and Ivor's beloved regiment was to be divided along class lines. Dogras, Gurkhas and Sikhs to

India, Punjabi Musselmans and Pathans to Pakistan. All these men had fought with great gallantry and loyalty side by side in so many wars, and were now to split up and fight each other. British officers would never forgive the government, which, with unseemly haste, had brought this disaster about. Rumours were filtering through of the horrific massacres taking place in the Punjab and of the murder, misery and displacement that was going on. We couldn't believe it was happening. It was a heartbreaking time for the British officers of the Indian Army, who had served the various races of India with great devotion and affection and fashioned a fighting force second to none in the world. Looking back now in our old age, we can see that that work shines through in the successor regiments of the armies of the sub-continent to-day. From our personal point of view we were thankful that our belongings were stored in Bombay, as all communication with the emerging Pakistan had become very difficult if not impossible. Those British officers stationed in India who had bank accounts in Lahore or Karachi and their luggage stored there found it almost impossible either to get money, or to get instructions through about their belongings.

We attended the final parades of British Regiments leaving Madras. The Essex Regiment Beat the Retreat in Fort St. George on 1st August, followed on the 4th by the Inniskillins, who held their farewell ceremonial parade there. The great day came, on 15th August 1947, with lots of headaches for Ivor, who found himself and four British Military Police doing crowd control. In the evening the Indian officers gave a big party to say farewell to the British officers and we were entertained by some splendid Indian dancing. The following day we were all invited to a very good party on board HMIS *Kristna*, which was in port for the celebrations.

The heat was taking its toll of Antony and he had failed to put on weight for several weeks and was very reluctant to eat anything. Linda Walker had to go into hospital for an abdominal operation and I undertook to supervise the nursing for the first few critical days afterwards. It was decided that I should take Antony up to the Nilgiri hills and out of the heat. So we packed up the flat and Ivor arranged with a fellow officer, Tony Home, at Madras Sub-Area that he would p. g. with them whilst I was away. Ursula and Tony were very good to us and Ursula arranged rooms for me in Ootacamund. I set off on an overnight train journey on 1st September, with an ayah Ursula had found for me. We were to stay with a Miss Scott of Stone Ridge. It wasn't up to much but once Antony got over the journey, he began to pick up and put on half a pound in the first 10 days. He was getting quite mobile now and Ivor had managed to get a playpen for him in Madras which was to be a boon.

We all returned to Madras on 21st September, travelling in a very rickety bus to Metapalyalum, where we caught the train to Madras. Antony had put on one and a half pounds during our three weeks' stay. We all moved in with the Homes. We had decided to take Gretel home with us and she was seen off on a cargo vessel, *Clan Mackay*, to go straight into quarantine on arrival.

Our return to the hot and humid climate did not suit Antony and he grizzled and whined and went off his food. A fortnight later on 8th October he ran a high temperature and I called the doctor, who prescribed one of the new drugs, sulphadiazole. I spent another worrying week nursing Antony when Ivor heard that a hospital ship was coming into Madras on 26th October on its way home from the Far East. As Linda was slow to recover from her operation, Edward joined forces with Ivor to apply for passages for Linda and Antony. We got a Doctor's certificate for Antony and on 18th October Linda and he had to attend a medical board and I went as Antony's attendant. The weather was getting cooler but very wet. I weighed Antony on 21st October and he hit the scales at 16lbs 13ozs, aged eleven and a half months.

We finally embarked on the Hospital Ship *Oxfordshire* on 28th October 1947. We found ourselves in the families ward of 16 beds on the boat deck. Linda read the treatment book in the Sister's absence, and saw that the woman in the bunk next to Antony was a leper with three children. My diary records:

> Linda browned off, but quite amused by the awfulness of it! And on 29th October: Much grumbling about the food. However managed to feed Antony on Farex. The three awful children of the leper woman created general nuisance and I spend my time trying to keep them away from Antony. Had a moan to the M.O. about Antony being next to the leper, but he insisted that there was no infection. Later on 31st October: In evening eldest child was ill with fever. Feeling very worried about the wards, but Antony seems quite happy and thoroughly enjoying all the attention. And on 3rd November: Got Antony's playpen on deck, a great boon.

I wrote to my friend Elise:

19th December 1947.
Fairways, Aldeburgh, Suffolk.

My dear Elise,

I've been feeling very guilty about not having written before, but I was always waiting for some definite news to write you.

We had an appalling journey on the hospital ship. However Antony flourished even on sour oats and dried potato, which was his main diet, and put on two pounds whilst we were on board! We arrived on the 22nd November in Southampton and were met by Aunt Tat and Uncle Irvine, who were looking just the same as ever.

Mummy met us at Saxmundham. Antony was very good the whole time, thoroughly enjoyed everything, and fetched up beaming in Aldeburgh. Mummy and Daddy are in fine form and looking younger than ever and certainly more spritely than in the War years. Fairways just the same as ever, except for an extra front door and a sun porch off the sitting room. All our luggage had arrived from India, about 40 boxes and crates, piled high in the garage! I had a week at home before I went off to meet Ivor, who had sailed about a week after we had only from Bombay. I left Mummy looking after Antony and went to Dorchester, where I spent a night with Rosemary. Her children are sweet and Penelope most amusing. I hadn't seen her since she was four months old! Elspeth is just about the same size as Antony, only two months younger. I left her place at crack of dawn to get to Southampton in time to meet Ivor's ship. Of course, being a troopship, there were various difficulties about disembarking. We spent three days in London and stayed at Berners Hotel (do you remember, opposite Bourne and Hollingsworth in Berners Street?) Very near our old haunts. We had a simply wizard time. No Antony and a really civilised place again. We went to two shows and dined and danced once at the Landsdowne in Berkeley Square, the next night at Hatchets followed by a murky nightclub in Bond Street. The next night another show and dinner and dance at the Savoy! We now go to ground for a year to recover our finances! But it was certainly worth it. London has improved immensely since I last saw it, which was during the War, early 1945. And I must say the food was marvellous after what we've been used to in India. The fat ration is the worst in one's home, but Mummy is very lucky and gets parcels from abroad which make all the difference. But for us it is so marvellous to see fresh milk. Poor Antony had never had any fresh milk until we got here! After our three days in town, Ivor and I came to Aldeburgh and he was presented to the family. They all seem to get on very well. Ivor hadn't been here four days when he had to go off to meet his mother, who had arrived from Australia. She is staying in a boarding house in Aldeburgh for the time being and going to her relations in January. Ma was going to put her up, but of course there isn't room here with the three of us. We are leaving her high and dry for Christmas, I'm afraid, as Antony, Ivor and I are going to Rosemary's for Christmas and New Year. Mummy is having what she calls a 'Derby and Joan' Christmas with old C. Spencer and Tilly, I expect. She seems quite happy about it. You know her ideas about the 'young' all being together. Jolly sound ideas, I think! I must admit I flatly refuse to have Mother-in-law living with us. She can come and stay once in a while when we have anywhere we can offer her hospitality. We don't know what our future is yet. Ivor has applied for transfer to the RAF, and we are now waiting for an interview, so we can't do anything more about a job until that's over. We anticipate coming back here from Rosemary's to finish unpacking and re-packing our baggage and then we want to take a furnished flat or house.

Yours as ever, Eliza.

So it was home to Aldeburgh, but not for long as we were to settle elsewhere. But that is another story.

Appendices

Appendix 1

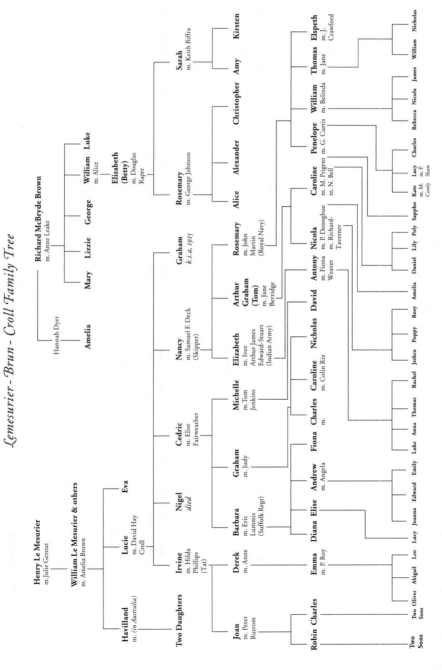

Lemesurier - Brun - Croll Family Tree

Deck Family Tree

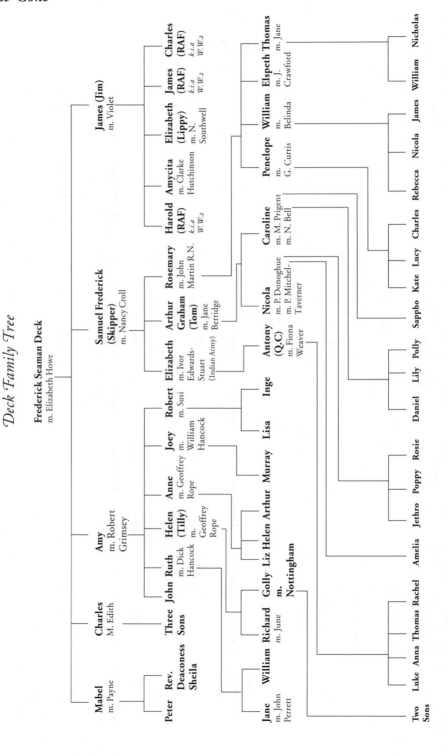

Edwards-Stuart Family Tree

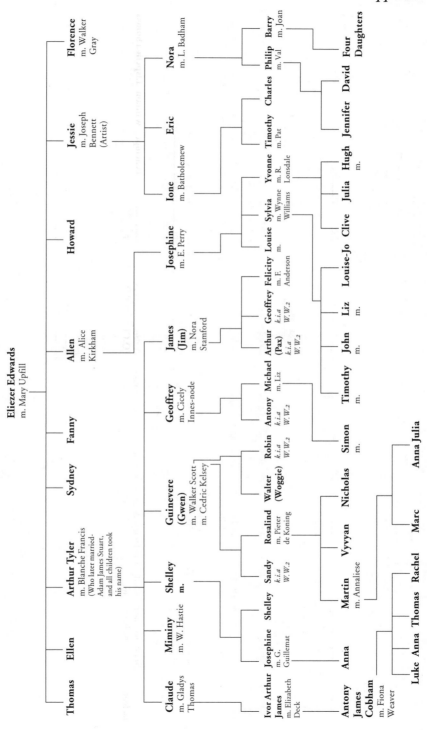

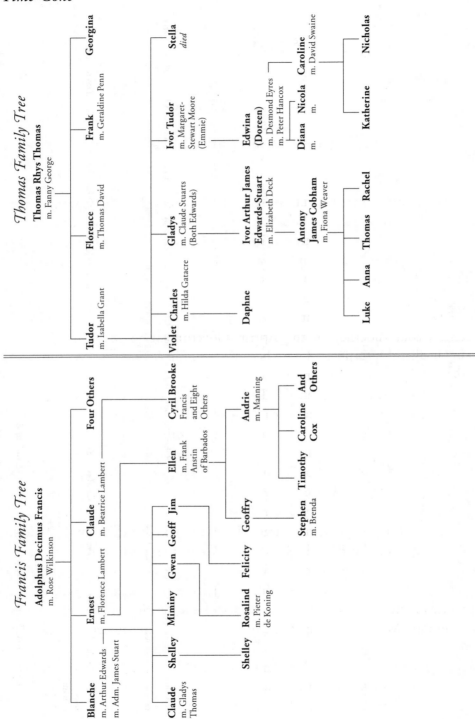

Thomas Family Tree

Thomas Rhys Thomas
m. Fanny George

Tudor — Florence — Frank — Georgina
m. Isabella Grant — m. Thomas David — m. Geraldine Penn

Violet Charles — Gladys — Ivor Tudor — Stella
m. Hilda Gatacre — m. Claude Stuarts (Both Edwards) — m. Margaret-Stewart Moore (Emmie) — *died*

Daphne — Ivor Arthur James Edwards-Stuart — Edwina (Doreen)
m. Elizabeth Deck — m. Desmond Eyres — m. Peter Hancox

Antony James Cobham — Caroline
m. Fiona Weaver — m. David Swaine

Diana Nicola — Katherine — Nicholas
m. — m.

Luke Anna Thomas Rachel

Francis Family Tree

Adolphus Decimus Francis
m. Rose Wilkinson

Blanche — Ernest — Claude — Four Others
m. Arthur Edwards — m. Florence Lambert — m. Beatrice Lambert
m. Adm. James Stuart

Ellen — Cyril Brooke
m. Frank Anstin of Barbados — Francis and Eight Others

Claude — Shelley — Miminy Gwen Geoff Jim
m. Gladys Thomas

Shelley — Rosalind Felicity — Geoffry — Andrie
m. Pieter de Koning — m. Manning

Stephen — Timothy Caroline And
m. Brenda — Cox Others

Appendix 2

The Le Mesuriers:
A Commissariat Family.

ETTERS FROM WILLIAM LE MESURIER, who served in the Commissariat
from 1842 to 1862, have been kept by his descendants and have led to
further research resulting in this article. William was the third generation of
his family to serve in the Commissariat.

The Le Mesuriers were a Guernsey family who not only provided more
than one Lord Mayor of London, but also four Hereditary Governors of
Alderney. Major-General John Le Mesurier, the last Hereditary Governor of
Alderney, sold Alderney to the British Government in 1825[1]. He had an
uncle Havilland born in 1758 who became Commissary General of Southern
District in 1798. He had commenced his service with the Commissariat in
1793 after commercial experience in Le Havre and London. He was appointed
Adjutant Commissary-General with the forces under command of the Duke
of York on the Continent. He gained high commendation from Count
Walmoden and General Dundas for his action during the retreat through
Holland and Westphalia to Bremen. As Commissary General Southern
District in 1798 he introduced a new system of supply which met with the
approval of Sir Charles Grey (later the 1st Earl Grey). This was based on
establishing stores depots in charge of reserve commissaries in Croydon,
Leatherhead, Guildford and elsewhere. When the post of Commissary-
General was restored in 1800, placing le Mesurier in a secondary position,
he resigned. But in March 1802 he was reinstated and sent to Egypt to
superintend the commissary requirements of the retiring Army. His duties
took him to Malta and Naples before returning home, where he died in
1806[2].

Havilland had two sons – Havilland and Henry. The younger, Havilland,
though never a member of the Commissariat, displayed in his short life all
the administrative flair of his father in addition to marked ability as an active

soldier, as his entry in the *Dictionary of National Biography* shows. Apart from following his father in Egypt and Italy, he held commissions in the Royal Staff Corps, the 20th and 83rd Foot and the 21st Fusiliers. He was DAQMG under Sir John Moore in Sweden and at Corunna. Later in Portugal as the Commanding Officer of the 14th (Algarve) Portuguese Infantry and Commandant of the fortress of Almeida he brought both unit and garrison to a high state of efficiency. At Almeida he raised corn and potatoes for the maintenance of the garrison and more. He was mentioned in despatches leading his Regiment (12 Portuguese Infantry). He was wounded on 28th July 1813 at the Battle of Sorauren (in the Battle of the Pyrenees) near Pamplona and died soon after. He was aged 30. Amongst other accomplishments was his work as translator of French military books and writer of Regulations for the Portuguese Army[3].

Henry, his younger brother, was born in 1791. He first held a clerkship in the Commissariat and was sent out to Portugal, where his elder brother, serving at Almeida, persuaded him to join the army. He engaged as a Volunteer but soon after in May 1812 he was commissioned as an Ensign in the 48th Foot. A few weeks later, at the battle of Salamanca, where he was carrying one of the Colours of the Regiment, he was badly wounded twice, losing an arm. After a period with the 3rd Garrison Battalion in the Peninsula, he was appointed Deputy Assistant Commissary General in 1814 and was posted to Canada. There in Quebec he served until going on half pay in 1818. He settled in Canada, marrying into a French Canadian family, and had 10 children[4].

One of these was William, who followed his father into the Commissariat as a Deputy Assistant Commissary General in 1842. He first saw service in Georgetown, Demerara and Gambia. In letters from Bathurst, Gambia, he painted a gloomy picture of the unhealthy conditions there. On arrival in September 1848 he found that out of 12 officers in the garrison, all were sick including the two doctors. The whole garrison at Macarthy Island 500 miles up river were down with fever. On average five Europeans out of seven died. A year later he was to report that 60% of fresh arrivals from Europe had been carried off in the last year; four surgeons had been lost and one crippled by disease. William was the only officer off the sick list. In that year he saw active service, according to *Hart's Army List*, at Bambacoo, Keenung and the plains of Quenealla. William was a very competent black and white (being colour-blind) artist and two drawings exist of the expedition, one showing the initial landing on the Gambia River, the other the submission of the local Chieftains as a result of this action[5].

After becoming Assistant Commissary General in 1850, he was posted to Fremantle, Western Australia in 1853. He found there a fellow Canadian from Quebec, Matthew Bell Irvine, who was to become Wolseley's right hand man as senior administrative officer in his Red River Expedition and Ashanti campaign.[6]. On arrival there, William seems to have got involved in rows with the Governor, the Commandant, the Controller of Convicts and his own chief. However, he wrote he had beaten them on all counts, and though having few friends, had won the Commandant round. He claimed he had effected several reforms in the convict service.

In December 1854 he married the daughter of Richard Broun who had been Government Resident in Fremantle and whose brother was Colonial Secretary. With his wife and son he left for Hong Kong in July 1856. He was to write about trouble with poisoning of food in Hong Kong and the arson of the flour store. His first experience of Indian troops' food requirements – the make-up of spices for curry and betel nut and panleaf – gave him cause for comment. Eighteen months later he had sent his wife and two children away from Hong Kong, because of the unhealthy conditions, to stay with his parents in Canada. Having been brought up in Western Australia, the wife with two small children were to arrive in bitter winter conditions on the south bank of the St Lawrence to a welcome from her one armed father-in-law and a perilous journey across the ice–infested river to Quebec in a canoe on a wild night in the middle of a howling snowstorm[7].

In Hong Kong William, as the senior Commissariat Officer acting as Deputy Commissary General, was getting very involved with the war with China. He reported on the return of the expedition from the Peiho River with nothing accomplished but after he himself had resolved three vexatious questions, he found himself in good standing with the General (Major General Sir Charles Straubenzee)[8], whom he went to see at Canton. In January 1859 he wrote of war again being likely in China and preparations for an expedition to Pekin. Though he had had another fight with the 'brass' at Canton, his affairs with both the Admiral (Sir Michael Seymour)[9] and General Straubenzee had taken a favourable turn. That same month he was able to report that he had had a good chit from the Commissary General in Chief for his Report on the new cash system[10]. He explained that the Report was based on 20 years experience in commissariat service duties and of matters of public accounts finance. He went on an expedition to Fatshan with 1000 troops, 9 gun boats and all the spare ship's boats in the river.

The next month he was to report that Lord Elgin had arrived at last and that the expedition had been decided upon. It would mean a lot more work for him, running up and down the river, and he had asked for three more officers. In April he was able to write that he had applied to be relieved in August after three years' service in Hong Kong, the equivalent of five years in the tropic. In the same letter he records that a cruiser, two despatch boats and four gunboats had left for Shanghai but that the news from Pekin was unsatisfactory; the forts demolished the previous year had been rebuilt.

In May 1859 he wrote to say that the new Admiral had arrived (Admiral Hope[11]) with a reputation as a martinet, but he had found him courteous; he had dropped 'HE' from his title; he wondered if HE, General Sir Charles Van Straubenzee would take the hint.

On 13th October he was to write that he had hoped to receive his passage order so as to leave that day. He had little doubt that the order was somewhere as he had received a letter from the General's wife to take to Malta. He was afraid he would be held back. His fears were realised. A fortnight later he wrote to say that the order arrived too late and though he could have gone by Jardine's steamer and waited at Singapore to avoid any news that would have made his detention necessary, he felt unable to do so; such a course would not have been consistent with his sense of duty. The next day, apparently, the 67th arrived with news of more troops on the way. He went at once to Canton to explain to the General why he had not left. He copied his letter of 19th October 1859 to the Military Secretary and the reply to it. He had requested permission to stay because of the arrival of more troops and the undesirability of weakening the Commissariat. The General agreed it was expedient not to weaken the Commissariat and expressed his gratification with the manner in which William had waived all personal consideration and volunteered to remain for the public service. William was instructed to resume as Head of the Commissariat in China as acting Deputy Commissary General. He hoped that he might be able to get away in three months' time. In the same letter he wrote of a big fire in Hong Kong and disasters in the North. He complained of Elgin's short-sighted diplomacy and gave news of the repulse on the Taku forts. A fortnight later he wrote that the 67th, a wing of the 3rd Buffs and an RE Company had reinforced the army from India. There had been great bungling as the troops were not required until April and there was no accommodation for large numbers if they arrived.

His hope of leaving within three months was clearly not realised. There is a gap of seven months in the sequence of letters that have been left. It is not difficult to guess at the tone of those that have not survived. In a letter dated 22 May 1860 we find references to despondency over incessant disappointment from his prolonged stay in Hong Kong. His letter went on to say how busy he was; there was a great deal of confusion and it was a mystery how 2000 would be fed. 200 ships were ready to start with the expedition. Lord Elgin's arrival was awaited. He intended to draw his portrait when he did.

The next letter is dated 10 August 1860 when William was waiting for mail. There was no news from the North, where forts were about to be attacked. Lord Elgin was quoted as saying he would eat his Christmas dinner in England. William felt that the Commissariat was giving satisfaction and was likely to come out with much credit[12]. He went on in sceptical fashion, which was probably justified[13], to write that it would take some time for the accounts to be audited, by which time all honours and promotions would have been granted before faults could be found in the arrangements. He reported that there had been about four months' incessant rain and the climate was very oppressive; the Town Major's wife, who had arrived two weeks before, had already left as it was too hot for her.

Before the end of August William was able to write and say that his promotion (to Deputy Commissary General dated 12 May 1860) did not gratify him much. He had been promised Canada and hoped to get away within three months. The campaign in the North was going slowly. Peitang had been sacked and every atrocity committed, particularly by the French.

William was finally relieved in October 1860 and went home by the overland route. Because of two days' delay and very bad weather in the Mediterranean, he found himself four days behind instead of four days before the Southampton passengers. He still expected Canada but was worried he might get sent to Aldershot, which was not represented by an officer of sufficient seniority. He was not well, being unable to eat hot meat, though he found the cold agreeing with him.

His appointment to Canada was confirmed because on 6 January he embarked at Queenstown and arrived in Canada on 1st February 1861. On 14th February he was recorded as being in ill health and was medically boarded. He was to remain in Montreal for treatment, and sick leave until 1st June 1862 was granted. As a result of another Medical Board he embarked for England at the beginning of August 1862 and was granted three months' leave. In September his third child, a daughter, was born. Six weeks later he was dead at the age of 43. He left behind a widow with three young children to bring up on a pension of £80 a year. His father, the Peninsular War veteran, had predeceased him by a matter of months; the *Army List* for 1863 records both their deaths.

Havilland Le Mesurier, William's son born in Fremantle, did not follow his father into the Commissariat but he did become a soldier. He was commissioned in the Australian Army, saw active service in South Africa and died in Adelaide while still serving as Colonel Commandant South Australia, in 1913.

Notes:

1. History of the Le Mesurier Family – Alderney.
2. *Dictionary of National Biography*, Vol XI page 904.
3. *DNB* Vol XI p 905
4. *Army Lists*; Family Records including letter from James Bentick from Downing St to James Hamilton dated 18 October 1813.
5. The action was in the form of a punitive expedition against the King of Keenung who had been 'guilty of every enormity' and had considerable influence over neighbouring tribes; the expedition consisted of men from the 2nd and 3rd West India Regiments, Enrolled Pensioners and the Royal Gambia Volunteers, totalling 295, all ranks with two guns. The action consisted of shelling and attacking the stockaded towns of Bambacoo and Keenung forcing their evacuation. Some 3 to 4000 casualties were inflicted for a loss of 5 killed and 21 wounded. (*One Hundred Years' History of the 2nd Batt. West India Regiment* by Col J E Caulfield, London 1899; and *Naval and Military Gazette* no 862 14 July 1849).
6. Matthew Bell Irvine – served Turkey and Crimea 1855–6; Red River Expedition 1870– CMG; Ashanti War 1873–4 – CB, Mention in Despatches, medal with clasp Capture of Coomassi, Order of Medjidie 5th col; Deputy Commissary General 1874; retired 1881, Hon Commissary General; best man to Wm. Le Mesurier at wedding 1854; married Charlotte Wood (née Guerout) first cousin of Wm. Le Mesurier 1874.
7. Article by George Gale in Montreal paper *Montreal Gazette* dated 29 Jan 1931.
8. General Sir Charles Straubenzee; GCB; born 1812; Commanded 39th Foot Maharajahpore 1843; Brigade in Crimea; Division in Bengal 1860–5; Governor and C-in-C Malta 1872–8; Colonel 39th Foot 1867.
9. Admiral Sir Michael Seymour GCB; born 1802; Captain of Baltic Fleet 1854; C-in-C India and China stations 1856–8; MP Devonport 1859–63.
10. Commissary-General wrote from London, 20 November 1858: 'I beg to acknowledge

with many thanks your note of 23 August as well as the very ably written paper which accompanied it. I fully concur in the observations you make on our new cash system. They are the clearest and most practical of any yet brought forward, and I will take care that they are exhibited in quarters where they will be profusely appreciated'.

11. Rear Admiral James Hope relieved Admiral Seymour as C-in-C East Indies and China Apr 1859; commanded disastrous attempt to force Taku Forts June 1859 where wounded twice; Admiral GCB; died 1881.

12. Fortescue *History of the British Army* Ch LV reports on the continual friction between the Commissariat responsible for supply and the Naval and Military Train responsible for transport afloat and ashore but declined to take the orders or respect the wishes of the Commissariat; Wolseley quoted as saying 'one of the best organized expeditions in the history of the army'.

13. General Sir Hope Grant's Despatches in the *London Gazette* contain no reference to the Commissariat. The *Report of the Strathnairn Committee on Transport and Supply Services in the Army* (1867; PRO XHL 1/1743) contain several accounts from various members of the Commissariat and others involved in supply and transport services in the campaigns in China in the period 1858–60, when William Le Mesurier was the Senior Commissariat Officer in China but make no reference to him; William was dead before the Committee was set up.

Further information came to Eric Lummis from a copy of extracts from *The War of 1812 Journal of Lieutenant John Le Couteur, 104th Foot* titled *Merry Hearts Make Light Days* and edited by Donald E. Graves.

October 1815

I had some very pleasant trips to Fort St. Jean on Richelieu River, south of Montreal, where Harry LeMesurier my cousin was quartered in charge of the Commissariat Department there. He became attached to a very sweet person, a Miss Guerute of St. Denys, the daughter of an old Norman gentleman who settled in Canada, reputed to be very rich. His second daughter, Sophy, was a haughty beauty. LeMesurier was much afraid that I should fall in love with her. I found her and Miss Amelia Caldwell, another sweeter and prettier girl, the bridesmaids at their wedding which took place at St. Denys October 27th in Monsieur Guerate's fine old house, with great hospitality and French gaiety.

---

27 October 1815

I have been to Harry LeMesurier's wedding which took place at St. Denys at the house of Monsieur Guerute, a French Protestant Gentleman from Rouen in Normandy.

Sources

1. *Kenya Pioneers* – Errol Trebinski

2. *Jubaland and Northern Frontier Province*

3. *Frontiersman*

4. *A Nurses War* – Brenda McBryde

5. *Before the Dawn* – General Sir John Smythe V.C.

6. *Defeat into Victory* – General Slim

7. *The Longest Retreat* – Tim Carew

8. *Back to the Pavilion* – Attiqur Rahman

9. *D-Day, An Illustrated History* – Stephen Badsay

10. *6 Armies in Normandy* – John Keegan

11. *Second World War* Vols 1–6 – Winston Churchill

12. *Spring Imperial* – Evelyn Hart